THE
COLLEGE
PRESS
NIV
COMMENTARY

JOSHUA

MARK ZIESE

Old Testament Series Co-Editors:

Terry Briley, Ph.D.   Paul Kissling, Ph.D.
Lipscomb University   Great Lakes Christian College

 COLLEGE PRESS
PUBLISHING COMPANY
Joplin, Missouri

International Standard Book Number 978-0-89900-880-6

A WORD
FROM THE PUBLISHER

Years ago a movement was begun with the dream of uniting all Christians on the basis of a common purpose (world evangelism) under a common authority (the Word of God). The College Press NIV Commentary Series is a serious effort to join the scholarship of two branches of this unity movement so as to speak with one voice concerning the Word of God. Our desire is to provide a resource for your study of the Old Testament that will benefit you whether you are preparing a Bible School lesson, a sermon, a college course, or your own personal devotions. Today as we survey the wreckage of a broken world, we must turn again to the Lord and his Word, unite under his banner and communicate the life-giving message to those who are in desperate need. This is our purpose.

ABBREVIATIONS

AB . . . . *Anchor Bible*
ABD . . . . . *Anchor Bible Dictionary*
Ant. . . . . . . Josephus, *Antiquities*
ASOR . . . . *American Schools of Oriental Research*
BA . . . . *Biblical Archaeologist*
BAR . . . . . *Biblical Archaeology Review*
BAS . . . . . . *Biblical Archaeology Society*
BASOR . . . *Bulletin of the American Schools of Oriental Research*
BDB . . . . . Brown, Driver, Briggs, *A Hebrew and English Lexicon of the Old Testament*
BHS . . . . . *Biblia Hebraica Stuttgartensia*
BRev . . . . . *Bible Review*
BT . . . . *The Bible Translator*
CBQ . . . . . *Catholic Biblical Quarterly*
EBA . . . . . *Early Bronze Age (3400–2000 B.C.)*
EDB . . . . . *Eerdmans Dictionary of the Bible*
HALOT . . . Koehler and Baumgartner, *The Hebrew and Aramaic Lexicon of the Old Testament*
HAR . . . . . *Hebrew Annual Review*
IEJ . . . . *Israel Exploration Journal*
IES . . . . . . *Israel Exploration Society*
Int . . . . *Interpretation*
ISBE . . . . . *International Standard Bible Encyclopedia*
JBL . . . . . . *Journal of Biblical Literature*
JETS . . . . . *Journal of the Evangelical Theological Society*
JSOT . . . . . *Journal for the Study of the Old Testament*
JSOTSupp . *Journal for the Study of the Old Testament Supplement Series*
LBA . . . . . *Late Bronze Age (1550–1200 B.C.)*
LXX . . . . . *Septuagint*

MBA ..... *Middle Bronze Age (2000–1550 B.C.)*
MT ...... *Masoretic Text*
NBD ..... *New Bible Dictionary*
NCB ..... *New Century Bible*
NEAEHL . *The New Encyclopedia of Archaeological Excavations in the Holy Land*
NEASB ... *Near East Archaeological Society Bulletin*
NIBC ..... *New International Biblical Commentary*
NICOT ... *New International Commentary on the Old Testament*
OEANE ... *The Oxford Encyclopedia of Archaeology in the Near East*
OTL ..... *Old Testament Library*
RB .... *Revue biblique*
RevExp ... *Review and Expositor*
SAW ..... *Saudi Aramco World*
TOTC .... *Tyndale Old Testament Commentaries*
TWOT ... *Theological Wordbook of the Old Testament*
TynBul ... *Tyndale Bulletin*
VT .... *Vetus Testamentum*
WBC ..... *Word Biblical Commentary*
ZAW ..... *Zeitschrift für die alttestamentliche Wissenschaft*

Simplified Guide to Hebrew Writing

Heb. letter	Translit.	Pronunciation guide
א	ʾ	Has no sound of its own; like smooth breathing mark in Greek
ב	b	Pronounced like English B *or* V
ג	g	Pronounced like English G
ד	d	Pronounced like English D
ה	h	Pronounced like English H, silent at the end of words in the combination āh
ו	w	As a consonant, pronounced like English V or German W
ו	û	Represents a vowel sound, pronounced like English long OO
ו	ô	Represents a vowel sound, pronounced like English long O
ז	z	Pronounced like English Z
ח	ḥ	Pronounced like German and Scottish CH and Greek χ (chi)
ט	ṭ	Pronounced like English T
י	y	Pronounced like English Y
כ/ך	k	Pronounced like English K
ל	l	Pronounced like English L
מ/ם	m	Pronounced like English M
נ/ן	n	Pronounced like English N
ס	s	Pronounced like English S
ע	ʿ	Stop in breath deep in throat before pronouncing the vowel
פ/ף	p/ph	Pronounced like English P *or* F
צ/ץ	ṣ	Pronounced like English TS/TZ
ק	q	Pronounced very much like כ (k)
ר	r	Pronounced like English R
שׂ	ś	Pronounced like English S, much the same as ס
שׁ	š	Pronounced like English SH
ת	t/th	Pronounced like English T *or* TH

Note that different forms of some letters appear at the end of the word (written right to left), as in כָּפַף (*kāphaph*, "bend") and מֶלֶךְ (*melek*, "king").

Vowels in Hebrew (except where the ו is used to represent a vowel sound), are represented by "vowel points" added to the consonant. For example: הַ (*ha*, "the"). The letter *yod* (י, *y*) also becomes a *part of* certain vowel sounds, as in the conjunction כִּי (*kî*, "that"). Originally, Hebrew was written as "unpointed" text, with just the consonants. For convenience, the different vowel points are shown below on the letter Aleph (א).

אָ	ā	Pronounced not like long A in English, but like the broad A or AH sound
אַ	a	The Hebrew short A sound, but more closely resembles the broad A (pronounced for a shorter period of time) than the English short A
אֶ	e	Pronounced like English short E

א	ē	Pronounced like English long A, or Greek η (eta)
א	i	Pronounced like English short I
א	î	The same vowel point is sometimes pronounced like אִי (see below)
אָ	o	This vowel point sometimes represents the short O sound
אֹ	ō	Pronounced like English long O
אֻ	u	The vowel point ֻ sometimes represents a shorter U sound and
אוּ	ū	is sometimes pronounced like the וּ (û, see above)
אֵי	ê	Pronounced much the same as אֵ
אֶי	ê	Pronounced much the same as אֶ
אִי	î	Pronounced like long I in many languages, or English long E
אְ	ə	An unstressed vowel sound, like the first E in the word "severe"
אֳ, אֲ, אֱ	ŏ, ă, ĕ	Shortened, unstressed forms of the vowels אָ, אַ, and אֶ, pronounced very similarly to אְ

PREFACE AND ACKNOWLEDGMENTS

This book could not have been written without the help of many people.

In the fall semester of 2006 and the spring semester of 2008, I had the privilege of offering graduate seminars on the book of Joshua on the campus of Cincinnati Christian University. The brave souls who signed on did so without knowing that the grist for this manuscript was being ground. They learned of it though, soon enough, and indulged me. I am thankful for that kindness and for the insights gained as a result of the give-and-take that characterized our meetings. At the time, David Toundas and Nick Miller worked out of my office as graduate assistants. They doggedly chased loose details of this manuscript and gave me many reasons to smile. Beyond these fine students, the institutional support of CCU channeled through the able leadership of Mike Shannon and Jon Weatherly was critical.

Just as students and administrators facilitate the task of writing, so do librarians. I take my hat off to Jim Lloyd and his excellent staff at the G.M. Elliott Library of CCU. They never blinked when presented with my requests, no matter how odd. The footnotes in this book give testimony to their help. Additionally, they kept the refrigerator in the back room full of cola.

If I exhausted the patience of Dru Ashwell and the other good people at College Press, they did not show it. Instead of giving me what my tardiness deserved, they gave me steady encouragement and prayers. Shy and Dan Rees caught a good many errors and improved the manuscript considerably. Obviously, any wrinkles that remain belong on my own face.

Words cannot express my love for Vicki, Tanner, and Moriah. I know that all of this took time from you. I hope you will understand.

Finally, I must acknowledge those who have set me on the tracks that run clear through this book. There are many deserving of mention, but for the moment, I will limit the discussion to just two. Willard (Wilkie) Winter went to be with the Lord on July 15, 1998, after 52 years of service at Cincinnati Christian University. Wilbur Fields is now retired after 35 years of service at Ozark Christian College. He still lives in Joplin, Missouri.

These two men were different in many ways, and yet they had much in common. Both loved the Old Testament and were convinced that its words are special and have relevance for the people of God today. Both were excellent teachers and churchmen. Both knew the archaeology of the *Heartland*, and, curiously enough, both scratched its surface in search of Joshua's *'Ai*. Winter served as Joe Callaway's registrar at et-Tell; Fields worked with David Livingston at Khirbet Nisya, and later, with Bryant Wood at Khirbet el-Maqatir. As a result of these seasons in the sun, both Winter and Fields were well-situated to illustrate their stories with color slides, to launch the ministries of others, and to stir faith in believers and nonbelievers alike.

Despite these similarities, these two men were also unique. Perhaps their differences are best measured at a personal level. Dr. Winter (never did I have the courage to address him otherwise) was the quintessential gentleman-scholar. Rarely was he found without coat and tie, and when outside, without a hat. In conversation with others, he always respectfully referred to his wife as "*Mrs.* Winter." He was conservative in all his ways, except when it came to helping others. In this he was most liberal. As his graduate assistant, not only did I grade his papers and fetch his mail, but I drove him to professional meetings, Cincinnati Reds baseball games (which he loved), church functions, and to many fine breakfasts. Wherever we went, from his seminary office to the deserts of the Hashemite Kingdom of Jordan, I observed his kind heart and steady consistency. To this day, I marvel at the way in which he was able to balance dignity and grace without missing a step. How honored I was—and remain so now—to be asked to participate in this new commentary series from College Press, knowing full well that the author of their original Bible Study Textbook Series, *Studies in Joshua, Judges, Ruth*, was Willard W. Winter!

In an earlier and very different stage of life I came to love Brother Fields (never did I have the desire to address him otherwise). He too wore a coat and tie, but never comfortably. Raw-boned and rangy, he blew into the classroom as gently as a Kansas tornado. And in like manner, his voice rose and fell: whispering, wheezing, roaring! He commanded the attention of a room full of undergraduates by force of presence alone. But this is not the reason he is remembered by all who sat under him. Never, before or since, have I experienced one who both knew and *shared* Scripture like Brother Fields. It erupted from his heart and came out of his mouth: here, there, on the stairs or in the parking lot, in conversation or in song (yes—now I remember—*especially*, in song!). It also came out of his large hands, and, seemingly, even out of his eyes. Every part of him communicated his devotion to the Lord and his care for each of us—despite our superior numbers. How else could he single us out by name, hometown, and family, and then check back later to inquire as to our prayer requests, long after everyone else had forgotten them? Certainly, I will not forget his classroom, his friendship, his prayers, his song, his own contributions to the Bible Study Textbook Series. Neither will I forget the opportunity to travel with him in the summer of 1984 from Missouri to the Mediterranean and back again. As with Dr. Winter, in Brother Fields I witnessed the Word and Ways of God, modeled in human form. I am changed as a result. For this reason, I humbly dedicate this work to the ministry and memory of these two men.

For Bro. Fields and Dr. Winter
"There were giants in those days."

Mark Ziese
May 1, 2008

INTRODUCTION

The Law of Moses (hereafter, *torah*) asks and answers questions essential to the reading of Scripture. Some of these questions are launched upwards: Who is YHWH[1]? What are his credentials, promises, and expectations? Can he be trusted? Other questions of *torah* are launched outwardly: Who is this Moses? What are his credentials? Can he be regarded as a reliable guide? Finally, questions of *torah* are launched inwardly: What does it mean to be the people of God? How are such people identified? Where do they come from? Where do they go? Far more than a mishmash of short stories, endless genealogies, and odd rules; *torah* makes specific claims about the nature of Yahweh, Moses, and the people of God. Like any living document, it must be remembered, interpreted, and applied afresh by each generation.

The book of Joshua attempts to do just this. Scripturally, it snaps on the end of *torah*, offering the story of the first generation to venture beyond the scarps of Mt. Nebo where the tracks of Moses stop abruptly, then disappear. For the *Exodus* generation, and indeed for Moses himself, a walkabout in a land of promise could only be appreciated by proxy, unless, of course, one were to include a deep-down ache for a place to call home. For the *Eisodos* generation, on

---

[1]The personal/covenant name of God in Hebrew is spelled with four consonants, represented by the Latin letters YHWH (Hebrew originally gave no direct indication of vowels). As such, it is often referred to as the Tetragrammaton (Greek for "four letters"). Because the Jews avoided pronouncing the holy name, they did not add the "proper" vowel signs to the Tetragrammaton when they started writing in the vowels, and we do not know with certainty what those vowels should be. The author would prefer to represent it just with the consonants, as it appears here, but for the convenience of the readers, College Press has added in the most widely accepted vowels for this name.

the other hand, a walkabout will become reality.[2] To fully appreciate their position, though, the words of *torah* and its stories of men whose feet trod this land centuries earlier must be remembered. By the late second millennium B.C., the trail of these early walkers is already old, but not yet cold; *torah* retrieves the pathways of Abraham, Isaac, and Jacob.

Beyond the task of remembering, the text of Joshua will also interpret *torah*. Moses is clear about the rules of Canaanite engagement (e.g., Deuteronomy 7 and 20), the division of land among the tribes (e.g., Num 26:52-56; 33:50-54), the establishment of cities of refuge (e.g., Num 35:6-34), and a host of other issues. These instructions must be relocated and reconsidered in light of contemporary events. Given the twists of real life, the practice of law seldom hinges on a single point (oh, if only it were so easy!); more often it flexes longways through a whole set of variables. Put differently, *torah* is uncompromising with regard to Canaan's residents. So how, then, should this code be read in the case of Rahab, the alien, or the Gibeonites? Similarly, *torah* is clear that once God's people are in the land, Yahweh will select one place of sacrifice and dwelling. How, then, should the "imposing altar" of the Transjordan tribes be understood? Clearly, one cannot read Joshua the text — much less Joshua the man — without sensing the challenge of interpreting a living document. There are no comfortable precedents here. Moses laid it down in the past, but Joshua must live it out in the present.

Just as the text will reach back to make contact with *torah* before reaching forward to touch contemporary situations, Joshua will also use *torah* as a base from which to advance a case of its own. While

---

[2]The city of Athens is conveniently marked . . . if you can read Greek! Over the door in the back of the public bus is a sign, lettered in block characters, ΕΞΟΔΟΣ, *exodus*, or the "way out." Every Bible reader immediately recognizes the idea; Israel's "exodus" experience is described in a book with the same label. It tells the story of how Israel "got off the bus of slavery," by leaving Egypt.

The bus in Athens, however, has another sign. This one is over the front door. It reads, in block characters, *eisodos*, the "way in." For those getting on the bus this is the entrance. While there is no book of the Bible by this name, it would be an appropriate way to consider how Israel enters the *Heartland*. It is, for them, a kind of *eisodos*.

the whole of this present work is given to isolating and describing the particulars of that case, three may be mentioned up front as they are worth watching. First, as already stated, *torah* inquires as to the identity and authority of Yahweh. Joshua will continue to infill this theme, but adds significantly to the picture of Yahweh as both prom- ise-keeper and war-maker. Israel cannot achieve victory by its own savvy; only when the people move in conjunction with "a great com- mission" and — more importantly — "a great commissioner" can any ground (or "earth") be gained. Second, *torah* inquires as to the iden- tity and credibility of Moses. Again, this base will be confirmed and developed. As expected, the role of Moses as the legitimate inter- preter of *torah* will eventually give way to his successor, Joshua. What is unexpected is the slowness with which this conclusion comes. Third and finally, *torah* inquires as to the identity and conduct of God's people. On this point, a most startling conclusion awaits the reader who grinds it out to the very end. The story of Joshua turns out to be less about fighting and more about walking, less about cheering and more about choosing, and less about erecting barriers and more about penetrating them. Finally, arising in a most unex- pected irony, the text will offer one answer to the question of how Israel itself is to be defined. Given the number of geographical par- ticulars that litter the book — and ballyhoo about the modern state of Israel that litters the evangelical church — it is interesting that this final measure is quite indifferent to any lines on the ground.

However, before proceeding directly to details of the text and its contents, other introductory points should be considered as impor- tant background material to Joshua study. Those who have given attention to the literature will quickly recognize the bulk of what fol- lows; if there is anything new here, it is merely the voice or the arrangement. To assist the latter, four heads serve as organizers: his- tory and prophecy, language and text, strategy and structure, and setting and archaeology.

HISTORY AND PROPHECY

Within the Christian Bible, Joshua is considered the first of twelve books of Old Testament history. These extend from Joshua to Esther, follow the Pentateuch, and precede the books of poetry and prophecy. Structurally, this fourfold arrangement (Pentateuch-History-Poetry-Prophecy) is a legacy of an earlier text tradition, the Greek Old Testament or Septuagint (hereafter abbreviated LXX). It groups biblical books according to literary type and has been embraced as Scripture since the earliest centuries of the church's existence.

The question of "history," and hence, "books of history" as a literary type has attracted the concern of some in the modern period. One might argue that the purest "history" is a grocery list of facts, i.e., names, dates, places, etc. But even then, would not selectivity and arrangement govern the presentation? Clearly, the "books of history" not only muster select tidbits, but do so in a string of sorts, in a context of "story," offered in quest of a particular goal. This narrated thoughtfulness need not relegate these dozen books into the class of wild invention as extremists argue. After all, effective — and even entertaining — rhetoric has never been the sole domain of the novelist. On the other hand, as V. Philips Long suggests, history writing has always been representational art, "constrained by the actualities of the subject matter."[3] His conclusion is helpful; it offers slack to the reins of "story-telling" without turning them loose altogether. Biblical prose may not constitute historiography in a modern sense, but only one with extraordinary faith could dismiss the whole lot as pure fiction! The "books of history," therefore, thoughtfully explain critical moments and key figures in Israel's story. They do so upon the sturdy conviction that there is a relationship between past, present, and future realities. God moves; men choose; history complies. Everything points this direction.

Efforts to read the book of Joshua as a historically invested text are few in the present age.[4] Among commentaries, Marten H. Woudstra's work remains the champion of conservative approaches.[5]

---

[3]V. Philips Long, *The Art of Biblical History*, vol. 5 of Foundations of Contemporary Interpretation, ed. by Moises Silva (Grand Rapids: Zondervan 1994), p. 68.

[4]Reasons for this are many, but may be specifically tied to the difficulty of linking archaeological results with the story of the text, alleged contradictions between the books of Joshua and Judges, preconceptions about the origins of biblical text, and a predisposition against the miraculous.

[5]Marten H. Woudstra, *The Book of Joshua*, NICOT (Grand Rapids: Eerdmans, 1981).

Trent Butler's volume is far more thorough, but shot through with source-critical theory.[6] Both vie to integrate textual and historical approaches into their readings. For Woudstra, the purpose of Joshua is ultimately tied to a life-truth: the author wants his audience "to know how the promise made to the forefathers was fulfilled during the Conquest so his chosen people would trust and obey him in future generations."[7] Butler is less straightforward, preferring to see Joshua as a revelation that arrived "in a protracted period of tradition formation and preservation."[8] It carries essential truths regarding the identity of Israel and the promises of Yahweh into everyday life.[9] Voices like Woudstra and Butler, while different from each other and from our own reading at many points, represent the spirit of investigation embraced here: historical interests must be blended with textual study.[10]

In order to accomplish this blending, assistance must be sought in many corners. One cannot overlook Yohanan Aharoni's timeless contributions[11] or recent works by Daniel Hillel,[12] and Anson F. Rainey and R. Steven Notley.[13] Valuable writings such as these offer portals to the larger sweep of historical and geographical concerns. Likewise, perspectives offered by K.A. Kitchen,[14] K. Lawson Younger Jr.[15] and Amihai Mazar[16] demonstrate that the text of Joshua is not far removed from a late second millennium B.C. context.

---

[6]Trent Butler, *Joshua*, vol. 7 of WBC, ed. by David A. Hubbard and Glenn W. Barker (Waco: Word Books, 1983).

[7]Woudstra, *Joshua*, p. 18.

[8]Butler, *Joshua*, p. xl.

[9]Ibid., p. xlii.

[10]This encouragement is needed now more than ever. Consider the essay by Gary N. Knoppers, "The Historical Study of the Monarchy: Developments and Detours," in *The Face of Old Testament Studies: A Survey of Contemporary Approaches*, ed. by David W. Baker and Bill T. Arnold (Grand Rapids: Baker, 1999), pp. 207-235.

[11]Yohanan Aharoni, *The Land of the Bible: A Historical Geography*, rev. ed., trans. by A.F. Rainey (Philadelphia: Westminster, 1979).

[12]Daniel Hillel, *The Natural History of the Bible: An Environmental Exploration of the Hebrew Scriptures* (New York: Columbia University, 2006).

[13]Anson F. Rainey and R. Steven Notley, *The Sacred Bridge: Carta's Atlas of the Biblical World* (Jerusalem: Carta, 2006).

[14]K.A. Kitchen, *On the Reliability of the Old Testament* (Grand Rapids: Eerdmans, 2003).

[15]K. Lawson Younger Jr., *Ancient Conquest Accounts: A Study in Ancient Near*

Oddly, this problem of "history," so absorbing to moderns, does not appear to be an issue within the Hebrew canon. No such formal category of biblical texts even exists! In the traditional Jewish organization of biblical books (attested by the Masoretic Text or, hereafter, MT), Joshua is found dancing in the company of the $N^{\partial}bi'\hat{i}m$, or "Prophets." Here, Joshua leads Judges, Samuel, and Kings in a line known as the "Former Prophets." With respect to load, these four carry the twin burden of "theological testimony" and "interpretative commentary."[17] With respect to contents, these four present a kind of arcing trajectory that begins with the *Heartland* won and concludes with the *Heartland* lost.[18] The dance that begins as a fling fades to the floor at the end. This crisis is worth pondering; we will return to it below.

That Joshua is a "book of prophecy" or that Joshua the man functions as a "prophet" should come as no surprise. After all, is not Moses the נָבִיא (*nābî'*, "prophet") without equal (Deut 34:10) and Joshua his attendant (מְשָׁרֵת מֹשֶׁה, *m^ə šārēth mōšeh*)?[19] Like Moses, Joshua engages Yahweh in direct conversation and reliably represents his voice to others. This relationship endows Joshua with the authority to function prophetically in his community. Unlike Moses, however, Joshua's character is much more opaque and guarded; only through inference can the reader gain access to his inner thoughts and feelings. So despite his very public role, the Joshua of

---

Eastern and Biblical History Writing, JSOTSupp 98 (Sheffield: JSOT Press, 1990).

[16]Amihai Mazar, *Archaeology of the Land of the Bible 10,000–586 B.C.E.,* The Anchor Bible Reference Library (New York: Doubleday, 1990).

[17]These categories are drawn from the work of Walter Brueggemann, *An Introduction to the Old Testament: The Canon and Christian Imagination* (Louisville, KY: Westminster John Knox, 2003), pp. 103-104. For Brueggemann, "theological testimony" is all about proclaiming the work of God, while "interpretative commentary" suggests that the work of the Former Prophets draws freely from other literature available to the narrator.

[18]Throughout this work, the term *Heartland* is used to describe the geographical core of the biblical story. This term avoids the political connotations aroused by reference to the modern states of Israel, Jordan, and Palestine.

[19]Although it should be noted that the text never explicitly describes Joshua by the terms/titles commonly used of prophets, i.e., *nābî'* ("prophet"), רֹאֶה (*rō'eh*, "seer"), or חֹזֶה (*ḥōzeh*, "visionary").

the text is a very private character. This insulation both blinds and bends him before the reader. Why does Joshua acquiesce to the arrogant scouts from The *'Ay*? How can he be so easily snookered by the Gibeonite ruse? What is his role with regards to the delegation of manipulation sent to Transjordan? These textual moments suggest that, despite the occasional shaft of access to the Divine, this prophet must toil "a little lower than the angels," not to mention the more obvious horizon of the narrator and reader.

Mention of the narrator leads to a final word on the subject of history and prophecy. It should be remembered that each of the books of the Former Prophets is written anonymously; this is true of Joshua as well. Only much later do interpreters cast about for possible authors and editors. The usual list of suspects are those who loom large in the biblical story: Samuel, Nathan, Gad, and, of course, Joshua himself. Investigation nets nothing more than traditions of speculation.[20] Unlike we moderns, the text itself cares little for the question of authorship. Instead, it is efficiently steered by an omniscient narrator who sets scenes, musters voices, manages time, and, for the most part, keeps well out of sight. Instead of wrangling over the question of authorship, a better — and more biblical — investment would be to give energy toward an understanding of the language, strategy, and context of the narration.

LANGUAGE AND TEXT

Early texts of Joshua are preserved in Hebrew and Greek. The Leningrad Codex (B19[A]), dated A.D. 1009 or 1008, represents "the oldest dated manuscript of the complete Hebrew Bible."[21] Its very existence is a credit to the Masoretes who responsibly preserved and transmitted it. Their text critical work (oftentimes called the Masoretic Text, or "MT" for short) is the basis for many close read-

---

[20]According to the Talmud (*Baba Bathra* 14b, 15a), Joshua the son of Nun is responsible for writing the book by his name. However, it also acknowledges that Joshua's death was subsequently recorded by Eleazar son of Aaron, and that the death of Eleazar son of Aaron was recorded by Phinehas son of David. See Woudstra, *Joshua*, p. 5.

[21]K. Elliger and W. Rudolph, *Biblia Hebraica Stuttgartensia* (Stuttgart: Deutsche Bibelstiftung, 1967/1977), p. XI.

ings of the 656 verses of Joshua, including the present one. It is widely available with apparatus under the title of *Biblia Hebraica Stuttgartensia*. This text is well preserved; the Masoretes suggest few adjustments.[22] Students in the future may have access to the next generation of critical text, the *Biblia Hebraica Quinta*, currently being released in sections. Unfortunately, the pace of the study has not yet brought a Joshua volume forward to publication. Anticipation over this future work runs high, as it promises to add unpublished evidence from the Dead Sea Scrolls to the discussion.[23]

The Septuagint (LXX) gives testimony to the early Greek text of Joshua. This is available in critical form through the Cambridge[24] effort, although students may have more ready access to the concise work of A. Rahlfs.[25] Finally, one must also note the careful work of Max L. Margolis to reconstruct a "proto-LXX" version of the Joshua text.[26] That such an attempt could even be made reveals the edge of the storm when it comes to textual criticism and the book of Joshua. Numerous and, at times, significant differences between the Hebrew and Greek text traditions have placed this text at the center of the swirling debate.[27] This is hardly the place to test its currents though; suffice it to say that those responsible for the Joshua of the LXX were not inclined to settle for a wooden translation. Awkward passages in the MT are pruned or smoothed. Idioms are glossed. Occa-

---

[22]The Masoretes proposed only 32 adjustments of the *qere* ("as read") and *kethib* ("as written") variety for the entire book.

[23]Fragments from "two distinct manuscripts" were found in Cave 4 at Qumran. Other citations from Joshua were found among Dead Sea Scroll materials, and in one case, among fragments found at Masada. See Leonard Greenspoon, "The Book of Joshua—Part 1: Texts and Versions," *Currents in Biblical Research* 3 (2005): 236.

[24]A.E. Brook and N. McLean, *Joshua, Judges and Ruth*, vol. 1, part IV, in The Old Testament in Greek (Cambridge: Cambridge University, 1917).

[25]A. Rahlfs, ed., *Septuaginta* (Stuttgart: Württembergische Bibelanstalt, 1935).

[26]Max L. Margolis, *The Book of Joshua in Greek* (Paris: Geuthner, 1931–1938).

[27]Greenspoon observes how the Greek text is "approximately 4-5 percent shorter" than the Hebrew text. He continues: "Such figures mislead for there are places where the LXX is longer than MT; further, there are quite a few passages where the number of words in each tradition is about the same, but many of the words are different in meaning or structured differently" ("Book of Joshua," p. 234).

sionally, insertions are added and paragraphs are even rearranged, to make the text less cumbersome for its Greek readership. Clearly, the guarded approach of the Masoretes does not extend to these Hellenists. For the latter, the Old Testament is much more open to dynamic interpretation. That this effort is likely the work of the church (rather than the synagogue) is interesting indeed, and is deserving of future investigation concerning Hellenistic Christians and Scripture. In the meantime, to satisfy the curious, the work of A. Graeme Auld on the text of Joshua is probably the best place to begin.[28] For the rest, expedience demands that one eye be closed to the problem and that the priority of the MT be simply assumed. Only occasionally, will a quick peep be given to the LXX. Of course, to be consistent with the series in which this volume appears, all direct quotes (indicated in bold face) are drawn from the New International Version of the English Bible.

STRATEGY AND STRUCTURE

Conclusions concerning the literary context for Joshua have, in many ways, controlled ideas concerning the book's strategy and structure. Early critics recognized what has been observed here, namely, that Joshua is deeply connected to *torah*. At the beginning of the 19th century, W.M.L. DeWctte made this relationship formal, linking the book of Joshua to Deuteronomy.[29] This recognition prompted the thought that Joshua be considered as a part of the *torah* itself, and hence, in the minds of some, the Pentateuch (five books of Law) grew into a Hexateuch (six books of law). The same dissecting search for "sources" (the "JEDP" or "documentary hypothesis") that had been previously been applied to Genesis through Deuteronomy was extended to Joshua. Various voicings of the quest angled off in many directions.

---

[28]G. Graeme Auld, *Joshua Retold: Synoptic Perspectives* (Edinburgh: T & T Clark, 1998).

[29]See the summary of the idea of the "Deuteronomistic History" by S.L. Richter in *Dictionary of the Old Testament Historical Books*, ed. by Bill T. Arnold and H.G.M. Williamson (Downers Grove, IL: InterVarsity, 2005), pp. 219-230.

These were brought back together again in 1943 through the hypothesis of Martin Noth.[30] Noth began by recognizing the intimate connection between Deuteronomy and Joshua, but took this observation in a new direction. For him, the Former Prophets (Joshua, Judges, Samuel, and Kings) was too unified in style and substance to be the work of multiple hands. He therefore proposed that they be considered the work of a single historian or "compiler." The introduction to this sweeping work and, hence, the source of its controlling ideas was the book of Deuteronomy. Thus was born the idea of the "Deuteronomistic History," an elongated account describing how Israel first won, and subsequently lost, the *Heartland*. For Noth, the anonymous teller of this story hailed from the time of the exile (called simply the "Deuteronomist"), and therefore had the long view needed to observe how God had worked with Israel through the course of time. This effort involved repeated promises of blessing and warnings of destruction. But in the end, when the warnings went unheeded, God sent Israel into exile. The Deuteronomistic history was therefore an apology of sorts, a tragedy that justified divine choice in the face of human defiance. Much attention has been given to Noth's hypothesis in the years since it was first offered, to refine the process whereby the text reached its present state and to the ultimate meaning behind it.

One does not have to accept the presuppositions of critical scholarship to appreciate its partial grip on the truth. Without a doubt, the text of Joshua peers beyond itself. For those of DeWette's generation, seizing upon the fact that Joshua looks intently back to *torah*, and perhaps even to Deuteronomy in particular, is a point gained. Likewise, to the credit of Noth and his generation, the recognition that Joshua rightly anticipates specific events in Israel's future story is also helpful. Clearly, Joshua functions within a larger intertextual process stretching *both* backward and forward; it shares momentum, personalities, theology, and language not just with *torah*, the Former Prophets, and the rest of the Old Testament, but with the New Testament as well. One cannot wrench the book out of any one of these contexts without severing essential links.

---

[30]Martin Noth, *The Deuteronomistic History*, JSOTSupp 15 (Sheffield: JSOT, 1981 [1943]).

Since the mid-1980s, the recognition of "narrative art" has nudged the discipline of Old Testament study off of the mark of "compositional investigation" and has granted it new life. Instead of investing more effort in sorting out theories of editorial layering, more fruitful research may investigate character description, plot development, the play of voices, intertextuality, gapping, and similar dynamics. These are liberally mustered here, as pioneered within the field of biblical studies by Robert Alter,[31] Meir Sternberg,[32] H. Chanan Brichto,[33] and Adele Berlin,[34] among others. In this vein, Robert Polzin's *Moses and the Deuteronomist*[35] and L. Daniel Hawk's *Joshua*[36] are excellent examples of literary approaches to the book of Joshua. I have learned much from them; it is an indebtedness that will reveal itself.

This kind of literary sensitivity reveals that the text of Joshua is composed of several kinds of materials. It gives the book an uneven appearance, as prose narrative, geographical lists, boundary descriptions, inventories, legal interpretations, and exhortations are stitched together into a single tapestry. This can be puzzling not only for the unprepared reader, but for the expositor venturing into the recesses of the Old Testament! The prose of Joshua 1–12 lends itself well enough to pulpit use; from chapter 13 on, however, difficulties mount. Only by understanding the structure and goals of the text as a whole — a task most appropriately investigated through literary tools — may assistance be found in first appreciating, and then appropriating the larger message in a contemporary age.

That message may be outlined in three moves. The first is here titled, "How Yahweh Led Israel into Canaan" (1:1–12:24). This

---

[31]Robert Alter, *The Art of Biblical Narrative* (New York: Basic, 1981).

[32]Meir Sternberg, *The Poetics of Biblical Narrative: Ideological Literature and the Drama of Reading* (Bloomington: Indiana Press, 1985).

[33]Herbert Chanan Brichto, *Toward a Grammar of Biblical Poetics. Tales of the Prophets* (New York: Oxford, 1992).

[34]Adele Berlin, *Poetics and Interpretation of Biblical Narrative* (Sheffield: Almond, 1983).

[35]Robert Polzin, *Moses and the Deuteronomist: Deuteronomy, Joshua, Judges*. A Literary Study of the Deuteronomic History (Bloomington: Indiana University, 1980).

[36]L. Daniel Hawk, *Joshua*, Berit Olam. Studies in Hebrew Narrative & Poetry (Collegeville, MN: The Liturgical Press, 2000).

entrance is nothing short of miraculous: waters are parted at Israel's approach, and the occupants of Canaan either shrink back in fear, foolishly expose themselves, or fight each other. Setbacks for Israel are limited, and divine assistance is great. This culminates in the inventory of conquered chiefs.

In the second move of the book, Israel finds itself in the *Heartland*, hence, the title: "What Happened after Israel Arrived in Canaan" (13:1–21:45). Here, action is arrested; a progress report is given. It becomes clear that despite the initial successes, there is much work to be done. Village by village, region by region, tribe by tribe, land grants are detailed and distributed. Included here are special grants for the sake of religious and judicial institutions.

Far from an irrelevant appendix, the pieces are reeled together in the third and final move: "How to Be Israel" (22:1–24:35). Here, a series of speeches press a summary for the book. The definition of Israel is reexamined, as are the role of torah loyalty and choice-making in serving Yahweh.

Through it all, the subject of the *Heartland* is never too far out of sight. As a vibrant symbol for Israel, it recalls verbs of promising and gifting and resting, not to mention the figures of Abraham, Isaac, and Jacob. It also anticipates the partial success of occupation and the eventual loss of home in the exile. Still, one gets the distinct feeling, that while the *Heartland* is an important aspect of the story, it is not at the center. It is the view through the windshield, but not the reason for the journey. Certainly the revealed journey travels through the *Heartland*, noting physical boundaries along the way, but is more concerned with other, less tangible issues. To reduce these to bullet points may damage the presentation either by simplification or by leaping ahead of the evidence, but with that risk in mind, three objectives may be highlighted here. Perhaps this advance notice will assist in the hunt.

First, the book of Joshua is concerned with *torah* obedience. The primer for this plot is "a great commission" issued by Yahweh, distributed among his people, and used to induce courage, comfort, and, above all else, obedience. From the start, therefore, the question arises: will *torah* be instinctively recalled on the field and correctly adapted to ever-changing circumstances? The exhortation "to be strong and courageous" is raised. That energy is given a specific direction: strength and courage must be mustered in order "to carefully obey all the law my servant Moses gave you" (1:7). To obey Moses is to obey *torah*. To obey *torah* is to obey Yahweh.

Growing from the first concern is a second: the book of Joshua seeks to communicate the identity and ongoing program of Yahweh. A "pedestrian campaign" by the people will only be successful to the degree that it follows the lead of Yahweh. This will be no contest of arms. Here, the question is voiced: is Yahweh dependable as war-maker and promise-giver? A positive answer assists in the matter of obedience. It also integrates this book into the largest context: Joshua's story joins the ongoing story.

Third and finally, the book of Joshua is concerned with rightly defining the people of God. With so much attention given to bound-aries on the ground, the temptation is to identify Israel on the basis of landlines alone. While obviously these physical boundaries will be important, the narrator is keen to keep the balance of God's people in view. And fascinatingly, examples of faith are repeatedly drawn from unexpected corners. These examples underline a conclusion that suggests that those who *become* Israel are those who are chosen and rescued by Yahweh. Those who *remain* Israel are those who choose and serve Yahweh. If this message is marvelous in modern ears where "individual choice" is a way of life, imagine how much more so (and dangerous!) it sounds when voiced in a closed society where identity, rank, and power are not just predetermined, but group-determined.[37] This setting is crucial for appropriating the message of Joshua.

SETTING AND ARCHAEOLOGY

The tumultuous period of time known by archaeologists of the *Heartland* as the Late Bronze Age (hereafter LBA) stretches from

---

[37]Describing the social structure of ancient Israel is admittedly difficult. Help here is coming, however, as biblical scholars begin to develop and use new tools of analysis. Consider Bruce J. Malina, *Windows on the World of Jesus: Time Travel to Ancient Judea* (Louisville, KY: Westminster John Knox, 1993); John J. Pilch and Bruce J. Malina, eds., *Handbook of Biblical Social Values* (Peabody, MA: Hendrickson, 1998); and K.C. Hanson and Douglas E. Oakman, *Palestine in the Time of Jesus: Social Structures and Social Conflicts* (Minneapolis: Fortress, 1998).

approximately 1550–1200 B.C. (See Supplemental Study on Archaeological Periods p. 35.) Its arrival is signaled by a resurgence of Egyptian power, as a series of foreign rulers (Hyksos) were driven from the Nile basin. The effects of this revolt are significant, locally and internationally; an invigorated Egypt recenters itself, then expands its interests in all directions. In fact, the Egyptian shadow cast across Canaan is a characteristic but irregular feature of the two centuries to follow.[38]

If one follows this shadow to the other side of the Late Bronze Age, its end is signaled by the presence of large-scale upheavals across the eastern Mediterranean. These are noted on one point of the compass by the smoldering ruins of Priam's Troy and on other points by the wholesale collapse of regimes connected to centers at Mycenae, Hattusus, and Ugarit. A domino effect spurs refugee groups such as the Philistines to jostle for new homes on foreign shores. Robert Drews describes the curtain drawn over the ancient world in this moment with crisp efficiency: it is "The Catastrophe."[39] Hence, the LBA is framed by the renewal of Egypt in 1550 B.C. and the tumultuous upheavals of 1200 B.C. Obviously much will happen on the ground in the intervening 350-year period.

Patterns of settlement in the LBA are being uncovered and analyzed by *Heartland* archaeologists. Broadly speaking, when compared to previous centuries (Middle Bronze Age, or MBA, ca. 2000–1550 B.C.), cultural trends in the LBA signal a region in decline. Lines of trade are slowed and severed. Smaller villages dry up and disappear. Nomadism appears on the rise. Technology slumps. Areas located on the fringes of good land are deserted. Even some old urban centers located in very viable zones suggest crisis by their impoverishment and reduction in size. New constructions may appear on the other side of occupation gaps, but these cannot arrest the larger downward spiral. Ancient defensive earthworks are ignored or patched up for reuse. It is possible that this "urban" decline slows somewhat about halfway through the period (ca. 1400 B.C.) although further exploration is needed to confirm this suspicion.

---

[38]Mazar uses the metaphor of the Egyptian "shadow" to characterize the whole of the LBA. See his "In the Shadow of Egyptian Domination," in *Archaeology and the Land of the Bible*, pp. 232-294.

[39]Robert Drews, *The End of the Bronze Age: Changes in Warfare and the Catastrophe, ca. 1200 B.C.* (Princeton: Princeton University, 1993).

For readers of the Old Testament, this setting is important, as
interpreters who regard the text of Joshua as historically credible,
often insert the arrival of Israel in Canaan somewhere in the midst
of this LBA spiral. Passages such as 1 Kings 6:1 and Judges 11:26,
taken literally, suggest this. However, as it is understood from
archaeological data alone, no clear corresponding pattern of widespread destruction exists, either early or late in the period. Israel's
arrival in Canaan refuses to be measured in ashes.

What is measurable, and relevant in the spiral, may be summa-
rized using three kinds of evidence: the record of Egyptian raids,
clay tablets associated with the site of el-Amarna, and the appearance of new settlements in the highlands of the *Heartland*. The literary character of the first two is balanced by the nonliterary character of the third. A quick sketch of these three items is helpful for
establishing a context for reading Joshua.

The 18th and 19th Dynasties of New Kingdom Egypt align with
the LBA of the *Heartland*. Rulers of these dynasties were, for the
most part, eager to control the region, if for no other reason than
to profit from its trade goods and use its space as a buffer against
northern enemies. The bickering city-states of LBA Canaan may
have even been organized into a formal province governed from
Gaza. Secondary control points were established along lowland high-
ways at some half-dozen places like Aphek, Megiddo, and Beth
Sha'an. These Nile-born fingers should not be confused with a cultural invasion, however. Egyptian policy seems to be one of simple
subjugation, extortion, and exploitation. To ratchet up the "fear factor" among the Canaanite city-states and to ensure compliance, peri-
odic raids by Thutmose III, Amenhotep II, Thutmose IV, and others
were mounted.

These Egyptian raids assist the reader of Joshua in at least two
ways. First, of course, is in the matter of map making. More than 350
site names in Canaan and Syria are preserved in these royal records.[40]
They may, in part, be coordinated with site names found in the biblical text.[41] While not the highest priority of this study, the attempt

[40]Aharoni, *Land of the Bible*, p. 154.
[41]Consider the example of 119 names offered in the topographical list of
Thutmose III and discussed by Rainey and Notley, *Sacred Bridge*, pp. 72-74.

to identify and evaluate Joshua's site names on the ground will be an important feature.[42] Second, these raids help clarify a picture of Egyptian foreign policy in Canaan. Mirroring the trajectory of the LBA itself, the 18th Dynasty begins with strength, wavers, and then wanes before giving way to the 19th Dynasty. Moreover, Egyptian interest seems to be directed toward the more profitable (and strategic) lowlands of the Mediterranean coast and the Jezreel Valley. The central highlands of the *Heartland*, particularly in the south where the roads lead nowhere, appear irrelevant to their concerns. This uneven and piecemeal foreign policy of Egypt may be significant for reasons that will be seen.

Beyond the record of New Kingdom raids in Canaan, tablets associated with the site of Tell el-Amarna in Egypt help fix the context of LBA. At this site, the capital of Amenhotep IV (or Akhenaten), some 350 clay tablets were found. These were pressed with the diplomatic languages of the day[43] and represent a valuable archive of letters sent to the Pharaoh. Approximately half of these are dispatched from city-state leaders in Canaan; the rest hail from other corners of the ancient Near East. Together they paint a picture of weakening Egyptian power during the first half of the 14th century B.C. (the approximate middle of the LBA).

Canaanite chiefs complain of bully alliances, conspiring arms dealers, and roving gangs. They appeal to the Pharaoh for military aid in buttressing "Egyptian" interests, which, more often than not, are really their own interests (no surprises here!). As in the case of the record of Egyptian raids, the el-Amarna tablets preserve the names of numerous LBA centers; many correspond with biblical mentions. Most intriguing, however, are complaints about *'Apîru* men: mercenaries without property rights, who, at times, work both for and against the Canaanite chiefs. Not surprisingly, they seem to

---

[42]This effort is facilitated by regular reference to J. Monson, *Student Map Manual: Historical Geography of the Bible Lands* (Jerusalem: Pictorial Archive, 1979); Aharoni, *Land of the Bible*; Burton MacDonald, *"East of the Jordan": Territories and Sites of the Hebrew Scriptures* (Boston: ASOR, 2000); Yoel Elitzur, *Ancient Place Names in the Holy Land: Preservation and History* (Winona Lake, IN: Eisenbrauns, 2004); and Rainey and Notley, *Sacred Bridge*.

[43]Several languages and dialects have been identified in the Amarna archive. The bulk is in various dialects of Akkadian, while Hurrian, and Hittite are also attested (Rainey and Notley, *Sacred Bridge*, p. 88).

be a real threat in the highlands, where Egyptian leverage is most remote. Every scholar who has contemplated the period under review has considered the relationship between these troublemaking '*Apîru* (or *Habiru/Hapiru*) men and the biblical Hebrews. Could the Canaanites grousing at the '*Apîru* be leveled at the *Hebrews*? It is an attractive connection at a glance, but one that does not hold up under the evidence, be it linguistic, geographic, or social. What the '*Apîru* men really do for the Joshua reader is to suggest the degree to which the region has destabilized by 1400 B.C., the nature of Egyptian weakness (or selective disinterest) in its northeastern flank, and the havoc that a relatively small group of armed troublemakers can wreak among the city-states of LBA Canaan.

Finally, to sketch a context for this work, the appearance of new settlements in the highlands must be mentioned. This topic presses the discussion to the very end of the LBA and considers its collapse against the appearance of a new cast of characters in a new era. *Heartland* archaeologists agree that the human landscape changes dramatically when one moves from the end of the Bronze Age to the beginning of the Iron Age. This trend was noticed early on by Lawrence E. Stager, whose numbers are used here.[44] Diminishing site size and density in the LBA produced a situation where only 23 urban sites are known in the hill country stretching between the Jezreel Valley and Beer-sheba corridor. These sites are, on average, some seven and a half acres in area. By contrast, when one moves across the threshold of ca. 1200 B.C. into the beginning of the Iron Age, the number of highland sites soars from 23 to 114 in the same area. Of the 114, at least 97 are newly founded. In size, they are half that of their LBA predecessors, averaging slightly more than four acres. Stager goes on to point out how those who occupied these sites also adapted (or developed?) lifeway strategies appropriate for

---

[44]Lawrence E. Stager's seminal article on this subject is "The Archaeology of the Family in Ancient Israel," *BASOR* 260 (1985): 1-35.

The ongoing publication of work such as the Manasseh Hill Country Survey will undoubtedly force some reassessment of these numbers. The hard numbers described only generally by Adam Zertal ("Israel Enters Canaan—Following the Pottery Trail," *BAR* 17 [Sept./Oct. 1991]: 28-47) are slowly being disseminated. See Adam Zertal, *The Shechem Syncline*, vol. 1 in The Manasseh Hill Country Survey (Leiden: Brill, 2004), and *The Eastern Valleys and the Fringes of the Desert*, vol. 2 (Leiden: Brill, 2008).

hill country living. These include tactics of deforestation, terrace farming, the use of cisterns for water storage, houses that doubled as stables, and multigenerational family compounds.

Naturally, interest in this data has been great, and debates over how it is to be interpreted continue to the present.[45] The material-cultural nature of the evidence has lent itself to other angles of analysis; the contribution of social-scientific approaches here has been substantial, and yet, far from conclusive.[46] For some, elements of continuity from lowland to highland sites suggest that the settlers were not new to the region, but merely bands of locals moving upland. Others point to elements of discontinuity in order to suggest that these settlers were newcomers from outside. Stager navigates the debate carefully to reach his conclusion: "clearly there was a sizable influx of people into the highlands of central Palestine in the 12th century B.C."[47] That no one truly doubts that this is the presence of "early Israel" is telling. In fact, confirmation of the matter comes by way of the so-called "Israel Stela." Dated to the closing decades of the previous century (ca. 1212 B.C.), an engraved stone records the exploits of one Merneptah, an Egyptian pharaoh of the 19th Dynasty. Among his victims in Canaan is a tribal group known as "Israel."[48] Apparently their "demise" is worth bragging about. Hence, as the curtain of the LBA closes, Israel is already in its place posing some kind of challenge to Egypt. The proof is carved in a granite monument standing more than seven feet tall!

---

[45]As a sample of the debate, consider Israel Finkelstein, *The Archaeology of the Israelite Settlement* (Jerusalem: IES, 1988); Israel Finkelstein and Nadav Na'aman, eds., *From Nomadism to Monarchy. Archaeological and Historical Aspects of Early Israel* (Washington: BAS, 1994); William G. Dever, *Who Were the Early Israelites and Where Did They Come From?* (Grand Rapids: Eerdmans, 2003).

[46]As examples, see Robert B. Coote and Keith W. Whitelam, *The Emergence of Early Israel in Historical Perspective,* The Social World of Biblical Antiquity Series 5 (Sheffield: Almond, 1987); T.E. Levy, ed., *The Archaeology of Society in the Holy Land* (London: Leicester University, 1995); or Robert D. Miller, *Chieftains of the Highland Clans: A History of Israel in the 12th and 11th Centuries B.C.* (Grand Rapids: Eerdmans, 2005).

[47]Stager, "Archaeology of the Family," p. 3.

[48]There is some debate however, over how to interpret this "Israel" in Canaan. See Michael G. Hasel, "*Israel* in the Merneptah Stela," *BASOR* 296 (1994): 45-61.

Hence, the question lingering today does not concern the timing of Israel's arrival; highland settlements and Merneptah have all but settled that. The question concerns Israel's true origins and nature. Did this "early Israel" come from within the *Heartland,* from outside it, or is it the result of some combination thereof? Three models give voice to the options: an infiltration model, a revolt model, and a conquest model. Issues of continuity and discontinuity with respect to material culture are vital pieces to assessing each, as are the perceived strength and weaknesses of sociological analogies. Finally, presuppositions concerning the rootage of Joshua 1–12 in history also figure into weighing these ideas. A quick overview of these three models of Israel's origins will close this discussion.[49]

The infiltration model holds that Israel entered Canaan from without, coming peacefully as semi-nomadic tribesmen from neighboring deserts. Entering Cisjordan[50] annually with their herds, in search of grass and water, they eventually settled down, joined together in a community of equals, and became a part of the historical record as "Israel." This view seeks support by appealing to the patriarchal stories of Genesis that depict rustic herders and by appealing to life patterns of semi-nomads rediscovered by explorers in the 19th century. The model was formally voiced in the 1920s and 1930s by Albrecht Alt and Martin Noth.[51] While attractive in some ways, the model elevates sociological analogs over clear descriptions in the biblical text. Moreover, as more thorough study of semi-nomadic groups has shown, the infiltration model is founded upon exaggerations and misconceptions about how and why herders operate the way they do.[52]

---

[49]Overviews and evaluations of these three models are found in many places. Particularly helpful is the effort by K. Lawson Younger Jr., "Early Israel in Recent Biblical Scholarship," in *The Face of Old Testament Studies: A Survey of Contemporary Approaches,* ed. by David W. Baker and Bill T. Arnold (Grand Rapids: Baker, 1999), pp. 176-206.

[50]The term "Cisjordan" is explained on p. 103 in Chapter 3.

[51]See Martin Noth, *The History of Israel,* 2nd ed. (London: Adam & Charles Black, 1965).

[52]However Fritz has argued for a modified approach to this model, utilizing a more sensitive understanding of nomadism. See Volkmar Fritz, "Conquest or Settlement? The Early Iron Age in Palestine," *BA* 50 (1987): 84-100.

A second model of Israel's origins in Canaan hinges on a potent mix of contemporary social, historical, and political ideas. Sometimes called the "peasant revolt model," this view begins with a downward spiral of the LBA and the observed disparity between the "haves" and the "have-nots" of the land. It suggests that in a tumultuous "class struggle," the heavy-handed elites of Canaan lost control of those they sought to exploit. The exploited individuals fled the urban lowlands and settled in the more remote highlands. There, they coalesced into a group and under Joshua's leadership set about establishing a new order. As understood, Israel's arrival comes not from outside of Canaan, but as a result of a socio-economic struggle within the land. This theory was initially advanced by George Mendenhall,[53] but found modification in the work of Norman Gottwald, Israel Finkelstein, and others.[54] As a child of the 1960s and 1970s (revolutionary decades in their own right) the model reads the biblical story as myth, a cover story invented to hide a less-than-glorious past. The overt influences of liberation theology, Marxism, historical reductionism, and a selective reading of the biblical and archaeological evidence are clear.

The third and final voicing of Israel's origins in Canaan is the conquest model. By far, the most traditional of the three views presented here, the conquest model takes its cue from a positivist reading of the text of Joshua. Archaeological and sociological evidence is then used to fill in the missing details. Here, Israel surges into the land in a single onslaught and is overwhelmingly (and militarily) successful. Advocates of the conquest model such as W.F. Albright[55] or Yigael Yadin[56] sought widespread destructions in Canaan to pinpoint the arrival of Israel. However, when these levels did not materialize as expected, some either dismissed the text or sought to con-

---

[53]G.E. Mendenhall, "The Hebrew Conquest of Palestine," *BA* 25 (1962): 66-87.

[54]See Younger for the evolution of this model ("Early Israel," pp. 181-191).

[55]For example, see W.F. Albright, "Archaeology and the Date of the Hebrew Conquest of Palestine," *BASOR* 58 (1935): 10-18.

[56]To see Yigael Yadin's views toward the end of his life, see his "Is the Biblical Account of the Israelite Conquest of Canaan Historically Reliable? *BAR* 7 (1982): 16-23.

tort the archaeological record.[57] As argued here, neither of these conclusions is necessary. It is suggested that Joshua reveals far less destruction than the advocates of the conquest model first believed. Similarly, apparent "contradictions" between the text of Joshua and the text of Judges melt when simplistic readings are elevated to give room for literary concerns.

Hence, in the end, each of these three models selectively reads the biblical text, pulling some details from it while ignoring others. The text, like the historical formation of early Israel itself, is a complex production. Elements of peaceful infiltration, local assimilation, and violent conflict are all attested to some degree.[58] Overall, however, it is here concluded that "early Israel" comes from outside the *Heartland*. It moves in with varying degrees of success: scouting and shouting, dealing and stealing, waiting and measuring, but at all times, walking. Any continuity with respect to material culture is a matter of lingering locals, for after all, even when taken at face value, the biblical story of Joshua is a pedestrian expedition that eventually leads to a less-than-glorious conclusion. Needless to say, every walker is changed as a result of the experience.

SUPPLEMENTAL STUDY
ARCHAEOLOGICAL PERIODS

Systems of time reckoning used in the study of the *Heartland* grow from the outline of Christian Jürgensen Thomsen, first offered in the 19th century. Thomsen's "Three Age System" drew its primary categories from the presumed development of technology, hence "Stone Age," "Bronze Age," and "Iron Age." While it is realized that this development was more complex than that which Thomsen envisioned, the labels he created have stuck and continue to be used up to the present day.

---

[57]For an example of the latter, see J. Bimson, *Redating the Exodus and Conquest* (Sheffield: University of Sheffield, 1981).

[58]The "mixed multitude theory" seems to be sensitive to these dynamics (Ann E. Killebrew, *The Archaeology of Ethnicity in the Biblical World: Canaanites, Egyptians, Philistines, and Israelites 1300–1100 B.C.E.* [Atlanta: SBL, 2005], pp. 184-185). We await a fuller presentation of this idea.

Most relevant for the current study is the period of time known as the Bronze Age. While not everyone agrees on the details, scholars have divided and subdivided this block into ever-finer segments for the sake of organization and communication. As these may assist descriptions of historical and archaeological issues in the study of Joshua, some general comments on the subject of periodization are in order.

The beginning of the Bronze Age corresponds with the beginnings of urbanization in the *Heartland,* a threshold crossed around 3400 B.C. The end of the Bronze Age is aligned with a series of disruptions corresponding with 1200 B.C. The 2,200 years that passed between these two endpoints is usually divided into three blocks, known as the Early, Middle, and Late Bronze Ages. The Early Bronze Age, or EBA, (3400–2000 B.C.) witnessed a rise and fall of cultures; in this time the great pyramids of Egypt were built, the Sumerians settled in Mesopotamia, and quite possibly, at the very end of this period, Abraham left Ur for the Promised Land. The Middle Bronze Age, or MBA, (2000–1550 B.C.) follows the EBA, and, in the case of the *Heartland,* appears to be a moment of high culture. Canaanite art, pottery, jewelry, literature, city-building, and defensive systems reach a level of sophistication unmatched in the region for centuries on either side of the mark. It is unlikely that Israel had anything to do with this, however; they were occupied in Egypt, laboring in obscurity as slaves. However, the cultural climax reached in the *Heartland* during this time would leave a lasting legacy. The Canaan faced by Joshua was likely the residues from this MBA achievement. Hence, the Late Bronze Age, or LBA, (1550–1200 B.C.), believed to be the setting for Israel's arrival, was already suffering in a downward spiral that would continue to the collapse that marks the horizon between the Bronze and Iron Ages. The moment of Joshua's arrival therefore, would correspond with a stretch of great unrest as the surviving city-states squabbled with each other for limited resources and appealed to Egypt for help.

As the Bronze Age gives way to the Iron Age, new dynamics come into play, new people groups come to the fore, and new lines and labels are drawn. Temporally speaking, the Iron Age begins where the Bronze Age leaves off, in the collapse of 1200 B.C. Its other end is usually marked by the fall of Jerusalem at the hands of the Babylonians in 586 B.C. Hence, the six-century stretch called the Iron Age is, by far, of shorter duration than the Bronze Age that preceded it. Still, it is a most critical period for the reader of the biblical text. The Iron Age is a time of smallish kingdoms in competition with each other; one of these will be the Israel of Saul, David, and Hezekiah. To facilitate the descriptive task here, the Iron Age is divided into two blocks: Iron Age I and Iron Age II. The Iron Age I endures for two centuries, from 1200 to 1000 B.C. In this time Israel settles comfortably into a monarchial mode. In the four centuries that follow, known as Iron Age II, that united monarchy will fragment, struggle, and be dissolved. The same could be said of Israel's competitors, for, as the Iron Age comes to an end — and Thomsen's Three Age System with it — the following period will not be characterized by technological labels. It will be an Age of Empires.

OUTLINE

I. HOW YAHWEH LED ISRAEL INTO CANAAN — 1:1–12:24
A. A Great Commission Given — 1:1-18
   1. The Charge of Yahweh — 1:1-9
   2. The Charge of Joshua — 1:10-15
   3. The Charge of the People — 1:16-18
B. Behind Enemy Lines — 2:1-24
   1. Scouts Deployed — 2:1-7
   2. An Unexpected Betrayal and an Uncomfortable
      Covenant — 2:8-14,17-20
   3. The Escape and the Report — 2:15-16,21-24
C. Crossing over the Jordan — 3:1–4:24
   1. The People, the Priests, and Joshua Prepare — 3:1-14
   2. Israel's Riverwalk — 3:15-17
   3. The Crossing Over Memorialized in Israel — 4:1-8
   4. Joshua's Leadership Emphasized in Israel — 4:9
   5. The Crossing Over Completed — 4:10-18
   6. The Memorial Established — 4:19-24
D. Camping in Canaan's Land — 5:1-12
   1. The Canaanite Paralysis — 5:1
   2. The Israelite Pardon — 5:2-9
   3. The Passover Party — 5:10-12
E. Victory at Jericho — 5:13–6:27
   1. An Unexpected Meeting Described — 5:13-15
   2. An Unusual Strategy Prescribed — 6:1-5
   3. An Unusual Strategy Prosecuted — 6:6-27
F. A Secret Disobedience Revealed and Corrected — 7:1-26
   1. A Secret Disobedience — 7:1
   2. A Setback at the 'Ay — 7:2-5
   3. A Search for Answers — 7:6-9
   4. A Stern Warning — 7:10-13
   5. A Special Lottery — 7:14-26
G. The 'Ay Revisited — 8:1-29

TABLE OF SUPPLEMENTAL STUDIES

BIBLIOGRAPHY

Aharoni, Yohanan. *The Land of the Bible: A Historical Geography*. Rev. ed. Trans. by A.F. Rainey. Philadelphia: Westminster, 1979.

Ahituv, S., and B.A. Levine, eds. *The Early Biblical Period: Historical Studies*. Jerusalem: Israel Exploration Society, 1986.

Albright, W.F. "Archaeology and the Date of the Hebrew Conquest of Palestine." *Bulletin of the American Schools of Oriental Research* 58 (1935): 10-18.

—————. "The Israelite Conquest of Canaan in the Light of Archaeology." *Bulletin of the American Schools of Oriental Research* 74 (1939): 11-23.

Alter, Robert. *The Art of Biblical Narrative*. New York: Basic, 1981.

Anderson, Francis I. "Israelite Kinship Terminology and Social Structure." *Bible Translator* 20 (1969): 29-39.

Arnold, Bill T., and H.G.M. Williamson, eds. *Dictionary of the Old Testament Historical Books*. Downers Grove, IL: InterVarsity, 2005.

Auld, G. Graeme. *Joshua Retold: Synoptic Perspectives*. Edinburgh: T&T Clark, 1998.

Baker, David W., and Bill T. Arnold, eds. *The Face of Old Testament Studies: A Survey of Contemporary Approaches*. Grand Rapids: Baker, 1999.

Baly, Denis. *The Geography of the Bible*. New York: Harper & Row, 1974.

Bar-Efrat, Shimon. *Narrative Art in the Bible*. 2nd ed. Decator: Almond, 1984.

Bartlett, John R. *Cities of the Biblical World: Jericho*. Grand Rapids: Eerdmans, 1982.

Beck, John A. "Why Do Joshua's Readers Keep Crossing the River?

The Narrative-Geographical Shaping of Joshua 3–4." *Journal of the Evangelical Theological Society* 48 (Dec. 2005): 689-699.

Beitzel, Barry, ed. *Biblica: The Bible Atlas: A Social and Historical Journey through the Lands of the Bible.* Lane Cove: Global, 2006.

Ben Tor, A. "Excavating Hazor, Part II: Did the Israelites Destroy the Canaanite City?" *Biblical Archaeology Review* 25 (Mar./Apr. 1999): 22-39.

Berlin, Adele. *Poetics and Interpretation of Biblical Narrative.* Sheffield: Almond, 1983.

Bimson, J. *Redating the Exodus and Conquest.* Sheffield: University of Sheffield, 1981.

Bimson, John J., et al., eds. *New Bible Atlas.* Downers Grove, IL: InterVarsity, 1994.

Boling, Robert G. *Joshua: A New Translation with Notes and Commentary.* The Anchor Bible. Garden City, NY: Doubleday, 1982.

Borowski, Oded. *Every Living Thing: Daily Use of Animals in Ancient Israel.* Walnut Creek, CA: Alta Mira, 1998.

Bottero, J. *Mesopotamia: Writing, Reasoning, and the Gods.* Chicago: University of Chicago, 1992.

Botterweck, G. Johannes, Helmer Ringgren, and Heinz-Josef Fabry, eds. *Theological Dictionary of the Old Testament.* 15 vols. Grand Rapids: Eerdmans, 1974–2006.

Brichto, Herbert Chanan. *The Problem of "Curse" in the Hebrew Bible.* Philadelphia: Society of Biblical Literature, 1963.

_____ . *Toward a Grammar of Biblical Poetics: Tales of the Prophets.* Oxford: Oxford University, 1992.

Bromiley, Geoffrey W., ed. *International Standard Bible Encyclopedia.* Rev. ed. 4 vols. Grand Rapids: Eerdmans, 1988.

Brook, A.E., and N. McLean. *Joshua, Judges and Ruth.* Vol. I. Part IV. *The Old Testament in Greek.* Cambridge: Cambridge University, 1917.

Brown, F., S.R. Driver, and C.A. Briggs. *A Hebrew and English Lexicon of the Old Testament.* Oxford: Clarendon Press, 1952.

Brueggemann, Walter. *An Introduction to the Old Testament: The*

Canon and Christian Imagination. Louisville, KY: Westminster John Knox, 2003.

_____ . *A Social Reading of the Old Testament: Prophetic Approaches to Israel's Communal Life*. Ed. by Patrick D. Miller. Minneapolis: Fortress, 1994.

_____ . *Theology of the Old Testament: Testimony, Dispute, Advocacy*. Minneapolis: Fortress, 1997.

Bunimovitz, Shlomo. "Socio-Political Transformation in the Central Hill Country in the Late Bronze–Iron I Transition." In *From Nomadism to Monarchy: Archaeological and Historical Aspects of Early Israel*. Ed. by Israel Finkelstein and Nadav Na'aman. Pp. 179-202. Jerusalem: Israel Exploration Society, 1994.

Butler, Trent. *Joshua*. Vol. 7. Word Biblical Commentary. Ed. by David A. Hubbard and Glenn W. Barker. Waco: Word, 1983.

Callaway, Joseph A. "Ai (Et-Tell): Problem Site for Biblical Archaeologists." In *Archaeology and Biblical Interpretation: Essays in Memory of D. Glenn Rose*. Ed. by Leo G. Perdue, Lawrence E. Toombs, and Gary L. Johnson. Pp. 87-99. Atlanta: John Knox, 1987.

Campbell, K.M. "Rahab's Covenant." *Vetus Testamentum* 22 (1972): 243-244.

Carter, Renae. "Property, Jubilee, and Redemption in Ancient Israel." M.A. Thesis, Cincinnati Christian University, 2005.

Childs, John. "The Military Revolution I." In *The Oxford History of Modern War*. New ed. Ed. by Charles Townshend. Pp. 20-39. Oxford: Oxford University, 2005.

Chouinard, Larry, David Fiensy, and George Pickens, eds. *Christian Ethics: The Issues of Life and Death*. Joplin, MO: Parma, 2003.

Clausewitz, Carl von. *On War*. Trans by Michael Howard and Peter Paret. Oxford: Oxford University, 2007.

Cleave, Richard, et al. *The Holy Land Satellite Atlas*: Vol. 1, *Terrain Recognition*, and Vol. 2, *The Regions*. Nicosia: Røhr Productions, 1999.

Cohen, Chaim, Avi Hurvitz, and M. Shalom, eds. *Sefer Moshe: The Moshe Weinfeld Jubilee Volume: Studies in the Bible and the Ancient Near East, Qumran, and Post-Biblical Judaism*. Winona Lake, IN: Eisenbrauns, 2004.

Coogan, Michael D., ed. *The Oxford History of the Biblical World*. New York: Oxford, 1998.

Coote, Robert B. "Tribalism: Social Organization in the Biblical Israels." In *Ancient Israel: The Old Testament in Its Social Context*. Ed. by Philip F. Esler. Pp. 35-49. Minneapolis: Fortress, 2006.

Coote, Robert B., and Keith W. Whitelam. *The Emergence of Early Israel in Historical Perspective: The Social World of Biblical Antiquity Series, 5*. Sheffield: Almond, 1987.

Crawford, T.G. "Taking the Promised Land, Leaving the Promised Land: Luke's Use of Joshua for a Christian Foundation Story." *Review and Expositor* 95 (1998): 251-261.

Creach, Jerome F.D. *Joshua*. Interpretation: A Bible Commentary for Teaching and Preaching. Louisville, KY: Westminster John Knox, 2003.

Danby, Herbert, trans. *The Mishnah*. London: Oxford University, 1933.

Davidson, Richard M. *Typology in Scripture: A Study of Hermeneutical Typos Structure*. Berrien Springs, MI: Andrews University, 1981.

Davis, Dale Ralph. *No Falling Words: Expositions of the Book of Joshua*. Grand Rapids: Baker, 1988.

Demsky, Aaron. "The Boundary of the Tribe of Dan (Joshua 19:41-46)." In *Sefer Moshe: The Moshe Weinfeld Jubilee Volume: Studies in the Bible and the Ancient Near East, Qumran, and Post-Biblical Judaism*. Ed. by Chaim Cohen, Avi Hurvitz, and M. Shalom. Pp. 261-284. Winona Lake, IN: Eisenbrauns, 2004.

de Vaux, Roland. *Ancient Israel: Its Life and Institutions*. Trans. by John McHugh. New York: McGraw-Hill, 1961.

Dever, William G. "How to Tell a Canaanite from an Israelite." In *The Rise of Ancient Israel*. Symposium at the Smithsonian Institution, October 26, 1991. Pp. 26-60. Washington DC: Biblical Archaeology Society, 1992.

Dever, William G. *Who Were the Early Israelites and Where Did They Come From?* Grand Rapids: Eerdmans, 2003.

Dothan, Trude. *The Philistines and Their Material Culture*. New Haven: Yale, 1982.

Drews, Robert. "The 'Chariots of Iron' of Joshua and Judges." *Journal for the Study of the Old Testament* 45 (1989): 15-23.

_____ . *The End of the Bronze Age: Changes in Warfare and the Catastrophe ca. 1200 B.C.* Princeton: Princeton University, 1993.

Drinkard, J.F. Jr., G.L. Mattingly, and J.M. Miller, eds. *Benchmarks in Time and Culture: Essays in Honor of Joseph A Callaway.* Atlanta: Scholars, 1988.

Elitzur, Yoel. *Ancient Place Names in the Holy Land: Preservation and History.* Winona Lake, IN: Eisenbrauns, 2004.

Elliger, K., and W. Rudolph. *Biblia Hebraica Stuttgartensia.* Stuttgart: Deutsche Bibelstiftung, 1967/1977.

Ellis, Earle E. *The Old Testament in Early Christianity: Canon and Interpretation in the Light of Modern Research.* Grand Rapids: Eerdmans, 1991.

Epstein, I. *The Babylonian Talmud: Seder Mo'ed Megillah.* London: Soncino, 1938.

Eshel, H. "A Note on Joshua 1:61-62 and the Identification of the City of Salt." *Israel Exploration Journal* 4 (1995): 37-40.

Esler, Philip F. "Social-Scientific Models in Biblical Interpretation." In *Ancient Israel: The Old Testament in Its Social Context.* Ed. by Philip F. Esler. Pp. 3-14. Minneapolis: Fortress, 2006.

Finkelstein, Israel. *The Archaeology of the Israelite Settlement.* Jerusalem: Israel Exploration Society, 1988.

Finkelstein, Israel, and Nadav Na'aman, eds. *From Nomadism to Monarchy: Archaeological and Historical Aspects of Early Israel.* Jerusalem: Israel Exploration Society, 1994.

Freedman, David Noel, Allen C. Myers, and Astrid B. Beck, eds. *Eerdmans Dictionary of the Bible.* Grand Rapids: Eerdmans, 2000.

Freedman, David Noel, and David Frank Graf, eds. *Palestine in Transition: The Emergence of Ancient Israel.* The Social World of Biblical Antiquities Series 2. Sheffield: Almond, 1983.

Fritz, Volkmar. *The City in Ancient Israel.* Sheffield: Sheffield Academic, 1995.

_____ . "Conquest or Settlement? The Early Iron Age in Palestine." *Biblical Archaeologist* 50 (1987): 84-100.

Gal, Zvi. "Iron I in Lower Galilee and the Margins of the Jezreel Valley." In *From Nomadism to Monarchy: Archaeological and Historical Aspects of Early Israel*. Ed. by Israel Finkelstein and Nadav Na'aman. Pp. 43-44. Jerusalem: Israel Exploration Society, 1994.

Garstang, J. *Joshua, Judges*. London: Constable, 1931.

Glueck, Nelson. *Ḥesed in the Bible*. Trans. by A. Gottschalk. Cincinnati: Hebrew Union College, 1967.

—————— . *The River Jordan: Being an Illustrated Account of Earth's Most Storied River*. Philadelphia: Westminster, 1946.

Gorny, Ronald L. "Hittites." In *Eerdmans Dictionary of the Bible*. Ed. by D.N. Freedman. Pp. 595-597. Grand Rapids: Eerdmans, 2000.

Gray, John. *Joshua, Judges, and Ruth*. New Century Bible. Rev. ed. Greenwood: Attic, 1977.

Greenspoon, Leonard. "The Book of Joshua—Part 1: Texts and Versions." *Currents in Biblical Research* 3 (2005): 236.

Gundry, Stanley N., ed. *Show Them No Mercy: 4 Views on God and Canaanite Genocide*. Grand Rapids: Zondervan, 2003.

Gunn, David M., and Danna Nolan Fewell. *Narrative in the Hebrew Bible*. Oxford: Oxford University, 1993.

Hall, Gary. "Violence in the Name of God: Israel's Holy Wars." In *Christian Ethics: The Issues of Life and Death*. Ed. by Larry Chouinard, David Fiensy, and George Pickens. Pp. 261-284. Joplin, MO: Parma, 2003.

Halligan, John M. "The Role of the Peasant in the Amarna Period." In *Palestine in Transition: The Emergence of Ancient Israel*. The Social World of Biblical Antiquities Series 2. Ed. by David Noel Freedman and David Frank Graf. Pp. 15-24. Sheffield: Almond, 1983.

Hallo, W.W. "The First Purim." *Biblical Archaeologist* 46 (1983): 19-29.

Hanson, K.C., and Douglas E. Oakman. *Palestine in the Time of Jesus: Social Structures and Social Conflicts*. Minneapolis: Fortress, 1998.

Harris, J. Gordon, Cheryl A. Brown, and Michael S. Moore. *Joshua, Judges, Ruth*. Vol. 5. New International Biblical Commentary. Ed. by Robert L. Hubbard Jr. and Robert K. Johnston. Peabody, MA: Hendrickson, 2000.

Harris, R. Laird, Gleason L. Archer, and Bruce Waltke, eds. *Theological Wordbook of the Old Testament*. 2 vols. Chicago: Moody, 1980.

Hasel, Michael G. "*Israel* in the Merneptah Stela." *Bulletin of the American Schools of Oriental Research* 296 (1994): 45-61.

Hawk, L. Daniel. *Every Promise Fulfilled: Contesting Plots in Joshua*. Louisville, KY: Westminster John Knox, 1991.

_____. *Joshua. Berit Olam: Studies in Hebrew Narrative & Poetry*. Collegeville, MN: The Liturgical Press, 2000.

_____. "Strange Houseguests: Rahab, Lot, and the Dynamics of Deliverance." In *Reading between the Texts: Intertexuality and the Hebrew Bible*. Ed. by D.N. Fewell. Pp. 89-97. Louisville, KY: Westminster John Knox, 1992.

Hepner, Gershon. "Israelites Should Conquer Israel: The Hidden Polemic of the First Creation Narrative." *Revue biblique* 113 (April 2006): 161-180.

Hepper, Nigel F. *Baker Encyclopedia of Bible Plants*. Grand Rapids: Baker, 1992.

Herzog, Chaim, and Mordechai Gichon. *Battles of the Bible: A Modern Military Evaluation of the Old Testament*. New York: Random House, 1978.

Hess, Richard S. "Achan and Achor: Names and Wordplay in Joshua." *Hebrew Annual Review* 14 (1994): 89-98.

_____. "Asking Historical Questions of Joshua 13–19: Recent Discussion Concerning the Date of the Boundary Lists." In *Faith, Tradition and Eastern Context*. Pp. 191-205. Ed. by A.R. Millard, James K. Hoffmeier, and David W. Baker. Winona Lake, IN: Eisenbrauns, 1994.

_____. "Non-Israelite Personal Names in the Book of Joshua." *Catholic Biblical Quarterly* 58 (April 1996): 205-214.

Hillel, Daniel. *The Natural History of the Bible: An Environmental Exploration of the Hebrew Scriptures*. New York: Columbia University, 2006.

Hoffmeier, James K. "The Structure of Joshua 1–11 and the Annals of Thutmose III." In *Faith, Tradition, and History: Old Testament Historiography in Its Near Eastern Context*. Ed. by A.R. Millard,

James K. Hoffmeier, and David W. Baker. Pp. 165-179. Winona Lake, IN: Eisenbrauns, 1994.

Hoftijzer, J., and G. Van der Kooij. *Aramaic Texts from Deir 'Alla.* Leiden: Brill, 1976.

Holliday, John. "Day(s) the Moon Stood Still." *Journal of Biblical Literature* 87 (1968): 166-178.

Howard Jr., David M. "'Three Days' in Joshua 1–3: Resolving a Chronological Conundrum." *Journal of the Evangelical Theological Society* 41 (Dec. 1998): 539-550.

Humphreys, Colin J. "The Number of People in the Exodus from Egypt: Decoding Mathematically the Very Large Numbers in I and XXVI." *Vetus Testamentum* 48 (April 1998): 196-213.

Jones, Gwilym H. "'Holy War' or 'Yahweh War'?" *Vetus Testamentum* 25 (1975): 642-658.

Jost, Lynn. "Warfare in the Old Testament: An Argument for Peacemaking in the New Millennium." *Direction* 27 (1998): 177-188.

Kaiser, Walter C. Jr. *Hard Sayings of the Old Testament.* Downers Grove, IL: InterVarsity, 1988.

_____. *Toward an Old Testament Theology.* Grand Rapids: Zondervan, 1979.

Keil, C.F. *Commentary on the Book of Joshua.* Trans. by J. Martin. London: T & T Clark, 1857.

Kempinski, Aharon. "Middle and Late Bronze Age Fortifications." In *The Architecture of Ancient Israel: From the Prehistoric to the Persian Periods.* Ed. by Aharon Kempinski and Ronny Reich. Pp. 127-142. Jerusalem: Israel Exploration Society, 1992.

Kempinski, Aharon, and Ronny Reich, eds. *The Architecture of Ancient Israel: From the Prehistoric to the Persian Periods.* Jerusalem: Israel Exploration Society, 1992.

Kenyon, Kathleen M. "Jericho." In *The New Encyclopedia of Archaeological Excavations in the Holy Land.* Vol. 2. Ed. by Ephraim Stern. Pp. 674-681. New York: Simon & Schuster, 1993.

Killebrew, Anne E. *The Archaeology of Ethnicity in the Biblical World: Canaanites, Egyptians, Philistines, and Israelites 1300–1100 BCE.* Atlanta: Society of Biblical Literature, 2005.

King, Philip J., and Lawrence E. Stager. *Life in Biblical Israel.* Louisville, KY: Westminster John Knox, 2001.

Kissling, Paul J. *Reliable Characters in the Primary History: Profiles of Moses, Joshua, Elijah and Elisha.* JSOT Supplement Series 224. Sheffield: Sheffield, 1996.

Kitchen, K.A. *On the Reliability of the Old Testament.* Grand Rapids: Eerdmans, 2003.

Knoppers, Gary N. "The Historical Study of the Monarchy: Developments and Detours." In *The Face of Old Testament Studies: A Survey of Contemporary Approaches.* Ed. by David W. Baker and Bill T. Arnold. Pp. 207-235. Grand Rapids: Baker, 1999.

Kochavi, Moshe. "Aphek." In *The Oxford Encyclopedia of Archaeology in the Near East.* Vol. 1. Ed. by Eric M. Meyers. Pp. 147-151. New York: Oxford, 1997.

Koehler, Ludwig, and Walter Baumgartner, eds. *The Hebrew and Aramaic Lexicon of the Old Testament.* Leiden: Brill, 1994–2000.

LaBianca, Øystein. *Sedentarization and Nomadization: Hesban 1.* Berrien Springs, MI: Andrews University, 1990.

Lambdin, T.O. *Introduction to Biblical Hebrew.* New York: Scribner, 1971.

Lawrence, Lee. "History's Curve." *Saudi Aramco World* 54 (Sept./ Oct. 2003): 2-11.

Lemaire, Andre. "Fragments from the Book of Balaam Found at Deir Alla." *Biblical Archaeology Review* 11 (Sept./Oct. 1985): 26-39.

Levy, T.E., ed. *The Archaeology of Society in the Holy Land.* London: Leicester University, 1995.

Linbolm, J. "Lot-Casting in the Old Testament." *Vetus Testamentum* 122 (April 1962): 164-178.

Liverani, M. "The Amorites." In *Peoples of Old Testament Times.* Ed. by D.J. Wiseman. Pp. 100-133. Oxford: Clarendon, 1975.

Livingston, David. "Further Considerations on the Location of Bethel at El-Bireh." *Palestine Exploration Quarterly* 126 (Jul.-Dec. 1994): 154-159.

_____ . "Location of Biblical Bethel and Ai Reconsidered." *Westminster Theological Journal* 33 (Nov. 1970): 20-44.

_____. "Traditional Site of Bethel Questioned." *Westminster Theological Journal* 34 (Nov. 1971): 39-50.

Long, Jesse C. Jr. *1 & 2 Kings.* The College Press NIV Commentary. Joplin, MO: College Press, 2002.

Long, V. Philips. *The Art of Biblical History.* Vol. 5. Foundations of Contemporary Interpretation. Ed. by Moises Silva. Grand Rapids: Zondervan, 1994.

MacDonald, Burton. *"East of the Jordan": Territories and Sites of the Hebrew Scriptures.* Boston: ASOR, 2000.

Machlin, Milt. *Joshua's Altar: The Dig at Mount Ebal.* New York: William Morrow, 1991.

Malamat, Abraham. "How Inferior Israelite Forces Conquered Fortified Canaanite Cities." *Biblical Archaeology Review* (Mar./Apr. 1982): 25-35.

Malina, Bruce J. *The New Testament World: Insights from Cultural Anthropology.* 3rd ed. Louisville, KY: Westminster John Knox, 2001.

_____. *Windows on the World of Jesus: Time Travel to Ancient Judea.* Louisville, KY: Westminster John Knox, 1993.

Margolis, Max L. *The Book of Joshua in Greek.* Paris: Geuthner, 1931–1938.

Marquet-Krause, J. *"La deuxième campagne de fouilles à 'Ay (1934): Rapport Sommaire."* *Syria* 16 (1935): 325-345.

Matthews, Victor. *Manners and Customs in the Bible.* Rev. ed. Peabody, MA: Hendrickson, 1991.

Matthews, Victor H., and Don C. Benjamin. *Social World of Ancient Israel 1250–587 BCE.* Hendrickson, MA: Peabody, 1993.

Mazar, Amihai. *Archaeology of the Land of the Bible 10,000–586 B.C.E.* The Anchor Bible Reference Library. New York: Doubleday, 1990.

_____. "Jerusalem and Its Vicinity in Iron Age I." In *From Nomadism to Monarchy: Archaeological and Historical Aspects of Early Israel.* Ed. by Israel Finkelstein and Nadav Na'aman. Pp. 70-91. Jerusalem: Israel Exploration Society, 1994.

Mazar, Benjamin. "Geshur and Maachah." In *The Early Biblical*

Period: Historical Studies. Ed. by S. Ahituv and B.A. Levine. Pp. 113-125. Jerusalem: Israel Exploration Society, 1986.

_____. "Lebo-hamath and the Northern Border of Canaan." In *The Early Biblical Period Historical Studies*. Ed. by Shmuel Ahituv and Baruch A. Levine. Pp. 189-202. Jerusalem: Israel Exploration Society, 1986.

McCarthy, Dennis J. "An Installation Genre?" *Journal of Biblical Literature* 90 (1971): 31-41.

McGarvey, J.W. *Lands of the Bible: A Geographical and Topographical Description of Palestine with Letters of Travel in Egypt, Syria, Asia Minor, and Greece*. Philadelphia: J.B. Lippencott, 1880.

Mendenhall, G.E. "The Hebrew Conquest of Palestine." *Biblical Archaeologist* 25 (1962): 66-87.

Merling, David Sr. *The Book of Joshua: Its Theme and Role in Archaeological Discussions*. Andrews University Doctoral Dissertation Series 23. Berrien Springs, MI: Andrews University, 1997.

_____. "Large Numbers at the Time of the Exodus." *Near East Archaeological Society Bulletin* 44 (1999): 15-27.

_____. "The Number of Israelites at the Exodus." Unpublished paper, 1998.

Meyers, Eric M., ed. *The Oxford Encyclopedia of Archaeology in the Near East*. 5 Vols. New York: Oxford, 1997.

Millard, A.R., James K. Hoffmeier, and David W. Baker, eds. *Faith, Tradition, and History: Old Testament Historiography in Its Near Eastern Context*. Winona Lake, IN: Eisenbrauns, 1994.

Miller, Patrick D. Jr. "The Gift of God: The Deuteronomic Theology of the Land." *Interpretation* 22 (1969): 451-461.

Miller, Robert D. *Chieftains of the Highland Clans: A History of Israel in the 12th and 11th Centuries B.C.* Grand Rapids: Eerdmans, 2005.

Monson, James M. *The Land Between: A Regional Study Guide to the Land of the Bible*. Jerusalem: n.p., 1983.

_____. *Student Map Manual: Historical Geography of the Bible Lands*. Jerusalem: Pictorial Archive, 1979.

Montagu, Jeremy. *Musical Instruments of the Bible*. Lanham, MD: Scarecrow, 2002.

Muilenburg, James. "The Site of Ancient Gilgal." *Bulletin of the American Schools of Oriental Research* 140 (Dec. 1955): 11-27.

Nelson, Richard D. *Joshua: A Commentary*. The Old Testament Library. Louisville, KY: Westminster John Knox, 1997.

Niditch, Susan. *War in the Hebrew Bible: A Study in the Ethics of Violence*. New York: Oxford, 1993.

Niehaus, Jeffrey. "*Pa'am 'Ehat* and the Israelite Conquest." *Vetus Testamentum* 30 (1980): 236-238.

Noth, Martin. *The Deuteronomistic History*. JSOT Supplement Series 15. Sheffield: JSOT, 1981.

_____. *The History of Israel*, 2nd ed. London: Adam & Charles Black, 1965.

Nugent, John C. "Biblical Warfare Revisited: Extending the Insights of John Howard Yoder." Parallel session presented at the 7th Annual *Stone-Campbell Journal* Conference. Cincinnati Christian University. April 12, 2008.

O'Connor, Jerome M. *The Holy Land: An Oxford Archaeological Guide from Earliest Times to 1700*. 4th ed. Oxford: Oxford University, 1998.

Origen. *Homilies on Joshua*. The Fathers of the Church, 105. Trans. by Barbara J. Bruce. Ed. by Cynthia White. Washington, DC: Catholic University of America, 2002.

Orni, Efraim, and Elisha Efrat. *Geography of Israel*. 4th ed. Jerusalem: Israel Universities, 1980.

Pao, David W. *Acts and the Isaianic New Exodus*. Grand Rapids: Baker, 2000.

Peterson, Eugene. *A Long Obedience in the Same Direction: Discipleship in an Instant Society*. 2nd ed. Downers Grove, IL: InterVarsity, 2000.

Pilch, John J., and Bruce J. Malina, eds. *Handbook of Biblical Social Values*. Peabody, MA: Hendrickson, 1998.

Pitard, Wayne T. "Before Israel: Syria-Palestine in the Bronze Age."

In *The Oxford History of the Biblical World*. Ed. by Michael D. Coogan. Pp. 33-77. New York: Oxford, 1998.

Pitre, Brant. *Jesus, the Tribulation, and the End of Exile: Restoration Eschatology and the Origin of the Atonement*. Grand Rapids: Baker, 2005.

Plevnik, Joseph. "Honor/Shame." In *Handbook of Biblical Social Values*. John J. Pilch and Bruce J. Malina, eds. Peabody, MA: Hendrickson, 1998.

Polzin, Robert. *Moses and the Deuteronomist: A Literary Study of the Deuteronomic History. Part One. Deuteronomy, Joshua, Judges*. Bloomington, IN: Indiana University, 1980.

Porter, J.R. "The Legal Aspects of the Concept of 'Corporate Personality' in the Old Testament." *Vetus Testamentum* 15 (1965): 361-380.

Rad, Gerhard von. "The Promised Land and Yahweh's Land in the Hexateuch." In *The Problem of the Hexateuch and Other Essays*. Trans. by E.W. Trueman. Pp. 79-93. New York: McGraw-Hill, 1966.

Rahlfs, A. ed. *Septuaginta*. Stuttgart: Württembergische Bibelanstalt, 1935.

Rainey, Anson F. "Bethel Is Still *BEITÎN*." *Westminster Theological Journal* 33 (May 1971): 175-188.

_____ . "Historical Geography." In *Benchmarks in Time and Culture: Essays in Honor of Joseph A Callaway*. Ed. by J.F. Drinkard Jr., G.L. Mattingly, and J.M. Miller. Pp. 353-368. Atlanta: Scholars, 1988.

Rainey, Anson F., and R. Steven Notley. *The Sacred Bridge: Carta's Atlas of the Biblical World*. Carta: Jerusalem, 2006.

Rhem, Kathleen T. "Aboard Lincoln, President Bush Proclaims End to Major Combat Ops in Iraq." *Navy News*. 2 May, 2003 [newspaper on-line]; accessed 28 April, 2008; available from http://www.news.navy.mil/search/display.asp?story_id=7239.

Richter, S.L. "Deuteronomisic History." In *Dictionary of the Old Testament Historical Books*. Ed. by Bill T. Arnold and H.G.M. Williamson. Pp. 219-230. Downers Grove, IL: InterVarsity, 2005.

Ritter, Carl. *The Comparative Geography of Palestine and the Sinaitic Peninsula.* New York: Appleton, 1866.

Robertson, Palmer O. *The Israel of God: Yesterday, Today, and Tomorrow.* Phillipsburg: P&R, 2003.

Robinson, H. Wheeler. *Corporate Personality in Ancient Israel.* Rev. ed. Philadelphia: Fortress, 1980.

Rothstein, David. "The Meaning of 'A Three-Days Journey' in 11 QT. The Evidence of Biblical and Post-Biblical Sources." *Revue biblique* 114 (Jan. 2007): 32-51.

Sailhamer, John H. *The Pentateuch as Narrative: A Biblical-Theological Commentary.* Grand Rapids: Zondervan, 1992.

Scott, R.B.Y. "Meteorological Phenomena and Terminology in the Old Testament." *Zeitschrift für die Alttestamentliche Wissenschaft* (1952): 19-20.

Smith, George Adam. *The Historical Geography of the Holy Land.* 25th ed. Reprint. NewYork: Harper & Row, 1966.

Smith, Mark S. *The Memoirs of God: History, Memory, and the Experience of the Divine in Ancient Israel.* Minneapolis: Fortress, 2004.

Spina, Frank Anthony. "Reversal of Fortune: Rahab the Israelite and Achan the Canaanite." *Bible Review* 17 (Aug. 2001): 30.

Stager, Lawrence E. "The Archaeology of the Family in Ancient Israel." *Bulletin of the American Schools of Oriental Research* 260 (1985): 1-35.

Steinsaltz, Adin. *The Essential Talmud.* Thirteenth Anniversary Edition. New York: Basic, 2006.

Stern, Ephraim, ed. The *New Encyclopedia of Archaeological Excavations in the Holy Land.* 4 vols. New York: Simon and Schuster, 1993.

Sternberg, Meir. *The Poetics of Biblical Narrative: Ideological Literature and the Drama of Reading.* Bloomington, IN: Indiana Press, 1985.

Stott, John. *The Spirit, The Church, and the World: The Message of Acts.* Downers Grove, IL: InterVarsity, 1990.

Theological Wordbook of the Old Testament. 2 vols. Ed. by R. Laird Harris, Gleason L. Archer, and Bruce Waltke. Chicago: Moody, 1980.

Townshend, Charles, ed. *The Oxford History of Modern War.* New ed. Oxford: Oxford University Press, 2005.

VanGemeren, William A. *Interpreting the Prophetic Word.* Grand Rapids: Zondervan, 1990.

Waldbaum, Jane C. "The First Archaeological Appearance of Iron and the Transition to the Iron Age." In *The Coming of the Age of Iron.* Ed. by Theodore A. Wertime and James D. Muhly. Pp. 69-98. New Haven, CT: Yale University, 1980.

Wallerstein, Immanuel. *The Capitalist World-Economy.* Cambridge: Cambridge University, 1979.

_____. *The Modern World-System, Vol. 1: Capitalist Agriculture and the Origins of the European World-Economy in the Sixteenth Century.* New York: Academic, 1974.

_____. *World-Systems Analysis: An Introduction.* Durham, NC: Duke University, 2004.

Waltke, Bruce K., and Michael Patrick O'Connor. *An Introduction to Biblical Hebrew Syntax.* Winona Lake, IN: Eisenbrauns, 1990.

Walton, John H. "Joshua 10:12-15 and Mesopotamia Celestial Omen Texts." In *Faith, Tradition, and History: Old Testament Historiography in Its Near Eastern Context.* Ed. by A.R. Millard, James K. Hoffmeier, and David W. Baker. Pp. 181-190. Winona Lake, IN: Eisenbrauns, 1994.

Weigley, Russell F. *The American Way of War: A History of United States Military Strategy and Policy.* Bloomington, IN: Indiana University, 1973.

Wenham, Gordon J. "The Deuteronomic Theology of the Book of Joshua." *Journal of Biblical Literature* 90 (Jun. 1971): 140-148.

_____. *Numbers: An Introduction and Commentary.* The Tyndale Old Testament Commentaries. Downers Grove, IL: InterVarsity, 1981.

Wenham, John W. "Large Numbers in the Old Testament." *Tyndale Bulletin* 18 (1967): 19-53.

Wertime, Theodore A., and James D. Muhly, eds. *The Coming of the Age of Iron.* New Haven, CT: Yale University, 1980.

Wiseman, D.J., ed. *Peoples of Old Testament Times*. Oxford: Clarendon, 1973.

_____. "Rahab of Jericho." *Tyndale Bulletin* 14 (1964): 8-11.

Wood, Bryant G. "From Ramesses to Shiloh: Archaeological Discoveries Bearing on the Exodus–Judges Period." In *Giving the Sense: Understanding and Using Old Testament Historical Texts*. Ed. by David M. Howard, Jr. and Michael A. Grisanti. Pp. 256-282. Grand Rapids: Kregel, 2003.

_____. "Did the Israelites Conquer Jericho? A New Look at the Archaeological Evidence." *Biblical Archaeology Review* 16 (March/April 1990): 44-57.

Woudstra, Marten H. *The Book of Joshua*. The New International Commentary on the Old Testament. Grand Rapids: Eerdmans, 1981.

Wright, C.J.H. "Ethics." In *The Dictionary of the Old Testament: Historical Books*. Ed. by Bill T. Arnold and H.G.M. Williamson. Pp. 259-268. Downers Grove, IL: InterVarsity, 2005.

_____. *God's People in God's Land: Family, Land, and Property in the Old Testament*. Grand Rapids: Eerdmans, 1990.

Wright, G.R.H. "Joseph's Grave under the Tree by the Omphalos at Shechem." *Vetus Testamentum* 22 (Oct. 1972): 476-486.

Wright, N.T. *The New Testament and the People of God*. Minneapolis: Fortress, 1992.

Yadin, Yigael. *The Art of Warfare in Biblical Lands*. New York: McGraw-Hill, 1963.

_____. "Is the Biblical Account of the Israelite Conquest of Canaan Historically Reliable?" *Biblical Archaeology Review* 8 (Mar./Apr. 1982): 16-23.

Yancey, Philip. *Disappointment with God: Three Questions That No One Asks Aloud*. Grand Rapids: Zondervan, 1988.

Yerushalmi, Yosef Hayim. *Zakhor: Jewish History and Jewish Memory*. Rev. ed. Seattle: University of Washington, 1989.

Yoder, John Howard. "To Your Tents, O Israel: The Legacy of Israel's Experience with Holy War." *Studies in Religion* 18 (1989): 345-362.

Younger, K. Lawson Jr. *Ancient Conquest Accounts: A Study in Ancient Near Eastern and Biblical History Writing.* JSOT Supplement Series 98. Sheffield: JSOT, 1990.

_____. "Early Israel in Recent Biblical Scholarship." In *The Face of Old Testament Studies: A Survey of Contemporary Approaches.* Ed. by David W. Baker and Bill T. Arnold. Pp. 176-206. Grand Rapids: Baker, 1999.

Zertal, Adam. *The Eastern Valleys and the Fringes of the Desert.* Vol. 2. The Manasseh Hill Country Survey. Leiden: Brill, 2008.

_____. "Has Joshua's Altar Been Found on Mt. Ebal?" *Biblical Archaeology Review* 11 (Jan./Feb. 1985): 26-43.

_____. "Israel Enters Canaan—Following the Pottery Trail." *Biblical Archaeological Review* 17 (Sept./Oct. 1991): 28-47.

_____. *The Shechem Syncline.* Vol. 1. The Manasseh Hill Country Survey. Leiden: Brill, 2004.

Zevit, Ziony. "Archaeology and Literary Stratigraphy in Joshua 7–8." *Bulletin of the American Schools of Oriental Research* 251 (1983): 26-222.

Ziese, Mark. "Bible Lands and Lifeways." In *A Humble Defense: Evidence for the Christian Faith. A Special Tribute Honoring Dr. Lynn Gardner.* Ed. by Mark Scott and Mark Moore. Pp. 89-106. Joplin, MO: College Press, 2004.

Ziese, Mark. "Plants and Animals." In *Eerdmans Handbook to the Bible.* Grand Rapids: Eerdmans, forthcoming.

JOSHUA 1

I. HOW YAHWEH LED ISRAEL INTO CANAAN (1:1–12:24)

A. A GREAT COMMISSION GIVEN (1:1-18)

Terse speeches, rather than thumping prose, set the stage for the Joshua narrative and integrate it with the ongoing story of the people of God. Values such as faithful leadership, the gift of land, and the importance of obedience are stressed. While such values are anticipated in *torah* and demonstrate continuity with it,[1] they also signal the arrival of a watershed moment, and hence, the opening of a fresh chapter, or indeed, a fresh book. A new generation under new management is poised to meet new challenges. But will they be ready this time? What will this new leadership look like? What will those challenges be? Answers to these and other questions may be found in the charge of Yahweh to Joshua (1:1-9), the charge of Joshua to the people (1:10-15), and the charge of the people to Joshua and to each other (1:16-18). This triad of speeches introduces the larger text and unites its message. In terms of form (or performance), little effort is expended in character arrangement, description, or other matters of indirect discourse so often minimized in biblical narration: Yahweh, Joshua, and the people simply utter words. In terms of plot, their combined message suggests the nearness of a critical mass. Not surprisingly, in terms of grammar, their mood is imperative, urgent, compelling. The priming for this

---

[1]Gordon J. Wenham argues more fully that Joshua is linked to Deuteronomy by five themes: holy war, distribution of land, the unity of Israel, Joshua as successor to Moses, and the covenant. All five of these appear in Joshua 1. See Gordon J. Wenham, "The Deuteronomic Theology of the Book of Joshua," *JBL* 90 (1971): 140-148.

plot comes by way of "a great commission" where divine directives are issued, distributed among the people of God, and used to induce courage, comfort, and, above all else, obedience.[2]

1. The Charge of Yahweh (1:1-9)

[1]**After the death of Moses the servant of the LORD, the LORD said to Joshua son of Nun, Moses' aide:** [2]**"Moses my servant is dead. Now then, you and all these people, get ready to cross the Jordan River into the land I am about to give to them—to the Israelites.** [3]**I will give you every place where you set your foot, as I promised Moses.** [4]**Your territory will extend from the desert to Lebanon, and from the great river, the Euphrates—all the Hittite country—to the Great Sea[a] on the west.** [5]**No one will be able to stand up against you all the days of your life. As I was with Moses, so I will be with you; I will never leave you nor forsake you.**

[6]**"Be strong and courageous, because you will lead these people to inherit the land I swore to their forefathers to give them.** [7]**Be strong and very courageous. Be careful to obey all the law my servant Moses gave you; do not turn from it to the right or to the left, that you may be successful wherever you go.** [8]**Do not let this Book of the Law depart from your mouth; meditate on it day and night, so that you may be careful to do everything written in it. Then you will be prosperous and successful.** [9]**Have I not commanded you?**

---

[2]Some parallels have been noted between the encouragement to Joshua here and the commission of Solomon by David in 1 Kings 2:1-4. See Dennis J. McCarthy, "An Installation Genre?" *JBL* 90 (1971): 31-41. Such investigation links Joshua to royal characters of Israel's monarchy and has many critical presumptions about the authorship of the book of Joshua at its root.

The parallels between Joshua 1 and Matthew 28:16-20 may be profitably explored. In both texts an authoritative charge is offered, a specific mission is described, and the assurance of divine presence is granted. In deference to the tradition that labels Matthew 28:16-20 "The Great Commission," I would label Joshua 1, and specifically the first speech of the chapter as "A Great Commission."

Such a context may provide an opportune moment for the creative expositor to consider the relationship between the Hebrew name, יְהוֹשֻׁעַ (Yᵉhôšuaʿ), and the Greek equivalent, *Iēsous*, Jesus.

Be strong and courageous. Do not be terrified; do not be discouraged, for the LORD your God will be with you wherever you go."

^a*4 That is, the Mediterranean*

1:1 Just as Yahweh spoke (וַיֹּאמֶר, *wayyō'mer*) regularly to Moses in the past, the divine communiqué is now directed to Joshua. These words may be divided into two segments (vv. 1-5 and vv. 6-9) that roughly parallel each other. Three facets are seen in each: a description of the present situation, a call to action, and an encouragement of presence.

The present situation is marked by **the death of Moses**. This hitch-up to Deuteronomy 34 raises the tension of succession afresh.[3] Moses is remembered as a prophet without peer, a man who led Israel out of Egypt, established the Law of Yahweh, forged a people in the wilderness, and brought them to the very edge of Canaan (Deut 34:10-12). With his death comes the mourning of community (Deut 34:8) and the very real question: who is able to pick up his heavy mantle? If no one could ever be his equal, can anyone possibly be his successor? The answer comes quickly through the utterance of Yahweh, empowering **Joshua son of Nun** to the task (vv. 2,6).[4] For the careful reader, Joshua is no new character; his appearance is not

---

[3]That this hitch-up is intentional is supported by the presence of the leading verb: an imperfect form of הָיָה (*hyh*) modified by a *waw* (וַיְהִי, *way^ehî*). This grammatical expression of succession (ASV, "now it came to pass"), makes it clear that Joshua 1:1 is meant to be understood as a logical continuation of that which preceded it. Naturally and canonically, this would be the end of Deuteronomy. For more on the use of *waw* conversive with the imperfect, see Bruce K. Waltke and M. O'Connor, *An Introduction to Biblical Hebrew Syntax* (Winona Lake, IN: Eisenbrauns, 1990), sec. 33.2.4b; or T.O. Lambdin, *Introduction to Biblical Hebrew* (New York: Scribner, 1971), p. 123.

As a point of relevance, Judges and Ruth begin the same way.

[4]*Y^ehôšua'* is a familiar theophoric name in Scripture, commonly understood as meaning "Yahweh saves," or the exclamatory "Save, Yahweh!" Related forms include the Hebrew הוֹשֵׁעַ (*Hôšēa'*, Joshua's original name, see Num 13:16), יְשַׁעְיָהוּ (*Y^eša'yâhû*), or Isaiah, and the Greek Ἰησοῦς (*Iēsous*), or Jesus. The individual יְהוֹשֻׁעַ בִּן־נוּן (*Y^ehôšua' bin-Nûn*) should be distinguished from יְהוֹשֻׁעַ בֶּן־יְהוֹצָדָק (*Y^ehôšua' ben-Y^ehôṣādāq*, the high priest or "branch" of Zechariah 3 and 6) and *Y^ehôšua'* of Beth Shemesh (known from the "traveling ark" passage of 1 Sam 6:14). For more on theophoric names, see the Supplemental Study on Theophoric Names in ch. 14, p. 273.

limited to the book by his name. His role as successor to Moses is anticipated through his introduction elsewhere as a military man (Exod 17:8-16), scout (Numbers 13), and aide (Exod 24:13; 32:17; Num 27:18-23). In fact, according to Deuteronomy 34:9, Joshua's qualification for leadership stems from the observation that he is ordained by Moses' own hands. Joshua's leadership, therefore, is not of unknown origin or quality, but is a predicted extension[5] of the "super-prophet" himself.[6] Moses may be physically dead, but his legacy will live on through the presence of his name (the throbbing appearances of "Moses" in this chapter alone cannot be missed), in the remembering of his words (1:7,13,14), and in the person of his *chargé d'affaires*. All told, management of the leadership transition from Moses to Joshua is one aspect of the present situation.[7]

1:2-3 A second aspect of the present situation may be inferred from the first of a series of issued imperatives.[8] Israel, as a people, is commanded to **get ready,** or better yet, to "gear up!"[9] As in the case of the discussion of leadership, the text of Joshua picks up where Deuteronomy leaves off: Israel sits, perched on the limestone rim of

---

[5]In the first verse of the book (1:1) Moses is specifically identified as the עֶבֶד יהוה (*'ebed YHWH*), "servant of Yahweh," and Joshua, in turn, is identified as the מְשָׁרֵת מֹשֶׁה (*mᵉšārēth Mōšeh*), "minister to Moses." Leading with this outline of relationships is fundamental in establishing Joshua as successor to Moses and therefore as a legitimate recipient of divine revelation and qualified mediator between God and Israel.

[6]Willem A. VanGemeren views Moses as the "fountainhead of the prophets" (*Interpreting the Prophetic Word* [Grand Rapids: Zondervan, 1990], p. 28). More recently, Mark S. Smith has referred to him as "super-prophet" (*The Memoirs of God: History, Memory, and the Experience of the Divine in Ancient Israel* [Minneapolis: Fortress, 2004], p. 163).

[7]The phrase וַיְהִי אַחֲרֵי מוֹת (*wayᵉhî 'aḥărê môth*, "It was after the death of . . .") is used elsewhere as a marker to bring closure to one story and to initiate another. Consider the following examples: "after Abraham's death, God blessed his son Isaac" (Gen 25:11); "After the death of Joshua, the Israelites asked the LORD" (Judg 1:1); and "After the death of Saul, David returned" (2 Sam 1:1).

[8]Grammatically, these imperatives are singular and are addressed to Joshua. However, all the "people" are regularly subordinated to Joshua and therefore share in the directive.

[9]קוּם (*qûm*, 1:2) is an imperative directing the listener to physically "get up," as from sleep, sickness, or mourning. It suggests that the time of inaction is over. It is frequently used in language preparing for a military engagement. See *TWOT*, s.v. "קוּם."

the land of promise, awaiting (with every antenna aquiver) for some
signal to move. In one sense, this is no new situation. For the
sojourning patriarchs, seeking the security of a place to call home is
a persistent theme (e.g., Gen 12:6-7; 15:16,18-20; 35:12). For wilderness wanderers, the idea of a "milk and honey" residence is a distant
dream (e.g., Lev 26:6-13; Numbers 34–35; Deut 26:1–27:8) appreciated only by proxy through the report of the returning scouts (Num
13:21-25). This latter example brings forward for examination a particular tragedy. Israel now hovers outside the Promised Land for a
second time. A previous generation lagged at land's end and did not
penetrate it due to a faith failure (Num 14:1-45). This memory col-
ors the opening chapter of Joshua with somber hues by deliberately
raising the question: will it be any different this go-round? Could it
possibly go better without the leadership of Moses? Could it go any
worse? The passing of years in desert wastes has pressed one generation beneath the weight of sand and has etched hard faces upon a
second. One wonders if windblown grit has the power to render new
features at a deeper level as well?

Building upon the present situation is a call to action. This call
centers on land (vv. 2-4) and law (vv. 7-8). It is snappy, direct, and
sequential to the death of Moses.[10] **Cross the Jordan River into the
land I am about to give to them—to the Israelites.** Key to the text is
the understanding that the land spread before Israel is *from God.*
Verbal expressions alternatively describe it as that which is "given"
(vv. 2,3,6) or as that which is "inherited" (v. 6). Both ideas pull at
strings knotted in the book of Genesis and laced throughout *torah.*[11]

---

[10]Despite unparalleled intimacy with Yahweh, Moses is disqualified from
personally leading Israel into the land of promise (Numbers 20). His death
and mourning must be completed before Israel enters Canaan. Joshua 1:2
picks up this idea by means of an adverb of time, עַתָּה (*'attāh*) that emphasizes the present moment, e.g., "Moses my servant is dead, *now* arise." See
BDB s.v. עַתָּה for other examples of this word followed by an imperative.

Further investigation may be given to the use of *'āttah* as a "disjunctive"
textual marker. In dialogue, it signals that change is afoot. This is certainly
true here. See Waltke and O'Connor, *Biblical Hebrew Syntax,* sec. 38.1e.

[11]Both ideas have also been worked as lenses through which the text of
Joshua may be contextualized and understood. For perspective on the land
as "gift," see Patrick D. Miller Jr., "The Gift of God: The Deuteronomic
Theology of the Land," *Int* 22 (1969): 451-461. For perspective on the land
as "inheritance," see G. Von Rad, "The Promised Land and Yahweh's Land

They alert the reader to promises past and future and hint that what is to come may be viewed as a commentary to that larger program.[12] For Israel, receiving the "gift" or claiming the "inheritance" must certainly begin with "gearing up," but it involves more. Israel must also "cross over." While this command is directed toward a specific object in view — the Jordan River — the idea of "crossing over" (עָבַר, *'ābar*) may also be tucked away and used as part of a book-wide thematic lens.[13] As a broader view will reveal, a number of boundaries will be drawn, encountered, or breeched in the book of Joshua. Some of these, like a river or city wall, are hard to miss: they are elemental, carved of ground itself. Others, no less referential, are composed of different stuff and will be harder to sense, much less penetrate (see Supplemental Study on Archaeological Periods, pp. 35-37).

1:4 In keeping with its introductory character, the speech of Yahweh offers one measure of this land on the far side of the Jordan. It is but a brief sketch, a geographical goal, suggesting borders that stretch **from the desert to Lebanon.**[14] The phrasing of the NIV suggests that the "desert" serves as one end point (the southern limit?) while the proper name "Lebanon" serves as another (the northern limit?).[15] These are followed by two more measures, **the great river, the Euphrates** (the eastern limit?) and the **Great** or Mediterranean **Sea** (the western limit). Finally, the cultural label, **all the Hittite country**, is appended to the definition, adding, if noth-

---

in the Hexateuch," in *The Problem of the Hexateuch and Other Essays,* trans. by E.W. Trueman Dicken (New York: McGraw-Hill, 1966); or Walter C. Kaiser Jr., *Toward an Old Testament Theology* (Grand Rapids: Zondervan, 1979), pp. 124-127.

[12]The role of the land as a feature of biblical theology may well begin in the garden where man was placed in a land of blessing (Gen 2:8,15-17). The subsequent fall separated man from that privileged position and put into motion a plan for renewal (3:15,17-18). O. Palmer Robertson introduces this developing idea in his *The Israel of God: Yesterday, Today, and Tomorrow* (Phillipsburg, NJ: P & R, 2000), pp. 3-31.

[13]The repetition of particular words in the text here is not viewed as accidental but as clues to purpose. Narrative studies often refer to such dynamics under the heading of word-motif or *leitwort.* For more on the function of these within Hebrew prose, see Robert Alter, *Art of Biblical Narrative,* pp. 92-95.

[14]Compare with Deut 11:24-25.

[15]This phase is less clear in the Hebrew text. A textual emendation is required to achieve the NIV reading.

ing else, a subtle reminder that this land is presently occupied.[16] Israel cannot settle here without first displacing others, dangerous others. The limits given here correspond to the largest measures of the land of promise issued elsewhere (Gen 15:18; Deut 1:7-8; 11:24-25). As will be seen, the measure of the land divided into territories in Joshua 13–21, and indeed, that controlled by the later monarchy, will be more modest in scope.

1:5 Within this call to action is perhaps the best known phrase of the book. Yahweh instructs Joshua to "be strong and courageous."[17] This stock phrase is repeated no less than three times in four verses. Such rhythms demand attention. Joshua is commanded to "be strong and courageous" in serving as a leader (v. 6), in keeping *torah* (vv. 7-8), and in facing terror and discouragement (v. 9). While each of these three injunctions is important, emphasis is placed upon strength and courage in light of the challenge of "living out" *torah*[18]

---

[16]Mention of the Hittites here (and in the context of the Patriarchs) is a subject of some debate. The question centers on whether the Hittites of the biblical texts are to be connected with the great Hittite empire of the second millennium B.C. or with other settlers. It should be noted that a political definition of "Hittite" and a cultural definition of "Hittite" might diverge considerably. Amalgamation of diverse groups in order to create a unified "national consciousness" may have been a tactic of expansion. In one case, a person dubbed "a man of Hatti" does not even speak the language of Hatti. For this and other examples, see, Ronald L Gorny, "Hittites," in *Eerdmans Dictionary of the Bible,* ed. by D.N. Freedman (Grand Rapids: Eerdmans, 2000), pp. 595-597.

[17]The root חזק (*ḥzq*) communicates the idea "to be strong," and may be achieved as a result of squeezing firmly with the hands or binding up with a rope. Objects with holes or leaks may be strengthened in this way (BDB, pp. 304-305). The imperative of *ḥzq* is frequently coupled with אמץ (*'mṣ*), "to be courageous," "alert," or "stout," in a formula of encouragement (BDB, s.v. חזק; *TWOT*, s.v. חזק). This formula first appears on the lips of Moses (Deut 31:6-7,23, but note also Deut 3:28), and is picked up in Joshua (here and in 10:25) and elsewhere (1 Chr 22:13; 28:20; 2 Chr 32:7). In the New Testament, Jesus strikingly continues this theme, "Be courageous—I have overcome the world!" (John 16:33).

[18]Note the addition of the adverb מְאֹד (*mᵉ'ōd*) in v. 7. "Only be strong and *very* courageous in living out all the *torah* that Moses, my servant, commanded you." Obscured by my translation is the awkward juxtaposition of two infinitive constructs, לִשְׁמֹר (*liš°mōr*, "to keep") and לַעֲשׂוֹת (*la'ăśôth*, "to do"). Perhaps by reading the second verb as a gerund salvages a more literal translation, i.e., "to keep doing . . . *torah.*" See Waltke and O'Connor,

(see Supplemental Study on The Nature of *Torah* in ch. 23, p. 355). Presuming that the Mosaic Law is firmly cast and available to Joshua in some form, the ongoing test will be to apply that code instinctively on the field and correctly to ever-changing circumstances.[19] In fact, when examined closely, this emphasis creates the tension from which the entire book of Joshua is suspended. The present context, rather than the popular view, makes this clear. A popular view to the book of Joshua considers the inhabitants of Canaan to be Israel's primary challenge.[20] Without a doubt, they are a formidable military opponent, established in defensive positions with stocks of supplies and weaponry (Num 13:31-33). However, a closer read of Yahweh's programmatic speech makes it clear that the inhabitants of the land are not the primary obstacle. On the contrary, their threat is summarily defanged by Yahweh's promises (anticipated in Deut 11:24-25), e.g., **no one will be able to stand up against you** or "I will give you every place where you set your foot" (v. 3)[21] The latter even rais-

---

Biblical Hebrew Syntax, sec. 36.2.3e, for more on the gerundive use of the infinitive construct. Compare also to the structure of Josh 23:6 where these same two infinitive constructs are separated by a conjunction.

[19]The exact nature of the סֵפֶר הַתּוֹרָה (*sēpher hattôrāh*), "book of the *torah*" (1:8) is not specifically defined here beyond its connection with Moses. Critical scholars tend to view the production of the Pentateuch (Genesis–Deuteronomy) as a late affair, completed no earlier than the 6th century B.C. However, the notion of a collected body of traditions known as *torah* is described early and often (Gen 26:5; Exod 13:9; 18:16-20; 24:12; Deut 1:5; 4:8, etc.). By the end of Deuteronomy, *torah* is described specifically as a written document or "book," ascribed to Moses (31:9-13,24-26). It is reasonable to expect that such a "book" at this point included the speeches of Deuteronomy, and possibly much more.

[20]Ironically, expository schemes typically view the field of battle as the appropriate place for the cry to "be strong and courageous." While this is not completely inappropriate, it is not wholly in keeping with the spirit of the Joshua mandate. Consider another alternative, Ps 27:14: "Be strong and courageous in your heart—wait for Yahweh!"

[21]L. Daniel Hawk, *Joshua* (Collegeville, MN: Liturgical Press, 2000), p. 2, has articulated this carefully. "The linking of divine gift, obedient response, and victory in the land suggests that the Canaanites will not pose a significant threat to Israel. Yahweh claims both the right and the power to deliver the land to Israel and promises to bring complete victory over the peoples (vv. 2b-4). The *real* obstacle to fulfillment is therefore not the formidable resolve of the Canaanites but a potential lack of resolve on the part of Joshua and Israel."

es the possibility that the ideal conquest of Canaan is to be achieved as much by simply walking around as by fighting — an odd kind of "stamping expedition"![22] In this, the echo of a more ancient directive is sensed, "Go, walk through the length and breadth of the land, for I am giving it to you" (Gen 13:17).

The true challenge for Israel finally emerges when this call to action is placed beside the third element of the present situation, the encouragement of presence (vv. 5,9). Joshua and Israel are told that this will be no solo flight: **I will be with you; I will never leave you nor forsake you**[23] (v. 5). This promise is an old one, given to others who worked in places of risk and danger, following Yahweh's agenda (e.g., Gen 28:15; 31:3; Exod 3:12). That Yahweh is a promise-maker is clear enough from ancient testimony. The question that must be freshly answered by each generation is this: is he a promise-keeper? Contemplating this question reveals that the zone between Yahweh's intentions and life's circumstances is hardly a no-man's land. It is every-man's land. Experience reveals that a loss of faith — or put more darkly, the triumph of despair — begins whenever promise is overwhelmed by circumstance.

1:6 With all these thoughts on the table, a view to the stiffer challenge — and hence, the essence of Israel's "great commission" — may be considered from the opening speech of Yahweh. Perhaps this is more easily recognized when the imperatives of the section are aligned with their polar opposites. The opposite of being strong and courageous (1:6,9) is being weak and fearful. The opposite of being careful (1:7) is being lax, and the opposite of being meditative (1:8) is being forgetful. Between these poles of choice the narrator casts the true challenge of the conquest. Will Israel be strong, courageous, careful, and meditative? Or will Israel be weak, fearful, lax, and forgetful? The stakes are enormous and must be carefully considered.

---

[22]The word order of v. 3 stresses this. It may be cast woodenly, "*every place* that the arches of your feet tread *upon it*." Leading with the direct object ("every place"), and, by doubling the object ("upon it"), suggests the rumble of many feet stamping about and emphasizes the certainty of the giving, i.e., once stamped, no corner will be missed or forgotten.

[23]The verb translated "forsake you" is built from a root (רפה, *rph*) meaning "to relax" or "go slack." The promise develops a picture of the fierce grip of God.

1:7-9 That this future is truly a choice and not some deal where blessings are "automatically" dispensed down the chute is clearly established. At the head of verse 7 stands a particle, רַק (*raq*), introducing a note of contingency.[24] For his part, God promises land to Israel. For Israel's part, the duty of obedience must stand — *only* "be very strong and courageous."

Finally, beyond this particle of restriction, two other terms require a closer look. In verse 7 the term translated "successful" is etymologically linked to true wisdom, and, in fact, is translated elsewhere as "prudence" or "understanding."[25] Not turning to the right or to the left means that the traveler will finish with gained insight. Success, by modern standards, tends to be measured in harder currency! The same word is used again in verse 8, but, in this case, is preceded by yet another loaded term. The NIV reads "prosperous," obscuring the nuance that this prosperity is the result of pressing, chopping through, or choosing a right path.[26] Taken together, these terms suggest that choosing the "strong and courageous" route means following a well-defined road to a true understanding, one that appreciates the rightful place of God's grace and man's duty in life. On the other hand, the choice of a "weak and fearful" route is connected to innovation, deviation, and ultimately, misunderstanding. Lurking in the shadows of this latter choice are ominous precedents: the record of Israel's rebellion in the wilderness, the recitation of "curses for disobedience" ordered by Moses (Deut 27:15-26; 28:15-68), and the prediction of Israel's future failure (Deut 31:14-18). Hence, in the end, the challenge offered to Israel by Yahweh may be pictured as two poles of choice, each complete with its own set of consequences. The choices are clear. Will Israel be strong or

---

[24]The particle *raq* is positioned between two commands to be strong and courageous. The first is connected to the promise of land (v. 6). The second is connected to the keeping of *torah* (v. 7). Syntactically, the use of *raq* functions to show how the first idea is restricted or defined by the second. For use of *raq* as a restrictive adverb, see Waltke and O'Connor, *Biblical Hebrew Syntax*, sec. 39.3.5.

[25]For שֵׂכֶל (*śēkel*) as "wisdom in action," see for example, Prov 1:3; 12:8; 1 Chr 22:12.

[26]The text of v. 8 may be more freely translated, "Do not let this *torah* leave your mouth, ruminate on it all the time, so that you will keep on doing everything written in it. Then, and only then, will *your life-path be prosperous* and *you will understand why.*"

weak? Courageous or afraid? Careful or lax? Meditative or forgetful? The consequences are likewise clear. Will Israel be comfortable and successful or uncomfortable and unsuccessful? Without a doubt, the charge of Yahweh is a great commission.

2. The Charge of Joshua (1:10-15)

[10]**So Joshua ordered the officers of the people:** [11]**"Go through the camp and tell the people, 'Get your supplies ready. Three days from now you will cross the Jordan here to go in and take possession of the land the LORD your God is giving you for your own.'"**

[12]**But to the Reubenites, the Gadites and the half-tribe of Manasseh, Joshua said,** [13]**"Remember the command that Moses the servant of the LORD gave you: 'The LORD your God is giving you rest and has granted you this land.'** [14]**Your wives, your children and your livestock may stay in the land that Moses gave you east of the Jordan, but all your fighting men, fully armed, must cross over ahead of your brothers. You are to help your brothers** [15]**until the LORD gives them rest, as he has done for you, and until they too have taken possession of the land that the LORD your God is giving them. After that, you may go back and occupy your own land, which Moses the servant of the LORD gave you east of the Jordan toward the sunrise."**

Joshua's speech to the people follows Yahweh's speech to Joshua (1:1-9) and parallels it in many ways. Just as Yahweh commanded Israel to "cross over," so too, Joshua commands the leaders of the people to "cross over." Similarly, as Yahweh encouraged Joshua by means of the assurance of divine presence, so too Joshua encourages the people to recognize the program of Yahweh. Through this cascading pattern, the narrator makes it clear that Joshua will serve in the place of Moses. Like his predecessor, Joshua will stand as authoritative mediator between Yahweh and the people.

1:10-11 Joshua's first directive is to **the officers of the people**. These officers have been previously identified as foremen (Exod 5:14), elders (Num 11:16; Deut 29:9) or military men (Deut 20:5).[27]

---

[27]Hebrew שֹׁטֵר (šōṭēr), "officer," has at its root the idea of one who writes lines, i.e., a secretary, arranger, or organizer. BDB, s.v. שֹׁטֵר.

They are now commissioned to "cross over" (in parallel with v. 2) through the "middle of the camp" with the message for all: prepare provisions. Bags must be packed, tents must be rolled up, food and drink must be secured and made portable for the journey ahead.[28] Furthermore, a notice of time is given to prepare the people to **cross over the Jordan**. This mention of "three days" is the first of several occasions where this phrase appears; it is worth watching. The notice of "crossing over" sustains the development of the narrative, as does the repeating vocabulary of "possessing" and "giving."[29]

SUPPLEMENTAL STUDY

"THREE DAYS"

The phrase יָמִים שְׁלֹשֶׁת (*šᵊlōšeth yāmîm*), "three days" appears no less than 27 times in the pages of the Old Testament. Five of these appearances are within the text of Joshua: 1:11; 2:16,22; 3:2; and 9:16. A variant, "on the third day," appears in 9:17. How is this measure to be understood? Is this phrase meant to be taken literally or figuratively? Does it indicate three 24-hour periods? Does it suggest one full day and some portion of two more? Does it mean something else? Consider the six mentions of the phrase within the text of Joshua.[30]

In 1:11 Joshua commands the people to get ready to move. After the death of Moses, Joshua passes the order, via the officers, that they will cross the Jordan בְּעוֹד שְׁלֹשֶׁת יָמִים (*bᵊ'ôd šᵊlōšeth yāmîm*), "within three days." This would seem to be a simple matter if not for

---

[28]It is possible that manna was a part of these provisions, as manna was available until after the celebration of Passover in Gilgal (Josh 5:12). However, storing manna could have been a problem (Exod 16:20).

[29]While "the land as gift" is an idea previously expressed, the verb "to possess" or "dispossess" (יָרַשׁ, *yāraš*) appears here for the first time in the text of Joshua. It is emphasized by the repetition, "you will cross over . . . *to possess* the land that Yahweh your God is giving for you *to possess it*." This choice of words draws from the language of patriarchal promises (e.g., Gen 15:7; 24:60) and from repeated mentions in the book of Deuteronomy (e.g., 2:12,24; 4:1, etc.). For an overview of the uses of this term in a theological context, see *TDOT*, s.v. יָרַשׁ.

[30]For an introduction to this problem and a creative solution, albeit different from our own, see David M. Howard, Jr., "'Three Days' in Joshua 1–3: Resolving a Chronological Conundrum," *JETS* 41 (Dec. 1998): 539-550.

the fact that, after this order is dispatched, the scouts are sent to Jericho, they spend some time with Rahab, and, according to the narrator in 2:22, they hide in the hills for *šᵊlōšeth yāmîm*, "three days," before returning to the Israelite camp. Only after all this is accomplished, do the people cross the Jordan. It is possible that the "three days" of 1:11 or of 2:22 be taken literally, but not both.

The situation is further aggravated by the words of the narrator in 3:2 suggesting that, after the scouts return, the camp is seemingly moved to the edge of the Jordan and once again, מִקְצֵה שְׁלֹשֶׁת יָמִים (*miqṣēh šᵊlōšeth yāmîm*), "at the end of three days," the officers pass instructions for crossing the Jordan among the people. Constructing anything more than a relative chronology of these events would seem impossible.

Similarly, in 9:16 it is *miqṣēh šᵊlōšeth yāmîm*, "at the end of three days," that Israel discovers the truth concerning the Gibeonite identity. This span of time separates the moment of covenant-making from the moment of startling revelation that the Gibeonites were inhabitants in the land. In the verse that follows, Israel then breaks camp and moves toward the villages of the Gibeonite coalition, arriving there בַּיּוֹם הַשְּׁלִישִׁי (*bayyôm haššᵊlîšî*), "on the third day." While this is not necessarily problematic, it is curious to place this description alongside of 10:9 where the same journey, seemingly from Gilgal to Gibeon, is accomplished in a single night's march. According to Soggin, who assumes a southern Gilgal location, this uphill climb of 3,500' over the course of eighteen miles could be reasonably accomplished in eight to ten hours.[31] That this same journey required "three days" in 9:17 raises the possibility that the "three-day" journey of 9:17 was possibly a leisurely affair. Alternatively, the "three days" of 9:17 may not be intended to represent three literal days. Under ordinary circumstances, it took "a while" to get from Gilgal to Gibeon.

Two observations may be offered on the problem of "three days" within the text of Joshua. One or both may be true. First, the appearance of "three days" may be a part of the narrator's literary craft. In the case of 1:11 and 3:2, these mentions do not seem to function as strict indications of time, but as a clause used to frame and reframe the same scene. Between them is the Jericho affair, a kind of paren-

---

[31]J.A. Soggin, *Joshua: A Commentary*, OTL (Philadelphia: Westminster, 1972), p. 127.

thesis that functions apart from the narrative flow of time. Use of "three days" in 3:2 places the narrative back on track, picking up where 1:11 left off.

A second observation requires further word study. Is it possible that *šᵊlōšeth yāmîm*, "three days," was a phrase never understood in the minds of Hebrew readers as an exact measure of time? Consider a possible parallel from the English language. If a person suggests that he or she will return "in a couple of days," a literal interpretation would require an understanding of exactly two days. A "couple" is, by definition, a pair. Functionally, however, a "couple of days" has a much wider point of reference. For English speakers, a "couple of days" suggests an inexact number of days greater than one but less than many. Could *šᵊlōšeth yāmîm* function in the same way? Joshua commands the people to ready themselves; they will cross the Jordan *very soon*. Rahab tells the scouts to hide in the hills for *a short time*, until their pursuers fade. The journey from Gilgal to Gibeon was accomplished with exceptional effort by an all-night march; normally, it takes *a little while* to get there.

The possibility that *šᵊlōšeth yāmîm* ("three days") is an ancient Hebrew idiom for "a little while" is supported by use in the Dead Sea Scrolls.[32] How this affects the interpretation of many other Old Testament texts where the phrase appears must be investigated.[33] The same is true for several key New Testament passages which would undoubtedly follow a Hebrew precedent, including Matthew 12:40; 26:61; Mark 8:31; and Acts 9:9.

1:12-15 However, to some of the people, an additional message is necessary. To the **Reubenites, the Gadites and the half-tribe of Manasseh**, Joshua gives special orders. To understand these, the

---

[32]Recent work in the text of the Dead Sea scrolls adds weight to this conclusion. Interestingly, it was suggested by students of the Bible long ago. For a summary of this understanding of "three," see the work of David Rothstein, "The Meaning of 'A Three-Days' Journey' in 11 QT*: The Evidence of Biblical and Post-Biblical Sources," in *RB* 114 (Jan. 2007): 32-51.

[33]Within the text of the Old Testament (and outside the book of Joshua), "three days" appears in many passages including the following: Gen 30:36; 40:12,13,18,19; 42:17; Exod 3:18; 5:3; 8:23; 10:22,23; 15:22; Num 10:33; 33:8; Judg 14:14; 19:4; 1 Sam 9:20; 30:12; 2 Sam 20:4; 2 Sam 24:13; 1 Kgs 12:5; 2 Kgs 2:17; 1 Chr 21:12; 2 Chr 10:5; Esth 4:16; and Jonah 1:17; 3:3.

text of Numbers 21:21-35 and Deuteronomy 3:1-20 must be reviewed. According to these texts, land to the east of the Jordan River (Transjordan), previously controlled by Og of Bashan and Sihon of Hesban, was acquired by Israel through military action. In this place, the speeches of Deuteronomy originate, Moses dies and is buried, and Israel now camps awaiting further orders (presumably at *Shittim*, cf. 2:1). Before his death, however, Moses awarded much of Transjordan as a land grant to the members of two and one-half tribes — Reuben, Gad, and a part of Manasseh. But to prevent them from immediately going about the business of settlement — presumably depleting not just the collective force of Israel's strength, but the larger witness to the coming work of Yahweh — the fighting men from these tribes were ordered to "cross over" with the rest of Israel and assist in the conquest of the western regions (Cisjordan). Only after the larger conquest is complete, will the goal of "rest" be possible for the members of these two and one-half tribes.[34]

The original command of Moses (Deut 3:18-20) regarding these matters is reiterated by Joshua (vv. 12-15) nearly verbatim. At the very least, this careful repetition underlines Joshua as the genuine mouthpiece of Moses. It also demonstrates Joshua's faithfulness in not allowing "the book of the law to depart from his mouth" (v. 8). In this, a strategy for reading the text of Joshua continues to be shaped: Deuteronomy reveals the program; Joshua reveals the program enacted. Key to connecting these dots throughout is the function of memory. By "remembering," and thus "appropriating" the past, the present may be shaped.[35] Hence, this activity is greater than the sparking of cognitive processes alone; biblically speaking, to "remember" is not the opposite of to "forget." To remember is to translate thought into real life, to choose and act accordingly.[36] This idea will arise in the text of Joshua again and again.

---

[34]"Rest" (נוּחַ, *nûaḥ*) may be read here in many ways. One appropriate context is "relief from war," or "relief from enemies." See the context of the original injunction (Deut 3:20), or elsewhere, i.e., Deut 12:10; Josh 21:44. As Butler states, "rest, not war is the ultimate goal of Israel." (*Joshua*, p. 22).

[35]Much ink has been spilt in recent years on the subject of social or collective memory. For a brief introduction to the subject and an overview of major players, see Mark Smith, *Memoirs of God*, pp. 126-140.

[36]No one has made this case more eloquently than Yosef Hayim Yerushalmi. Consider his *Zakhor: Jewish History and Jewish Memory*, rev. ed. (Seattle: University of Washington, 1989).

3. The Charge of the People (1:16-18)

¹⁶Then they answered Joshua, "Whatever you have commanded us we will do, and wherever you send us we will go. ¹⁷Just as we fully obeyed Moses, so we will obey you. Only may the LORD your God be with you as he was with Moses. ¹⁸Whoever rebels against your word and does not obey your words, whatever you may command them, will be put to death. Only be strong and courageous!"

The final speech of the chapter comes in response to the words of Joshua. This culmination is ambiguously set up as "they answered," leaving the reader wondering for a moment who the "they" are. This question of identity is critical and grows oddly from the front end of the book. Fortunately, the symmetry of presentation, unrealized until the tail end of the book swings back around, brings this subject into view. Not only is the question of "who?" given an answer, so too is the question of "why?"

In the meantime, a reminder is valuable. In this chapter of opening speeches — and, more importantly, the interlocking displays of intention that they demonstrate — no space is given to the actual execution of orders. Past action is sensed (e.g., Moses dies, Yahweh issued commands). Future action is anticipated (e.g., Yahweh will be with Joshua, the leaders will spread orders about the camp); but surprisingly, nothing is truly *done* beyond speaking and listening. One begins to recognize the hand of an artful narrator who is able to cast an agenda almost by proxy — with or without the reader's tacit consent — through the strategic selection and arrangement of voices. In this way, the initial trajectory of the book arcs almost effortlessly: no action is required; no true dialogue is needed; no editorial opinions are dropped. Even without these familiar tools, the plot glides forward, tensions mount, and tidbits of developments to come are offered. Obviously, this will be no humdrum ride.

1:16-17a In response to the penultimate speech of Joshua, two sentiments are expressed. The first appears as an oath of loyalty. "They" reply: **Whatever you have commanded us we will do, and wherever you send us we will go** (cp. Deut 11:31-32). This response is striking in expansiveness and devotion. The phrase כֹּל אֲשֶׁר (*kᵊkōl 'ăšer*), rendered "whatever" or "wherever" in the NIV, displays a steely no-limits ("no fear") kind of attitude. It suggests that the shift of leadership from Moses to Joshua has traction. Still, what follows quickly mires that determination. **Just as we fully obeyed Moses, so we will obey you.**[37] While sounding pious at a full run, these words grow ever more disturbing when contemplated against the larger context of the ministry of Moses. Is this response meant to be taken at face value or in some other way? Does this response represent the opinion of "all Israel" or just some part thereof? Is this response a deeply held sentiment or merely a breezy promise with a life span no longer than the honeymoon of Joshua's tenure?

The track record of how all Israel "fully obeyed Moses" in the wilderness is hardly reassuring. Theirs was a stormy relationship of conflict and disobedience, impatience and frustration. Israel did not fully "do" what Moses commanded them to do; neither did they "go" wherever Moses commanded them to go. Placing this "just as" exclamation in the mouth of "all Israel" would seem an odd move, one that generates irony, if not gushing humor. From Joshua's perspective, dealing with the Israel of the desert would be anything but encouraging! Might something else be at work here?

Contextually, the section beginning in verse 16 comes on the heels of Joshua's orders given specifically to members of the Transjordan-based tribes, namely, the Reubenites, Gadites, and members of the half-tribe of Manasseh (v. 12). While it is tempting to suggest that "the people" who speak these pious-sounding words are identified as "all Israel," contextual awareness whittles that chorus down to two and one-half tribes. Does this narrowing ease the tension raised by the wilderness track record? Possibly. Could this constriction prohibit a reading that uses the voice of one group as representative for the whole? Not necessarily. Might this move be placed to one side and held for future examination as part of a developing strategy? Absolutely. For the moment, it may be allowed to stand simply as a positive response to the leadership of Joshua from one corner of Israel.

1:17b-18 Beyond an oath of loyalty, a second sentiment is expressed. Just as Yahweh and Joshua issued charges, so too, the peo-

---

[37]In Hebrew, כְּכֹל אֲשֶׁר־שָׁמַעְנוּ אֶל־מֹשֶׁה כֵּן נִשְׁמַע אֵלֶיךָ (kᵊkōl 'ăšer-šāma'nû 'el-mōšeh kēn nišma' 'ēlêkā). The kōl 'ăšer, "whatever," phrase is carried forward and used a second time. Roughly, "whatever (the manner) we listened to — or obeyed — Moses, so too we will listen to — or obey — you."

ple of the corner. Their charge comes as a reciprocating shot, a potent mix of warning, prayer, and encouragement.

The warning concerns disobedience. **Whoever rebels against your word . . . will be put to death.** Striking is the use of the verbal root מָרָה (*mārāh*) to describe the rebellious one. Moses characterized all Israel by this same term (Deut 9:7). In the present context, the warning of death prepares the ground for Achan's story (7:1-26). Interestingly, the "whatever" phrase (*kōl 'ăšer*) appears for a fourth time in just three verses, in the end describing a kind of radical allegiance to Joshua, "*whatever* your orders." Such drill has the feel of a "blank check," a signed paper slipped in Joshua's pocket. He may seemingly fill in the amount for "whatever."

Closing encouragement and prayers moderate the "blank check" idea. Just as Yahweh insists on the duty of obedience (1:7) by way of the restrictive adverb, רַק (*raq*), so too, Joshua is held responsible by force of grammar.[38] His leadership must manifest divine presence, **Only** (*raq*) **may the Lord your God be with you.** Moreover, he must maintain a stance that is careful and meditative (per Yahweh's speech). **Only** (*raq*) **be strong and courageous.** Back and forth, the reciprocating charges spark an engine to life: Yahweh encourages Joshua to be responsible; Joshua encourages the people to be responsible; the voice of the people encourages Joshua to be responsible. Expositors working this text may explore the values of mutual encouragement and accountability within the context of good leadership.

Thus, a great commission is given. Those who respond to it in voice appear positive and ready to meet the challenge. Still, as presented, words alone are the only measure of compliance; actions have yet to confirm rhetoric. Is all Israel truly prepared to gear up, cross over, and faithfully begin this grand "pedestrian" campaign of land stamping? Will they be strong, careful, courageous, and meditative? Is Yahweh fully invested in this exercise? Will Joshua demonstrate the right kind of leadership to make it possible? Such questions will be answered in time.

---

[38]Waltke and O'Connor designate *raq* ("only," "surely") as a restrictive or limitive adverb. It typically rests in the center of a logical flow and in some way modifies or restricts it. See their discussion (39.3.5). In this case, the logic of the text is interrupted from v. 16 to v. 17. Pieced together, it runs as follows. The people say to Joshua, "we will unswervingly follow your lead, *just be sure* to be faithful, strong, and courageous." Their commitment to Joshua's leadership is conditioned by Joshua's commitment to Yahweh.

JOSHUA 2

B. BEHIND ENEMY LINES (2:1-24)

Behind enemy lines is a dangerous place to be. This is the realm of secret agents, unexpected betrayals, and narrow escapes. Such features render this well-told chapter one of the most dramatic in the book. In this initial encounter with the Canaanites, the chief of Jericho and a shady lady named Rahab reveal new information. Behind *their lines* lurks a play of perspectives so wholly unanticipated and deftly told that the reader, like a fugitive, is nabbed flat-footed. The arrest comes with a revelation: even before Israel arrives, Yahweh is at work in Canaan.

Three scenes compose the story. The first (2:1-7) depicts leaders sending out scouts: Joshua deploys his men; the chief of Jericho does the same. The second (2:8-14,17-20) communicates an unexpected betrayal and an uncomfortable covenant. The third (2:15-16,21-24) reveals the escape of Joshua's scouts, their confidential agreement with Rahab, and their report to Joshua.

1. Scouts Deployed (2:1-7)

¹**Then Joshua son of Nun secretly sent two spies from Shittim. "Go, look over the land," he said, "especially Jericho." So they went and entered the house of a prostitute**ᵃ **named Rahab and stayed there.**

²**The king of Jericho was told, "Look! Some of the Israelites have come here tonight to spy out the land."** ³**So the king of Jericho sent this message to Rahab: "Bring out the men who came to you and entered your house, because they have come to spy out the whole land."**

⁴**But the woman had taken the two men and hidden them. She said, "Yes, the men came to me, but I did not know where they had come from. ⁵At dusk, when it was time to close the city gate, the men left. I don't know which way they went. Go after them quickly. You may catch up with them." ⁶(But she had taken them up to the roof and hidden them under the stalks of flax she had laid out on the roof.) ⁷So the men set out in pursuit of the spies on the road that leads to the fords of the Jordan, and as soon as the pursuers had gone out, the gate was shut.**

ᵃ*1* Or possibly *an innkeeper*

2:1 Introductory comments are issued in two directions. The first concerns the dispatch of agents by Joshua; the second concerns the arrival of those men in Jericho. Momentum builds with one word piling upon another until the avalanche of sibilants is released: Joshua "sends out from *Shittim*,[1] two men, scouts,[2] silently!" As a veteran himself and as one of the scouts sent into the land in a previous generation (Num 13:1-33), Joshua understands the need for accurate reconnaissance.[3] This may explain why the men are sent at all, since no divine prompt for the action is issued.[4] The fact that the

---

[1]*Shittim* is the location of the Israelite camp mentioned in Num 25:1; Josh 2:1; 3:1; and Micah 6:5). It is likely the same as *Abel-Shittim*, or "meadow of the acacia trees" of Num 33:49. Context dictates its location east of the Jordan River, opposite Jericho. Two proposals have been offered to identify the site, Tell el-Kefrein and Tell-el-Hammam. The latter is most attractive, due to size and location. See MacDonald, *East of Jordan*, pp. 89-90; or Rainey and Notley, *Sacred Bridge*, p. 124.

[2]These are called מְרַגְּלִים (*mᵊraggᵊlîm*), literally, "pedestrians," but more specifically "scouts" or "spies."

[3]Is it possible that there were more than two scouts dispatched here? The precedent of Numbers 13 would suggest the sending of twelve men, representing different tribes. If these agents went to different areas of Canaan to gather current information, perhaps the general clause of v. 1, "see the land," applied to all the group and the "especially Jericho" part applied to just the two. Little can be made of this thought, however. The text offers no mention of any other agents.

[4]Given the fact that the fall of Jericho eventually occurs without military action, one wonders, why are any scouts needed at all? Of course, this assumes that the outcome is known from the start, a luxury afforded only to the reader. Still, it has been suggested that the sending of the scouts represents a needless act, and God's silence towards the whole affair confirms

scouts are dispatched from *Shittim* reminds the reader of the debacle of Numbers 25:1ff, a text that prefigures events to come by
underlining the problem of dangerous liaisons with the inhabitants
of the land. That the agents remain faceless, nameless, and lacking
entirely in description only emphasizes their clandestine role. They
are on the sly. Therefore it is not surprising that they are sent "quietly," although, curiously, it is not clear from whom their mission is
kept secret. Are they hidden from the view of the Canaanites, from
the Israelites, or both? One thing is certain: they are exposed to the
reader. This deliberate "leak" of intelligence on the part of the narrator pries open the mission's innermost circle and has the effect of
transforming the reader into the ultimate spy of the story, privileged
even beyond the faceless men themselves! Now, thanks to the narrator, the goals of their eyes-only assignment are seen by all who
read it. The mission is, broadly, an investigation of Cisjordan: "view
the land." Yet it is also dubbed more particularly "a Jericho affair."[5]

The second direction of comment concerns the arrival of the
scouts in Canaan. No details are offered as to the route taken or to

---

it. This might explain why the mission is "secret," hidden from the Israelites
as well as the Canaanites. Joshua wishes to nullify the "fear factor" that
stymied the report of the first exploration of the land (Numbers 13), and
possibly, bury a painful memory. Keeping it secret from Israelite ears may
help. For more thinking along this line see Polzin, *Moses and the
Deuteronomist*, pp. 85-86.

From a military perspective, however, the dispatching of scouts has always
been essential business. As Weigley comments in the context of the
Revolutionary War of the United States: "To act offensively at all demanded the best possible intelligence system and rapid movement. To hit detach-
ments and not the major strength of the enemy Washington must effect sur
prise. He must know the enemy's location and movements intimately, and
the enemy must not know his. No general in American history has sur-
passed, and probably none has matched, the care and thought which
Washington gave to his intelligence service." See Russell F. Weigley, *The
American Way of War: A History of United States Military Strategy and Policy*
(Bloomington, IN: Indiana University, 1973), p. 15.

[5]The verb "see" has two direct objects separated by a *waw* conjunction.
This is not unusual in the book of Joshua (e.g., 1:6). In this case, the first
object is general (land) while the second object is specific (Jericho). Later
translations attempt to smooth the reading by interpreting the second
object as a prepositional phrase modifying the first: "in the region of
Jericho." For more on a series of objects growing from a single transitive
verb, see Waltke and O'Connor, *Biblical Hebrew Syntax*, sec. 10.3.1.

the observations made by the men along the way. The narrator deftly gaps this information[6] and without further comment ushers them quickly to the house of a woman, a prostitute named Rahab. There, a center of gravity is developed; there, they catch their breath.[7]

In a book where personal names are almost begrudgingly offered, the attention given to this Jericho "hostess" is striking (consider how even the Jericho chief remains nameless!). Her name, רָחָב (*Rāḥāb*), comes from a family of words built around the Hebrew root רחב (*rḥb*). These communicate ideas of breadth, girth, or openness; רְחוֹב (*rᵊḥôb*, "Rechob") is still used today in Modern Hebrew to describe a plaza, esplanade, or wide street.[8] That a woman, and particularly, a זוֹנָה (*zônāh*) or "prostitute," is given such a label is indicative of her profession. She is a "street girl," or less discretely, she is "wide open," and hence, sexually approachable.[9] The temptation to reread this name as some kind of slangy metaphor is strong, yet historical evidence from outside the biblical record shows that the name "Rahab" was quite at home in Bronze Age Canaan.[10]

---

[6]For an introduction to gapping as narrative tool, see Sternberg, *Poetics of Biblical Narrative*, pp. 186-190.

[7]The hospitality to "strangers in danger" motif is familiar to biblical readers and is recognized by form critics as early as Gunkel (Butler, *Joshua*, p. 28). One might compare the Rahab story with that of Sisera and Jael (Judges 4 and 5), the Levite's concubine (Judges 19), or Ahimaaz and Jonathan (2 Sam 17:18-22). L. Daniel Hawk demonstrates parallels between this account of Rahab and the scouts in Joshua 2 and the account of Lot and the angels at Sodom in Genesis 19 and suggests that these parallels are purposive. See his "Strange Houseguests: Rahab, Lot, and the Dynamics of Deliverance," *Reading between the Texts: Intertextuality and the Hebrew Bible*, ed. by D.N. Fewell (Louisville, KY: Westminster, 1992), pp. 89-97.

[8]J. Bottero suggests that even the location of Rahab's house, "in the wall" (2:15) is consistent with other evidence describing prostitutes. See J. Bottero, *Mesopotamia: Writing, Reasoning, and the Gods* (Chicago: University of Chicago, 1992), pp. 190, 194.

[9]Some have proposed that Rahab was a cult prostitute who participated in sex as part of a system of pagan worship. Parallels between this passage and the story of Tamar (specifically, Gen 38:21-22), explored below, make this reasonable.

For a critique of Rahab as a cult prostitute view, see Frank Anthony Spina, "Reversal of Fortune: Rahab the Israelite and Achan the Canaanite," in *BRev* 17 (Aug. 2001): 30.

[10]Richard Hess has collected other forms of "Rahab" used as both a place and as a feminine personal name. Consider his "Non-Israelite Personal Names in the Book of Joshua," in *CBQ* 58 (Apr. 1996): 205-214.

Any discomfort prompted by the arrival of these scouts at what could very well be a brothel is prolonged without blush by the narrator.[11] The verb standing behind the NIV's polite rendering, they "stayed there" (root, שָׁכַב, *škb*), may refer to the act of resting or sleeping (e.g., Gen 28:13; 1 Sam 3:2; Ezek 4:4). However, as in English, it is also used euphemistically for the act of having sexual intercourse (e.g., Gen 26:10; Lev 15:24; Deut 22:22). Some interpreters are quick to point to this latter understanding as indicating an indiscretion here on the part of the scouts. This view may be buttressed by two other pieces, namely, the Jericho chief's accusation that the men "entered" (בּוֹא, *bô'*) Rahab (2:3),[12] and the narrator's "set up" sketch of 2:1, flash-backing the site of *Shittim*. Admittedly, viewing this sequence as merely a word fumble is unattractive; yet, taking the option of sexual innuendo at every turn hardly seems the way to go either. Is there another way out? How can the interpreter maneuver in this darkness?

The presence of ambiguity in the biblical text challenges the notion that sophisticated discourse is a modern product. Untangling the thin line that separates fact from judgment may provide work for some, but it is not always helpful and can possibly be harmful to the text. Ambiguity in narrative is *not* just a wrinkle in the fabric in need of more heat, steam, and pressure[13]; it is a complexity to be appreciated and, at times, even preserved as part of a crafted strategy. In this case, wrinkly edges are a good thing. A hard reality is replaced with the softer strokes of the *risque*, shadowed, uncertain, tense. Consider the emergence of two points in the immediate text, clear when viewed from the back end of the story: first, under scrutiny, the scouts are hardly role models for ethical behavior anyway;

---

[11]For ancient efforts to "reform" Rahab and present her as simply an innkeeper, barmaid, or landlord, see Josephus (*Ant* 5.7-15). D.J. Wiseman also contemplates this possibility in his "Rahab of Jericho," *TynBul* 14 (1964): 8-11.

[12]The verb *bô'* is used of "entering" a woman on a number of occasions, e.g., Gen 16:2; Deut 22:13; Judg 15:1; 16:1; Prov 6:29.

According to the narrator's perspective, the men only "enter" (*bô'*) Rahab's house. See 2:1.

[13]This work of "gap-filling" can result in wild and illegitimate readings that begin not with the world of the text but with the world of the reader. Sternberg, *Poetics of Biblical Narrative*, p. 188, must certainly be smirking with his dead-on observation: "Where there's a will, the midrash will always find a way."

and, second, wherever the truth lies with respect to their relationship with Rahab, it does not alter the plot one whit. More helpful is an approach that regards this build-up as an oblique suggestion of what *could* have happened, making it possible for others to *imagine* what did happen. This sort of play actually goes somewhere, working straight into Rahab's bluff of 2:4. Her raspy voice suggests that the men were nothing more to her than customers: her place is one where the faceless and nameless come and go regularly. No questions are asked. No alarms are sounded. Is this not what you would expect? Is she not a *zônāh*? Is she not *raḥab*?

2:2-7 Despite all cloaking tactics, the Canaanite chief of Jericho (see Supplemental Study on Canaanite Chiefs in ch. 12, p. 247) discovers the scouts' evening arrival, their identity (Israelite), hiding place (in Rahab's house), and mission ("to dig up information about the land"[14]). Action is prompt and marked by an exclamation of immediacy: "Just tonight some men came here."[15] Through his agents, the chief appeals to Rahab's self interest (these men have "come to spy") and demands that she expose them.[16] The chief's words not only catch the two men by surprise, they catch the reader as well. Who told the chief of these matters? How is this counter-intelligence obtained so quickly and accurately? Will Rahab turn the men over to the authorities? Is there any chance for an escape? Oddly, before this mission can develop, it is deeply compromised. Thoughts drift backward to Kadesh Barnea and forward to Micah's house,[17] other spy operations spinning out of control.

---

[14]The Qal infinitive לַחְפֹּר (*laḥpōr*) is built from a root idea "to dig" or "search out" a hidden thing. Wells are dug in this way, but so are pits or traps. See *TWOT*, s.v. חָפַר.

[15]The הִנֵּה (*hinnēh*) of 2:2 emphasizes the "here-and-now-ness of the situation" (Waltke and O'Connor, *Biblical Hebrew Syntax*, sec. 40.2.1).

[16]A striking parallel to this is drawn from second millennium Babylonia, where tavernkeepers are required by law to inform the authorities of rogues passing through. See Wiseman, "Rahab of Jericho," pp. 8-9.

[17]In Judg 18:2 members of the tribe of Dan dispatch scouts "to explore (לַחְקֹר, *lāḥqōr*) the land." Ironically, this is done in response to the failure of the group to occupy the territory assigned to them in the book of Joshua. These scouts bed down for the night, not in the house of a prostitute, but in the house of one Micah. Before their story is through, they burn a defenseless village (Laish), pillage the house of their host, and threaten its occupants. It is altogether less-than-stellar stuff.

Surprisingly, Rahab conceals the scouts in the stalks of flax[18] on her roof and offers disinformation to those who seek them. Some humor is also hidden in the fact that the men who come to "dig" end up being "buried." Before her interrogators, Rahab admits that the two fellows came to her — presumably as clients — but claims ignorance ("I did not know where they were from"), and, in a startling move, misdirects the search to outside the city wall. Her orders appear authoritative and crisp: "Quickly, go after them and catch them!" The pursuers respond immediately, not bothering to search her place, but dash in the direction of the Jordan crossing located some six miles away.[19] If the exit can be sealed, the Israelite scouts can be intercepted and prevented from returning to Joshua's camp with their precious intelligence. The deception is quick-witted and convincing on Rahab's part; it buys just enough time for complete darkness to fall — and, narratively, just enough space for a crucial speech.[20]

---

[18]Flax is a product of the wetland plant, *Linum usitatissimum*, and used to make oil, linen fabric, belts, twine, and lamp wicks. Fibers were obtained by pulling, drying, soaking, separating, and combing the stalks. Such stalks may be up to one meter in length and would have been stored or stacked in groups. The text of 2:6 suggests the possibility of a home industry. Rahab "arranged" flax stalks (lit. "woody flax") on the flat roof of her house, presumably drying them in parallel rows under the daytime sun. For more on flax, how it was processed, and specific evidence that it was grown in the region of Jericho, see Philip J. King and Lawrence E. Stager, *Life in Biblical Israel* (Louisville, KY: Westminster John Knox, 2001), pp. 148-152. For an excellent overview of flax production, see F. Nigel Hepper, *Baker Encyclopedia of Bible Plants* (Grand Rapids: Baker, 1992), pp. 166-168.

[19]Butler, *Joshua*, p. 31, comments on the humor of the presentation: "The king's intelligence system is so thorough it knows when strange men enter a prostitute's house, but so ignorant that it follows the advice of the prostitute without even searching the house or watching the window to discover the spies, who dangle tantalizingly within reach for such a long time (vv. 15-21)." He later suggests that this humor is not just a tool of the narrator but a fundamental purpose of the text. "The purpose of the story in its present setting is not so much to reconstruct history as to ridicule the original inhabitants of the land" (p. 33). Such a conclusion demonstrates a confusion of narrative art with narrative goals.

[20]Her action in lodging the spies and deceiving their pursuers is praised in James 2:25 (and again, partially, in Heb 11:31). This New Testament endorsement of Rahab places some interpreters in a bind and has produced a variety of contorted explanations for her behavior (since she is one of the "good guys," she must act like one). Some attempt to cast Rahab's deceptive

2. An Unexpected Betrayal and an Uncomfortable Covenant
(2:8-14,17-20)

[8]Before the spies lay down for the night, she went up on the roof [9]and said to them, "I know that the LORD has given this land to you and that a great fear of you has fallen on us, so that all who live in this country are melting in fear because of you. [10]We have heard how the LORD dried up the water of the Red Sea[a] for you when you came out of Egypt, and what you did to Sihon and Og, the two kings of the Amorites east of the Jordan, whom you completely destroyed.[b] [11]When we heard of it, our hearts melted and everyone's courage failed because of you, for the LORD your God is God in heaven above and on the earth below. [12]Now then, please swear to me by the LORD that you will show kindness to my family, because I have shown kindness to you. Give me a sure sign [13]that you will spare the lives of my father and mother, my brothers and sisters, and all who belong to them, and that you will save us from death."

[14]"Our lives for your lives!" the men assured her. "If you don't tell what we are doing, we will treat you kindly and faithfully when the LORD gives us the land."

[a]*10* Hebrew *Yam Suph*; that is, Sea of Reeds   [b]*10* The Hebrew term refers to the irrevocable giving over of things or persons to the LORD, often by totally destroying them.

-----

[17]The men said to her, "This oath you made us swear will not be binding on us [18]unless, when we enter the land, you have tied this scarlet cord in the window through which you let us down, and unless you have brought your father and mother, your brothers and all your family into your house. [19]If anyone goes outside your house

-----

words as a very narrowly defined truth rather than simply accepting them as a lie (see the impossible logic of Woudstra, *Joshua*, p. 71, n. 14). Others admit Rahab does tell an untruth, but argue that lying is never justified, and caution against using this text as an excuse for lying under certain conditions, the so-called "white lie," or "dutiful lie" (see Walter C. Kaiser Jr., *Hard Sayings of the Old Testament* [Downers Grove, IL: InterVarsity, 1988], pp. 95-97). This angle is better than the first, but is still enmeshed in a view to Scripture that is problematic. The difficulty is that Old Testament characters — and Canaanites in particular — are never going to act like good Christians! Why force them into this ethical mold?

into the street, his blood will be on his own head; we will not be responsible. As for anyone who is in the house with you, his blood will be on our head if a hand is laid on him. [20]But if you tell what we are doing, we will be released from the oath you made us swear."

The sequence of what follows is broken for reasons of presentation. Following a crucial speech (vv. 8-13), the scouts agree to an uncomfortable covenant (v. 14). However, as they make their escape, that covenant is further modified (vv. 17-20). To simplify the discussion here, analysis of their escape through the window-hole (vv. 15-16) is set aside momentarily, to be picked up in the next section.

2:8-11 The speech offered in the reprieve is marked with amazing insight and concludes with an astonishing request. Rahab reviews Israel's story including Yahweh's place in it. She is aware that the land of Canaan is a gift given by Yahweh to Israel. She understands how Israel came out of Egypt, crossed the Red Sea and defeated the chiefdoms of Transjordan in a "take no prisoners"-style conflict. In words that approach testimonial proportions, Rahab also confesses that Yahweh is sovereign over all creation, "for Yahweh, **your God is God in heaven above and on the earth below**." Finally, in an unexpected betrayal, Rahab offers the scouts the intelligence they seek: all Canaan knows about and fears the Israelite approach.[21] How Rahab acquires this information, or, is prompted to act on what seems to be a risky "faith position," is of no concern to the narrator.[22] What is clear is that these words, voiced as high credo, emerge from the lips of a surprising source. Rahab is a Canaanite, a woman, and a most impure one at that.[23] Yet, she is also firmly in control of the facts, capable of deflecting hostile inquisitors, and

---

[21]This passage is anticipated by Exod 23:27-28 suggesting that Yahweh will send his terror ahead of Israel. Compare with Deut 2:25.

[22]The same cannot be said of a source-critical perspective. Within this view, the words of Rahab are clearly those of another inserted into the text. Butler, *Joshua*, p. 31, puts it this way: "Here then is pre-Deuteronomic literature given a Deuteronomic stamp."

[23]Some contemporary readings arguing that "Israel" did not enter from outside Canaan, but emerged from within it, often champion Rahab as one example of a restless many. As a woman and a prostitute, Rahab occupies the lowest rung of an off-kilter society. She merely does what she needs to do to survive. This view casts her as victim of a corrupt economic system, engenders sympathy for her as a character, and binds her cause to that of

powerful enough to safeguard (at least temporally) the botched Israelite mission.[24] In short, she towers while the scouts cower! This contrast is striking, purposive, and effectively communicated through word and deed. The reader can only marvel over the narrator's sleight of hand. Roles are surprisingly reversed. Questions flutter down uneasily. Who is controlling this situation?

2:12-13 Beyond amazing insight, Rahab's speech also contains an astonishing request: **show kindness to my family, because I have shown kindness to you**. As Rahab clearly comprehends the Israelite agenda and the God who stands behind it, she requests an act of covenant mercy. In exchange for her action, she asks that Israel spare her life, as well as the lives of her father, mother, brothers and sisters in the upcoming campaign.[25] This request is astonishing in how it continues to reveal the depths of Rahab's knowledge. She is the first to describe Jericho's fall and is confident enough of this future fact to pin her own life (and the lives of her family) to it. She recognizes Israel's חֵרֶם-style (*ḥāram*) conquest, a striking first mention of this subject within the text of Joshua (see Supplemental Study on *Yahweh* War in ch. 6, p. 151). She even uses a very special technical word, חֶסֶד (*ḥesed*, "mercy"), often reserved for covenant discussions, to couch her request. The weight of this single word alone may suggest she has more in mind than simple self-preservation.[26]

---

the scouts as part of an anti-establishment groundswell. For more on this interpretive framework see the Supplemental Study on Playing Monopoly in ch. 11, p. 235.

[24]Richard D. Nelson (*Joshua: A Commentary*, OTL [Louisville, KY: Westminster John Knox, 1997], p. 42) regards Rahab as a trickster: "She seems to help the king, but tricks him. She seems to aid the spies, but traps them."

[25]Rahab requests that Israel "spare the lives of my father and mother, my brothers and sisters, and all who belong to them." This last clause is literally וְאֵת כָּל־אֲשֶׁר לָהֶם (*wəʾēth kol-ʾăšer lāhem*), and could be translated "all that belong to them." Does this refer to people only, or does this refer to the family's belongings as well? Given the Achan episode in chapter seven, this preservation of people and possessions under "the ban" is problematic.

[26]Nelson Glueck (*Hesed in the Bible*, trans. by A. Gottschalk [Cincinnati: Hebrew Union College Press, 1967], p. 102) argues that *ḥesed* is not to be understood as simply "love" or "mercy," but as "loyalty to covenant obligations." While Glueck's line of thinking continues to be debated, the discovery of this technical term in Rahab's vocabulary is enormous.

Consider the use of *ḥesed* elsewhere. In Exod 34:6-7, Yahweh is described

Rahab's use of special vocabulary culminates in her request: **Swear to me by the LORD.** This comes, astonishingly, out of a Canaanite mouth; the prostitute desires an oath from the scouts in the personal name of Israel's God![27] If a previous generation of Israelites seemingly did not know who (or what) Yahweh was and had to be informed by Moses (cf. Exod 3:13-14), how, then, can this strange woman in this backwater oasis know anything of Israel's God, much less appeal to his authority in an obligatory formula? Are her words to be regarded as a manipulative ploy (after all, in v. 11, Yahweh is *your* God") or are they to be regarded as an invocation of divine curse should the scouts fail to follow through with their promise ("May Yahweh do such-and-such or worse to me if I fail")? The source of Rahab's well-informed audacity remains a mystery but may account for the faith-tag given to her by later interpreters (Heb 11:31; Jas 2:25).

More to the point at hand, Rahab now places the scouts in a double bind. If they refuse her request, they risk being revealed to the authorities; if they grant her request, they risk breaking the divine mandate to "not leave alive anything that breathes" in the land (Deut 20:16). It is a tension that cannot be missed. The narrator, through the words of Rahab, offers another glimpse at the strategy of the larger text. The reader will not be permitted to coast along a pre-

---

as a "compassionate and gracious God, slow to anger, abounding in *ḥesed* and faithfulness, maintaining *ḥesed* to thousands, and forgiving wickedness, rebellion and sin." This text celebrates mercy on the other side of the "golden calf" incident, a pagan moment — and possibly a *Canaanite* pagan moment, given associations between Baal and bull images — in Israel's story. Could Rahab have known about this too?

Other uses of *ḥesed* in covenant contexts include Exod 20:6; Deut 5:10; 7:9,12; Ruth 1:8; Hos 6:6. For more examples and discussion of the use of *ḥesed* see *TWOT*, s.v. חסד.

[27]Similarly, in 1 Kgs 17:7-24 the widow at Zarephath, another female "outsider," speaks to an Israelite (in this case, Elijah) and surprisingly refers to Yahweh by name as "your God." Like Rahab, the widow also musters an oath formula in the name of Yahweh and takes unnatural risks in the direction of faith. Both women are the focal points of their respective stories and challenge hasty generalizations about doubt, belief, and ethnic identity. For the Phoenician widow, the culmination comes in the first person confession of v. 24: "Now I know that you are a man of God and that the word of the LORD from your mouth is truth." For the Canaanite Rahab, the last word is more subtle, but no less real, cast in third person through the narration of Josh 6:25.

dictable path. Given the well-ordered worldview in which the biblical authors operate, such feints and zigzags become all the more
effective. Rahab's careening words force all interpreters into a corner, wedged right between the two scouts. How is escape from this
double bind possible?

To begin to answer this question, the speech of Rahab must be
placed into the larger context. The speech gives testimony to the
work of Yahweh. As such, it peers backward in time, an outsider's
response to no less than three points: the inside message of *torah*,
the God who stands behind *torah*, and the risk of opposing either.
This much is clear, even to a Canaanite prostitute. One need not
personally experience forty years of desert to appreciate the God
behind it all. But just as the speech peers backward in time, it also
peers forward, ratcheting up the tension of the book. How will this
pedestrian expedition be prosecuted? What does it really mean to
"be careful to obey all the law" (1:7)? How is *torah* interpreted when
a faceless and nameless enemy is suddenly given a face and a name?
What happens if this named enemy expresses faith in Yahweh?
Taken in this way, Rahab's speech of chapter two drops with a thud
among the three speeches of chapter one. Yahweh has issued a great
commission. Joshua has ordered the people to follow. The two and
a half tribes have promised full obedience. Thus far, all indications
are positive, harmonious, smooth. But with Rahab's speech a new
voice is picked up; the trio becomes a quartet, an odd foursome.
This last part arises through the others in high counterpoint: thoroughly orthodox in sound, but unclean at the source. It is Canaanite, helpful, dangerous, disturbing, and, — in short — complicating.
How will Israel respond? What can the scouts possibly say?

2:14,17-20 Their answer is rushed and uncomfortable: **Our lives
for your lives!** They recognize that their personal future is clearly in
the hands of this unfamiliar woman who is all too familiar with their
past. They grant her request, but not without dropping a series of
"loophole" conditions. The first and last of these conditions to their
agreement is that Rahab remain silent about the whole affair
(2:14,20). The second is that Rahab pin her hope to a marked window-hole (2:18). The third is that those who are to be spared as a
result of Rahab's kindness, be gathered into her house when the city
is overrun (2:18-19). Any breech of these three conditions will result
in a nullification of their oath. It is also worth noting that adjust-

ments to the agreement accelerate once the spies are out the window-hole and seemingly free from the authorities in Jericho and —
perhaps even more significantly — from this woman who has, in one
move, both rescued and trapped them! Once down the wall, they
sniff the outside air and emphasize their own innocence should the
plan miscarry (2:19-20). They also emphasize that the agreement
between them is something *she made them swear*,[28] suggesting that it
was a matter of entrapment. Such "fine print" may be required to
seal the deal[29]; on the other hand, the words of the scouts reek of
second thoughts and reneging promises. One is left wondering if
the threads to this covenant are not already unraveling.

Mention of the "scarlet thread" in this passage is worth further
comment. It provides one example of how this rich passage has been
analyzed by expositors through the centuries. Church fathers discussed how this "thread" might relate to the blood of Christ and
how Rahab could be a symbol of the church.[30] Such typological
approaches have merit, but must be executed cautiously.[31] In doing
so here, two points may be explored, each prompted by a close reading of the text and attention to word choice.

---

[28]The causal nuance comes through the use of שבע (*šb'*) in the hiphil, "you
caused us to swear." See Supplemental Study on Swearing in ch. 9, pp. 199.

[29]The verbal contract between Rahab and the spies contains language and
themes common to covenant agreements. See K.M. Campbell, "Rahab's
Covenant," *VT* 22 (1972): 243-244.

[30]Consider the work of Origen of Alexandria (A.D. 185-250) on the matter. He writes of Rahab: "She herself puts the scarlet-colored sign in her
house, through which she is bound to be saved from the destruction of the
city. No other sign would have been accepted, except the scarlet-colored
one that carried the sign of blood. For she knew there was no salvation for
anyone except in the blood of Christ. . . .

"By that sign, all persons attain salvation, all those who are found in the
house of the one who was once a prostitute, all those cleansed in the water
and by the Holy Spirit and in the blood of our Lord and Savior Jesus Christ.
'to whom is the glory and the dominion forever and ever. Amen!'"

An English translation of Origen's twenty-six sermons on Joshua is available in *Origen: Homilies on Joshua*, trans. by Barbara J. Bruce, ed. by Cynthia
White, The Fathers of the Church 105 (Washington, DC: Catholic University of America, 2002), pp. 49-50.

[31]For a more responsible approach to typology, see Richard M. Davidson,
Typology in Scripture: A Study of Hermeneutical typos *Structure* (Berrien
Springs, MI: Andrews University, 1981).

First, in 2:15 the term חֶבֶל (*ḥebel*) occurs. The NIV reads this literally as a "rope": **she let them down by a rope through the window.**[32] This term may certainly describe a braided object used for
measuring distance or for tying things together. Interpreted in this
way, the *ḥebel* will facilitate the descent of the scouts out of the window-hole and down to the ground. However, another reading is possible.[33] The root from which the noun *ḥebel* is derived may also suggest the action of "binding" or even "seizing a pledge."[34] Given
Rahab's request of 2:12 for a "pledge" and a "sure sign,"[35] this passage may be understood as a direct response to her request. It summarizes the exchange between the scouts and Rahab at the moment
of their parting, hence: "she permitted their descent — *with a binding pledge* — through the window-hole." One way or the other, in a
playful double charge of a "binding rope" and a "binding pledge,"
the scouts are securely "roped" by Rahab. Promises are sworn as
they wiggle through the window-hole and drop into the night.[36]

A second term of interest — really a *phrase* of interest — is found
in 2:18 and 2:21. As in the case of the "rope/pledge" discussion, it
may be understood in more than one way. In verse 18 the phrase
appears as תִּקְוַת חוּט הַשָּׁנִי (*tiqwath ḥûṭ haššānî*); in verse 21 it appears
only as *tiqwath haššānî*. In both places it is typically read as a bright-
ly colored marker tied "in" (בַּחַלּוֹן, *baḥallôn*) the window-hole (possibly to some sort of lattice-work?). No questions hinder a reading of
the modifying *ḥûṭ haššānî* as a "red cord"[37] or a "crimson strip."[38] The

---

[32]The noun *ḥallôn* translated by the NIV as "window" suggests a hole in
the wall for the purpose of letting in light and air. It may also have vented
smoke from a brazier used for heating or cooking. Such holes were often
small in size, high in location, and few in number to prevent unwanted
drafts (or intruders!) from entering the house.

[33]*TWOT* offers four different families of words generated by the root חבל
(*ḥbl*).

[34]In fact, a slight variation in pointing produces the term חֲבֹל (*ḥăbōl*), an
economic term describing the "pledge" or "promise" that insures a loan.
See Ezek 18:12,16; 33:15; Micah 2:10.

[35]Note in the Passover context of Exod 12:13 that the blood on the houses is likewise described as a saving "sign" (אוֹת, *'ôth*).

[36]The LXX dodges this question of translation altogether, smoothing the
text as, "she let them down through the window."

[37]Dyes in the ancient Near East were obtained from a variety of sources
and used to tint fabrics such as clothing, curtains, coverings, and threads. It

same cannot be said of the modified noun *tiqwath*, however. It is uniquely interpreted in this passage as a "cord,"[39] "cord of thread," or, to put the whole phrase together, "the cord of a scarlet thread."[40]

How is this to be understood? If not confused with the rope from 2:15, the commonly interpreted image is that of a "red ribbon" (?) gaily fluttering from a window in a high wall. It is clearly a marker of some sort, but for whom? And to what end? The text is surprisingly mum. Is this marker large and conspicuous or tiny and secretive? Would it go unnoticed by the residents of Jericho? If it was noticed, would it be considered irrelevant to the current crisis, even after Rahab herself has been marked as a person of suspicion? If it is too small, and, ultimately for the sake of forces on the outside, will they be able to see it when they come? Finally, there is the logical issue over how this marker relates to the fact that Rahab's window-hole is "in" the wall, and yet the wall will eventually fall down. How will an escape be facilitated? No answers are found in the immediate text or in the description of Rahab's future rescue in chapter six. Because it will not reappear, the mystery of the "scarlet thread" must be addressed here.

Perhaps some of these questions are solved when this interpretative image is adjusted. A fresh start begins with the realization that a traditional reading of the text offers an odd twist of meaning for *tiqwath*. Understanding this word as "cord" or "rope" is without parallel in more than thirty occurrences of the word in the text of the Old Testament. In every other case, without exception, *tiqwath* is translated as "hope," or as one source puts it, the "expectations associated with the duration and quality of human life."[41] If the appearance of *tiqwath* here is read consistently with the unanimous voice of the rest of Scripture, a very different idea takes root. The scouts

---

is believed that this particular color — crimson or scarlet — was obtained from the insect known as the louse (from the family *Kermidae*). Consider Exod 28:5 among other places for the "scarlet worm." These insects are found in shrubby oaks native to the region. For more on this see *TWOT*, s.v. *šānî*.

[38]The same phrase is used in S of S 4:3 to describe the lips of a lover.

[39]The LXX translates *tiqwath* as the diminutive σπαρτίον (*spartion*), "a small cord."

[40]Is this cord made up of one strand dyed red, or of many red strands? In Eccl 4:12 the *ḥûṭ* ("thread") is composed of three strands.

[41]*TWOT*, s.v. תִּקְוָה.

demand that Rahab "connect" — not a "rope" — but "*the hope* of this scarlet stripe with the window-hole" (v. 18). Narratively, she then responds appropriately by merging "*the hope* of the scarlet with the window-hole" (v. 21). Read in this way, a new idea emerges. From it, several points may be drawn. First, the "hope of the scarlet" is for Rahab and not for the scouts. It is not their zip-line out of Jericho. It should not be confused with the *ḥebel* of verse 15. Second, the appropriation of the message is fixed upon a future deliverance symbolized by the term "scarlet." Even the syntax of the words from the mouths of the scouts (the object-first construction) emphasizes the importance of the symbol: "*As for the* hope *of this scarlet line* — connect *it* to the window-hole." Third and finally, in order for this deliverance to be activated, Rahab must choose to act. She must take action in order to merge the "scarlet" (color) with the window-hole.[42] In this, the role of the window-hole (through which the scouts wiggle) must not be lost. Hence, when examined closely, the text presents yet one more string in need of interpretation, a string of thought. The demand of Rahab is that she exhibit *hope*, that her hope be connected to the "*scarlet,*" which, in turn, is connected to the place of exit, the *window-hole*. As is so often true, one thing leads to another.

To set this reading into place, it must be remembered that the text of Joshua is, in so many ways, an exposition of *torah*. As such, deliberate shaping of the language and contours of the story connect the text to *torah* and should be expected.[43] It is therefore reasonable that "the hope of the scarlet" in Joshua is a reflection of the "the hope of the scarlet" found elsewhere. But where?

Two narratives come to mind: the story of Tamar found in Genesis 38 and the Passover story of Exodus 12. Of the two, the story of Tamar is lesser known, but perhaps more relevant. It highlights the less-than-stellar escapades of Judah, the struggle over seed

---

[42]The verbal root קשׁר (*qšr*) communicates the idea of affixing one thing to another. For example a stone may be tied to a scroll (Jer 51:63). More metaphorically, words may be tied to hands (Deut 6:8), or people may be deeply connected to one another (Gen 44:30; 1 Sam 18:1). Here, Rahab blends the scarlet (color) to the window-hole.

[43]This has been referred to as "implicit midrash." See E. Earle Ellis, *The Old Testament in Early Christianity: Canon and Interpretation in the Light of Modern Research* (Grand Rapids: Eerdmans, 1991), pp. 92-96.

(lineage), and the ingenious way in which Tamar — a Canaanite widow several times over — cunningly secures for herself a place inside the people of Yahweh.[44] The passage, bizarre enough even without the ending, concludes with the barren Tamar at long last birthing twin boys. Their birth-race is marked by the presence of a "scarlet thread" tied about the wrist of the false first; the true first becomes a progenitor of the royal house of David! Hence, the actions of Tamar, culminating in this twisting birth account, are presented as both bold and appropriate. The latter point falls from the lips of Judah himself: "she is more righteous than I" (38:26). The outsider moves in.

Language use and themes link the account of Tamar to the account of Rahab. Repeated vocabulary includes terms such as "prostitute," (זוֹנָה, zônāh; Gen 38:15,24; Josh 2:1) and the phrase "she tied . . . a 'scarlet' (marker)" (Gen 38:28; Josh 2:18,21). Other links include Judah's taking a Canaanite woman and "entering" her (Gen 38:2; Josh 2:3), the giving and taking of a "pledge" to secure a promise (Gen 38:17; Josh 2:12), the "cord" as a part of that "pledge" (Gen 38:18), the unrealized expectation of burning a "prostitute" to death (Gen 38:24; Josh 6:21-22), the breaching of a womb like a wall (Gen 38:29; Josh 2:15), the question of relative righteousness (Gen 38:26; Josh 6:25), and a presence in the lineage of David (Ruth 4:1,12,18). Through all this is the cunning with which Tamar moves toward an unlikely victory, an image easily transferred to Rahab. As a final supreme legacy, both "outsiders" appear in the lineage of Jesus (Matt 1:3,5). Connections lace together these Canaanite women, their stories, and their readers. Everyone cheers for the long shot; it is "the hope of the scarlet."

If the Tamar story makes Rahab's move from the outside to the inside of Yahweh's people plausible, the Passover account of Exodus 12 demonstrates it completely. Significant vocabulary common to both texts and used in key positions is limited (e.g., אוֹת, 'ôth, "sign," and בֵּית, bêth, "house"); more informal parallels accumulate quickly. When these accounts are placed side by side, they suggest that Rahab is about to experience a "passover" and "exodus" of her own, albeit of a backdoor variety, or — better put — a back window-hole

---

[44]See Alter's excellent analysis of this story in his *The Art of Biblical Narrative*, pp. 5-12.

variety! For Rahab, it is not an entrance with doorposts and lintels striped in red, but a tiny gap in a defensive wall. Language permits the possibility that this mark may consist of red paint splashed about the window-hole on the mud brick. It would be visible to those on the ground outside, but not to those on the inside or even to those above, on the ramparts. As will be seen later, death in Jericho comes miraculously and devastatingly by the hand of Yahweh, just as in Egypt. Yahweh's people on the inside will watch it happen, marked and therefore passed over. Not-Yahweh's people, unmarked and in the open, face a certain death. Both "passover" accounts (Exodus and Joshua) require the exercise of hope (faith) on the part of Yahweh's people. Embedded within both texts are warnings concerning the danger of disobedience, lost hope, and the foolishness of going outside the door of the appropriately marked dwelling (Exod 12:22; Josh 2:19). Both accounts describe the collecting of family (Exod 12:3-4; Josh 2:13,18) and perhaps most importantly, both stories result in the saving of specific individuals who will play a role in the ongoing narrative. While unstated, it is possible that the avenue of escape for Rahab's company will be the same window-hole used by the scouts. Just as she permitted others to descend from that marked opening, others will permit her and hers to do the same. In Jericho, the "hope of the scarlet," yields salvation for the harlot!

3. The Escape and the Report (2:15-16,21-24)

[15]So she let them down by a rope through the window, for the house she lived in was part of the city wall. [16]Now she had said to them, "Go to the hills so the pursuers will not find you. Hide yourselves there three days until they return, and then go on your way."

[21]"Agreed," she replied. "Let it be as you say." So she sent them away and they departed. And she tied the scarlet cord in the window.

[22]When they left, they went into the hills and stayed there three days, until the pursuers had searched all along the road and returned without finding them. [23]Then the two men started back. They went down out of the hills, forded the river and came to Joshua

son of Nun and told him everything that had happened to them.
**[24]They said to Joshua, "The LORD has surely given the whole land
into our hands; all the people are melting in fear because of us."**

2:15-16,21 Unfazed by the last-second conditions of the Israelite
scouts, Rahab facilitates their escape. In so doing, crucial facts about
the construction of Jericho are revealed. It is already clear that the
city is walled (cf. 6:1, "tightly shut up"): at the moment it has a
locked gate (2:7), undoubtedly guarded, and cannot be used by the
scouts. However, as it turns out, Rahab's house is described as "in
the wall," an odd expression for those unfamiliar with defense structures of the time.[45] Fortunately, excavations at Tell es-Sultan
(Jericho) have revealed an impressive MBA fortification system consisting of a double wall encircling the mound (see Supplemental
Study on Canaanite Fortifications below). Between these two walls
and along steep ramparts, some residences have been uncovered.
Given this vulnerable position of these residences (inside the first
wall but not inside the second) and their cheap construction (walls
are only one mud brick thick), it has been proposed that this would
be an appropriate position for a "red light" district. Such a structure
would literally be located "*in* the wall (system)" and could have had
a window-hole that peeped through the upper reaches of the outer
barrier. Through this portal, presumably under cover of darkness,
the scouts could escape the sealed city.

Curiously, even when the men are safely outside, Rahab continues to control the situation. She commands them to **Go to the hills**
and **hide yourselves.** As the Judean ridge rises sharply to the immediate west of Jericho, this advice is shrewd. The Canaanite pursuers
will likely seal the Jordan crossing and then scour the crusty flats
between it and Jericho. By traveling in the opposite way, into the
sculpted canyons and caves of the hill country, the scouts have the
best chance of escaping unnoticed. This they do, hiding out for

---

[45]Hawk, *Joshua*, p. 47, prefers to keep to literary lines and therefore handles Rahab's window in the wall only figuratively. "The information moves
the plot along by reporting how the scouts made their escape, but it also
underscores the sense that the boundary between Israel and Canaan is
porous. The city wall itself is a boundary, a meeting place between Israel
and others and the site of transformations."

three days (cf. 1:11),[46] until the hunt is abandoned. At last, the agents make their escape, undoubtedly skirting Jericho by a wide margin. Their original mandate to "look over the land" (v. 1) is only partially realized.

2:22-24 Returning to the camp, the men report to Joshua, telling **him everything that had happened**. While unstated, this undoubtedly includes their encounter with Rahab, as the words of the scouts are drawn directly from her mouth (cp. 2:9 with 2:24). Hence, in the end, the report Joshua seeks and receives is produced by a most unlikely source. Behind enemy lines is discovered an unmistakable truth: Yahweh is on the move in Canaan. This realization forces another question: will Israel follow this lead?

SUPPLEMENTAL STUDY

CANAANITE FORTIFICATIONS

The walls of Jericho are among the most celebrated defensive structures in the biblical text. They have been sung about, artistically painted, and recreated in film. Depictions range from something as elegant as an English castle to a bulwark of brutish wood and stone. But what were they really like? Can archaeology assist (or curb) the imagination?

As presented in the Introduction, the Canaan of Joshua's day was likely the *Heartland* of the LBA. With a handful of exceptions, many sites at this time lacked fortification walls, either because the instability of the age prevented their construction and upkeep, or because defensive systems were outlawed by Canaan's Egyptian overlords.[47] The exceptional sites that were fortified have revealed systems built centuries earlier in the Canaanite heyday of the MBA.[48]

---

[46]See Supplemental Study on "Three Days" in ch. 1, p. 72.

[47]It appears that Khirbet el-Ureima (Tel Kinrot) and Khirbet Rabud (Debir) were newly constructed in the LBA with fortification walls. They are exceptional. Sites that were fortified in the period, such as Hazor, Shechem, Jericho, and possibly Gezer, simply were MBA reuses.

[48]For more on this, see Aharon Kempinski, "Middle and Late Bronze Age Fortifications," in *The Architecture of Ancient Israel: From the Prehistoric to the Persian Periods*, ed. by Aharon Kempinski and Ronny Reich (Jerusalem: IES, 1992), pp. 127-142.

It is therefore necessary to begin in that time in order to construct an image of fortifications from Joshua's day.

Volkmar Fritz has suggested four types of MBA fortifications.[49] These commonly utilized some combination of sloping earthwork with a vertical wall. The earthworks would be set in such a steep pitch as to altogether prevent an ascent by chariot or greatly hinder an ascent by foot.[50] As one example, the exterior face of the earthworks at Tell el-Qadi (Dan) had a 38-degree slope and was topped by many layers of smooth plaster.[51] As besieging, scaling, and sapping (tunneling) appear to have been offensive tactics of choice in the Bronze Age, the vast scale of these enclosure systems would have proved to be quite a deterrent.

Fritz's first type of MBA fortification consists of a perimeter wall between eight and thirteen feet thick. This wall may be built of stone or of mud brick resting on a still larger stone foundation. A sloping ramp (or glacis) often protected the lower courses from easy access. Rectangular towers appeared at intervals for reinforcements. An example of this type may be clearly seen at Tell Balatah (Shechem).[52] The unhewn stones used to erect the wall were so large that they attracted the name "Cyclopean," as only a mythical Cyclops could lift them!

A second type of fortification consists simply of earthworks. Layers of beaten earth (*terre pisée*) piled in an encircling ridge might measure 80 to 100 feet wide at the base and 30 or 40 feet high at the crest. Tell el-Ajjul, near modern Gaza, had such a system.[53] At the outer foot of the defenses a deep ditch or "moat" (20 feet deep!) was dug into the sandstone bedrock to further hinder all approaches.

A third type of fortification was an earthwork topped by wall. This wall could be fashioned of stone, mud brick, or a combination

---

[49]Volkmar Fritz, *The City in Ancient Israel* (Sheffield: Sheffield, 1995), pp. 33-34.

[50]Kathleen Kenyon suggested that these ramparts were introduced in Canaan by the Hyksos, a military aristocracy driven from Egypt in 1550 B.C. In her view, these wide, sloping ramparts could be an answer to the great weapon of the day: the horse-drawn chariot. See John R. Bartlett, *Cities of the Biblical World: Jericho* (Grand Rapids: Eerdmans, 1982), p. 88.

[51]See *NEAEHL*, s.v. "Dan."

[52]See *NEAEHL*, s.v. "Shechem."

[53]See *NEAEHL*, s.v. "Ajjul, Tell el-."

of each. The MBA fortifications at Tell el-Fukhar (Acco) is a good example of this type.[54] The earliest phase of construction here appears to have been the construction of a clay rampart. Above this was raised a wall of stone. Later work would add still more to the accumulated mass, a second ramp covered the first; the wall was given additional height using mud bricks over the stone.

Fritz's fourth type of MBA defenses consisted of earthen rampart, as before, only in this case, anchored at the center by a stone core. This inner "wall" helped stabilize the earthwork; the same could be used as a base from which an even higher wall could project. An excellent example of this type of system is visible at Tell el-Qadi (Dan). When probed by recent excavations, the stone core of the rampart was still standing at a height of 36 feet![55]

At Jericho the settlement was enclosed by a system closely matching Fritz's third type of MBA fortification.[56] Evidence for a great rampart has been unearthed at several points on the edge of the mound. This rampart was improved on at least three occasions; plaster was used to surface and seal the exterior face each time. For the final phase, the most impressive of the improvements, a secondary wall of stone topped with a mud brick superstructure was raised at the foot of the revetment. This stone base of this skirting wall (still standing today in places) was 15 feet high and functioned as a first line of defense. From this point the revetment rose at a slope of 35 degrees, and, judging by the angle, rose to a height of about 45 feet. On the top of this crest arose a second wall, set back some 65 feet from the revetment base. No part of this upper wall has been discovered in situ, but evidence of its existence is visible in the mud brick debris discovered downslope. Hence, the MBA defenses of Jericho consisted of two concentric walls of mud brick, one resting at the base of a steep revetment and the other resting at the summit. Rising from the surrounding plain, the double rim of mud brick would have risen to a height equal to that of a six-story building.

No doubt the original construction of these defenses was completed well in advance of the Israelite arrival in Canaan. However,

---

[54]See *NEAEHL*, s.v. "Acco."

[55]See *NEAEHL*, s.v. "Dan."

[56]Archaeologists refer to the Jericho of this period as "City IV." For more on "City IV," see *NEAEHL*, s.v. "Jericho."

ceramic evidence, the evidence of Egyptian-style scarab seals, and one Carbon-14 sample all point to the conclusion that the fiery destruction of the bulwarks (and the enclosed city) did not occur until the end of the Late Bronze I period, a conclusion that corresponds closely with the arrival of Israel.[57]

---

[57]See a popularized presentation of this evidence by Bryant G. Wood in "Did the Israelites Conquer Jericho? A New Look at the Archaeological Evidence," *BAR* 16 (March/April 1990): 44-57.

JOSHUA 3

C. CROSSING OVER THE JORDAN (3:1–4:24)

The Jordan River does not unite the land, it divides it.[1] This truth is deeply embedded in the ground, down to the level of names. Land on the east bank of the Jordan River is called "Transjordan" or "Overjordan"[2]; land on the west bank of the Jordan River carries the name "Cisjordan." Between this ancient divide, the waters rush and rest irregularly, ever descending, and ever draining the region of precious rainfall. Rocky screes and heavy vegetation render the river largely unnavigable, but do provide dense habitat for wild creatures. In the end, after following a course that twists out of the Lebanon and through the scarps of the Great Rift Valley, the writhing flow empties into the Dead Sea. The area of its salty demise is visible from the crest at Jericho. Crossing this "Downrusher" is no simple task (see Supplemental Study on High Expectations for a Low River below).[3]

For Israel, the Jordan River represents more than simply a physical barrier. It symbolizes a true frontier: the end of a wilderness and the beginning of the land of settlement. After wandering for a generation in a dusty desert, it is ironic that the final barrier to entering that

---

[1]George Adam Smith makes this important point in his discussion in *The Historical Geography of the Holy Land,* 25th ed., 1931 (repr., New York: Harper & Row, 1966), p. 313. For more, see a popular presentation of the role played by this river throughout history in Nelson Glueck's *The River Jordan: Being an Illustrated Account of Earth's Most Storied River* (Philadelphia: Westminster, 1946).

[2]The term "Overjordan" is used by G.A. Smith, ibid., p. 335.

[3]The name of this river, the יַרְדֵּן (*Yardēn*), "Downrusher," is drawn from the verb "to go down." This is certainly true. The Jordan is born in the ice-cold springs of the Hula Basin (Upper Jordan Valley) at an elevation of about 220 feet above sea level. It only goes downhill from there, dropping briefly in and out of the Sea of Galilee before plunging into oblivion beneath the surface of the Dead Sea (at more than 1400 feet below sea level).

land of promise is liquid in nature. Perhaps this is appropriate. After all, leaving Egypt could not be accomplished until another body of water, the Red Sea, was opened and traversed. It is almost as if the story of the wilderness wanderings is written on a dry parchment with a soggy margin. As will be seen, the armies of the enemy watch in fear from beyond this liquid frame on either side. Egypt returns home to lick its wounds; Canaan braces for the incoming surge.

Within the text of Joshua, the importance of the Jordan crossing is enormous. Two whole chapters are devoted to its telling. Barking orders fill the page as preparations are made (3:1-13), the crossing is initiated, and a miracle occurs (3:14-17). In the chapter that follows, the crossing concludes with the building of two monuments. The first serves to memorialize the event (4:1-8,19-24), while the second serves to emphasize Joshua's leadership (4:9). Through this telling and retelling, crossing and recrossing, Yahweh is shown to be a mighty God who advances before his own, Joshua is exalted as Moses' successor, and the people appear as faithful followers.[4] Released in context, the crossing may even become paradigmatic for the larger preachment of the book. God leads. His people follow and obey, even into the torrent. This is what success looks like in a great commission enterprise.

SUPPLEMENTAL STUDY

HIGH EXPECTATIONS FOR A LOW RIVER

On Jordan's stormy banks I stand,
And cast a wishful eye
To Canaan's fair and happy land,
Where my possessions lie.
I am bound for the promised land,
I am bound for the promised land;
O who will come an go with me?
I am bound for the promised land.
—American Folk Hymn (Public Domain)

---

[4]John A. Beck argues for the same purpose in his article, "Why Do Joshua's Readers Keep Crossing the River? The Narrative-Geographical Shaping of Joshua 3–4," *JETS* 48 (Dec. 2005): 689-699.

Crossing the Jordan River is a persistent theme in Christian hymnody. Songs express the desire to see, experience, or meet someone on the far side of its banks. By means of such cherished expressions, the Jordan has become a powerful metaphor for the boundary between the sorrows of this world and the comfort of a world to come. In the language of hope, the "Promised Land" has become a code word for heaven and crossing the Jordan marks the final leg of that journey. Armed with these expectations, travelers who experience the watercourse that provides the inspiration of this image, unfortunately, may be disappointed. The "great divide" is not what it used to be, or, at the very least, it is far less impressive than the lyrics of old songs such as "Roll, Jordan, Roll" might suggest.

Some of this disappointment may come as a result of the "crossing" environment. Today, the Jordan River runs down a political boundary line between the modern state of Israel and the Hashemite Kingdom of Jordan. For this reason, both banks exhibit all the fearful trappings of security in the Middle East.[5] While recent improvements in the relations between these sovereigns have made the "crossing zone" less tense, approaching the Jordan inevitably means approaching barbed wire, minefields, checkpoints, vehicle searches, and gun emplacements. These high-security measures may detract from the spiritual appreciation of crossing the Jordan.[6]

Beyond this military threat is the hostility of the land itself. This is particularly true below the confluence of the Wadi Zerqa (Jabbok) and the Jordan. In this southernmost third of the valley, the rain-shadow created by the Judean Hills to the west deprives the region of precipitation. The Rift floor drops to more than a thousand feet below sea level and widens to more than ten miles across. The broken walls on either side of the valley tumble down upon crusty flats

---

[5]An exception to this rule is the area between the southern end of the Sea of Galilee and the mouth of the Yarmuk River. Because of the Israeli occupation of the Golan Heights, this short stretch of the Jordan is controlled by the State of Israel on both banks. Not surprisingly, entrepreneurs seeking to profit from the Christian impulse for baptism have built a facility there (Yardenit) to accommodate those willing to pay for access to the water.

[6]The opening of a park connected with "Bethany beyond the Jordan," near the Wadi al-Kharrar, offers the best opportunity to approach the river from the Jordanian side. Many future tourists will undoubtedly reward the development of this area with their business.

of lime, salt, and clay, the remains of a prehistoric lake.[7] These soft
sediments are, in turn, erosively carved into eerie shapes. Treeless
terraces, buttes, and mesas rise and crumble, forming an exhausting
barrier to even the most intrepid explorer. In the center of this ash-
gray badland coils the Jordan river itself, a muddied line of water
banked by thickets of thirsty vegetation. A watercourse here seems
so out of place; it surely must be imported from fairer regions.

A third cause for modern disappointment is the size of the
Jordan River itself. Because water is so precious in this part of the
world, runoff from the hills on either side of the valley is strategically captured and diverted for agricultural use. While these controls
are critical for maintaining life in the land (evident by the bold green
squares of drip-irrigated fields in the distance), they impact the size
and vigor of both the Jordan River and the Dead Sea.[8] A quick
glance from the bus window while crossing the King Hussein (or
Allenby) Bridge near Jericho may be the sum of the visual experience; one blink and the pilgrim may miss the Jordan channel altogether. It is more like a creek than a river. In the dry summer
months, it might measure ten feet across and be no deeper than two
or three feet.

To obtain a view unobscured by these developments, one must
slip away to another time and investigate the writing of premodern
travelers. Three quotes are offered here. This first is from the pen
of George Adam Smith. *The Historical Geography of the Holy Land* was
based upon four journeys through the land between 1880 and 1904.
Smith offers one impression of the Jordan.

> The river itself is from 90 to 100 feet broad, a rapid, muddy
> water with a zigzag current. The depth varies from 3 feet at
> some fords to as much as 10 or 12. In the sixty-five miles the

---

[7]Efraim Orni and Elisha Efrat, *Geography of Israel*, 4th rev. ed. (Jerusalem:
Israel Universities, 1980), p. 97.

[8]Reports on the diminishing of these waterways are common. With
respect to the Dead Sea, it has been suggested that the surface has fallen by
twelve meters in elevation since 1900 (Jerome Murphy O'Connor, *The Holy
Land: An Oxford Archaeological Guide from Earliest Times to 1700*, 4th ed.
[Oxford: Oxford University, 1998], p. 226). Indirect evidence of this depletion may also be sensed by those who maintain walkways for swimmers and
tourists. Sidewalks must be regularly lengthened to extend their reach to the
water's edge.

descent is 610 feet, or an average of 9 feet a mile. . . . The swiftness is rendered more dangerous by the muddy bed and curious zigzag current which will easily sweep a man from the side into the centre of the stream. In April the waters rise to the wider bed, but for the most of the year they keep to the channel of 90 feet. Here, with infrequent interruptions of shingle, mostly silent and black in spite of its speed, but now and then breaking into praise and whitening into foam, Jordan scours along, muddy between banks of mud, careless of beauty, careless of life, intent upon its own work, which for ages by decree of the Almighty has been that of separation.[9]

In Carl Ritter's classic *The Comparative Geography of Palestine and the Sinaitic Peninsula*, a second testimony is discovered:

In proportion to the difficulty in crossing the Jordan in the winter time, when it is almost impossible for any but the Beduins to pass from bank to bank, is the ease of crossing in the summer time, when it may be passed in countless places. Above Beisan these are very numerous; below they are less frequent, and yet the Arabs appear to cross with their flocks and herds, judging from the fact that they are found as often on the west as on the east bank of the river. In July, when Burckhardt passed over the Jordan at Sukkat, where it was eight paces wide, it was only three feet deep. When Irby and Mangles crossed at the same ford, on the 13th of March, it was about a hundred and forty feet wide; the water ran with much force, and reached up to the girth of the horses. When, twelve days later, they crossed by a ford yet more to the south, which they erroneously considered to be that of Gilgal, the Jordan was to their amazement so swollen, that the horses only reached the other side by swimming, and all the goods were wet through. Buckingham and Banks found a ford two hours north of Jericho, and near the Wadi Faisail, where the breadth of the stream on the 29th of January was twenty-five yards.[10]

Third and finally, the testimony of J.W. McGarvey may be considered.

[9]G.A. Smith, *Historical Geography*, p. 313.
[10]Carl Ritter, *The Comparative Geography of Palestine and the Sinaitic Peninsula* (New York: Appleton, 1866), pp. 50-51.

We cross by a ford almost due east from Elisha's Fountain called *Gharanizeh*, and sometimes the Jericho ford. . . . A ferryboat is kept in readiness, and must be used during a large part of the year, but just below the ferry-crossing the water breaks over a shoal, and at the head of this it can be forded when it is very deep above. The author's party forded here on the 5th of May, 1879, the water coming about half-way up our saddle-skirt.[11]

Observations from these three hands help the reader with high expectations for a low river.

1. The People, the Priests, and Joshua Prepare (3:1-14)

[1]**Early in the morning Joshua and all the Israelites set out from Shittim and went to the Jordan, where they camped before crossing over.** [2]**After three days the officers went throughout the camp,** [3]**giving orders to the people: "When you see the ark of the covenant of the LORD your God, and the priests, who are Levites, carrying it, you are to move out from your positions and follow it.** [4]**Then you will know which way to go, since you have never been this way before. But keep a distance of about a thousand yards[a] between you and the ark; do not go near it."**

[5]**Joshua told the people, "Consecrate yourselves, for tomorrow the LORD will do amazing things among you."**

[6]**Joshua said to the priests, "Take up the ark of the covenant and pass on ahead of the people." So they took it up and went ahead of them.**

[7]**And the LORD said to Joshua, "Today I will begin to exalt you in the eyes of all Israel, so they may know that I am with you as I was with Moses.** [8]**Tell the priests who carry the ark of the covenant: 'When you reach the edge of the Jordan's waters, go and stand in the river.'"**

[9]**Joshua said to the Israelites, "Come here and listen to the words of the LORD your God.** [10]**This is how you will know that the**

---

[11]J.W. McGarvey, *Lands of the Bible: A Geographical and Topographical Description of Palestine with Letters of Travel in Egypt, Syria, Asia Minor, and Greece* (Philadelphia: J.B. Lippencott, 1880), pp. 345-346.

**living God is among you and that he will certainly drive out before
you the Canaanites, Hittites, Hivites, Perizzites, Girgashites,
Amorites and Jebusites. ¹¹See, the ark of the covenant of the Lord
of all the earth will go into the Jordan ahead of you. ¹²Now then,
choose twelve men from the tribes of Israel, one from each tribe.
¹³And as soon as the priests who carry the ark of the LORD—the
Lord of all the earth—set foot in the Jordan, its waters flowing
downstream will be cut off and stand up in a heap."**

**¹⁴So when the people broke camp to cross the Jordan, the
priests carrying the ark of the covenant went ahead of them.**

ᵃ*4 Hebrew about two thousand cubits* (about 900 meters)

3:1 Preparations for crossing the Jordan River begin with relo-
cating to the river's edge. Joshua and the people "pull up the tent
pegs"[12] early in the morning[13] and begin the logistical challenge of
transferring themselves and their belongings to a new place. The
language of moving reminds the reader that this generation of Israel
is familiar with a mobile lifestyle. They were likely born in the wilderness — on the march from Egypt — and have yet to realize, ever, the
possession of land. *Shittim* has been their campsite since before the
death of Moses. Now for the first time under Joshua's leadership,
they move again.

3:2 The repeating of phrases such as "three days,"[14] "the officers," and "crossing through the middle of the camp" place the narrative back on track following the scouting fiasco of chapter 2, and
reconnect it to the original commission given in chapter 1 (cf. 3:2
with 1:10-11). As in chapter 1, orders are delivered from the officers
to the people (vv. 3-4), from Joshua to the people (vv. 5,9-13), from
Joshua to the priests (v. 6), and from Yahweh to Joshua (vv. 7-8).
Such abrupt voice changes and snapping commands suggest a
tumultuous scene of motion, color, and high excitement.[15]

---

[12]The term נָסַע (*nāsaʿ*) suggests the action of pulling up tent pegs, and by
extension, "to break camp." Jer 31:24 provides a clear contrast between the
plowman, who is sedentary, and the herder, who "moves about," or "breaks
camp."

[13]See Waltke and O'Connor, *Biblical Hebrew Syntax*, sec. 27.4b

[14]See notes at 1:11 and 9:16.

[15]Such a reading, sensitive to the evocative mood of the text, is preferred
to that of Nelson, *Joshua*, p. 57, who confesses after some struggle to identi-

3:3-4 Initial instructions flow from the officers to the people. The people are instructed to take their cue from the movement of the Ark of the Covenant. When the Ark-box moves, the people are to move.[16] Where the Ark-box goes, the people are to go. This is important as the people prepare to enter territory that *is not*, and yet *is*, familiar.[17] It is not familiar in the sense that this generation has never physically set foot in the land. For this reason they need a guide. On the other hand, this land has indeed been visited by their ancestors and therefore, in a figurative sense, *they have been there before* — just not recently.[18] This nuance is important for the larger biblical presentation that views entering Canaan as a kind of homecoming.[19]

---

fy literary strands and overlapping redaction efforts that "further attempts to reconstruct the literary history of chapters 3–4 are probably doomed to failure." This impenetrable nature of the text, as he seemingly regards it, is odd, given a later sentence in the same paragraph: "Although the resulting logic and narrative flow is disjointed, by using moderate effort the reader actually has no trouble making sense of the story line." One wonders if the disjunction he senses is more an issue of his method and less an issue of his text!

Nelson's sentiments are often repeated by critical commentators who struggle to identify a neat structure for chapters 3–4. While admittedly, there is some truth to their claims of disjunction and open-endedness, a good number of the so-called problems are easily explained as literary tactics, e.g., suspense-building, prolepsis, flashback, and even metaphor.

[16]This is reminiscent of their *modus operandi* in the desert. Cf. Exod 40:36-38; Num 10:33.

[17]The clause מִתְּמוֹל שִׁלְשׁוֹם (*mittᵊmôl šilšôm*) is usually rendered as a temporal adverb ("you have never been this way *before*" NIV, or "you have not been this way *previously*.") Waltke and O'Connor argue that "it never has the supported 'literal' sense." (*Biblical Hebrew Syntax*, p. 658, fn. 44). This conclusion should be softened, however, in light of use elsewhere (e.g., Josh 4:18 or Ruth 2:11) and in light of the fact that even the absolute may be expressed differently. I suggest taking the phrase as referring to the *recent* past, as "you have not passed this way *recently*." This opens up the idea that Canaan is familiar ground.

[18]Within the Christian tradition is an old song, "Were You There When They Crucified My Lord?" Butler points out how this song uses the same tactic to draw the listener into the event and involve him/her in the action (*Joshua*, p. 51). Such appeals can be both dramatic and confessional.

[19]John H. Sailhamer raises this point in his discussion of Abraham's entry into the land of Canaan. See his comments on Gen 12:1-9 in *The Pentateuch as Narrative. A Biblical-Theological Commentary* (Grand Rapids: Zondervan, 1992), pp. 139-141. Note also his description of the principle of contemporization (p. 31).

Beyond the order to follow the Ark-box (and, more importantly, the God that it represents) is the stipulation that the people keep their distance from it, coming no closer than a thousand cubits, or, approximately **a thousand yards**. This separation is substantial in many ways; it not only underlines the "otherness" of Yahweh, but perceptually, it renders the holy entourage "other" as well: unapproachable, mysterious, dangerous.

3:5-6 Joshua directs the people and the priests. The people are commanded to consecrate themselves.[20] This act continues the idea of separation by putting distance between the sacred and profane (see Lev 20:7-8). Why is this necessary? Yahweh is about to **do amazing things**. The word translated as "amazing things" is used elsewhere of acts beyond the control of man but not beyond the control of God (the root strikingly appears in Exod 15:11, in Miriam's "Song of the Sea").[21] The priests are commanded to lift the Ark-box from the ground to their shoulders and "cross over" with all eyes watching. Viewing this spectacle would bring to mind the so-called "Song of the Ark-box" found in Numbers 10:35:

> Rise up, O Lord!
> May your enemies be scattered;
> may your foes flee before you.

This song is sung by Moses whenever the Ark-box is hoisted for movement. It reminds the people of a power beyond themselves[22]; this special container functioned as a symbol for יהוה צְבָאוֹת יֹשֵׁב הַכְּרֻבִים (*YHWH ṣᵊbā'ôth yōšēb hakkᵊrûbîm*), "Yahweh of omnipotence enthroned between the Cherubim" (1 Sam 4:4). When this kind of force arises, all opposition turns and beats a hasty retreat.

---

[20]The same order is given by Moses prior to the giving of the Law at Sinai. There, the act of consecration is further defined by the command to the people to wash their clothes and abstain from sexual relations. See Exod 19:10-15.

[21]It also appears in Exod 3:20 anticipating the events leading up to the Exodus of Israel from Egypt.

[22]Drifting forward in Scripture brings the careful reader to 2 Kings 2 where Elijah and Elisha also cross the Jordan on "dry ground." In this case, it was not a staff or an Ark-box that facilitated the "splitting" of the water, but the mantle of Elijah (2:8,14). No doubt, this story is meant to be read while reflecting upon Joshua 3–4. Israel is introduced to Canaan (and the residents of Jericho) as Yahweh's new people. Elisha is introduced to Israel (and the prophets from Jericho) as Yahweh's new prophet.

3:7-8 Orders flow from Yahweh to Joshua in two segments. The first almost appears as a private aside. Joshua learns that the amazing experience of the day will confirm his leadership role among the people. Again, harking back to elements of chapter 1, the responsibilities of Moses have now become the responsibilities of Joshua. To facilitate this transfer, Yahweh is going to magnify Joshua as a credible successor.

In the second segment, Yahweh issues the directive for the campaign of Canaan to truly begin. "Crossing over" will commence at the edge of the Jordan River with the priests bearing the Ark-box. The holy entourage is to press to the riverbank, and surprisingly, in the words of Yahweh, "stand *in* the Jordan." Exactly how this will work is not clear. One would suspect that the small group is to stand *on the riverbank*, however, use of the preposition *in* clearly proposes movement beyond that foaming edge. Interest is stirred.

3:9-14 Armed with this information, Joshua turns and passes on orders to the people. The people are to draw near, listen, look, and choose. They are to draw near and listen because the words they are about to hear are authoritative. They come from a **living God** who can offer assurance that Israel will be victorious over their enemies (see Supplemental Study on Ethnicity in chapter 10, p. 212). The people are to look because the Ark-box, the visible manifestation of the Lord of all the *land* (repeated twice in this passage), will move ahead of them.[23] They are to follow. The divine nature of this leading is suggested by Joshua's preview of a sign to come: the crossing of the Jordan will be possible because the waters **will be cut off and stand up in a heap.** This detail is revealed here for the first time, is assumed to have been part of Yahweh's previous message, and will be accomplished at the moment when the feet of the priests who bear the Ark-box "rest" in the Jordan.[24] Finally, the people are to choose twelve men for an unspecified future action. That these men

---

[23]Yahweh is described as the master "of all the אֶרֶץ (*'ereṣ*)," a term often tied to a specific land or country, but sometimes referring to all land, or by extension, "the earth" (e.g., Deut 10:14; Micah 4:13). The question at hand is whether the narrator is referring here to the whole world/universe or simply the land immediately before Israel, i.e., Canaan. Assuming continuity between this text and Rahab's very similar words (2:9), the latter is an attractive option. Still, see Rahab's words in 2:11.

[24]Similarly the text does not describe a command from Yahweh for the priests to exit the Jordan, yet Joshua will command them to do this too

are representative of the people is clear. The original text drums: "one man (and) one man (only) per tribe."[25] With these directions in place, the crossing is ready to begin.

2. Israel's Riverwalk (3:15-17)

[15]**Now the Jordan is at flood stage all during harvest. Yet as soon as the priests who carried the ark reached the Jordan and their feet touched the water's edge,** [16]**the water from upstream stopped flowing. It piled up in a heap a great distance away, at a town called Adam in the vicinity of Zarethan, while the water flowing down to the Sea of the Arabah (the Salt Sea**[a]**) was completely cut off. So the people crossed over opposite Jericho.** [17]**The priests who carried the ark of the covenant of the LORD stood firm on dry ground in the middle of the Jordan, while all Israel passed by until the whole nation had completed the crossing on dry ground.**

[a]*16* **That is, the Dead Sea**

3:15-16 At this point, the narrator both masterfully reels the action to climax and releases new information. Both create tension. The tempo of the telling is arrested by means of a complex sentence structure: The priests who bear the Ark-box enter the Jordan . . . their feet splash into the water's edge . . . and suddenly, the narrative freezes, interrupted by a new revelation: the Jordan is in flood stage! Understanding this interruption requires a glance at the terrain. While only a narrow border of land on either side of the river is usually in direct contact with the lapping water, the Jordan could overflow these limits during flood season and be up to a mile wide in places.[26] Surging currents, floating debris, and underwater obsta-

---

(4:17). Obviously, not every command is necessary for Joshua's sake or for the sake of the reader.

[25]Literally, אִישׁ־אֶחָד אִישׁ־אֶחָד לַשָּׁבֶט (*'îš-'eḥād 'îš-'eḥād laššābeṭ*). For more on this kind of distributive repetition, see Waltke and O'Connor, *Biblical Hebrew Syntax*, sec. 7.2.3.

[26]See Aharoni, *Land of the Bible*, p. 33. Such a scene seems impossible to the contemporary tourist. This is because enormous amounts of water are taken from the Jordan River today for agricultural purposes.

The text accurately records the season of flood near the traditional date of Passover (5:10). At this time, in March or April, the river would be running at its highest due to the melting of snow in the highlands.

cles present a hazardous, if not impossible, situation.[27] It is into *this kind of torrent* that the priests' feet venture! Only now does the narrator return to the expected. Per Joshua's preview of "amazing things," the water upstream stops flowing or "stands still,"[28] plashing **a great distance away.**[29] It has been proposed that biblical Zarethan be located at Tell Umm Hamad[30] and Adam, at Tell ed-Damiya.[31] Neither proposal has been confirmed, but if correct, would put the "pile (נֵד, *nêd*) of water" somewhere near the confluence of the Jordan and Zerqa (יַבֹּק, *Yabbōq*) Rivers, approximately eighteen air miles above the fords of Jericho.[32] Presumably, the water below the "pile" continues to drain away, opening a zone of more than twenty miles in length where all Israel may "cross over" conspicuously "before" Jericho. That this could be the result of natural causes, miraculously timed, is not out of the question. Collapses of the soft, marl banks due to erosion or earthquake activity in the region of Tell ed-Damiya have periodically blocked the Jordan River in the recent past (A.D. 1267, 1906, and 1927). In the case of the last example, an enormous slide took out more than 150 feet of the riverbank including the modern roadbed. As a result the Jordan was completely stopped up for a period of 21 hours.[33]

---

[27]This danger may be discovered in early Christian pilgrim diaries. Guides visiting the river in this area instructed their visitors not to dive into the water or attempt to swim to the other bank. Unfortunately, these rules were not always heeded and lives were lost by those who entered the rushing stream in an attempt to have a divine experience. They were, undoubtedly, not disappointed! See Beck, "Joshua's Readers," p. 696.

[28]Two verbs describe what happens to the water. First it "stands still, motionless, or upright" (יַעֲמְדוּ, *ya'amdû*) as a man might arise from a prone position. Second, it rises into a single heap or mass, as "if gathered in a bottle" Consult *HALOT*, s.v. 'amd.

[29]Not to be overlooked is the parallel use of the term נֵד (*nêd*), translated "heap" or "pile" to describe the Red Sea in Exod 15:8.

[30]See Aharoni, *Land of the Bible*, p. 443. Four miles northeast of Tell Umm Hamad is Tell es-Saidiyeh, another possibility for Zarethan. See Glueck here (*The River Jordan*, pp. 155-158).

[31]Aharoni, *Land of the Bible*, p. 429.

[32]And, incidentally, near a northern proposal for the site of Gilgal. Consider Zertal, "Israel Enters Canaan," pp. 38, 42-43, and *Eastern Valleys*, pp. 111-112.

[33]See John Garstang, *Joshua, Judges* (London: Constable, 1931), pp. 136-138, for descriptions, maps, and photographs.

McGarvey paints an imaginative picture of what this may have looked like:

> When the vast multitude broke up their camp and marched to the bank of the overflowing Jordan . . . the river was cut off from their extreme right down to the Dead Sea. . . . Even after the waters were thus cut off it was no easy task for the host to move across. The shortness of time did not admit of their forming into narrow columns and crossing at fords or other places of easy approach, which would have required several days, but they were compelled to move forward in a mass, descend the bluff, push their way through the brushwood of the muddy bottom-land, climb down into the wet bed of the river, and clamber over similar obstacles on the other side as best they could. It must have required a long and toilsome day's march for all the people to pass clean over Jordan.[34]

3:17 Throughout the crossing by all the people, the priests hold their position, bearing the Ark-box. Their feet are on **dry ground in the middle of the Jordan**.[35] Significantly, the rare term translated as "dry ground" (חָרָבָה, *ḥārābāh*) also appears in Exodus 14:21 to describe the floor of the Red Sea during the miracle of the exodus from Egypt. Here, too, the whole nation completes the journey successfully, but the telling is not yet done. Through synoptic/resumptive tactics, the narrator will replay specific elements of the story in order to highlight critical themes.[36] These themes are the focus of the next chapter.

---

[34]J.W. McGarvey, *Lands of the Bible*, p. 347.

[35]Hawk, *Joshua*, p. 66, highlights the careful wordplays of the passage. The Jordan River, like the people, stay "far away" from the Ark-box (cp. vv. 4 and 16). The waters "stand up" as do the priests (cp. vv. 16 and 17). Finally, the waters are "completely" cut off, as the people "completely" cross (cp. vv. 16 and 17). Such wordplay bespeaks the unity of chapters 3–4.

[36]This technique of narrative art has been described by many scholars. Dale Ralph Davis refers to it as "a summary-expansion pattern" and offers a number of examples. See his *No Falling Words: Expositions of the Book of Joshua* (Grand Rapids: Baker, 1988), pp. 86-87. My own teacher referred to it in the classroom and later described it under the heading the "synoptic/resumptive technique" in one of his last publications. See Brichto, *Toward a Grammar of Biblical Poetics*, pp. 13-14.

JOSHUA 4

3. The Crossing Over Memorialized in Israel (4:1-8)

[1]When the whole nation had finished crossing the Jordan, the LORD said to Joshua, [2]"Choose twelve men from among the people, one from each tribe, [3]and tell them to take up twelve stones from the middle of the Jordan from right where the priests stood and to carry them over with you and put them down at the place where you stay tonight."

[4]So Joshua called together the twelve men he had appointed from the Israelites, one from each tribe, [5]and said to them, "Go over before the ark of the LORD your God into the middle of the Jordan. Each of you is to take up a stone on his shoulder, according to the number of the tribes of the Israelites, [6]to serve as a sign among you. In the future, when your children ask you, 'What do these stones mean?' [7]tell them that the flow of the Jordan was cut off before the ark of the covenant of the LORD. When it crossed the Jordan, the waters of the Jordan were cut off. These stones are to be a memorial to the people of Israel forever."

[8]So the Israelites did as Joshua commanded them. They took twelve stones from the middle of the Jordan, according to the number of the tribes of the Israelites, as the LORD had told Joshua; and they carried them over with them to their camp, where they put them down.

4:1-3 With the people safely across the Jordan River, Yahweh gives directions for a memorial to be built. This directive pulls forward a previous command from Joshua left open-ended, namely, to choose twelve men to represent the twelve tribes. The correspondence is exact, both with respect to man to tribe (one to one) and from text (3:12) to text (4:2-3).[1] The task of this appointed crew is

---

[1]A grammatical link helps make this connection across chapters. In both

now spelled out: **Take up twelve stones from the middle of the Jordan from right where the priests stood.** It is assumed that the special nature of this assignment abrogates the previous command to the people to keep their distance from the Ark-box company. The crew is commanded to choose[2] stones out of the riverbed of the Jordan, from the place where the Ark-box is stationed.[3] The stones are to be carried out, or more literally, caused to "cross over" mimicking the motion of the people. They, too, will be brought "to rest" in a new camp.

4:4-7 Joshua takes the words of Yahweh and delivers them faithfully, adding some interpretive details in Moseslike fashion. New information from Joshua's mouth includes mention of a "teachable moment" for future generations. These stones will **serve as a sign among you** and as **a memorial to the people of Israel forever.** A biblical "sign" may be a simple physical marker, a divine act, or anything between (cf. 2:12). Similarly, a biblical "memorial" is an object that prompts a memory. In this case, the stones may spark future questions and afford an opportunity to offer witness and thereby relive the unrepeatable events of that day.[4] From Joshua's perspec-

---

3:12 and in 4:2 the repeating distributive, *'îš-'eḥād 'îš-'eḥād* ("one-man, one-man") is found. The only difference is in the choice of preposition: 3:12 uses *laššābeṭ* whereas 4:2 reads מִשֵּׁבֶט (*miššābeṭ*, "according to the tribe," or "from the tribe").

[2]The hiphil infinitive construct, הָכִין (*hākîn*), "to fix, appoint, or prepare," makes for difficult translation here. It is the second verbal form in an extended construction beginning with the transitive verb, שְׂאוּ (*śᵊ'û*), "lift up" (from נשׂא, *nś'*). Both *śᵊ'û* and *hākîn* are completed by the direct object, "twelve stones," although no conjunctive *waw* explicitly connects them. See Waltke and O'Connor (*Biblical Hebrew Syntax*, sec. 35.5.1) for a discussion of the use of the infinitive absolute in command formulas. A wooden proposal reads, "Pull up from the middle of this Jordan . . . (and) select twelve stones."

The verbal root of *hākîn* appears again in v. 4 in a wordplay. In this case, it is the twelve men who are selected. As a result of this construction, chosen men shoulder chosen stones.

[3]The noun מַצָּב (*maṣṣab*) describes the standing place of the priests' feet. It may connote a "standing place" but is usually interpreted less literally, representing a garrison or military post (cf. 1 Sam 13:23; 14:1,4,6,11,15; 2 Sam 23:14). Viewed from this perspective, the Ark-box company serves as a kind of outpost, checking dangerous forces and ensuring the safety of the population while they cross.

[4]Compare with Exod 12:24-27 or 13:14-16 where Moses likewise urges use

tive, key to the interpretation of this event is the role of the Ark-box in "cutting off" the waters of the Jordan. Like the staff of Moses stretched over the Red Sea, the Ark-box functions as a visible symbol of the presence and power of Yahweh (cf. Exod 14:16). From the perspective of literary composition, this role of the stones as "memorial" must be kept in mind for understanding the narrative future; a misreading of motive behind another "memorial" toward the end of the book will nearly precipitate a civil war (22:10-12,24-28).

4:8 With these directives given, the men carry out their duty. Stones are fetched, "carried over," and brought to the camp where they are "laid down" (lit., "caused to rest") in preparation for the closing scene of the chapter. This memorial will give expression to the Jordan crossing in the collective memory of the people. This specific purpose is worth noting as a contrast to the expression suggested by a second memorial.

4. Joshua's Leadership Emphasized in Israel (4:9)

[9]**Joshua set up the twelve stones that had been**[a] **in the middle of the Jordan at the spot where the priests who carried the ark of the covenant had stood. And they are there to this day.**

[a]**9** Or *Joshua also set up twelve stones*

4:9 In addition to this first stone construction prepared by the crew of tribal representatives, a second construction will be built. Like the first, the second is created from twelve stones drawn from the place where the Ark-box company stood. Unlike the first, however, the second is erected down in the riverbed, "under" the feet of the priests. This site is dry at the moment of construction, but as soon as the river resumes its course, it will slip beneath the surface of the water. It can hardly serve a visible (or public) purpose.

---

of the Passover story in a question-answer discussion between parent and child. Here too, the act of Yahweh (in 13:16) is termed an אוֹת (*'ôth*), "sign."

Walter Brueggemann refers to this kind of repetition as a "pedagogy of saturation," a way to keep the articulation of reality before the community. See his excellent discussion of "The Constitutive Power of Israel's Testimony" in his *Theology of the Old Testament: Testimony, Dispute, Advocacy* (Minneapolis: Fortress, 1997): 721-725.

Moreover, it is worth noting that while the first monument was commissioned by Yahweh and required the help of twelve men to gather the stones, the second monument is unprompted by Yahweh and
built by Joshua alone. These differences are important enough to
challenge those who would argue that some sort of confusion has
crept into the text, causing these two monument stories to be tele-
scoped into one.[5] There are two separate acts here, two separate
constructions, with, undoubtedly, two separate meanings.[6]

While the meaning of the first monument is clearly stated in the
text, the meaning of the second must be inferred from other clues.
Beyond the narrator's affirmation that this second monument is
there to this day (a claim difficult to prove or dispute!) no further
comments are offered. Perhaps by considering the differences and
the larger context, help may be gained. The fact that this second
construction is built by Joshua alone is useful. It is not the result of
a group effort, but an unprompted personal response on the part of
Joshua. Such "faith" memorials have antecedents and problems.[7]
Still more, however, may be adduced as a result of context. In
advance of the crossing, the reader is informed that Joshua will be
exalted as a result of the events of the day. Moreover, Yahweh
declares that the people will recognize that Joshua's leadership is
like Moses' leadership (3:7-8). Most fascinating is the parallel
between Joshua's activities here and the activity of Moses at Sinai,
just after communicating *torah* to the people and witnessing their
response. In the case of Moses, an altar of twelve stones is built, lit-

---

[5]For a brief discussion, see Jerome F.D. Creach, *Joshua*, Interpretation: A
Bible Commentary for Preaching and Teaching (Louisville, KY: Westminster John Knox, 2003), pp. 47-48.

[6]To emphasize the reading of two separate constructions here, the LXX
modifies v. 9 by adding the adjective ἄλλους (*allous*), or "other": Joshua set
up "the *other* twelve stones."

[7]Personal memorials appear regularly in the text of the Old Testament.
Some of these are termed מַצֵּבָה (*maṣṣêbāh*, sg.) or מַצֵּבוֹת (*maṣṣēbôth*, pl.) and
are recognized in many *torah* texts, e.g., Gen 28:18,22; 31:13,45; 35:14,20.
Curious in this context is the prohibition of Deut 16:22. The question remains, if Joshua's construction is really a *maṣṣêbāh*; true *maṣṣēbôth* seem to be
constructed of not many stones, but of one.

Another term for a personal memorial is יָד (*yād*, lit., "hand"). In the case
of 2 Sam 18:18 a *maṣṣêbāh* is termed a *yād*. Other uses of *yād* in this way
include 1 Sam 15:12 and Isa 56:5.

erally, "*under* the mountain" (Exod 24:4) after the people obediently and unanimously followed Yahweh's words. In the case of Joshua,
Yahweh's instructions have been delivered and responded to in
faith. This first great miracle with Joshua as leader has been accomplished. It may be proposed, therefore, that Joshua responds to the
crossing-over event with an act of thanksgiving that literarily imitates
the pattern and specific vocabulary of Moses.[8] Here the construction
is built, in a sense, under the feet of the priests, those bearing the
tablets *from Sinai*. If the first construction memorializes the "crossing over" in the collective memory of Israel; the second emphasizes
the personal leadership of Joshua in the collective activity of Israel.
The exaltation foretold in 3:7-8 is realized implicitly in 4:9 and again,
explicitly, in 4:14. Viewed in this way, the "confusion" of the two
memorials is easily resolved and the point of the text is driven home:
Joshua is just like Moses.

5. The Crossing Over Completed (4:10-18)

[10]**Now the priests who carried the ark remained standing in the
middle of the Jordan until everything the LORD had commanded
Joshua was done by the people, just as Moses had directed Joshua.
The people hurried over, [11]and as soon as all of them had crossed,
the ark of the LORD and the priests came to the other side while
the people watched. [12]The men of Reuben, Gad and the half-tribe
of Manasseh crossed over, armed, in front of the Israelites, as
Moses had directed them. [13]About forty thousand armed for battle
crossed over before the LORD to the plains of Jericho for war.**

[14]**That day the LORD exalted Joshua in the sight of all Israel; and
they revered him all the days of his life, just as they had revered
Moses.**

[15]**Then the LORD said to Joshua, [16]"Command the priests carrying the ark of the Testimony to come up out of the Jordan."**

[17]**So Joshua commanded the priests, "Come up out of the
Jordan."**

[18]**And the priests came up out of the river carrying the ark of
the covenant of the LORD. No sooner had they set their feet on the**

[8]Hawk, *Joshua*, pp. 69-70.

dry ground than the waters of the Jordan returned to their place and ran at flood stage as before.

4:10-18 Throughout the "crossing over" the priests shouldering the Ark-box remain stationed in the riverbed. That **the people hurried over** is to be expected in light of the circumstances. With them are the fighting men of the tribes given land in Transjordan, namely, Reuben, Gad, and half of Manasseh (cf. 1:12-15). The number and disposition of these men is given: they number forty "squads" and are **armed for battle**[9] (see Supplemental Study on Counting Israel opposite).[10] Notice of the way in which this process of crossing is accomplished by these groups is patterned by means of the repeating adverbial construction, לִפְנֵי (liphnê), translated as "before." Given the nonsequential nature in which the crossing over is narrated, "before" should not be understood in the sense of priority in time (this group goes first, second, or third), but rather, "before" in the sense of witnessing presence.[11] Viewed this way, even the pairing of identified action and identified eyes has testimonial significance. In verse 11 the Ark-box company crosses over *before* the people. All the people look and recognize the means by which this act is accomplished. In verse 12 the Transjordan tribes cross over *before* Israel. The tribes of Cisjordan look and recognize the contribution made by the tribes of Transjordan.[12] Finally, in verse 13 the armed men

---

[9]Men from two and one-half tribes proceed חֲמֻשִׁים (hămušîm, "ordered by fives" or "fifties"), possibly referring to a specific formation (cf. 1:14). For one understanding of this formation, see Roland de Vaux, *Ancient Israel: Social Institutions* (New York: McGraw-Hill, 1961), pp. 216-217. Those described in v. 13 cross over חֲלוּצֵי הַצָּבָא (hălûṣî haṣṣābā', "equipped" or "girded for war"). This latter phrase communicates a picture of skirts hiked up and tucked in (to prevent interference with legs in motion) and weapons tied about the hips (at the ready). See *TDOT*, s.v. חָלֵץ.

[10]Does the figure of forty armed squads refer specifically to the Transjordan fighters or more generally to the Israelite force? Context suggests the former.

[11]The construction *liphnê* is a combination of the preposition *lᵉ-* often read as "to" or "toward" and the plural construct of the noun פָּנִים (pānîm), "face." Together they suggest something done literally "in the face" of another or "in the presence" of another.

[12]For the sake of the interpretive angle taken later in this commentary, it should be noted that the crossing over of the two and one-half tribes is witnessed by "Israel."

cross over *before* Yahweh. The One who issues "a great commission" looks and recognizes the thumping of the pedestrian expedition. Hence, all orders are executed and witnessed appropriately; everything goes according to plan. The groups arrive safely on the plain between the Jordan River and the oasis of Jericho.

With the people across, Yahweh again issues an order that is passed down the line by Joshua. In this case, word reaches the priests to "come up" from the Jordan.[13] They move forward in unison. No sooner than the last step is drawn — the verbal form suggests the smacking sound of a foot pulling out of the mud[14] — the river rushes down as before in a flooded state.[15] The footprints of the people, Joshua's Sinailike stack of rocks, and the path of retreat all disappear beneath the surging foam. The rushing sound carries a chord of finality; turning back is not an option. For better or worse, for life or death, Israel is now in Canaan.

SUPPLEMENTAL STUDY

COUNTING ISRAEL

How many Israelites came into the *Heartland* under the leadership of Joshua? A discussion of this vexing question must acknowledge at least three points.

First, according to what is known of settlement patterns in the LBA (1550–1200 B.C.), population in the southern highlands appears to be quite thin. This is surprising, given the fact that in the preceding period, the MBA, the region was thickly settled. Raw numbers alone put this into perspective. The 220 sites of the MBA

---

[13]Note that when the priests' feet touch the water, the Jordan stops (3:13,15). As their feet pull free of its mud, the Jordan runs again (4:18). Note also that the stones for the memorial are drawn from the ground about the priests' "feet" (4:3) and that Joshua's monument is built at the priests' feet (4:9). This repeating patter of רַגְלַיִם (*raglayim*), "feet," reminds the reader of the inaugural promise of Yahweh to grant victory in every place where their "feet" tread (1:3). This continues to be a pedestrian affair!

[14]The verb נָתַק (*nāthaq*) is used of things "torn" or "snapped," such as tent cords or sandal-thongs. Note the possibility of onomatopoeia. See BDB, s.v. נָתַק.

[15]For כִּתְמוֹל־שִׁלְשׁוֹם (*kithmôl šilšôm*, "as before") see note on 3:4.

are reduced to just twenty sites in the LBA.[16] These surviving urban centers range from three to five hectares each. Taken together, the total occupied area suggests a Canaanite population of approximately 63,000 persons.[17]

Second, according to the NIV, more than 600,000 fighting men were a part of the wilderness wanderings (Num 1:46 and 26:51). If each member of this force had a family, the additional women and children would easily swell the ranks beyond the one million mark and could possibly press upwards to two million. Consistent with this count is Joshua 4:13, where "forty thousand" armed men from just two and a half Transjordan tribes cross over the Jordan to help in the campaign.[18]

Third, when comparing Canaanite population and Israelite population, Deuteronomy 7:1 and 7:7 cast a particular spin. Here, Moses tells Israel that the occupants of Canaan are "larger and stronger than you." Later, he adds that Israel is an object of Yahweh's love for reasons that have nothing to do with their own power or prowess. It is *not* "because you were more numerous than other peoples, for you were the fewest of all peoples."

How is it possible to engage these three points simultaneously? Do the absurdly large numbers in the text damage its testimony beyond repair?[19] Why would Israel fear the Canaanites (or even require divine assistance!) if they outnumber the enemy by twenty

---

[16]These figures are drawn from the work of Shlomo Bunimovitz, "Socio-Political Transformation in the Central Hill Country in the Late Bronze-Iron I Transition," in *From Nomadism to Monarchy: Archaeological and Historical Aspects of Early Israel*, ed. by Israel Finkelstein and Nadav Na'aman (Jerusalem: IES, 1994), p. 193.

[17]There is, understandably, great interest in this fall-off. Many archaeologists believe that Canaanite centers came apart at the seams due to a variety of reasons including internal pressure due to local conflict and external pressure from Egypt. It may be that for some locals, a sedentary lifestyle was exchanged for a more nomadic existence. For the Biblicist, it is attractive to see something of the "hornet" promised by Yahweh (Exod 23:28) in this Canaanite disintegration.

[18]Even this figure is problematic as the numbers of fighting men given elsewhere for Reuben (Num 1:20-21), Gad (Num 1:24-25), and Manasseh (Num 1:34-35) are more than three times the total given here. Where are the rest of the fighters?

[19]In an unpublished paper entitled "The Number of Israelites at the Exodus" (1988) David Merling suggests that if two and one half million peo-

or thirty to one?[20] But even if this is set aside momentarily, how are such numbers to be squared with the clear statements of Deuteronomy 7 about Israel's weakness? And how does one truly reckon with the logistical problems of moving a million-plus people anywhere, let alone supporting their pastoralist lifestyle once they arrive in a land that is marginal in so many ways?[21] Clearly, there are problems here, throbbing at several levels.

Students of the text have wrestled with these problems, and while many wrinkles still remain, some answers have been discovered. Most helpful is the realization that the term translated into English as "thousand" (אֶלֶף, 'eleph) in the texts of Exodus, Numbers, and Joshua, has other meanings.[22] One option is to read 'eleph poetically as an extraordinarily large number (e.g., Num 10:36). While useful in some contexts, this is of little assistance here. A second option is to translate 'eleph as "squad," "unit," "company," or even "tent group." This meaning seems consistent with the tribal character of ancient Israel, and may allude to the original grouping along the line of a people's militia.[23] A third option is to voice the term as

---

ple marched in rows ten abreast with three feet between each row, the line would stretch slightly more than 141 miles. Of course, dealing with the old, the young, the flocks, wagons, and carts would complicate this picture considerably. In this scenario, the front of the column would be 15 days ahead of the rear. Given the size of the Sinai Peninsula, it is not impossible to imagine a scene where those in the lead would enter Canaan before the stragglers emerge from the Red Sea! For a more serious presentation of this thinking, see his "Large Numbers at the Time of the Exodus," in *NEASB* 44 (1999): 15-27.

[20]Similarly, how could a million or so people be overcome by wild beasts (Exod 23:29-30), or why would a million or so people be given to despair when facing a chariot force numbering only in the hundreds (Exod 14:7)? Could they not overwhelm the charioteers by force of numbers alone?

[21]Consider that the population of the current state of Israel numbered 3,653,000 in 1977. This modern number strains the natural resources of the land and is only achievable through significant financial support from abroad and through sophisticated technologies for raising food and safeguarding water. See Orni and Efrat, *Geography of Israel*, p. 263.

[22]Following the presentation of J.W. Wenham, "Large Numbers in the Old Testament," *TynBul* 18 (1967): 24-25.

[23]Here the text of Josh 22:14 is helpful. The description of this delegation is significant for understanding the use of the Hebrew term 'eleph in the book of Joshua. Each of the men clearly represents one Cisjordan tribe. But the last clause of 22:14 reads: וְאִישׁ רֹאשׁ בֵּית־אֲבוֹתָם הֵמָּה לְאַלְפֵי יִשְׂרָאֵל (wᵊ 'îš

'allûph, "commando" or "trained warrior." It is possible that the
presence of *'allûph* in the text represents a single "commando" or a
group under the lead of such, i.e., "a commando (unit)." Using
either this second or third option, the large numbers of Israelites
may be seriously reduced.[24] By this means, J.W. Wenham reduces
Israel's militia from a traditional reading of more than a half million
to some 18,000.[25] Colin Humphreys goes even farther. Citing examples from the contemporary texts (Amarna Letters) where squads of
fighting men are frequently mentioned, he suggests that the *'eleph*
represented a squad of nine or ten persons. This thinking reduces
Israel's total fighting force to a mere five thousand men.[26] Suddenly
the loss of thirty-six individuals at the battle of The *'Ay* (Josh 7:5)
becomes meaningful. If this militia of five thousand men had families, the total number of Israelites under Joshua's charge is now
reduced to somewhere between ten and twenty thousand persons.
While it would still be a logistical headache to organize and move
this kind of mob, the reduction makes it possible to take the archaeological data, the geographical reality, and the biblical text seriously. Moreover, it renders other statements of Scripture intelligible,
such as the "fear factor" on the part of Israel, their real need for
divine assistance, and the smugness of the Canaanite opposition.[27]
An indigenous population of 63,000 people, in fortified settlements

---

rō'š bêth-'ăbôthām hēmmāh l°'alphê yiśrā'ēl). In this case, the NIV translates:
"each (man was) the head of a family division among the Israelite clans."
The term "clans" here is rendered elsewhere in the NIV as "thousands."
Clearly, to conclude that *'eleph* must represent a whole number is not a foregone conclusion; even the inconsistency of the NIV points this way.

[24]As an example, Num 1:21 suggests that the number of members of the
tribe of Reuben is forty-six *'eleph* and five hundred. The NIV translates this
as a whole number, 46,500. Could it be read instead as "46 'clans,' that is,
500 men"? In this case the *waw* is read with in an appositional sense (Waltke
and O'Connor, *Biblical Hebrew Syntax*, sec. 39.2.1, example 6).

[25]Wenham, "Large Numbers," p. 31. He therefore numbers the total
Israelite congregation at 72,000 persons.

[26]Colin J. Humphreys, "The Number of People in the Exodus from Egypt:
Decoding Mathematically the Very Large Numbers in Numbers I and
XXVI," *VT* 48 (April 1998):196-213.

[27]Regardless of how this presentation of numbers appears, it is not our
intention to undermine the biblical text, but to undermine interpretations
of the text based upon bad information or layers of tradition. Sadly, some
interpretations do more to damage the text than to explain it.

and armed with superior technology (chariots and bows) would be a
God-sized challenge for a group of ten or twenty thousand Israelites.

6. The Memorial Established (4:19-24)

**[19]On the tenth day of the first month the people went up from
the Jordan and camped at Gilgal on the eastern border of Jericho.
[20]And Joshua set up at Gilgal the twelve stones they had taken out
of the Jordan. [21]He said to the Israelites, "In the future when your
descendants ask their fathers, 'What do these stones mean?' [22]tell
them, 'Israel crossed the Jordan on dry ground.' [23]For the LORD
your God dried up the Jordan before you until you had crossed
over. The LORD your God did to the Jordan just what he had done
to the Red Sea[a] when he dried it up before us until we had crossed
over. [24]He did this so that all the peoples of the earth might know
that the hand of the LORD is powerful and so that you might always
fear the LORD your God."**

[a]23 Hebrew *Yam Suph*; that is, Sea of Reeds

Past, present, and future come together with the establishment
of the memorial of "crossing over." That memorial is established at
a site located on the "eastern edge" of Jericho.[28] The name of the site
is anticipated — Gilgal — but is not formally "named" until 5:9. Here,
the twelve stones shouldered by the twelve tribal representatives are
arranged by Joshua (possibly together in the form of a dry, stacked
altar or apart in some kind of circular array). Following this action
Joshua offers a speech.

The future is referenced by means of a hypothetical dialogue
made in reaction to the memorial: "What do these stones mean?"
This repetition of the question and answer in the chapter (compare
with 4:6-7) drives home the central character of the memorial as a
reminder. This visible symbol will prompt the young to wonder, the
old to testify, and all who hear to reconsider their view of Yahweh.

---

[28]The location of Gilgal continues to be elusive. Here, it is described as
בִּקְצֵה מִזְרַח יְרִיחוֹ (*biqṣēh mizraḥ yᵉrîḥō*), or "on the edge" or "outskirts, east
(of) Jericho." In question is the sense of *qāṣēh* ("end," "edge," "border")
intended here. Is the relationship between Jericho and Gilgal to be understood in a physical or political sense, or in some other way?

4:19 The present is referenced by means of Joshua's words and actions, but also by a note of the specific date: it is **the tenth day of the first month**. This glance at the calendar creates anticipation for events described in the next chapter. After all, does not memory flow through both recital and ritual?[29]

4:20-24 Finally, the past is referenced in a way that makes clear the relationship between Israel "crossing over" the Jordan and "crossing over" the Red Sea. The Jordan crossing, under the leadership of Joshua, is presented as a kind of Red Sea crossing, an act accomplished under the leadership of Moses. Both events are a testimony to Yahweh, and a reason for reverence in Canaan: **"All the peoples of the land might know that the hand of the LORD is powerful and so that you might always fear the LORD your God."** Thus, in the end, the clasp between these two events is locked, but equally important is the rhetorical move that binds together the one who sees (at the present) with the one who hears (in the future). Because the fathers truly experienced it, the children may truly believe it. Joshua will return to this plea again and again.

---

[29]Yerushalmi, *Zakhor*, pp. 11-12.

JOSHUA 5

D. CAMPING IN CANAAN'S LAND (5:1-12)

With the Jordan River behind and Canaan's land looming ahead, pause is made to take care of some important matters. These are presented in this chapter in four parts. In the first part, Canaan responds to Israel's "crossing over" (5:1). In the second part, Israel receives a pardon (5:2-9). In the third part, Israel celebrates the Passover (5:10-12). Finally, in anticipation of the next section, Joshua has an unexpected meeting (5:13-15). The entire chapter presupposes familiarity with two rites rooted in *torah*: circumcision and Passover. These are experienced by Israel as they leave the shame of the past behind and press forward to claim the land under divine guidance.

1. The Canaanite Paralysis (5:1)

¹Now when all the Amorite kings west of the Jordan and all the Canaanite kings along the coast heard how the LORD had dried up the Jordan before the Israelites until we had crossed over, their hearts melted and they no longer had the courage to face the Israelites.

5:1 The aftershocks of Israel's "crossing over" the Jordan rock Canaan. The two clauses, "all the Amorite chiefs west of the Jordan" and "all the Canaanite chiefs along the coast," represent the totality of the inhabitants of Cisjordan (see the Supplemental Study on Amorites on p. 130). These leaders hear not only of Israel's approach, but that Yahweh is responsible for facilitating it.[1] Their resulting fear

---

[1] Cf. 5:1 with 9:1-2; 10:1-2; and 11:1-3. In the case of each chapter head, the chiefs of Canaan will "hear" (וַיְהִי כִשְׁמֹעַ, *wayᵉhî kišmōaʿ*) something about

is described in the language of Rahab (2:10-11) and confirms the prediction of Yahweh (1:5): hearts are melted and breath is lost. While this statement may seem more appropriately connected to the previous chapter, it may also explain the lull in the action. The momentary paralysis in Canaan offers the necessary space for the following events to unfold.[2]

SUPPLEMENTAL STUDY

AMORITES

Rahab is the first in the book of Joshua to describe Sihon and Og as "Amorite" chiefs (2:10). She will not be the last (e.g., 9:10; 24:12). This designation is a familiar one to the reader of the Bible; it picks up where Deuteronomy left off (31:4). Other references to "Amorites" in the text of Joshua go beyond the description of these occupants of Transjordan and refer generally to chiefs in Cisjordan (5:1), to the five chiefs who opposed the Gibeonite-Israelite coalition (10:5-6,12), and to one of the seven groups who occupied Canaan and resisted the Israelite campaign (24:11). The use of "Amorite" can therefore be confusing. Is it just another name for "Canaanites"? Is it a group distinct from the "Canaanites"? Is it a name for all non-Israelites in the *Heartland*?

Study of the Ancient Near East has revealed both a language and a people group known as Amorite. The tongue belongs to the family of languages called Northwest Semitic and is likely an early ancestor to Hebrew, Aramaic, Moabite, and others. Study suggests that use of the Amorite language was widespread in time and place. Amorite speakers hail from Canaan to Mesopotamia and may date anywhere from the third to second millennium B.C. The name

---

Israel and act in a particular way (e.g., become afraid and withdraw or organize for war and engage). This structuring move sets the stage for the narrative that follows.

[2]Consider Gen 34:25 where the adult males of Shechem are incapacitated for a period of several days as a result of being circumcised. Because they are incapable of defending themselves, an entire settlement is susceptible and wiped out by only two men. Likewise, if all the adult males in Israel submit to circumcision at the same time, they would become easy targets in what is likely an open and unfortified camp.

"Amorite" (*Mar.tu* in Sumerian and *Amurrû[m]* in Akkadian), means something like "Westerners" and adds support to the view that the origins of these folk/language are probably in the area of Syria today. In the eyes of the cultured Mesopotamians, this region was more like the "Wild Wild West," and the people who lived there were considered ignorant barbarians!

M. Liverani suggests that the Amorites were originally a unique people group, but by the second millennium they became so widespread and mixed into local cultures that they were no longer conscious of their common roots.[3] This may very well be true. Second millennium uses may alternate between a term for non-Akkadian westerners living in Mesopotamia, an Amorite kingdom/Egyptian province located in the mountain folds of modern Lebanon and Syria, or those perceived to be "old rustics" running about the *Heartland*. The biblical memory of "Amorites" may mix these last two categories. In the case of Joshua 13:4, the use of the phrase "region of the Amorites" in the context of geographical borders may reference the Amorite state in a strict sense, while other uses, as in the case of Og and Sihon, refer to ancient inhabitants of the region. The same may be true of Joshua 5:1; 11:3; or 10:5-6,12. Here, Amorites are among the Canaanites, yet somehow distinct from them (cf. Num 13:29). Perhaps reading "Amorite" as "old rustics" may help; consider how the folk of pre-Israelite Jerusalem may be considered both "Jebusite" (2 Sam 24:18) and "Amorite" (10:5). Clearly, more work on this subject is needed.

2. The Israelite Pardon (5:2-9)

[2]**At that time the LORD said to Joshua, "Make flint knives and circumcise the Israelites again." [3]So Joshua made flint knives and circumcised the Israelites at Gibeath Haaraloth.**[a]

[4]Now this is why he did so: All those who came out of Egypt— all the men of military age—died in the desert on the way after leaving Egypt. [5]All the people that came out had been circumcised, but all the people born in the desert during the journey from Egypt

---

[3]M. Liverani on "The Amorites," in *Peoples of Old Testament Times*, ed. by D.J. Wiseman (Oxford: Clarendon, 1973), p. 115.

had not. [6]The Israelites had moved about in the desert forty years until all the men who were of military age when they left Egypt had died, since they had not obeyed the LORD. For the LORD had sworn to them that they would not see the land that he had solemnly promised their fathers to give us, a land flowing with milk and honey. [7]So he raised up their sons in their place, and these were the ones Joshua circumcised. They were still uncircumcised because they had not been circumcised on the way. [8]And after the whole nation had been circumcised, they remained where they were in camp until they were healed.

[9]Then the LORD said to Joshua, "Today I have rolled away the reproach of Egypt from you." So the place has been called Gilgal[b] to this day.

[a]*3 Gibeath Haaraloth* means *hill of foreskins.*   [b]*9 Gilgal* sounds like the Hebrew for *roll.*

5:2-3 Yahweh commands Joshua to make **flint knives**[4] and circumcise Israel a second time. Unfortunately, translators lumber over the placement of the Hebrew verb, שׁוּב (*šûb*, "to turn," "return," or "repair"). The NIV smothers it completely, while the NASB brings it out awkwardly as an adverb, "circumcise *again* the sons of Israel the second time."[5] If one is bold enough to disregard accents however,[6] a very different reading of verse 2 may emerge, one that eases the

---

[4]Despite sounding crude, a flint or obsidian blade (one possibility for צֹר, *ṣor*) would be much sharper (and hence, more effective) than one of metal. Chipped-stone technologies were well known in earlier periods in the Ancient Near East and continue throughout the Bronze and Iron Ages. Fine-grained brown flint was readily available in the region.

These facts scrape the view of Butler, who muses over the passage: "Time honored, old-fashioned materials are used in the cult even when more 'modern' equipment is available. Such utensils yield an awesome aura to the cultic event" (*Joshua*, p. 58). While Butler's explanation may sound attractive, the choice of a flint or obsidian blade has little to do with the production of an "awesome aura" and everything to do with using the sharpest edge available to make an incision that minimizes tearing. A "clean" cut simply heals faster than a jagged one.

[5]The LXX opts for yet another alternative reading. Instead of assuming the pointing as *šûb*, it reads the text as שֵׁב (*šēb*, impv. of יָשַׁב, *yāšab* "to sit down"), suggesting that Joshua needs to "sit down" to do the job!

[6]Note the disjunctive *'atnaḥ* ( ) under the word צֻרִים (*ṣurîm*), breaking the clause at this point.

translation and supports the larger context: "Yahweh told Joshua, 'Make yourself flint knives and be restored! Circumcise Israel a second time." Reading *šûb* as an imperative of restoration[7] reveals how Israel is urged to choose obedience and life as mandated in *torah* and detailed in the covenant with Abraham (Genesis 17).[8] As will be borne out below, this reading also connects nicely with 5:8, where, on the other side of the procedure, Israel is not just physically healed, Israel now *lives* in the truest sense of the word! The place of fulfillment is remembered (grimacingly) as the **Gibeath Haaraloth**, or the "pile of foreskins."[9] Such a place is not a site that would be preserved — much less identified — in the archaeological record, but is simply an activity area in or near the camp.[10]

5:4-7 Following the statement of compliance, the narrator backs up to explain why this act is even necessary. Packed into this preachment are several elements of significance that distinguish between the generation born in Egypt and the generation born in the wilderness. The first generation of Israelites, those born in Egypt, are circumcised according to *torah* instruction. Despite possessing this physical mark, they are disobedient in heart and hands and prevented from entering the land of promise (Deut 1:19-35; 9:12-24). By contrast, the second generation of Israelites, those born in the wilderness, are those who are now entering the land of promise.[11]

---

[7]Reading *šûb* with an eye toward restoration finds expression in Job 33:25; Hos 6:1; 1 Kgs 13:6, and elsewhere.

[8]The reading may also provide a unique reflection on the problematic description of the circumcision of Moses' son (Exod 4:24-26).

[9]Some translations, including the NIV, treat this descriptor as a proper name. It is difficult to imagine a site bearing such a name prior to the Israelite arrival, and the event described here; rather, the text offers a proleptic — or "after the fact"— naming of the place. See Woudstra, *Joshua*, p. 100.

[10]Incidentally, the attempt to naturalize this event by grappling with logistics of how, where, and when this event may have happened only assists the effort to downgrade the large numbers of Israelites.

[11]The description of this land as a place "flowing with milk and honey" is taken directly from Exod 3:8 and Deut 26:15. These coordinating objects refer to the land as a place of bounty, where food may be cultivated (milk from grazing animals) or hunted (honey from wild bees), or possibly a place of domestic (sheep, goats, and cattle) and wild animals (bees). However understood, it is clearly presented as rich in potential (contains many zones of possibility) and stands in stark contrast with the wilderness (a zone of impossibility). Consider the author's own brief presentation on "Plants and Animals" in *Eerdmans Handbook to the Bible* (Grand Rapids: Eerdmans, forthcoming).

They have not been circumcised in a physical sense. The reason?
The narrator insinuates that this is yet another failure on the part of
the first generation: they did not circumcise their sons **on the way**.
Understood in this sense, "the way" may refer literally to the journey
taken, hence, they did not circumcise "along the path" or "route"
taken out of Egypt. However, "the way" may also refer to the execution of custom or command, hence, they did not circumcise according to "The Practice" (of *torah*).[12] It was a failure of habit. Read
in either direction, a contrast of two generations emerges. It is a contrast between those who exit and those who enter, between those
who disobey and those who obey, and finally, between those who
died landless and those who are about to become landed. Cunningly,
the narrator advances *torah*. Through the text of Joshua, "The Practice" of circumcision is held up for examination, but oddly enough,
so is the conclusion that a physical mark alone can never be the full
measure of God's people. In this, the reader is forced to grapple
again with the question of what it really means to be *Israel*.

By seizing upon the need for circumcision, the narrator continues to present the process of consecration whereby Israel prepares
to enter the land (cf. 1:7,8; 3:5).[13] But by including issues of greater
obedience to check this defining mark, the narrator seizes upon the
torah teaching that true circumcision also has a spiritual dimension
that cannot be ignored (Lev 12:3; Deut 10:16; 30:6). The spirit, as
well as the letter of *torah*, finds interpretation in Joshua.

5:8 It is natural that the camp be immobilized following this procedure. However, such a focus may miss the point of the text. On
the other side of the event, the NIV offers the idea that Israel
"remained where they were." This glosses an odd arrangement of
words possibly rendered as they "sat (convolutedly) under them-

---

[12]The NIV translates the pausal בַּדָּרֶךְ (*baddārek*) as "in the way." The noun
derek may refer literally to a "road," "path," or "journey." However, other
examples suggest that this "road" is one of customary "manner," "behavior,"
or "conduct." See Gen 31:35 for the use of *derek* to refer to the menstrual
bleeding of Rachel, Jer 10:2 for the use of *derek* to refer to the idolatrous
behavior of Gentiles, or 1 Sam 15:18 for the use of *derek* to refer to the stated mission of Saul.

[13]See also Genesis 17, a pivotal passage for interpreting the conquest of
Canaan. Here, a direct link is made between the claim to the land of Canaan
(v. 8) and the covenant of circumcision (vv. 9-14).

selves"! But even this pained reading (!) does not fully do justice to
the text. A pruning of a more interpretive nature is needed!

An important phrase that appears here is יֵשְׁבוּ תַחְתָּם (yēšbû taḥtām), a combination of terms that appears only five times in the
Hebrew Bible. In every other instance, the sense communicated is
that of displacement; one people group pushes another people
group out of the way and assumes their position/possession. Consider the following examples: "the descendants of Esau destroyed the
Horites and *settled in their place*" (Deut 2:12,22); the Ammonites
drove out the Rephaites and *settled in their place*" (Deut 2:21); the
Caphtorites destroyed the Avvites and *settled in their place*" (Deut
2:23). Assuming the line of thinking previously advanced, namely,
that this new generation of Israelites is in the process of replacing the
old generation, a reading that is in keeping with the biblical use of
yēšbû taḥtām in verse 8 emerges: "and after the whole nation was circumcised, *they* replaced *them* in the camp." But who are *they*? Who are
them? And what is *the camp*? Only a moment's thought is needed. The
them are clearly the old generation that is being replaced. The *they* are
the recently circumcised new generation that is pushing forward into
the place of the old generation. The "camp" may refer to a military
bivouac (e.g., Judg 4:16), but is used of the whole congregation of
Israel as well (Josh 6:18).[14] This is a likely choice here. Outlined,
therefore, is a contrast between the old camp of Israel that died in
the wilderness and the new camp of Israel that is entering Canaan.
This idea must be suspended in the air for a moment longer.

As hinted above, the clincher for this reading comes through the
last words of 5:8, עַד חֲיוֹתָם ('ad ḥăyôthām), glossed by the NIV, "until
they were healed." Two adjustments may be offered. First, rather
than reading the particle *'ad* as indicative of time ("until"), it is possible to understand it as indicative of degree ("to the point that," or
"so that even").[15] Coupled with the particle is an infinitive built from
the verb of life (and the antonym of death), חָיָה (ḥāyāh). Taken
together, these suggest an end result, "to the point that they lived,"
or more roughly, "even to their survival." Hence, a second adjustment is added to the first: context is used to suggest the antecedents

---

[14]The description of Israel throughout the wilderness wandering follows
military lines (cf. Exod 14:19; Num 2:3; Deut 23:9-10; etc.).
[15]This is particularly true in the case of comparisons. See BDB, s.v. עַד.

of pronouns in 5:8b. Again, this must be done remembering the idea of comparison and displacement.

When all these pieces are carried forward and assembled, a proposal for reading verse 8 may be offered, "after all the nation had been circumcised, they (the second generation) replaced them (the first generation) in the camp with the result that they (the second generation) lived." The point of the text is not to explain why no one moved around during a painful healing process. While this may have been true, a more profound take-away is ripe for picking. It falls appropriately on the heels of the Jordan crossing and at the conclusion of the wilderness wandering. The point is this: the end of the second generation will be different than that of the first. The second generation will live! Through negative and positive examples a teaching about obedience is laid down. It is consistent with the opening mandate that links those who are careful to do *torah* with those who are prosperous and successful (1:8).

5:9 A summary statement comes by way of Yahweh, declaring this moment special. As a result of this circumcision event and the announcement of life, the **reproach of Egypt** is **rolled away.** While many proposals have been offered to explain how or what this reproach might be,[16] context suggests that this "reproach of Egypt" is more specifically, the "reproach of *the previous generation from* Egypt." Simply put, the omission of the fathers is rectified by the act of Joshua. On this side of the Jordan, Israel can now truly put the wilderness sentence-of-death behind them. Amid the wordplay is yet another naming: the camp is named "Wheeling" or **Gilgal,**[17] a circular place of

---

[16]One understanding of this reproach connects it with the state of uncircumcision. A common suggestion is that this "reproach" refers to the degradation of slavery and landlessness in Egypt experienced by the previous generation. For an example of this approach, see J. Gordon Harris, Cheryl A. Brown, and Michael S. Moore, *Joshua, Judges, Ruth,* vol 5, NIBC, ed. by Robert L. Hubbard Jr., and Robert K. Johnston (Peabody, MA: Hendrickson, 2000), p. 41.

[17]The location of this site — or campsite (?) — has been problematic. For southern possibilities near Jericho, see James Muilenburg, "The Site of Ancient Gilgal," *BASOR* 140 (Dec. 1955): 11-27. For an attractive northern proposal, consider Zertal, "Israel Enters Canaan," pp. 38, 42-43, and *Eastern Valleys,* pp. 111-112 (see Supplemental Study on the Survey of Manasseh in ch. 17, p. 307).

"rolling" because in this place Yahweh "rolled away" their shame.[18] As elsewhere, this matter is remembered **to this day**, suggesting some distance between the event itself and the time of writing.

3. The Passover Party (5:10-12)

[10]**On the evening of the fourteenth day of the month, while camped at Gilgal on the plains of Jericho, the Israelites celebrated the Passover. [11]The day after the Passover, that very day, they ate some of the produce of the land: unleavened bread and roasted grain. [12]The manna stopped the day after[a] they ate this food from the land; there was no longer any manna for the Israelites, but that year they ate of the produce of Canaan.**

[a]*12 Or the day*

5:10 While encamped on the desert plains of Jericho, Israel celebrates the Passover. This is the first Passover observed in the Promised Land, and as such, is a significant marker. Anticipation for this marker has already grown as a result of indicators, such as 4:19, announcing the arrival on the tenth day of the first month, as well as the circumcision event. In fact, while the connection is not explicitly drawn here, it cannot be overlooked: according to the instructions of Moses, no uncircumcised male may eat the Passover meal (Exod 12:44,48). This realization adds further clarity to the action described previously (vv. 2-9). It also, incidentally, continues to demonstrate the execution of *torah* by Joshua. As the evening of the 14th day of the first month approaches (Lev 23:5), Israel is now fully prepared, ritualistically — and perhaps even psychologically by means of Yahweh's pardon — for celebration. Despite this dramatic ramp-up, little descriptive attention is given to the event itself. Passover is the

---

[18]Cf. the use of (Heb.) Gilgal as a common noun in Isa 28:28, גִּלְגַּל עֶגְלָתוֹ (*gilgal 'eglāthô*, "wheel of his cart"). The noun grows from the verbal root, גָּלַל (*gll*), "to roll (away)." See BDB, s.v. גָּלַל.

Another play on the word "Gilgal" has been put forward. The Manasseh Hill Country Survey conducted under the direction of Adam Zertal has revealed a series of "wheel shaped" enclosure sites, e.g., el-Unuq, Yafit, Bedat esh-Sha'ab. It is possible that a *gilgal* refers not to the proper name of a site, but to a kind of site (Zertal, "Israel Enters Canaan," p. 43).

quiet climax; it is simply "made" in the Gilgal camp. Contextual awareness of the liturgy, meal, and activities recollecting the Exodus event must be imported (Exod 12:1-30; Lev 23:4-8; Deut 16:1-8).

5:11 More significant than the details of the celebration is the recognition of **that very day**; Israel's first Passover in Canaan is a special marker. This is communicated through the events that immediately follow. For the first time, the people eat the produce of the Land of Promise: unleavened bread and roasted grain. Such repast may seem mundane, but is important for two reasons. First, it is a meal provided by the miracle of the land itself. Second, in the seven days following Passover (Exod 12:15-20), only unleavened bread is to be eaten. The unspoken conclusion is that Israel continues to honor *torah* by acting and eating appropriately.

5:12 Connected to the notice of diet is the narrator's announcement that manna now ceases to be given. As manna was strictly survival rations, particular to the generation of wandering (Exod 16:4-5), it is no longer necessary. Hence, the exchange of the exceptional for the ordinary, heavenly manna for local produce, offers additional closure to the wilderness experience. A sad chapter in Israel's history is given closure at last; a new one is ready to be written.

This last thought prompts a glance over the shoulder. Visible is a balanced structure of events, hardly accidental. This narrative design spans great distances measured in texts, locations, and conditions. Connecting lines may be drawn from the muddy banks of the Nile to the plains above the Jordan, from the book of Exodus to the text of Joshua, and from the squalid conditions of slavery to an open campsite of freedom. In the center of it all is the Law and the shadow of the Lawgiver, outlines that will continue to be framed and adjusted as the conquest of Canaan begins in earnest.

E. VICTORY AT JERICHO (5:13–6:27)

Across the Jordan River lies the city of Jericho. While certainly not the largest challenge of Israel's Canaanite campaign, it is a celebrated first. Steep ramparts and high walls remind the reader of the original Israelite fear and failure in Canaan (e.g., Num 13:28) as well as the difficulties of the recent scouting expedition (2:1-24). How can such an obstacle be overcome? What will happen to Rahab?

How will Joshua interpret and apply the "Yahweh war" instructions? Answers are revealed in stages. An unexpected meeting (5:13-15) precedes the prescription (6:1-5) and prosecution (6:6-27) of an unusual strategy.

1. An Unexpected Meeting Described (5:13-15)

[13]**Now when Joshua was near Jericho, he looked up and saw a man standing in front of him with a drawn sword in his hand. Joshua went up to him and asked, "Are you for us or for our enemies?"**

[14]**"Neither," he replied, "but as commander of the army of the LORD I have now come." Then Joshua fell facedown to the ground in reverence, and asked him, "What message does my Lord[a] have for his servant?"**

[15]**The commander of the LORD's army replied, "Take off your sandals, for the place where you are standing is holy." And Joshua did so.**

[a]*14 Or lord*

5:13 No temporal indicators are given; sometime later, Joshua, according to the NIV, is simply **near Jericho.**[19] That an aging commander-in-chief would be close enough to the enemy to accidentally encounter or engage him, possibly without attendant, is difficult to fathom. As all Israel is, in a sense, "near Jericho," a circumstantial reading of the preposition בְּ (b^e-) is preferred: "Now when Joshua was (set) *against* Jericho. . . ."[20] This adversative reading of the clause more clearly establishes the context for the scene that follows. Anticipating conflict with Jericho in the near future, Joshua looks up and sees a figure (אִישׁ, *'îš*) standing opposite him, armed, at the ready, with sword unsheathed. While the circumstances prompting the meeting are ambiguous, the language of the encounter is not. The syntax of "raising his eyes," "looking," and "behold" is used else-

---

[19]The text reads literally בִּירִיחוֹ (*bîrîḥô*), "in Jericho." A narrow, spatial understanding of the preposition *b*- is unlikely. The NIV suggests a looser reading, "in the territory" or "vicinity" of Jericho, cf. 4:19.

[20]For the adversative reading of the preposition *b*-, see Waltke and O'Connor, *Biblical Hebrew Syntax*, sec. 11.2.5d, example 18.

where of surprise encounters with the divine (cf. Gen 18:2; 22:13). By the use of such stylized clues, the narrator slips a secret to the reader: this is no ordinary mortal. Still, Joshua must discover this by himself. His cool inquiry is appropriate to a sentry at his post: **"Are you for us or for our enemies?"**

5:14-15 The answer is irascible, curt, and altogether inappropriate for Joshua's either-or question. **"No!"**[21] The identity of this mysterious stranger cannot be understood in human categories. He does not serve at the whim of any warlord, Israelite or Canaanite, but instead, functions as captain of Yahweh's hosts![22] Moreover, his timing is opportune: "Now, I come!" Such words are puzzling; are they meant to be comforting or ominous? With blade exposed but even fewer words, a warrior halted Balaam's donkey in its tracks (Num 22:23).[23] Needless to say, the tension mounts.

Just as the appearance of the divine representative is described in biblically recognizable terms, so too is Joshua's response. Once the realization of his privileged position sinks in, he falls forward to the ground, stretches out in humility, and addresses the figure again — this time, more appropriately. The stranger becomes **my liege** or lord and the language of the Israelite leader shifts into 3rd person, Joshua becomes **his servant.**[24]

With all roles now properly established, Joshua inquires as to the divine message. The response is uncanny. It does not concern the expected campaign strategy or directions for war, but instead, is directed in an odd way: **Take off your sandals for the place where you are standing is holy.** Such a message prompts thoughts in two directions. First, the worship that it demands dovetails neatly with themes raised in the "Great Commission" of Yahweh (1:3,5,7,9). The coming campaign is to be unique, ideally prosecuted by courageous, careful, and meditative personnel. As prefigured by this armed cap-

---

[21]The LXX reads this לֹא (lō'), "no," as לֹ (lô), "to him."

[22]The specific title of this character, שַׂר־צְבָא (śar-ṣᵉbā'), appears elsewhere as the supreme commander of the forces from Hazor (1 Sam 12:9), Israel and Judah (1 Kgs 2:32), or Aram (2 Kgs 5:1). When applied in spiritual spheres, the title is only found in Dan 8:11.

[23]Another figure of divine judgment appears in 1 Chr 21:16.

[24]This shifted point of view where one refers to himself in the 3rd person is well attested in dialogues with authority figures. Compare the self-effacement here with examples in 1 Sam 26:18,19 or 2 Sam 9:11.

tain, the forces of Yahweh will go before the forces of Israel. This
meeting confirms it. Second, the specific vocabulary of the message
prompts yet another flashback for the alert reader. The command
to Joshua to pull off his sandals is identical to the command given to
Moses at the burning bush (Exod 3:5). This too, dovetails with
themes previously raised: Joshua, in so many ways, is *like* Moses (e.g.,
1:5; 3:7). The theophany experienced by Moses in the text of Exodus
is clear enough: he is called into action as a leader of God's people
and given promises of assurance. One assumes the same is true of
Joshua. However, here, the theophany that begins in a dangerous
and expected way, falls off abruptly. Joshua removes his sandals, the
chapter ends, and a notice of the situation of Jericho (6:1) starts a
whole new trajectory. Hence, the resulting picture can only be
appreciated as a silhouette at best. God is at work. Joshua is like
Moses. Beyond these outlines, the reader is left to his/her own
resources. Perhaps casting the text into the guise of film may provide an insight of a different order. With Joshua on the ground
before the holy captain, the screen slowly blurs before fading to
black. All who see it strain to capture the fading voices, realizing that
much more is said than heard, much more is shown than seen. In
the end, though, just before the total silence overtakes the scene, a
whisper of just three syllables drifts out: Je-ri-cho.

JOSHUA 6

2. An Unusual Strategy Prescribed (6:1-5)

¹Now Jericho was tightly shut up because of the Israelites. No one went out and no one came in.

²Then the LORD said to Joshua, "See, I have delivered Jericho into your hands, along with its king and its fighting men. ³March around the city once with all the armed men. Do this for six days. ⁴Have seven priests carry trumpets of rams' horns in front of the ark. On the seventh day, march around the city seven times, with the priests blowing the trumpets. ⁵When you hear them sound a long blast on the trumpets, have all the people give a loud shout; then the wall of the city will collapse and the people will go up, every man straight in."

6:1 Inside Jericho, the inhabitants adjust for a prolonged siege. None dare enter; none dare leave the grim city.[1] While this knotty situation is likely due to efforts from without (the Israelites nearby) and efforts from within (the defenses are hopelessly insurmountable), it also provides a context for understanding what follows. While Israel may not be capable of assaulting the walls directly, they may move about freely outside the range of a bowshot.[2] At least there will be no sorties with which to contend.[3]

---

[1] The unusual phrase, סֹגֶרֶת וּמְסֻגֶּרֶת (sōgereth ûmsuggereth), "tightly shut up," combines two participles (Qal active and Pual) built on the same root, sgr, "to be shut, locked, or bolted." Josh 2:5,7 suggest that the gate was regularly "shut" at night. This "shutting," here in 6:1, however, appears of a greater degree or intensity, possibly referring to the "barricading" of more than one door (as in a chambered gate or gate between towers), the throwing of deadbolts, or the dropping of crossbars.

[2] The use of the composite bow in the LBA was widespread. Such bows were fashioned of laminated layers of horn, wood, and animal sinew and could be used with deadly accuracy at distances up to 150 yards. For more

6:2-5 Faced with this stalemate, Yahweh reveals a battle plan to Joshua. One is tempted to associate this revelation with the previous scene involving the divine captain. However, no explicit connections are made. Narratively, the presence of the captain communicated the sovereignty of Yahweh; now, the words of Yahweh communicate encouragement and instruction. What is clear from the beginning is the end of the story: this fortified site, its chief, and fighting men will be given over into Joshua's power.[4] To accomplish this, however, a most unusual strategy is prescribed. **March around the city once with all the armed men. Do this for six days**. This is no magical invocation and certainly not a description of conventional besieging tactics. If anything, it is a parade of symbolic action, perhaps even a snapshot representing the conquest as a whole. Heart and hands, belief and action are blended. Once a day for six days, priests and warriors will march, rank and file, around the city. Seven priests are to carry seven ram horns and precede the Ark-box.[5] Finally, on the seventh day, the city is to be circled seven times.[6] At this time, the

---

on efforts to manufacture and fire modern replicas of ancient composite bows, see Lee Lawrence, "History's Curve," *SAW* 54 (Sept/Oct 2003): 2-11.

[3]For more on the role of the chariot in the MBA and LBA, see Drews, *The End of the Bronze Age*, pp. 104-134.

[4]One should not be too troubled by verbal tenses used here. Butler suggests that throughout this chapter the narrator presents scenes that take place contemporaneously rather that successively (*Joshua*, p. 65, n. 1.a.).

[5]Different words are used to describe these horns. In vv. 4 and 8, they are called שׁוֹפְרוֹת הַיּוֹבְלִים (*šôphrôth hayyôblîm*), a wind instrument used for signaling and made from the curving horn of a buck or ram. These instruments may be used to herald a battle (e.g., Judg 3:27) or the arrival of a year of Jubilee (Lev 25:9). This latter use is curious; does it suggest that the conquest will be a kind of land "release"? Such has been recently suggested by Hawk (*Joshua*, pp. 95-96) and pursued in an unpublished master's thesis by M. Renae Carter ("Property, Jubilee, and Redemption in Ancient Israel," M.A. Thesis, Cincinnati Christian University, 2005).

In v. 5, the instrument of the priests is called a קֶרֶן הַיּוֹבֵל (*qeren hayyôbēl*), a more common term that likewise refers to an instrument fashioned from the horn of an animal.

For discussions of these and other musical instruments. See Jeremy Montagu, *Musical Instruments of the Bible* (Lanham, MD: Scarecrow, 2002).

[6]The repeating of the number seven is a notable feature of the text: there are seven days of "siege," seven priests with ram horns, and seven circuits on the seventh day. What is the significance of this repetition? Several suggestions have been offered. Perhaps the repetition recognizes that the Hebrew term for seven derives from the verbal idea "to take an oath." By

priests will blow the trumpets, the people will shout, and the fortifications of Jericho will give way downward, seemingly, "under their
own weight."[7] This collapse will allow the city to be broadly penetrated and effectively taken. Such an image echoes the "pedestrian
expedition" (1:3) raised previously by Yahweh.

3. An Unusual Strategy Prosecuted (6:6-27)

[6]**So Joshua son of Nun called the priests and said to them,
"Take up the ark of the covenant of the LORD and have seven
priests carry trumpets in front of it." [7]And he ordered the people,
"Advance! March around the city, with the armed guard going
ahead of the ark of the LORD."**

[8]**When Joshua had spoken to the people, the seven priests carrying the seven trumpets before the LORD went forward, blowing
their trumpets, and the ark of the LORD's covenant followed them.
[9]The armed guard marched ahead of the priests who blew the
trumpets, and the rear guard followed the ark. All this time the
trumpets were sounding. [10]But Joshua had commanded the people,
"Do not give a war cry, do not raise your voices, do not say a word
until the day I tell you to shout. Then shout!" [11]So he had the ark
of the LORD carried around the city, circling it once. Then the people returned to camp and spent the night there.**

[12]**Joshua got up early the next morning and the priests took up
the ark of the LORD. [13]The seven priests carrying the seven trum-**

---

this cue, the use of seven may remind Israel of the importance of oath taking, e.g., that which is offered to Rahab (Hawk, *Joshua*, p. 98). On the other
hand, some vocabulary choices are evocative of the "year of jubilee" (as
mentioned above), a celebration observed after seven sabbaths of years,
"seven times seven years" (Lev 25:8). Alternatively, the passage may have a
symbolic relationship with creation and the sabbath (seventh day), remind-
ing the people of both creation and redemption (Woudstra, *Joshua*, p. 110).
Finally, seven often signals the notion of completeness, and may signal "the
successful realization of a task or event" (Creach, *Joshua*, p. 63).

[7]The preposition plus suffix, תַּחְתֶּיהָ (*taḥtêhā*), is either included as part of
the verbal expression, "collapse," or rendered as an adverb, i.e., "fall *down
flat*." Alternatively, it might be suggested that the wall will fall down "under
itself," or "under *its own weight*." This is the direction taken by the LXX that
suggests the wall will "fall down of its own accord," or "by itself," without
any physical action on the part of Israel.

pets went forward, marching before the ark of the LORD and blowing the trumpets. The armed men went ahead of them and the rear
guard followed the ark of the LORD, while the trumpets kept
sounding. ¹⁴So on the second day they marched around the city
once and returned to the camp. They did this for six days.

¹⁵On the seventh day, they got up at daybreak and marched
around the city seven times in the same manner, except that on
that day they circled the city seven times. ¹⁶The seventh time
around, when the priests sounded the trumpet blast, Joshua commanded the people, "Shout! For the LORD has given you the city!
¹⁷The city and all that is in it are to be devoted[a] to the LORD. Only
Rahab the prostitute[b] and all who are with her in her house shall
be spared, because she hid the spies we sent. ¹⁸But keep away from
the devoted things, so that you will not bring about your own
destruction by taking any of them. Otherwise you will make the
camp of Israel liable to destruction and bring trouble on it. ¹⁹All
the silver and gold and the articles of bronze and iron are sacred
to the LORD and must go into his treasury."

²⁰When the trumpets sounded, the people shouted, and at the
sound of the trumpet, when the people gave a loud shout, the wall
collapsed; so every man charged straight in, and they took the city.
²¹They devoted the city to the LORD and destroyed with the sword
every living thing in it—men and women, young and old, cattle,
sheep and donkeys.

[a]17 The Hebrew term refers to the irrevocable giving over of things or
persons to the LORD, often by totally destroying them; also in verses 18
and 21.   [b]17 Or possibly *innkeeper*; also in verses 22 and 25

6:6-11 While the reader is struck by the incredible nature of the
plan, Joshua exhibits no qualms or hesitations. He assembles the
priests and people, and relays the orders. As elsewhere, the narrative gains momentum as the plan is filled in with additional details
in its execution. To the people, the thematic charge to "cross over"
(NIV, "advance") is given.[8] An equipped unit is ordered to the fore,
followed by horn-blowing priests, who, in turn, precede the Ark-box
company. Behind the Ark-box company is a rear guard. Contrast is
drawn between the clamorous priests who sound the ram horns, and

---

[8]Here the familiar root עָבַר (*'ābar*), "cross over," appears yet again, cf.
1:2,11; 3:2, etc.

the other members of the parade who move silently. This display of sound and sight is accomplished on the first day. It involves many elements, but in the end, is described with the Ark-box of Yahweh at the focal point: it is the Ark-box of Yahweh that "follows" the trumpeting priests; it is the Ark-box of Yahweh that "circles" the city. All return to the camp, presumably in Gilgal, for the night.

Assuming that the modern mound known as Tell es-Sultan corresponds to the Jericho of the text, the journey around its walls would not have been a lengthy one. The site itself rises some sixty-five feet above the surrounding plain (and would undoubtedly have reached still higher with the defenses intact). Viewed from above, the fortifications would have enclosed an area no larger than three football fields.[9] The encircling track, keeping outside of bowshot, might measure a mile in length, but not much more. Pressing Israelite numbers into possible scenarios would be possible if the length or depth of the rank and file were known (or if the location of Gilgal was certain). Still, even if the total number of Israelite soldiers is downgraded significantly from hundreds *of* thousands to simply hundreds *or* thousands (see Supplemental Study on Counting Israel in ch. 4, pp. 125-129), it is likely that the fortification walls of Jericho would have been completely surrounded, at times, by a rotating, marching, human "wall." This disquieting vision could produce the "melting hearts" and "loss of breath" previously described by the narrator (5:1) and by Rahab (2:11), who undoubtedly peeps at this strange procession from her window-hole with no little apprehension.

6:12-15 The pattern established on the first day is followed on the second, and again, on the days that follow. Only on the seventh day is there a modification. Per Yahweh's instructions, instead of encircling the city once, the group marches around it seven times. This change of habit would certainly arouse Canaanite suspicion.[10]

---

[9]Due to erosion on the east side of Tell es-Sultan it is difficult to come by an exact measurement. Estimates suggest the site covered approximately three and a half hectares. Using a coefficient of 200 persons per hectare for calculating population density, the number of persons living within the walls would not have been many, perhaps 700 total. Of course, in a time of crisis, people living in the vicinity would have fled to the fortress, swelling its number. Still, the number of persons in Jericho may be numbered in the hundreds, but certainly not in the tens of thousands.

[10]Contra Malamat and others who suggest that the repeated circling of the city would have conditioned the Canaanites, causing them to lower their

6:16-19 Suddenly, the ram horns wail; Joshua bellows for all to shout. With imagination, the reader can feel the vacuum created as Israel singularly draws its collective breath, can see the Canaanites all boggle-eyed from atop the walls, and can remember in Yahweh's words that victory will come in a moment of rolling cacophony. All expectations rise, and — at this crucial point of climax — the narrator abruptly pauses. Open mouths and eyes freeze momentarily as Joshua proceeds to offer the "fine print" of Jericho's conquest deal.[11] This "fine print" concerns old, new, and surprising information. Old information includes the fact that Yahweh has given the city to Israel. New information lies in the fact that Jericho is to be "completely devoted" to Yahweh. Surprising information is the exclusion of specific objects and people from the destruction.

Of these three items of information, the second and third require further comment. Both fall under the חֵרֶם (ḥērem) instructions (see Supplemental Study on *Yahweh* War below). Significant is the command to Israel to "keep" from that which is "devoted to destruction," not only because the command sets up the Achan episode that follows (7:1-26), but also because it revisits familiar vocabulary: recall how the "great commission" of 1:7 encourages Israel to be careful "keepers." Failure in this endeavor will stir up trouble and may relegate Israel to the same fate as the Canaanites. For this reason, Joshua's order to spare Rahab and her clan from the fate of the rest of Jericho's inhabitants is all the more surprising. Up to this point, the reader may wonder if Joshua has been fully apprised of her situation (2:23-24), and, if he were, would agree to honor the scouts' oath — given the conditions under which it was extracted? Perhaps even more troubling is his compliance with the oath given the writ of execution issued against the inhabitants of Canaan (Deut 7:2-4; 20:16-18). The thin wire stretched between the

---

guard, and allow for a decisive blow by Israel. See his "How Inferior Israelite Forces Conquered Fortified Canaanite Cities," *BAR* (Mar./Apr. 1982): 25-35. The same thought is mustered by Chaim Herzog and Mordechai Gichon in their *Battles of the Bible: A Modern Military Evaluation of the Old Testament* (New York: Random House, 1978), p. 29.

[11]This scenario reminds me of radio and television commercials for automobiles that blare the news in a steady strong voice. However, when it comes to the details or "fine print" of interest rates or financing, the voice shifts to a softer and faster "auctioneer" patter.

desire to keep the scouts' oath to Rahab (in the name of Yahweh) and the desire to keep Yahweh's order to exterminate the Canaanites is taut with a pressure that cannot be sustained indefinitely. Both promises cannot be kept; something must *snap* soon and every close reader knows it.

In the midst of this tension, and seemingly without any specific direction from Yahweh, Joshua announces Rahab's salvation. Ostensibly, this is because **she hid the spies**. A closer look, however, may reveal more. Context here and below (6:24-25) likens Rahab to other items rescued from destruction, namely the **silver and gold and the articles of bronze and iron.** This careful juxtaposition of what is to be rescued, animate and inanimate, personal and impersonal is frequently overlooked, but is the key to understanding the inner resolution of the text. According to Joshua's "fine print" instructions offered prior to Jericho's fall, precious metals are to go into the "treasury" of Yahweh (v. 19), or even more powerfully stated, into the "treasury of the house of Yahweh" (v. 24). The language of the latter is often used in reference to the Jerusalem temple, a building clearly out of place in this context. If, however, such "house" language is allowed to function metaphorically (as "household") — and many other examples demonstrate that this would not be an exceptional case — a very different view emerges.[12] Precious objects are to be rescued from destruction because they **are sacred**, holy, special. Such exceptional qualities warrant exceptional treatment, and hence a different fate. The narrator's careful juxtaposition of these objects *with* Rahab and her clan are emphatically repeated (6:17-19 and 6:24-25) and advance the conclusion that a rescue effort will not only be directed toward certain objects, it will also be directed toward certain people. In this prominent example within the text of Joshua, the reader observes the journey of Rahab as she "crosses over" into the "treasury" or more specifically, into the "household" of Yahweh, a move that disturbs dullish thinking about the boundaries of "Israel." It also, in the end, provides an escape from the oath/ban

---

[12]Other examples of persons or objects entering into Yahweh's "household" or "possession" — but clearly not to the Jerusalem temple — may be found in Exod 23:19; 34:26; Deut 23:18[H 19]; and Judg 19:18. In a few other instances, Yahweh's "house" refers to the tabernacle. See 1 Sam 1:24; 3:15; or 2 Sam 12:20.

dilemma.[13] Consider the point: if Rahab becomes an "Israelite," must she share in the Canaanite destruction? Already, she has voiced the name of Yahweh, acknowledged his sovereignty, demonstrated familiarity with Israel's story, and risked her life to save the scouts. By virtue of her words and actions (not to mention her position "in the wall," or in the "interface" between Israel and Canaan), Rahab's identity as Canaanite is blurred. As her journey is not yet complete, this idea must be held aloft for a moment longer while another thought is pressed: just as the words of Joshua call for the deliverance of a woman with an ambiguous identity, the words of the narrator (or more precisely, the structure of the narrative itself that suggests Rahab = precious metal) calls for the deliverance of Joshua from those who would attack his role as a reliable character and interpreter. Joshua cannot be held responsible for breaking *torah*.

6:20-21 Only after this patter of "fine print" is exhausted, can the action resume. When the pause is released, the ram horns blast, the people raise a great whoop,[14] and incredibly, the walls crumble downward as predicted.[15] In this miracle, the role of the Ark-box company may be brought forward again. In the case of the Jordan River crossing, the Ark-box is a visible representative of the power that

---

[13]Polzin, *Moses and the Deuteronomist*, p. 114, seizes upon this same point, but casts it within a context of mercy: "The mercy that allows Rahab to continue to live in the land is not very different from the mercy that allows Israel to occupy the land in the first place. Neither party *deserves* the land. Possession of it by one party depends to a certain extent upon the wickedness of the other party, and both parties benefit from a merciful application of the law of God. What Moses accomplished for Israel in Deuteronomy 9-10, Joshua accomplishes for Rahab here in Joshua 6."

[14]This noise, translated here as "whoop," suggests a tumultuous roar. The verbal form (from the root רוּעַ, *rûa‘*) is often used in the context of battle, as forces surge or retreat to the accompaniment of shouts or horn blasts (e.g., Judg 7:21; 1 Sam 17:52). However, when modified with "great" as in the case in this text, תְּרוּעָה גְדוֹלָה (*t*ʳ*rû‘āh g*ᵉ*dôlāh*), it is always associated with contexts of celebratory worship (1 Sam 4:5; Ezra 3:11,13). This double meaning of war and worship continues to be imbedded in the text and communicates the idea that the conquest of Jericho is a sacred enterprise.

[15]Those who choose to explore a natural explanation for this collapse recognize the position of Jericho in an earthquake-prone region. The Great Rift Valley represents the fault between great tectonic plates; Transjordan rides on the Arabian Shield while Cisjordan is a part of the African plate. Jericho and the Jordan River snuggle between. Earthquakes are common

created a "wall" (of water). In the case of the fall of Jericho, the Ark-box is a visible representative of the power that destroyed a wall of mud brick and stone. Either way, through creating or destroying walls, the Ark-box of Yahweh facilitates passage.[16] Certainly this is true here; the footmen charge the city. There are no bottlenecks, no narrow entries.[17] The defenses are opened widely. The attackers penetrate easily, possibly ascending the stone ramparts by means of the rubble from the collapsed mud brick superstructure

Oddly, after such elaborate details are given to the preparation for the Jericho conquest, little attention is given to the assault itself. Every living thing inside is simply "devoted": **men and women, young and old, cattle, sheep and donkeys.** This selectivity serves to emphasize the fact that it is *not* the assault of Jericho that is the point of the narrative per se; it is Yahweh's miracle-working role in making this impossible attempt possible. Any effort to explain the victory in lesser terms grows from an agenda different from that of the narrator. As stated elsewhere, "Yahweh, the God of Israel, fights for Israel" (10:42).

SUPPLEMENTAL STUDY

YAHWEH WAR

Barbaric acts in the late 20th and early 21st centuries have pressed the discussion of "holy war" into the public forum. Ethnic "cleansings" in Rwanda and the former Yugoslavia, the attack against the World Trade Centers in New York City, suicide bombers in Tel Aviv, Baghdad, and elsewhere, have taken hundreds of thousands of innocent lives. Commentators are quick to point out con-

---

here up to the present day. For an overview of the geological situation, see Denis Baly, *The Geography of the Bible* (New York: Harper & Row, 1974), pp. 22-26. Even if such an approach is adopted, one cannot dismiss the miracle of the timing!

[16]Within this observation is a popular message that the expositor may choose to develop, e.g., God makes a way, God breaks down walls, etc.

[17]The phrase אִישׁ נֶגְדּוֹ (*'îš negdô*) suggests that the attackers climb into the city, literally, "a man to his front" or "each in a straightforward fashion." The collapse of the walls is so wholesale, so widespread, that no zigzagging is even necessary. It is a straight-up affair.

nections between these horrendous acts and the religious orienta-
tions that seemingly encourage them. Inevitably, as the world grap-
ples with the question of how or why such awful things happen
today, the text of Joshua is remembered. Passages such as 6:21 come
into play: "they devoted the city to the LORD and destroyed with the
sword every living thing in it — men and women, young and old, cattle, sheep, and donkeys." Without a doubt, the action described is
harsh, bloody, and disturbing. Many questions are raised by modern
readers. How can such acts be a part of a sacred story? Does
Scripture condone them? How does one "square" such activity with
passages that present a portrait of a loving God, much less with the
teachings of Jesus found in the New Testament? Answers to these
and similar questions are often asked but not easily answered.[18]

The language of Yahweh war[19] in the book of Joshua centers on
the Hebrew root חרם (ḥrm). The verbal idea communicates the
removing of an object or person from human use by giving it totally to God. Such removal requires radical surrender, and once an
object or person is so separated, it cannot be bought back (Lev
27:28). It is forbidden (to man) and holy (to God). In English translations, the verbal idea of ḥāram is translated "to devote" or "utterly
destroy." As a noun, it may be read as a "devoted thing," or in the
older versions, it becomes the "ban." In the same family of words is
the familiar Arabic term herem: such refers to the special quarters for
Muslim wives or even the wives themselves. They are off limits to all
because they are devoted to one.

Pressing this idea of this ḥāram-style war through a distinctly
Christian ethical grid is a daunting task. At risk is not just the relationship between the Testaments, but the consistency of the God

_____

[18]The body of literature on the subject of Yahweh War in Joshua is large
and diverse. Helpful entry points into this debate are found in Stanley N.
Gundry, ed., *Show Them No Mercy: 4 Views on God and Canaanite Genocide*,
(Grand Rapids: Zondervan, 2003); Gary Hall, "Violence in the Name of
God: Israel's Holy Wars," in *Christian Ethics: The Issues of Life and Death*, ed.
by Larry Chouinard, David Fiensy, and George Pickens (Joplin, MO: Parma,
2003), pp. 261-284; and John Howard Yoder, "To Your Tents, O Israel: The
Legacy of Israel's Experience with Holy War," *Studies in Religion* 18 (1989):
345-362.

[19]Despite the traditional use of the term "Holy War," it is preferable to use
the term "Yahweh War." On this question, consider the answer of Gwilym
H. Jones, "'Holy War' or 'Yahweh War'?" *VT* 25 (1975): 658.

who stands behind them. Setting aside those views that understand the text as simply a spiritual truth (with no "real" historical antecedent) leaves open ground in or between one of three camps.[20]

The first camp views the relationship between the Testaments as dualistic and discontinuous. For these readers, the Old Testament is, at best, a pre-Christian document. At worst, it is a sub-Christian document. Either way, it has little or no value for contemporary ethics. Israel's violent ways demonstrate a flawed understanding of God's perfect will, or, as C.S. Cowles puts it: "Joshua's perception of what God was telling him to do kept changing according to the exigencies of the moment."[21] While this angle does relieve the ethical dilemma by creating space between divine will and human action, it comes at a price. The value of the Old Testament as an authoritative word is diminished.

A second camp suggests that the Old Testament preserves a lively debate over acts of violence. Susan Niditch opens her *War in the Hebrew Bible* with the presumption of pluralism: "we should expect the emergence of a complex spectrum of attitudes, a range of ways in which war is justified, and some disagreement about what is considered allowable behavior in war."[22] Not surprisingly, her search reveals no less than seven different voices, each vying for the attention of the reader. Christian authors who share her view may also identify competing strands (e.g., violent vs. nonviolent) in the Old Testament, but often find that tension relieved in the message of Jesus, who ends the debate on the side of nonviolence.[23] As with the first camp, this second camp does eventually find a way through the ethical problem of Yahweh war, but not without raising other questions about the nature of revelation and consistency of God.

---

[20]Surveys are available in several places. John C. Nugent has recently detailed them in a presentation titled, "Biblical Warfare Revisited: Extending the Insights of John Howard Yoder," parallel session presented at the 7th Annual *Stone-Campbell Journal* Conference, Cincinnati Christian University, April 12, 2008. His paper is forthcoming in a book titled, *Power and Practices* (Herald Press).

[21]C.S. Cowles champions this view in Gundry, *Show Them No Mercy*, p. 40.

[22]Susan Niditch, *War in the Hebrew Bible: A Study in the Ethics of Violence* (New York: Oxford, 1993), p. 27.

[23]See Lynn Jost, "Warfare in the Old Testament: An Argument for Peacemaking in the New Millennium," *Direction* 27 (1998): 177-188.

A third view stresses that the relationship between the Testaments is continuous and that only in exceptional circumstances is bloodshed permitted.[24] Perhaps thinking through the four points of C.J.H. Wright would be helpful.[25] First, he suggests that this conquest is a limited event. Other military conflicts appear in the text of Scripture, but none are pursued along similar lines. The exceptional nature of the conquest of Canaan must be noted in Israel's story. Second, Wright observes that the text itself places the conquest into an ethical framework. It is not random violence, but action voiced in terms of divine justice (Gen 15:16; Lev 18:24; 20:23; Deut 9:5; 12:29-31). This perspective finds its way into the New Testament as well (Heb 11:31). Third, this occasion of Yahweh war is consistent with God's judgment elsewhere. One need not venture too far from the text of Joshua to recall the flood of Noah (Genesis 6–8), the destruction of Sodom and Gomorrah (Genesis 19), or even the notion that Israel itself will be similarly judged if they behave like Canaanites (Lev 18:28; Deut 28:25-68). Fourth and finally, Wright argues that the wider view of Scripture reveals how the wicked have been judged in the past and will be judged in the future. God answers prayers: those who desire to live apart from grace will receive exactly what they ask for. In this way, the destruction of the Canaanites is described in terms that anticipate what prophets term "The Day of the Lord" or what theologians consider to be "the final vindication of God's ethical justice."[26]

---

[24]Daniel L. Gard and Tremper Longman III champion this view in Gundry (*Show Them No Mercy*). Both confess that there is some measure of discontinuity between the Testaments ("Phase I," "Phase II"?), but this is not to be regarded as contradiction. Indeed, Gard emphasizes the judgment of God (against the Canaanites in the past and the ungodly in the future) as the way to tie the Testaments together (pp. 113-141), whereas Longman seems to emphasize the role of God/Christ as divine warrior against spiritual forces (p. 187).

[25]See his article on "Ethics" in the *Dictionary of the Old Testament: Historical Books*, ed. by Bill T. Arnold and H.G.M Williamson (Downers Grove, IL: InterVarsity, 2005), pp. 259-268.

[26]Ibid., p. 267.

[22]Joshua said to the two men who had spied out the land, "Go into the prostitute's house and bring her out and all who belong to her, in accordance with your oath to her." [23]So the young men who had done the spying went in and brought out Rahab, her father and mother and brothers and all who belonged to her. They brought out her entire family and put them in a place outside the camp of Israel.

[24]Then they burned the whole city and everything in it, but they put the silver and gold and the articles of bronze and iron into the treasury of the LORD's house. [25]But Joshua spared Rahab the prostitute, with her family and all who belonged to her, because she hid the men Joshua had sent as spies to Jericho—and she lives among the Israelites to this day.

[26]At that time Joshua pronounced this solemn oath: "Cursed before the LORD is the man who undertakes to rebuild this city, Jericho:

"At the cost of his firstborn son
    will he lay its foundations;
at the cost of his youngest
    will he set up its gates."

[27]So the LORD was with Joshua, and his fame spread throughout the land.

6:22-23 The only survivors of the devastation are Rahab and those belonging to her. Joshua orders the two oath-giving scouts to bring her and them out. This is accomplished as Rahab and her relatives are rescued, possibly by means of her window hole. The presence of the scarlet marker from 2:18 is assumed, as is the conclusion that the miracle of the collapsed defensive system also extends to the preservation of her house "in" it.[27] After this rescue is accomplished, Rahab and her family are placed **outside the camp of Israel**. By this, the narrator suggests that an immediate assimilation is not possible.

---

[27]Butler, *Joshua*, p. 67, concludes: "her house on the wall is basically incompatible with the ch. 6 tradition where the walls come tumbling down before she is rescued." This view is only possible if one assumes a strict chronology of the events in ch. 6 (ignoring literary artistry) and adopts a narrow view of Bronze Age architecture (ignoring the archaeological evidence).

For some time Rahab will continue to occupy an ambiguous "in-between" place, not quite "in Canaan" but not yet "in Israel" either.

6:24-25 The combustible portions of city are burned by fire.[28] Again, exceptions are noted as directed by Joshua. Treasure items are not destroyed, but put into the treasury of "Yahweh's house." In a parallel way, Rahab and her family are not destroyed, but enter into the "household" of Yahweh: **she lives among the Israelites to this day**.[29] Her transition from Canaanite to Israelite is completed, and with it, the dilemma involving her and the *ḥāram* order evaporates as well.

6:26 A curse, unprompted by Yahweh, is uttered by Joshua.[30] It is directed toward the one who rebuilds **this city**, although the invocation may specifically have the city *defenses* in view. Such a curse may function as a warning against anyone who would dare to rebuild what Yahweh himself has destroyed (cf. Deut 13:16). Alternatively, it may function as a solemn declaration or ominous prophecy of future events. The language of the text is vaguer than the NIV suggests: laying the foundations (the beginning of construction) will seemingly require the life of the builder's firstborn; setting the gateway doors on hinge (the end of construction) will seemingly require the life of the builder's youngest.[31] Whether these

---

[28]Kitchen, *Reliability*, p. 182, offers the timely reminder of how "the text of Joshua does *not* imply huge and massive fiery destructions of every site visited (only Jericho, Ai, and Hazor were burned). The Egyptians did not usually burn cities, preferring to make them into profitable tax-paying vassals; the Hebrews under Joshua sought basically to kill off the Canaanite leadership and manpower, to facilitate later occupation. These Egyptian and Hebrew policies are not readily detectable in the excavated ruins on sites."

[29]The preposition קֶרֶב (*qereb*), describing Rahab's position "among" or "in" Israel, argues that she is granted a position "within the inward parts" of Israel. It is difficult to see this as anything less than full assimilation. The notice that she is later remembered as "Rahab the prostitute" need not suggest a permanent marginalization; it simply fixes her unique role in the Jericho story within the collective memory of Israel.

Incidentally, ancient Jewish tradition suggests Joshua married Rahab! See I. Epstein, *The Babylonian Talmud: Seder Mo'ed. Megillah* (London, Soncino, 1938), pp. 14b-15a.

[30]The scouts have *sworn* (6:22); the interval of *seven* has repeatedly appeared (6:4). Now Joshua *forces an oath* (Hiphel imperfect of שָׁבַע (*šābaʿ*), a fitting conclusion to this chapter.

[31]Evidence for the Iron Age resettlement of Tell es-Sultan is not wide-

lives will be lost as a result of divine judgment, a construction "accident," or even as a result of human sacrifice is unclear.[32] What is certain is that these words are repeated and fulfilled in 1 Kings 16:34, a narrative move that does more than simply underline the power of the curse, it emphasizes the role of Joshua as a prophetic authority.[33] His words are true.

6:27 Time and circumstance will honor the assertion that Yahweh is **with Joshua**. At that moment, however, it is because of the most unusual victory at Jericho that his **fame** or "report" is widely circulated. Such dispatches reinforce what has already been told (2:10-11,24) and possibly keep the military forces of Canaan at bay by word of mouth alone. As in 5:1, the reprieve gained as a result of this miracle will be spent taking corrective measures within Israel.

spread. Kenyon identified several successive building levels on the flanks of the tell, including a large building with a tripartite plan (typical Iron II). The site was abandoned for good in the Persian period. See Kathleen M. Kenyon, "Jericho" in *NEAEHL*, vol. 2., ed. by Ephraim Stern (New York: Simon & Schuster, 1993).

[32]de Vaux suggests the possibility that this is some kind of "foundation-sacrifice," a Phoenician practice that made its way into Israel. See his *Ancient Israel*, p. 442.

[33]See Jesse C. Long Jr., *1 & 2 Kings,* The College Press NIV Commentary (Joplin, MO: College Press, 2002), p. 202.

JOSHUA 7

F. A SECRET DISOBEDIENCE REVEALED AND CORRECTED (7:1-26)

With Jericho now a smoldering heap, one would expect Israel to push forward into Canaan triumphantly. Unfortunately, this is not the case. A secret disobedience (7:1) has disastrous consequences, and, until corrected, no progress can be made. A setback at a site known as The 'Ay (7:2-5), prompts a search for answers (7:6-9) and a stern warning from Yahweh (7:10-12). A special lottery to locate and remedy the secret disobedience is commanded (7:13-15) and carried out (7:16-26). Along the way, issues of justice, mercy, and Yahweh war, continue to be raised and adjusted, as does the very definition of what it means to be "Israel."

1. A Secret Disobedience (7:1)

[1]**But the Israelites acted unfaithfully in regard to the devoted things[a]; Achan son of Carmi, the son of Zimri,[b] the son of Zerah, of the tribe of Judah, took some of them. So the LORD's anger burned against Israel.**

[a]*1 The Hebrew term refers to the irrevocable giving over of things or persons to the LORD, often by totally destroying them; also in verses 11, 12, 13 and 15.   [b]1 See Septuagint and 1 Chron. 2:6; Hebrew Zabdi; also in verses 17 and 18.*

7:1 As a preface to what follows, the narrator offers an aside to the reader: all Israel shares in the guilt of a secret disobedience.[1]

---

[1]Sternberg, *Poetics of Biblical Narrative*, pp. 164-165, refers to this kind of narrative as "reader elevating," i.e., the reader is given privileged knowledge at the expense of the characters.

Israel has been unfaithful by not fully following the prescribed
Yahweh war.[2] At the center of this collective guilt is a man named
Achan[3] who has sinned by taking from the category of that which is
"devoted" (cf. 6:18-19). His full lineage by kin, clan, and tribe is
offered, anticipating how he will eventually be identified. The reader, but not Joshua, is privy to these asides. Such revelation does not
bode well for coming events (see Supplemental Study on Personal
Sin, Corporate Results below) and places the reader on alert. Moreover, irony develops out of the fact that the curse of the previous
chapter against the Jericho (re)builder is juxtaposed against the
notice that Israel itself has attracted **the LORD's anger.**[4] Ignorant to
its own peril, Israel makes plans for the future.

SUPPLEMENTAL STUDY

PERSONAL SIN, CORPORATE RESULTS

The presentation of Achan's sin in Joshua 7 is, in some ways, baf-
fling to modern readers.[5] In an age of rugged individualism, sin is
popularly understood as a single act committed by one person.
Because sin is a personal choice, it is believed that the consequences
of sin, be they immediate or more distant, are thought to be personal as well. Notions of collective liability are thought to be "primitive," "pre-logical," or superseded by later revelation (e.g., Deut
24:16; Jer 31:29-34; or Ezekiel 18). Sketches of each of these positions may be found.[6]

---

[2]The root מעל (*m'l*) appears twice here (as a verb and a noun) as part of
a well-worn formula describing a conscious sin against God. On occasion,
the expression may describe marital infidelity (e.g., Num 5:12). See *TDOT*,
s.v. מָעַל.

[3]The name *Achan* is transmitted into the LXX as *Achar* and may very well
be a play on the Hebrew word for "trouble." See 7:26.

[4]An inescapable conclusion to be drawn from this passage is that covenant
violation can be fatal. Divine privilege and human obligation are inexorably
linked; Israel cannot take her position as covenant people nor her possession of land simply as an entitlement. This conclusion fits into larger thrusts
offered in advance of the Babylonian exile (e.g., Deut 6:15; 7:4; 11:17) and
in response to it (e.g., 2 Kgs 13:3; 23:26; 24:3-4; Jer 52:2-3).

[5]The same is true of 2 Sam 21:1-14.

[6]The classic survey of this subject is H. Wheeler Robinson, *Corporate*

However, Scripture points out that sin is interpersonal in many ways. Paul describes this in the broadest sense when he writes: "sin entered the world through one man, and death through sin" (Rom 5:12). Elsewhere the proverb echoes, "the fathers eat sour grapes and the children's teeth are set on edge" (e.g., Ezek 18:2). Observation in our own world reveals how alcoholism, child abuse, divorce, and many other tragedies seem to be passed on from generation to generation, in many cases, oddly, by those who suffered indirectly from the actions of others.

In the presentation of Joshua 7, Achan sins and the consequences of that sin ripple throughout all Israel. In fact, thirty-six "innocent" individuals die as a result of Achan's choice. This example is consistent with a larger reading of the text of the Old Testament that demonstrates how the covenant life of the people of God is critical of any view that elevates the wants of self above the needs of the community. Israel is never called to be self-indulgent, self-protecting, self-accumulating, or self-absorbed. On the other hand, Israel is called to be relational, invested in community, and preoccupied with the lives of one's neighbors. Consider how the term used by Achan, "I coveted them" (אֶחְמְדֵם, 'eḥmᵊdēm), also surfaces in the decalogue, "You shall not covet" (תַחְמֹד לֹא, lō' taḥmōd) your neighbor's house, wife, servant, etc. (Exod 20:17). Equally relevant is the prophetic use of the same term:

> Woe to those who plan iniquity, to those who plot evil on their beds! At morning's light they carry it out because it is in their power to do it. They covet [וְחָמְדוּ, ḥāmdû] fields and seize them, and homes, and take them. They defraud a man of his home, a fellowman of his inheritance. Therefore, the Lord says: "I am planning disaster against this people, from which you cannot save yourselves (Micah 2:1-3a).

Clearly, one private act can damage the larger community and keep it from becoming that which God intends it to be.

Personality in Ancient Israel, rev. (Philadelphia: Fortress, 1980). Interestingly, the story of Achan found in Joshua 7 is the first example encountered in this book.

More recent work on this subject has been done by Bruce J. Malina. Consider his *The New Testament World: Insights from Cultural Anthropology*, 3rd ed. (Louisville, KY: Westminster John Knox, 2001), or the work he has jointly edited with John J. Pilch, *Handbook of Biblical Social Values*.

The interpreter's dilemma in dealing with Joshua 7 often gives undue attention to the fairness/unfairness of God's response in this equation. While this is certainly an appropriate domain for theological speculation, the more accessible application redirects the focus to the human side of the matter. In this, little speculation is needed, and much profit may be gained. Achan's story is so very familiar to every reader: "I saw," "I desired," "I took." One line of thought may trace the verbal motion from eye to heart to hand; this much has already been offered in commentary. The other line of thought is more easily overlooked grammatically, but of equal, or, perhaps, greater importance. The common denominator in each of these three clauses of verse 21, אֵרֶא ('ēre'), "I saw," אֶחְמְדֵם ('ehm³dēm), "I desired them," and אֶקָּחֵם ('eqqāḥēm), "I took them," is the first person pronoun: "I." It is egoism that leads these crucial verbs in every sense, challenging the priorities of God, the leadership of Joshua, and the basic values of a community in joint pursuit of a great commission.

2. A Setback at The 'Ay (7:2-5)

²Now Joshua sent men from Jericho to Ai, which is near Beth Aven to the east of Bethel, and told them, "Go up and spy out the region." So the men went up and spied out Ai.
³When they returned to Joshua, they said, "Not all the people will have to go up against Ai. Send two or three thousand men to take it and do not weary all the people, for only a few men are there." ⁴So about three thousand men went up; but they were routed by the men of Ai, ⁵who killed about thirty-six of them. They chased the Israelites from the city gate as far as the stone quarries[a] and struck them down on the slopes. At this the hearts of the people melted and became like water.

[a]5 Or as far as Shebarim

7:2 As in the case of Jericho (2:1), Joshua sends footmen ahead to scout out the land. This action, coupled with the aside of 7:1, produces a nervous air. Such expeditions have thus far yielded results bordering on disaster. Will it be any different this time? The target of the expedition is a settlement named "The 'Ay," (NIV, "Ai") a curious label indeed.[7] The text offers no explanation as to how this particular site was known or selected by Joshua; details offered here concern only its location. The *'Ay* is **near Beth Aven** ("house of iniquity") and **east of Bethel** ("house of God").

This is hardly gratuitous detail. For the careful reader, these location markers jog the memory. It was in this same location that Abram camped when he arrived in the land. Perhaps even more importantly, it was in this exact location that he first "called on the name of the LORD" (Gen 12:8). As presented, Israel's probe into the *Heartland* mimics that of Abram and demonstrates the realization of Yahweh's declaration to give a home to his descendants. Similarly, it was at Bethel that Jacob dreamed of the heavenly portal and experienced a verbal promise to receive "the land on which you are lying" (Gen 28:13). Such "coincidences" of place can hardly be viewed as accidental, but underscore once again the intertextual artistry linking the text of Joshua with *torah*. The weight of this realization grows. Israel left The *'Ay* and went to Bethel as one man; now Israel returns in the form of a sprawling nation. Much has changed in the intervening years. The question now is this: will Israel still "call upon the name of the LORD"?

Along lines less theologically charged, the identification of this trio of sites — The *'Ay*,[8] Beth Aven,[9] and Bethel[10] — has generated considerable discussion. Certainly, their general location is recog-

---

[7]The term regularly occurs in this story with the definite article, הָעַי (*hā'ay*), leading many to suggest "The Ruin" as a rendering of "color" (e.g., Butler, *Joshua*, fn. 7:2b). However, as Zevit points out, this is not a foregone conclusion. The LXX renders the Hebrew *'ayin* with a *gamma*, suggesting an original pronunciation as *gai* (akin to the Arabic *gazza*), and an etymology different from that which is usually assumed. He proposes that the Hebrew *'ay* refers to "some topographical or geographical feature characteristic of the site's location." See Ziony Zevit, "Archaeology and Literary Stratigraphy in Joshua 7–8," *BASOR* 251 (1983): 26. For this reason, the presentation here will simply use The *'Ay* to refer to the site's name.

[8]The site of the *'Ay* is traditionally located at et-Tell, a site located near the village of Deir Dibwan immediately to the east of modern Ramalla/el-Bira. Excavations there have produced little evidence that may be coordinated with the biblical description of The *'Ay*. To sense the disappointment of the excavator, see the essay by Joseph A. Callaway, "Ai (Et-Tell): Problem Site for Biblical Archaeologists," in *Archaeology and Biblical Interpretation: Essays in Memory of D. Glenn Rose*, ed. by Leo G. Perdue, Lawrence E. Toombs, and Gary L. Johnson (Atlanta: John Knox, 1987), pp. 87-99. On the other hand,

nized on the eastern edge of the region known as the "Saddle of
Benjamin," but unfortunately, modern urban sprawl coupled with
local political instability has made identification and excavation of
sites here difficult. This region rests in a natural "saddle" slung
between the higher elevations of Judah and Samaria. To reach this
area from the vicinity of Jericho requires a steep and difficult ascent
of more than 3,000 vertical feet in a short stretch of ten miles.

7:3 No details of the reconnaissance effort are offered (there is
no "Rahab" character in The *'Ay*); only the final report is given. The
site is judged to be quite insignificant and not worth troubling all
the people. Effortlessly, the scouts shift roles from mere reporters to
directing strategists. They suggest that only a portion of the total
fighting force be dispatched, possibly two or three commando
squads.[11] This fragmentation of the group, at a glance, seems reasonable. It may even appeal to the greater good of those concerned:
do not weary all the people. Why exhaust everyone unnecessarily?[12]
However, this thinking runs counter to previous emphases of unity

---

it is possible that this effort is misdirected and the site of The *'Ay* is located
elsewhere. (See fn. 6 on p. 178 for more details.)

[9]Beth Aven has been tentatively identified by Aharoni, *Land of the Bible*, p.
256, with Tell Maryam. More poetically, Hosea seems to apply the term to
the sanctuary in Bethel itself (Hos 4:15; 5:8; 10:5), although other passages
suggest that Beth Aven is distinct from Bethel (Josh 18:12). See also 1 Sam
13:5 and 14:23.

[10]Linguistically, there is little doubt that the name Bethel is preserved by
the modern Arabic *Beitin*, according to Elitzur, *Ancient Place Names*, pp. 181-
183. This is echoed by Rainey and Notley, *The Sacred Bridge*, pp. 116-118.
Excavations at Tell Beitin were conducted in the middle of the 20th century, but poorly published. What is clear is that Tell Beitin was occupied
throughout the MBA and LBA, and was destroyed at the end of each of
these periods. Against the position that Bethel was located in Beitin, see the
exchange between David Livingston and A.F. Rainey in *WTJ* 33 (1970): 20-
44; 33 (1971): 175-188; 34 (1971): 39-50.

[11]Once again the term *'eleph* is read as "commando units" or "squads,"
rather than "thousands." Consult Supplemental Study on Counting Israel,
in ch. 4, pp. 123-127.

[12]The term translated here as "weary" or "toil" is derived from the Piel
form of the root יגע (*yg'*). It is famously remembered in Isa 40:28-31 and in
the book of Ecclesiastes where many kinds of activity are declared "exhausting" or "wearisome" (1:8; 10:15; 12:12). Interestingly, the term appears
again in the text of Joshua in 24:13 where Yahweh declares that he has given
Israel many good gifts including land upon which they did not "toil."

(cf. 1:2,12-15) and is shot through with the arrogance of power. The sweet taste of victory at Jericho may still be in Israel's mouth. The fact that **only a few men** have been observed at The '*Ay* seemingly reduces it to easy prey in the eyes of the scouts; in the eyes of the reader, the reported imbalance appears as a prelude to disaster.

7:4-5 The scouts' suggestion is followed with fatal results. Three commando squads attempt the assault, but are put to flight. They tumble out of the hill country pursued by angry locals and thirty-six individuals are killed along the way, possibly a majority of those involved in the action. In the end, the words originally used to describe the inhabitants of Canaan are now twisted and applied to Israel: **the hearts of the people melted** (cf. 2:11,24; 5:1). This sticking reversal hints at the identification of Israel with the enemy. Furthermore, it is curious that no mention of Yahweh is discovered in "The '*Ay*-spy" episode.[13] The entire excursion appears to be contrived, executed, and aborted apart from the initiative of Yahweh. The distance between Jericho and The '*Ay* may not be great on the ground, but in execution, the two engagements are worlds apart!

3. A Search for Answers (7:6-9)

⁶**Then Joshua tore his clothes and fell facedown to the ground before the ark of the LORD, remaining there till evening. The elders of Israel did the same, and sprinkled dust on their heads. ⁷And Joshua said, "Ah, Sovereign LORD, why did you ever bring this people across the Jordan to deliver us into the hands of the Amorites to destroy us? If only we had been content to stay on the other side of the Jordan! ⁸O Lord, what can I say, now that Israel has been routed by its enemies? ⁹The Canaanites and the other people of the country will hear about this and they will surround us and wipe out our name from the earth. What then will you do for your own great name?"**

7:6 Stunned by this unexpected rout, Joshua and Israel's elders mourn. This display of grief is appropriately demonstrated **before**

---

[13]The delightful assonance of "Ai-Spy" is discovered in the work of Hawk, *Joshua*, p. 107.

the ark and is accompanied by the tearing of clothes and the rub-
bing of dry earth in the hair and face. Such acts of disfigurement are
traditional responses to death or national calamity. All share the
assumption that Israel's defeat is a specific result of Yahweh's action.

7:7-9 Confused, Joshua seeks an explanation. He asks three questions of Yahweh, each couched in his deep grief, but quite bold in
nature. His first question has an upward thrust and asks, in essence,
why all the trouble spent in causing Israel to "cross over" the Jordan,
only to be destroyed on the other side? Joshua's second question has
an inward thrust. He asks himself what can be said in view of this
retreat?[14] His third question returns to an upward thrust and connects Israel's defeat to God's reputation. If Israel's name is erased,
will not the name of Yahweh likewise suffer? This probing gives
voice to Joshua's inability to understand God's motives, his inability
to explain Israel's behavior, and his inability to separate the defeat
of Israel from the defeat of God.

Connections between Joshua's questions and the prayers of
Moses (Exod 32:11-13; Num 14:13-16) encourage comparison
between the two leaders. In the teeth of disaster, they address Yahweh in similar ways.[15] Such cross-examinations[16] have an odd, and
perhaps even a manipulative edge in modern ears, particularly when
restated in terms that emphasize the self-interest of the speaker. A
more balanced approach is possible, however, if one assumes that a
man can truly care for God's "best interests," and, if one remembers

---

[14]Literally, "What can I say since Israel has turned their head before their
enemies?" Revealing the backside of the head or neck (עֹרֶף, *ʿōreph*), is tantamount to the act of flight or abandonment. This is the same Hebrew root
from which the personal name עָרְפָּה (*ʿOrpāh*) is formed, and thought by
some to account for it; cf. Ruth 1:14.

[15]Woudstra, *Joshua*, p. 125, suggests that the bold prayers of Moses may
have served as models for Joshua.

[16]Brueggemann, *Introduction to the OT*, p. 325, uses the phrase "cross-
examinations" to refer to arguments of disputation, common to the Old
Testament. Such speeches of friction are a challenge to Christian interpreters, but are seemingly characteristic of Jewish interpretation and dialogue. Perhaps it may be reduced to a question of spiritual honesty; is it possible to grapple seriously with God without being arrogant? Oddly, this kind
of honest "protest" is seldom given public voice in the Protestant world.

For more on "honest to God" approaches, consider Philip Yancey's *Disappointment with God: Three Questions That No One Asks Aloud* (Grand Rapids:
Zondervan, 1988).

COLLEGE PRESS NIV COMMENTARY

the covenantal contract between Yahweh and Israel. Here it is significant that the reader — but not Joshua — realizes the true reason
for the defeat at The 'Ay. For his part, Joshua is unaware of Israel's
covenant failure. His inquiry is directed toward what appears to be
an unprompted breach on the part of Yahweh. Is it a matter of cal-
loused disengagement or is Yahweh actively opposing Israel? Either
way, a vigorous and hopeful protest is in order.

4. A Stern Warning (7:10-13)

[10]The LORD said to Joshua, "Stand up! What are you doing
down on your face? [11]Israel has sinned; they have violated my
covenant, which I commanded them to keep. They have taken
some of the devoted things; they have stolen, they have lied, they
have put them with their own possessions. [12]That is why the
Israelites cannot stand against their enemies; they turn their backs
and run because they have been made liable to destruction. I will
not be with you anymore unless you destroy whatever among you
is devoted to destruction.

[13]"Go, consecrate the people. Tell them, 'Consecrate yourselves
in preparation for tomorrow; for this is what the LORD, the God of
Israel, says: That which is devoted is among you, O Israel. You
cannot stand against your enemies until you remove it.

7:10-13 The answer is stern and immediate. Joshua is commanded to **Stand up!** This is not a time for groveling; it is a time for
action. The reason? That which the reader discovered earlier is now
revealed to Joshua: **Israel has sinned.** Defeat at The 'Ay is *not* the
result of an unprompted breach of covenant on Yahweh's part. Rather,
Israel has transgressed, or "crossed over," the covenant.[17] Verb upon
verb adds to the indictment: Israel has taken, stolen, and set among
her own baggage that which should have been "devoted." The חֵרֶם
(ḥērem) is contagious! Limited contact has rendered Israel herself a
"devoted" thing and thus subject to destruction. This is the reason
for the deaths of thirty-six men, and perhaps even more seriously,
the reason for the impending departure of Yahweh's assuring pres-

---

[17]Note again the presence of the keyword עָבַר ('ābar, "to cross over").

ence.[18] As Butler puts it, "Israel must choose."[19] Something has to go. They cannot keep both the presence of God (v. 12) and the presence of the *ḥērem* (v. 13).

5. A Special Lottery (7:14-26)

[14]**"'In the morning, present yourselves tribe by tribe. The tribe that the LORD takes shall come forward clan by clan; the clan that the LORD takes shall come forward family by family; and the family that the LORD takes shall come forward man by man. [15]He who is caught with the devoted things shall be destroyed by fire, along with all that belongs to him. He has violated the covenant of the LORD and has done a disgraceful thing in Israel!'"**

[16]**Early the next morning Joshua had Israel come forward by tribes, and Judah was taken. [17]The clans of Judah came forward, and he took the Zerahites. He had the clan of the Zerahites come forward by families, and Zimri was taken. [18]Joshua had his family come forward man by man, and Achan son of Carmi, the son of Zimri, the son of Zerah, of the tribe of Judah, was taken.**

[19]**Then Joshua said to Achan, "My son, give glory to the LORD,[a] the God of Israel, and give him the praise.[b] Tell me what you have done; do not hide it from me."**

[20]**Achan replied, "It is true! I have sinned against the LORD, the God of Israel. This is what I have done: [21]When I saw in the plunder a beautiful robe from Babylonia,[c] two hundred shekels[d] of silver and a wedge of gold weighing fifty shekels,[e] I coveted them and took them. They are hidden in the ground inside my tent, with the silver underneath."**

[22]**So Joshua sent messengers, and they ran to the tent, and there it was, hidden in his tent, with the silver underneath. [23]They took the things from the tent, brought them to Joshua and all the Israelites and spread them out before the LORD.**

---

[18]Yahweh's presence has been thematic. It is an essential part of "a great commission" (1:5), the key to Joshua's credibility as leader (3:7), and the force behind the conquest of Canaan (3:10). At risk here is the baseline for the entire presentation.

[19]Butler, *Joshua*, p. 85.

²⁴**Then Joshua, together with all Israel, took Achan son of Zerah, the silver, the robe, the gold wedge, his sons and daughters, his cattle, donkeys and sheep, his tent and all that he had, to the Valley of Achor. ²⁵Joshua said, "Why have you brought this trouble on us? The LORD will bring trouble on you today."**

Then all Israel stoned him, and after they had stoned the rest, they burned them. ²⁶Over Achan they heaped up a large pile of rocks, which remains to this day. Then the LORD turned from his fierce anger. Therefore that place has been called the Valley of Achor[f] ever since.

ª*19* A solemn charge to tell the truth   ᵇ*19* Or *and confess to him*
ᶜ*21* Hebrew *Shinar*   ᵈ*21* That is, about 5 pounds (about 2.3 kilograms)
ᵉ*21* That is, about 1¼ pounds (about 0.6 kilogram)   ᶠ*26* Achor means trouble.

To correct this situation, directives are offered by Yahweh (vv. 14-15) and followed by Joshua and the people (vv. 16-26). Yahweh commands Israel to rise up (v. 13), be consecrated (v. 13), identify the perpetrator (v. 14), and destroy him (v. 15). The command to Israel to **consecrate yourselves in preparation for tomorrow** is reminiscent of 3:5 and signals a fresh start. Healing involves the whole body. Still, the contagion must be eliminated.

7:14-15 In the morning, the time of action (cf. 3:1; 6:12; 7:14,16; 8:14), Israel is to "draw near," tribe by tribe, clan by clan, family by family, and finally, man by man (see Supplemental Study on the Family in Ancient Israel in ch. 8, p. 186). **The LORD will take**, or single out, the guilty from among them. Some hint of this process is offered by the use of the verb לָכַד (*lākad*). Elsewhere this verbal idea is used to describe how individuals are captured on the battlefield, animals are snared in a trap, or choices are determined by lot. While the word for "lot" does not appear in this particular text, it may be inferred (see Supplemental Study on Lot Casting in ch. 16, p. 298). More significantly, within the text of Joshua the word translated "to take" is regularly used in context with חָרַם (*ḥāram*) to express the Canaanite fate (Josh 6:20f.; 8:19,21; 10:28,32,35,37,39,42). Due to his unlawful possession, the transgressor has, in effect, become non-Israel, and therefore must be taken and destroyed. This greater point should not be overlooked amid the search to discover the specifics of the revelatory process. If Rahab's story reveals how an "outsider" can "cross over" into Israel, Achan's story reveals exactly the opposite.[20] His pedigree by tribe, clan, and family is impeccable. Just as Rahab is the ultimate "outsider," Achan is the ultimate "insider." This fundamental contrast ought to give the careful reader pause. It is no accident that the stories of Rahab and Achan are carefully placed side by side; they are signboards nailed to the same post but pointing in opposite directions. Both purposively explore the larger question, "Who is an Israelite?" Rahab provides one answer; Achan, another. To keep the idea from falling out, one could even measure the quantity of text devoted to the discussion. If there is any correspondence between narrative weight and authorial intention, the Rahab–Achan contrast is given far more attention than even the miracle of Jericho's collapsing walls, a miracle so often celebrated as "the point" of the Joshua text.

7:16-18 One can imagine the horror growing within Achan as he realizes that his secret can no longer be hidden. Narratively, this process is drawn out to uncomfortably enforce the point: nothing is hidden from God. Yahweh's words to David are thus anticipated: "You acted in secret, but I will do this thing before all Israel" (2 Sam 12:12). As expected, the trail to Achan follows family lines previously revealed (7:1), and, in the end, he is successfully netted. Joshua implores him to **give glory** and **thanks** to Yahweh. Such doxology is an invitation to tell the truth. Achan is guilty. The only mystery that remains is in the offering of details.

7:20-21 No praise to God is found on Achan's lips. Instead, his response is a hollow אָמְנָה (*'ām⁽ʾ⁾nāh*), **It is true!** He condemns himself and specifically identifies his sin as not just a sin against God, but against "Yahweh the God *of Israel*." Note how Yahweh is described. Beyond this, his confession takes three parts, "I saw," "I desired," "I took." Such actions are as old as Eden itself (cf. Gen 3:6; Deut 7:25-26). It may also speak to the dynamic of covetousness. As Brueggemann points out, "there is something odd and insidious about the

---

[20]Interestingly, both Achan and Rahab are judged by what they bury and why. Achan buries booty that is supposed to be given to Yahweh. He is motivated by greed. Rahab, on the other hand, buries the scouts and is motivated, in part, by self-preservation. Other parallels exist: the messengers of Achan's story find that which is buried. In Rahab's case, it is the scouts themselves that are buried!

These contrasting stories are contemplated by Spina, "Reversal of Fortune."

fact that *having* makes persons more greedy."[21] Not surprisingly, Achan's selfish sin emerges at the precise moment when Israel moves from landless to landed, from scarcity to plenty.

The objects of Achan's greed consist of a **beautiful robe from Babylonia, two hundred shekels of silver, and a wedge of gold.** This booty is sleek and significant, but not beyond what a single man could conceal and carry. The robe is recognized as a foreign import, coming hundreds of miles from Mesopotamia.[22] Two hundred shekels of silver may have weighed about five pounds or 2.3 kilograms. The gold is likely a single wedge, bar, or "tongue," weighing 50 shekels, approximately 1¼ pounds, or .6 kilograms. With respect to these objects, it should also be remembered that prior to the conquest of Jericho, Israel was commanded not to take any booty from the city, and specifically told not to take any precious metals. These were designated as "holy to Yahweh" and, like Rahab, were destined for "his treasury" (6:19). By taking these objects as a personal possession, Achan flew directly into the teeth of Joshua's warning (6:18), robbed God, and brought trouble on all Israel.[23] The fact that these items were deliberately hidden makes it clear that Achan was aware of the shameful nature of his actions. This is no accident.

7:22-23 Messengers are dispatched to the tent and the stolen items are found as described, even down to the detail of how the silver is deposited. These are retrieved and **spread** out or "poured out" before Yahweh.[24] Achan's secret is exposed for all to see and with it, the reason behind the stunning defeat at The 'Ay.

---

[21]See Brueggemann, *Introduction to the OT*, p. 483, fn. 68.

[22]The text literally reads שִׁנְעָר (*Šin'ār*), an old and exotic name for Babylon. This term was used in the 16th to 13th centuries B.C., and, according to Kitchen, *Reliability*, p. 177 and fn. 44, gives the text an authentic edge. Kitchen also points to three examples in the 14th century when Babylonian merchants were murdered and robbed in Canaan.

[23]Several students of the text have noted a parallel between Joshua 7 and Acts 5:1-11 (e.g., Woudstra, *Joshua*, p. 119, fn. 1). The Achan–Ananias parallel is sketched in even more detail in the discussion of T.G. Crawford in his clever "Taking the Promised Land, Leaving the Promised Land: Luke's Use of Joshua for a Christian Foundation Story," *RevExp* 95 (1998): 251-261.

[24]The use of יָצַק (*yāṣaq*) here, "to pour out" is curious. It may simply refer to the action of dropping or spilling these items upon the ground, one at a time. The term is also used in sacred contexts, particularly when describing anointing oil that is poured out on a stone or upon a person's head. When used in connection with metals, however, *yāṣaq* may describe the casting of

7:24-26 As Achan's sin is tantamount to becoming "Canaanite," Joshua treats him as a Canaanite.[25] He is taken to the **Valley of Achor** (lit., "Taboo" or "Trouble Valley"), a place otherwise unknown.[26] There, Achan is asked a single, rhetorical, question: **Why have you brought this trouble on us?** This trouble is then turned upon him, trouble originating with Yahweh, but anticipated in the words of the people (1:18), and ultimately carried out by their hands. Achan, his family, and possessions are stoned to death, burned, and buried. His fate is inexorably tied to Canaanite Jericho; he, too, in the end, becomes a smoldering heap of rubble.

An editorial aside follows, as a conclusion, pointing in two directions. First, it is noted that the execution of Achan assuages the anger of Yahweh. The problem of 7:1 is resolved by 7:26. Disobedience leads to death. The campaign of Canaan can now continue. Second, it is noted that Achan's ruin heap is still visible **to this day** (cf. 4:9). Achan's trouble attaches itself to the area and accounts for the name of the place, still remembered at the time of writing. It is one more "memorial" that dots the landscape.

---

metal. Of course, the items here are silver and gold. While it is possible that these items coveted by Achan were in some sort of ingot or raw form (coinage was not yet in use), it is more likely that they were in the form of jewelry or perhaps even the form of local idols. If the latter is the case, it is not impossible that they were here literally melted down and poured into some other — less offensive — form.

[25]Hawk muses that there may even be a wordplay in Achan's name here (*Joshua*, p. 120). Achan (עָכָן, *'ākān*), as it stands, is a nonsensical word in Hebrew, but is built upon the same root letters as the name Canaan (כנע, *kn'*). Could this be purposive? Could Achan be preserved in the narrative as some sort of mumbly "Canaanite"? It is an interesting proposal.

More typical is the conclusion that Achan, as it appears, is a scribal error, and should be corrected to Achor ("trouble"). For more on this, see R.S. Hess, "Achan and Achor: Names and Wordplay in Joshua 7," *HAR* 14 (1994): 89-98.

[26]Invisible in the NIV is the Hebrew reading that Israel took Achan and company "up" (וַיַּעֲלוּ, *wayya'ălû*) to the Valley of Achor. If, however, this journey originated in Gilgal on the Jordan Valley floor, the Valley of Achor could have been any number of dry (and stony) watercourses that cut through the Ghor walls and scar the plain below. One suggestion is that the Valley of Achor be identified with el-Buqei'ah, but this is a guess at best. Other mentions of this valley include Josh 15:7; Isa 65:10; and Hos 2:15. See Nelson, *Joshua*, p. 99, fn. 2.

JOSHUA 8

G. THE '*AY* REVISITED (8:1-29)

United in purpose again, Israel and Yahweh renew the conquest of Canaan. A second attempt to capture The '*Ay* is mounted. Unfinished details from the first attempt are carried forward, as are larger compositional themes. Divine leadership and faithful obedience, are pitted against greed, impatience, and hubris. Interestingly, in this second attempt on The '*Ay*, the tools of entrapment previously used to seduce and destroy Israel, are now turned on the Canaanites themselves. This is presented in four sections: the relationship restored (8:1-2), the people in place (8:2-13), the trap triggered (8:14-23), and the pile portends (8:24-29).

1. The Relationship Restored (8:1-2)

¹**Then the LORD said to Joshua, "Do not be afraid; do not be discouraged. Take the whole army with you, and go up and attack Ai. For I have delivered into your hands the king of Ai, his people, his city and his land. ²You shall do to Ai and its king as you did to Jericho and its king, except that you may carry off their plunder and livestock for yourselves. Set an ambush behind the city."**

8:1-2 Yahweh delivers encouragement and instruction to Joshua. The encouragement, **Do not be afraid; do not be discouraged,** is needed on the heels of the Achan debacle. While this phrase is similar to the encouragement found elsewhere (e.g., 1:6-7,9), it is drawn directly from the words of Moses found in Deuteronomy 1:21. Significantly, these words were given on that occasion to Israel in advance of their first view of Canaan, prior to the dispatching of Joshua, Caleb, and ten other scouts to investigate the land. Now, as Israel prepares to return to this Canaanite *Heartland* where a fear of failure — once only imagined — has been realized, such a boost is crucial. It has a steadying effect; Israel's relationship with Yahweh has been restored.

Yahweh's instruction calls for a return to The *'Ay*, but the campaign must be reconfigured.[1] First, *all* the forces are mustered. The error of the scouts who counseled arrogantly for a limited show of force (7:3) will not be repeated. Israel may be confident, but their confidence comes not as a result of overwhelming numbers or military prowess. Instead it comes through the results of divine assurance. Yahweh states, **I have delivered** the chief of The *'Ay*, the settlement itself, and its land holdings, into Israel's hands. United behind Yahweh, Israel may proceed.

Second, in this reconfiguration, the rules for plunder are relaxed. Whereas at Jericho, no personal looting was permitted and all valuables were "devoted" to God, now, **plunder and livestock** may be taken. This relaxation need not be seen as a change of strategy (somehow in deference to Achan's sin), but may simply be a result of having completed the collection of the "firstfruits" of war.[2] Ironically, had Achan waited a little longer, the kind of reward he desired could have been his.

Third, this campaign is reconfigured tactically: the ambush is introduced.[3] Rather than taking the settlement by divine power, as was the case with the tumbling of Jericho's walls, The *'Ay* will fall by

---

[1] Joshua is literally told to "arise [קוּם, *qûm*] and go up to The *'Ay*" (8:1). Here, as elsewhere, the use of the imperative *qûm* signals a new narrative venture, a fresh start.

[2] The principle of the firstfruit offering demands that the first harvest of the crop in a given year be dedicated completely to God. This is sketched out in *torah* (Exod 23:16,19; 34:26; Num 18:12-16; Deut 26:1-11). The principle similarly applies to the firstborn of man and beast (e.g., Exod 13:2). New Testament writers broaden the application of this idea from grain, wine, and oil to include the Holy Spirit (Rom 8:23), the resurrected Christ (1 Cor 15:20,23), first converts (Rom 16:5; 1 Cor 16:15), and believers (Jas 1:18). For more on the Hebrew term, see *TDOT*, s.v. בְּכוֹר. For mention of this "firstfruit principle," with respect to Jericho, see by C.F. Keil, *Commentary on the Book of Joshua*, trans. by J. Martin (London: T & T Clark, 1857), pp. 169-170, fn. 1.

[3] The word translated in the NIV as "ambush" (אֹרֵב, *'ôrēb*) connotes a cunning act of lying in wait. Such stalking may be accomplished by a lion or bear (Ps 10:9; Lam 3:10), a whore (Prov 7:12), or by one who seeks to meet and take the life of another (e.g., Micah 7:2).

means of divine craft, albeit carried out by human hands. This go-round, however, there are no secrets, no hidden agendas at work from within. The narrator, the reader, Joshua, and all Israel are clearly aboard, together.

2. The People in Place (8:3-13)

[3]So Joshua and the whole army moved out to attack Ai. He chose thirty thousand of his best fighting men and sent them out at night [4]with these orders: "Listen carefully. You are to set an ambush behind the city. Don't go very far from it. All of you be on the alert. [5]I and all those with me will advance on the city, and when the men come out against us, as they did before, we will flee from them. [6]They will pursue us until we have lured them away from the city, for they will say, 'They are running away from us as they did before.' So when we flee from them, [7]you are to rise up from ambush and take the city. The LORD your God will give it into your hand. [8]When you have taken the city, set it on fire. Do what the LORD has commanded. See to it; you have my orders."

[9]Then Joshua sent them off, and they went to the place of ambush and lay in wait between Bethel and Ai, to the west of Ai—but Joshua spent that night with the people.

[10]Early the next morning Joshua mustered his men, and he and the leaders of Israel marched before them to Ai. [11]The entire force that was with him marched up and approached the city and arrived in front of it. They set up camp north of Ai, with the valley between them and the city. [12]Joshua had taken about five thousand men and set them in ambush between Bethel and Ai, to the west of the city. [13]They had the soldiers take up their positions—all those in the camp to the north of the city and the ambush to the west of it. That night Joshua went into the valley.

8:3-8 Joshua responds faithfully to this encouragement and instruction. He mobilizes his men to go up to The 'Ay, secretly dispatching an advance team of thirty crack[4] commando squads.[5] The

---

[4]These men will be working behind enemy lines and therefore must be stout fighters. They are described as גִּבּוֹרֵי הַחַיִל (gibbôrê haḥayil), "mighty

plan exploits the experiences gained from the first aborted attempt to take The 'Ay. With an ambush hidden in the folded landscape behind the city, Joshua and the rest of the militia will attempt a frontal approach, engage the enemy, and feign retreat. Once the Canaanite fighters are lured out into the open, away from high ground and the city's defenses, the ambush will rise up, penetrate the city, and kindle a blaze inside.[6] These larger details are shared with the advance team, although other crucial pieces are left out,

---

men," a phrase used elsewhere of men of valor (e.g., Josh 1:14; 2 Kgs 24:14). They are distinguished above others in prowess or skill (cf. Josh 10:7).

[5]The mention of "thirty commando squads" in 8:3 and "five commando squads" in 8:12 has been variously construed by students of the text. It is possible that the thirty squads represent the entire fighting force, whereas the five squads represent the ambush group only. It is also possible that there were two separate ambush groups (see Davis, No Falling Words, p. 66). The solution argued here is that the thirty squads represents a group sent secretly ("by night") in advance of the rest of the men. These have special jobs including advance scouting, holding of critical routes and junctions, and serving as "trip wires" to protect the rest of the group from enemy ambush. This argument solves several chronological/logistic problems and seems to make the most sense from a tactical perspective.

[6]In order for this story to be intelligible, The 'Ay must have been a fortified city. It had to have a gateway and walls connected to that gateway. Excavations at et-Tell, the site commonly identified with The 'Ay, give a very different picture of the town. As Callaway ["Ai (Et-Tell)," p. 97], the excavator, reports, "The evidence (from et-Tell) does not support at any point the account of the conquest of Ai in Joshua 7–8."

W.F. Albright believed that the Joshua description of the conquest of The 'Ay is really a description of the destruction of nearby Bethel. The problem is one of scene "shifting." See his "The Israelite Conquest of Canaan in the Light of Archaeology," BASOR 74 (1939): 17. Others believe the story to be legendary, a construct that was only used later to explain the massive ruins at et-Tell (e.g., J. Marquet-Krause, "La deuxième campagne de fouilles à 'Ay (1934): Rapport sommaire," Syria 16 [1935]: 341). Of course, another option is that et-Tell is the wrong site and remains of The 'Ay should be sought elsewhere. In light of this possibility, recent work (in the late 1990s) by Bryant Wood at Khirbet el-Maqatir is intriguing. Khirbet el-Maqatir is about one mile due west of et-Tell. Unfortunately, published finds from this effort are scant. For a glimpse, see a portion of Wood's article, "From Ramesses to Shiloh: Archaeological Discoveries Bearing on the Exodus–Judges Period," in Giving the Sense: Understanding and Using Old Testament Historical Texts, ed. by David M. Howard Jr. and Michael A. Grisanti (Grand Rapids: Kregel, 2003), pp. 264-268. Obviously, the final verdict on the location of The 'Ay is still out.

such as the raised javelin/sword signal (8:18-19) and the participation of the ambush team in the final pincers movement outside the city (8:22). This information may be withheld by the narrator for a dramatic effect or possibly left out of the instructions because it was not critical to the specific job of these men.

No question is left as to the authorization of this plan, however. The men are to **see to it,** because it is the word of Yahweh as commanded through Joshua. Again, the theme of Joshua as the legitimate interpreter of God for the community is brought forward (cf. 1:16-18; 3:7, etc).

8:9 The advance team deploys, presumably to scout and clear the approach, while Joshua remains behind in the main camp. The detail that **Joshua spent that night with the people** may be offered to provide contrast with his nocturnal activities of 8:13.

8:10-13 The bulk of the Israelite force rises in the morning and begins a long day's ascent into the hill country. Of interest is the presence of **the leaders of Israel** at the fore with Joshua. Their position leading a military column is unusual, but may be explained by their recent involvement in the story (7:6). Following the failed attempt to take The 'Ay, these elders mourned together with Joshua. Their presence now may be a show of solidarity before Joshua, the people, and Yahweh. At Jericho, the Ark-box and the power of God was on parade. This time there is no such display; instead, all eyes focus on the leadership of Israel and their ability to faithfully follow Yahweh. While part of the same campaign, this is a battle of a different order.

This group eventually arrives in the front of The 'Ay, and encamps on a ridge opposite it, **to the north.** Positions are established: the Israelite base presumably has a clear view to The 'Ay (and vice versa), five units of men are dispatched as an ambush team. These are secretly placed behind the settlement, **to the west.** It is assumed that the advance team deployed the day before either reintegrates with one of the two main contingents or continues to lie in wait, securing Israel's flank.

At dusk, Joshua goes **into the valley,** presumably between the occupied ridge and The 'Ay. There, he momentarily — and curiously — disappears from view. Literarily, it is attractive to contemplate a scene as when Israel was camped "near Jericho" (5:13-15). There, in advance of the conflict, Joshua had a mysterious meeting with the "commander of the army of the LORD." Could the same be true

177

here, "near The *'Ay*"? Possibly. On the other hand, he may simply be meeting with members of the scouts or the ambush team. However this literary gap is filled, it appears that despite the darkness, everyone is in place; all is well.

A further word must be offered on the hiding place of those in ambush. It is set west of The *'Ay*, between it and Bethel. As previously noted, the significance of this location arises from the early chapters of Genesis. When Abram responded to the call of God and entered Canaan, he camped quite near this exact location, "with Bethel on the west and The *'Ay* on the east" (Gen 12:8). Here, for the first time, Abram "called on the name of the LORD." This recollection of geographical space and spiritual longing brings forward a striking intertextual connection. Assuming that the waiting forces of Joshua knew Abram's story at least as well as the modern reader, the door of the imaginative process creaks open. It is easy to visualize the ambush team, bivouacking in silence, gazing into the starry sky and recognizing that many centuries earlier — perhaps on a night like this one — Abram breathlessly beheld that same view. Ancient promises are still at work, however cryptic, dormant, or slow. What is new and different now is that for the bivouac team these promises are being fulfilled, in part, by their own hands! However conceived, they are suddenly — and personally — taking a role in this grand story! They are the children of Abraham camping in Abraham's land.

3. The Trap Triggered (8:14-23)

[14]When the king of Ai saw this, he and all the men of the city hurried out early in the morning to meet Israel in battle at a certain place overlooking the Arabah. But he did not know that an ambush had been set against him behind the city. [15]Joshua and all Israel let themselves be driven back before them, and they fled toward the desert. [16]All the men of Ai were called to pursue them, and they pursued Joshua and were lured away from the city. [17]Not a man remained in Ai or Bethel who did not go after Israel. They left the city open and went in pursuit of Israel.

[18]Then the LORD said to Joshua, "Hold out toward Ai the javelin that is in your hand, for into your hand I will deliver the city." So Joshua held out his javelin toward Ai. [19]As soon as he did this, the

men in the ambush rose quickly from their position and rushed forward. They entered the city and captured it and quickly set it on fire.

[20]**The men of Ai looked back and saw the smoke of the city rising against the sky, but they had no chance to escape in any direction, for the Israelites who had been fleeing toward the desert had turned back against their pursuers.** [21]**For when Joshua and all Israel saw that the ambush had taken the city and that smoke was going up from the city, they turned around and attacked the men of Ai.** [22]**The men of the ambush also came out of the city against them, so that they were caught in the middle, with Israelites on both sides. Israel cut them down, leaving them neither survivors nor fugitives.** [23]**But they took the king of Ai alive and brought him to Joshua.**

8:14-17 As presented, **in the morning** the chief of The *'Ay* is eager to engage Israel again. He sees the forces deployed before him. He rises early, he hurries, and he goes out to do battle. Correspondingly, the pace of the action accelerates. The site of conflict is loosely described as "a certain" or "appointed place," **overlooking the Arabah**,[7] possibly along a well-defined path of decent. As in the first battle, Israel initially engages, and then tumbles backward toward that valley, put to flight. Now it is the Canaanite chief who is confident of victory, hotly pursuing them, encouraging all the people to abandon the safety of defensive positions within the city and join in the rout. The consequences of this choice will be catastrophic as **they left the city open.**

At this point, a new piece of information is dropped.[8] Not only do the able-bodied men of The *'Ay* give chase to Israel, but also those from their sister settlement of Bethel. Previously, Bethel had only been a point of reference; now it is learned that fighters from

---

[7]The term הָעֲרָבָה (*hā'ărābāh*) refers to the deep valley between the Dead Sea and the Gulf of Aqaba. It is part of the Great Rift system and therefore is a desert extension of the Lower Jordan Valley. From the area of The *'Ay*, the Great Rift is clearly visible in the west; the unnamed "site overlooking the *Arabah*" could rest in the Wilderness of Judea, somewhere between the Saddle of Benjamin above and the Lower Jordan Valley below.

[8]This reference to Bethel is present in the MT but absent in the shorter version of the conquest of The *'Ay* preserved in the LXX.

this city are also armed, alert, and apprised of the situation (or so they believe).

8:18-19 In the midst of these rapid developments, Yahweh instructs Joshua to act. Joshua motions toward The 'Ay with a weapon in his hand.[9] If the pose looks familiar it is because the same verb is used (נָטָה, *nāṭāh*, "to stretch out") to describe Moses on several occasions. He "stretches out" his hand/staff to initiate or end plagues (Exod 9:23; 10:13,22) and does the same to open and close the Red Sea (14:21,27). Like his mentor, Joshua brings judgment upon the enemies of God's people by outstretched arm. Here, Joshua activates a plague of a different order. The ambush force enters the open settlement, secures it, and quickly kindles a flame. The trap is sprung!

8:20-23 For the men of The 'Ay, the smoke from the city is a signal of death. They realize, all too late, that they have been caught in a pincers movement and have no path of retreat. Those who are pursued suddenly wheel about, trapping their pursuers in the open country. Israel savagely cuts them down from both front and rear, **leaving them neither survivors nor fugitives.** The reader is reminded of the earlier hubris of the Israelite scouts (7:3) and the secret of Achan that leads to destruction (7:22). This time the tables are turned. It is the hubris of the unnamed Canaanite chief (8:14,16) and the secret of Yahweh (8:2) that leads to destruction. The chief of The 'Ay is cornered, captured, and brought to Joshua.

4. The Pile Portends (8:24-29)

[24]**When Israel had finished killing all the men of Ai in the fields and in the desert where they had chased them, and when every one of them had been put to the sword, all the Israelites returned to Ai and killed those who were in it.** [25]**Twelve thousand men and women fell that day—all the people of Ai.** [26]**For Joshua did not draw back the hand that held out his javelin until he had destroyed[a] all**

---

[9]The term translated as "javelin" (כִּידוֹן, *kîdôn*), may refer to a curved sickle sword, a Bronze Age weapon well known in Egypt. See Yigael Yadin, *The Art of Warfare in Biblical Lands* (New York: McGraw-Hill, 1963), 1:204. Such a weapon was also carried by the *Goliath* (1 Sam 17:6).

who lived in Ai. [27]But Israel did carry off for themselves the live-stock and plunder of this city, as the LORD had instructed Joshua.

[28]So Joshua burned Ai and made it a permanent heap of ruins, a desolate place to this day. [29]He hung the king of Ai on a tree and left him there until evening. At sunset, Joshua ordered them to take his body from the tree and throw it down at the entrance of the city gate. And they raised a large pile of rocks over it, which remains to this day.

[a]26 The Hebrew term refers to the irrevocable giving over of things or persons to the LORD, often by totally destroying them.

8:24-29 The body count that day is high. Twelve units[10] of Canaan-ites are killed in the action, men of course, but apparently women as well.[11] As commanded, Joshua stands with outstretched weapon; he does **not draw back the hand** until the grizzly work is accomplished. Again, the statuesque pose is reminiscent of Moses in another mili-tary victory (Exod 17:11). The settlement is plundered, burned,[12] and reduced to a ruin-mound (תֵּל, *tēl*). As for the chief of The *'Ay*, he is executed and his lifeless body is hung from a tree like a crimi-nal.[13] There it dangles until sunset, after which time it is flung into the gateway and buried beneath the rubble. In another kind of throw, the narrator uses a symbol to lasso the disaster of chapter 7

---

[10]This is another good example of the problem of translating *'eleph* ("thou-sand" or "unit") in this context. How can a village with a population of "twelve thousand" persons be considered a small place and (even more oddly) require only two or three thousand men to take it (cf. 7:3)? See Supplemental Study on Counting Israel in ch. 4, p. 123.

[11]The preposition (*'ad*) in the phrase וְעַד־אִשָּׁה (*wᵊ'ad-'iššāh*) often express-es a sense of measure or degree, e.g., the men were killed "up to the women," or "as far as the women," suggesting the women were the place where the line of killing ceased. However, it may also express a more privitive sense, e.g., "All who fell that day numbered twelve units, men *as well as* women." See Waltke and O'Connor, *Biblical Hebrew Syntax*, sec. 11.2.12.

[12]A needless problem posed by critics suggests that the city was burned twice, once by the ambushers (8:19) and once by Joshua (8:28). Such twisting is altogether unnecessary, and is ignorant of the nature of ancient stone/mud villages and how they burn (piecemeal at best). Moreover, such twisting ignores the nature of the literary telling: 8:28 is clearly a summary statement of the event, not a precise description of whose hand sparked the blaze!

[13]Note in 10:26-27 how other chiefs are not hung to death, but rather, exe-cuted, and then their bodies are hung for a time, in humiliating display. Cf. Deut 21:22-23.

together with the victory of chapter 8: a rubble-cairn is erected. Like the stones piled over Achan's body, the stones piled over the dead chief present a visible portent of the seductive dangers posed by Canaan. Such dangers are obviously at work both within (in the case of Achan) and without (in the case of the chief of The *'Ay*) the Israelite camp. Achieving success somewhere, somehow, in the context of this dangerous mix of lust and violence is only possible when the people of God follow their leaders, who, in turn, follow Yahweh.

H. ISRAEL RENEWED (8:30-35)

What follows the dramatic telling of the fall of The *'Ay* may seem anticlimactic or even awkward at a glance. Without a word of transition, Joshua and all Israel abruptly appear in the center of the Canaanite *Heartland*. Here, they assemble, build an altar, sacrifice, and read *torah*. This sudden shift from war to worship may seem jolting, but when carefully examined, turns out to be a tidy knot at the end of the narrative string stretching from Jericho to The *'Ay*.[14]

1. Preparing People (8:30-33)

[30]**Then Joshua built on Mount Ebal an altar to the LORD, the God of Israel, [31]as Moses the servant of the LORD had commanded the Israelites. He built it according to what is written in the Book of the Law of Moses—an altar of uncut stones, on which no iron tool had been used. On it they offered to the LORD burnt offerings and sacrificed fellowship offerings.[a] [32]There, in the presence of the Israelites, Joshua copied on stones the law of Moses, which he had written. [33]All Israel, aliens and citizens alike, with their elders, officials and judges, were standing on both sides of the ark of the**

---

[14]The LXX locates this passage elsewhere. Here the text of 8:30-35 is placed after Josh 9:2. It should also be noted that 4QJosh[a], from the library of the Dead Sea Scrolls, places this passage immediately before 5:2. Some view these variants and conclude that the passage as it stands in the MT is "manifestly disconnected from its context whichever of the three possible locations one chooses" (Nelson, *Joshua*, p. 117). This skepticism is unwarranted, however, as a close reading reveals that the MT position is a good fit.

covenant of the LORD, facing those who carried it—the priests, who were Levites. Half of the people stood in front of Mount Gerizim and half of them in front of Mount Ebal, as Moses the servant of the LORD had formerly commanded when he gave instructions to bless the people of Israel.

ª*31* Traditionally *peace offerings*

8:30-31 Joshua builds an altar upon Mt. Ebal, the modern Jebel Islaméye, "the mountain of the oath." (See Supplemental Study on the Survey of Manasseh in ch. 17, p. 307.) This 3,100-foot scarp rises as part of the Central Ridge of Palestine and stands immediately adjacent to Mt. Gerizim, the modern Jebel et-Tor. Nestled between these peaks rests the settlement of Shechem, well-known biblically, but curiously not mentioned by name here.[15] This key area lies some twenty miles due north of the vicinity of The '*Ay* and represents a considerable Israelite incursion into Canaanite land. Because no divine prompting immediately precedes Israelite action and because there are no descriptions of troop movements or engagements to open up the region, this sudden Israelite appearance here is surprising.[16] Perhaps an observation may help relieve some difficulty: in the aftermath of the victory at The '*Ay*, local resistance simply retreated into fortified settlements. When Israel approached Jericho, Canaan was "tightly shut up. . . . No one went out and no one came in" (6:1). If an historical (rather than a literary) angle is

---

[15]Excavations at Tell el-Balatah (biblical Shechem) demonstrate continuity in occupation between the Bronze and Iron Ages. However, the site appears to diminish significantly as one moves from Stratum XIII to Stratum XI. It is possible that the settlement posed no threat at the moment of Israel's arrival, and therefore slips by without comment. To follow this line of thinking, see Kitchen, *Reliability*, p. 186.

[16]As discussed in note 14, some have suggested that this passage is out of place chronologically. In this scenario, Israel gains access as a result of later fighting, but the passage is placed here for effect (Butler, *Joshua*, p. 94). Another scenario suggests that Israel gains access to the region due to former alliances in the region of Shechem. This was the position of Noth, who argued that the penetration of Canaan was more gradual than the text of Joshua suggests. The Shechem region was open due to an earlier Israelite settlement. See Noth, *The History of Israel*, pp. 91, 145.

Of course, if Zertal's northern proposal for Gilgal is correct ("Israel Enters Canaan," pp. 38, 42-43; *Eastern Valleys*, pp. 111-112), much of this problem goes away!

sought to explain 8:30-35, the same dynamics may be at work. Alternatively, as Davis suggests, the contextual abruptness may not be an historical issue at all, but rather, a kind of "literary violence" in which the reader is propelled headlong into the question of priority: which is *most* important, the act of worship or the act of conquest?[17] One must be suspended in order to complete the other. However attractive this view may be, Davis forces a false choice: the key tension of the book of Joshua is strung between the external challenge of the Canaanites and the internal challenge of obedience. While odd sounding in modern ears, the preachment throughout the book is that the act of the pedestrian conquest *is* an act of worship. Within Joshua, it is difficult to prioritize or separate these two actions.

Joshua builds an altar on the summit of Mt. Ebal. The altar is **of uncut stone, on which no iron tool had been used.**[18] This style of construction demonstrates attention to *torah* (Exod 20:25) and to the specific command of Moses to meet on this mountain when the land is penetrated (Deut 11:26-32; 27:1–28:68). It is hardly surprising that the name of Moses is regularly encountered (8:31,32,33,35), and linkage to the beginning of the book is made via the phrase **Moses, the servant of the LORD** (cf. Deut 34:5; Josh 1:1,13,15). The economy of the telling in Joshua 8:30-35 presumes familiarity with the text of Deuteronomy and simply evokes the infilling of details from there. Beyond these connections, further witness to the enormous significance of the moment and place may be drawn from Genesis 12:6-7. Here, Abram, like Israel, succeeds in reaching Canaan. His first iden-

---

[17]Davis, *No Falling Words*, p. 72, writes, "The situation is like the interruption of normal television programming with a special news bulletin. The news bulletin is deemed of sufficient importance and priority to preempt normal telecasting. That is why the biblical writer makes us victims of his literary violence: to underscore the fact that covenant obedience has priority over military victory (indeed, that the former is the basis of the latter — remember chapt. 7); to show that heeding God's word is more crucial than fighting God's war."

[18]Perhaps the command to use fieldstones is a preventative measure. By forbidding the use of worked stone, the temptation to cut the stone into a particular shape (i.e., "graven images") is reduced.

The rabbis of old found other explanations as de Vaux communicates: "The altar prolongs life, but iron cuts it short," or "The altar is for forgiving, and iron is for punishing." See his *Ancient Israel*, p. 408.

tified stop is at Shechem, nestled between the mountains of Ebal and Gerizim. The careful reader notes not only that the promise of "this land" is offered to the Patriarch by God, but that Abram responds to the revelation by building an altar (Gen 12:7).

Hence, despite its clipped delivery, the ceremony of 8:30-35 carries tremendous weight. First, it is weighty because it continues the demonstration of the theme that Joshua is not just the successor of Moses, but a scrupulous interpreter of *torah* to his generation. This is the reason behind the sudden move to Ebal and his actions there. Second, it is weighty because it identifies Joshua's campaign as the fulfillment of ancient promises offered by Yahweh. Read in this way, the narrative of the assembly — described on the heels of the initial battles at Jericho and The '*Ay* — is hardly out of place, but is skillfully inserted. With their rubble-cairns now behind them, a united and faithful Israel experiences a fresh start following faithful leaders. As at Sinai, **burnt offerings and sacrificed fellowship offerings** are given (Exod 20:24).

8:32 Beyond building an altar and sacrificing on it, Joshua copies **on stones the law of Moses**. The ambiguity of this passage is difficult to crack, in part because what is represented is a narrative of covenant enactment rather than some direct quote from the covenant itself. Are the stones upon which Joshua wrote the same as the uncut stones used to build the altar? What exactly did Joshua write? Blessings and curses? A list of commandments? The book of Deuteronomy? The whole of *torah*? Satisfactory answers to these questions are elusive. What is clear is that Joshua's effort is to promulgate Moses' original words, and that it was done, somehow, in a public way, **in the presence of the Israelites**.[19]

While stone engraving is well known in the ancient Near East, it is difficult and time consuming. An easier alternative is to coat the stone in plaster and cut the letters into this smooth, soft surface. Such plaster inscriptions are well known and may be quite lengthy.[20]

---

[19]It is also clear that parallels between this ceremony enacted and the ceremony prescribed in Deuteronomy may be identified in covenant presentations discovered elsewhere in the ancient world. See Kitchen, *Reliability*, pp. 283-307, for a discussion of the elements, sequences, idioms, and chronology of these agreements.

[20]The Deir Allah inscription is the most conspicuous example of this kind of recovered artifact. See J. Hoftijzer and G. Van der Kooij, *Aramaic Texts*

In the prescription for this event in Deuteronomy 27:2, Moses makes clear that Joshua is to write *torah* upon plastered stones standing upright for display. As elsewhere (4:20-24), the construction will cause people to look and remember.

8:33 Elders, officials, judges, and priests participate in the ceremony. The sense of inclusiveness is hammered by the repetition of the word "all": *all Israel* listens as *all the law* is read. Newcomers (גֵּר, *gēr*) and old-timers (אֶזְרָח, *'ezrāḥ*) alike stand shoulder to shoulder, with half the congregation positioned on the slopes of Mt. Gerizim and half positioned on the slopes of Mt. Ebal (see Supplemental Study on The Family in Ancient Israel below). These face each other with the Ark-box between them, a powerful and central symbol of both Yahweh's presence and the people's unity. With respect to the latter, the *gēr*,[21] or the "newcomers," are particularly conspicuous, since the careful reader now knows the story of Rahab and how she is incorporated into the midst of Israel (6:23,25). Again, this theme of "Israelite" identity continues to be thoughtfully kneaded and pressed.

SUPPLEMENTAL STUDY

THE FAMILY IN ANCIENT ISRAEL

The concept of family is the cornerstone of society in ancient Israel. Village honor and shame, religious practice, military order, marriage customs, heritage, inheritance, and other issues critical for ensuring the identification and survival of a people are reckoned down family lines. Not surprisingly, basic notions of "in-group" and "out-group" also find their beginning point here. For this reason, the text of Joshua 7:14,16-17 is illuminating. The immediate context describes the process by which a guilty party is identified; taken

---

from Deir 'Allā (Leiden: Brill, 1976), or André Lemaire, "Fragments from the Book of Balaam found at Deir Alla," *BAR* 11 (1985): 26-39.

[21]The term *gēr* refers to one who takes up residence among a people not his/her own. As an immigrant or sojourner, a *gēr* is dependent upon the hospitality of others. According to *TWOT* (s.v. גּוּר) the *gēr* occupies a place somewhere between a native and a foreigner, although in time, the idea blends with that of proselyte, one who converts to the position of God-fearer. According to *torah*, the *gēr* is a protected citizen who is not to be oppressed (Exod 22:21[H 20]; 23:9).

more broadly, however, the passage offers a glimpse as to how family is structured.[22]

At the largest level is the notion of "tribe" (שֵׁבֶט, *šēbeṭ*). Biblically, the tribes of Israel expanded from the sons and grandsons of Jacob. These "patriarchs" were gathered and blessed in Egypt (Genesis 49); their names became patronymic for their descendants (e.g., "The tribe of Benjamin," "Issachar," "Judah," etc.). It is these descendants who left Egypt with a mixed multitude (Exod 12:38), wandered in the wilderness, and eventually entered Canaan. Twelve seems to be the ideal number for this group, although thirteen or even fourteen segments are specifically identified by name (depending on how the two Joseph tribes and the tribe of Levi are counted). Such elasticity hints at gaps between what may have been the ideal and what was the practice of tribalism, a thought that comes as no surprise to anthropologists. Observations made among human societies elsewhere demonstrate that while tribal boundaries offer a way to order the world (and one's self in it), in practice, they are far more flexible and porous than memory alone would suggest.[23] Curiously, the word translated as "tribe" may also be translated as "rod" or "staff," possibly alluding to the authoritarian "glue" or *realpolitik* that binds the unit together! One last observation in the direction of tribalism points out the difficulty of making the political shift from a decentralized, kin-based pattern to the more centralized of monarchy. When Israel is upset with royal policies and shouts, "to your tents, O Israel" (1 Kgs 12:16), one wonders if this is not the voiced yearning for the "good ol'" tribal days.[24]

Tribes are further subdivided by "sibs," "clans," or "families" (מִשְׁפָּחָה, *mišpāḥāh*). These mid-sized groups appear to be self-sufficient and self-protecting. Leadership, resources, property, labor,

---

[22]A parallel passage may be Num 1:2 where the "congregation of Israel" is divided into "clans" and "households."

[23]An introduction to the subject of tribalism has been written by Robert B. Coote. It emphasizes this fluid character and offers a window to contemporary critical views. See Robert B. Coote, "Tribalism: Social Organization in the Biblical Israels," in *Ancient Israel. The Old Testament in Its Social Context*, ed. by Philip F. Esler (Minneapolis: Fortress, 2006), pp. 35-49.

[24]I owe this thought to David Merling who first voiced it in my hearing somewhere near the water fountain in the Horn Archaeological Museum, Andrews University.

and brides were shared inside this group. Within the text of Joshua, this specific term is used repeatedly in the distribution lists where land is given to tribes לְמִשְׁפְּחֹתָם (l³mišp³ḥōtām, "according to family," or "clan by clan"; e.g., 13:15,24,29; 15:1, etc.; see also Judg 21:24). This land-blood connection was so strong, that according to one study, to offer the name of one's family was tantamount to offering one's address.[25] Furthermore, to distinguish between administrative and ethnic districts in the land would never have occurred to the ancient Israelite. They are one and the same. Whole villages would be composed of a single extended "family," led by elders, and able, if needed, to muster its own fighting force. As an example, some 600 men of a single mišpāḥāh gather for battle in Judges 18:11.

Beyond tribe and clan, the most fundamental level of social organization is the "household" or beth. It is from this level that essential identity and status are derived. The root word from which this comes is בַּיִת (bayith, typically used of a "dwelling place" or "house"). Town names may be remembered as the "house" of a founder (e.g., Beth-Gader, 1 Chr 2:51; Josh 12:13; Beth-el, "house of God," Josh 7:2). Elliptically, the term bayith may refer to those who live under one roof. These are, at times, described more fully as a בֵּית אָב (bêth 'āb) or "house of a father," suggestive of a two- or three-generational nuclear family unit (i.e., father, mother, children, grandchildren) living together. In the case of Achan, he has a wife and children, indicating a maturity of his own, but is still identified by the house of his father (e.g., 7:24). Other, possibly better examples, may be collected (Judg 6:11,15).

From this context it is interesting to project these lines biblically forward. The arrival of Christianity challenged many core ideas about family.[26] It understandably found a cool reception in some corners. In a universe where authority was traditionally a measure of social rank, the New Testament introduced authority gained through service. In a system where bloodlines were the difference between "in-group" and "out-group" identity and behavior, the New Testament offered the church as a community accessible to all who embraced the gospel message. In a worldview where tradition gov-

---

[25]Francis I. Andersen, "Israelite Kinship Terminology and Social Structure," BT 20 (1969): 29-39.

[26]This is noted in Pilch and Malina, Handbook, p. 78.

erned choices, both moral and social, the New Testament introduced new standards to a new community living in a new age. The retooling of "family" within the Kingdom of God, a process already hinted at in Joshua, is completed.

2. Reading *Torah* (8:34-35)

³⁴Afterward, Joshua read all the words of the law—the blessings and the curses—just as it is written in the Book of the Law. ³⁵There was not a word of all that Moses had commanded that Joshua did not read to the whole assembly of Israel, including the women and children, and the aliens who lived among them.

8:34-35 Before the people, Joshua reads *torah,* the highpoint of the ceremony. He reads specifically from the blessings and the curses (Deuteronomy 27–28) and the congregation likely responds in hearty agreement, *"Amen."* Recent experiences at Jericho (where blessings were realized) and The *'Ay* (where curses were realized) give this material timely application and deprive listeners of the excuse of ignorance. Legal questions looming on the horizon (e.g., the Gibeonite Maneuver of 9:1-27) will require regular fallback to the text of *torah* and special care in its interpretation. Through this exercise of testimony, therefore, Joshua models leadership for successive generations. This model will reach its zenith in a dramatic return to Shechem at the close of the book (24:1-27).

At the moment, emphasis is placed upon Israel's total participation. It is fascinating to discover how those who tend to be otherwise marginalized, the **women and children, and the aliens who lived among them**, are explicitly included. The point grows ever clearer: gender, age, and even ethnicity do not disqualify one from the congregation. That which binds "Israel" together is the recognition of Yahweh's presence, symbolized by the Ark-box, at the center of life and a mutual commitment to obey *torah.* This benchmark will be the reference for understanding the chapter that follows.

JOSHUA 9

I. THE GIBEONITE MANEUVER (9:1-27)

As word of Israel's victory at Jericho and The 'Ay spreads, all Canaan prepares for war. The inhabitants of Gibeon, however, choose a different response; they devise a ruse. Elaborate preparations are concocted. Their encounter with Israel wryly bundles humor with wonder: could such a maneuver possibly work? How should the reader judge the attempt?[1] What do the Gibeonites know of Israel's commission, and even more perplexing, how do they know it? Less obvious but more to the point of the story are the questions, how are the Gibeonites like or unlike Israel? How are they like or unlike Rahab? Altogether, the chapter continues to refine the idea of Israelite identity and serves as a prelude for battles to come.

The text breaks into four sections. The response to Israel's arrival in Cisjordan is detailed. The larger Canaanite response is sketched (9:1-2), as is an exceptional move successfully carried out by the residents of Gibeon (9:3-15). Eventually, however, the maneuver is discovered (9:16-21), and an uncomfortable confrontation occurs (9:22-27).

---

[1]The notion of "maneuver," expressed here by use of the Heb. עׇרְמׇה ('ormāh), is a fascinating study in wordplay and authorial intention. One expects the term to carry a condemnatory force. This is certainly true in the case of a premeditated murder — committed with "guile" — as the KJV presents it (Exod 21:14). However, in Proverbs, 'ormāh shares the podium with wisdom (it is translated as "prudence" in 1:4 and 8:12), a trait to be actively sought and rewarded! This brings back the question: In the case of Gibeonite 'ormāh, how should it be regarded? Does the narrator regard it as treacherous "guile" or wise "prudence"?

1. A Coordinated Response (9:1-2)

¹**Now when all the kings west of the Jordan heard about these
things—those in the hill country, in the western foothills, and along
the entire coast of the Great Sea^a as far as Lebanon (the kings of the
Hittites, Amorites, Canaanites, Perizzites, Hivites and Jebusites)—
²they came together to make war against Joshua and Israel.**

^a*1 That is, the Mediterranean*

9:1-2 News travels fast, especially bad news. For the inhabitants
of Cisjordan, every antenna is set aquiver by word from Jericho and
The ʿAy. The news cascades down from the **hill country**, or Central
Ridge above, where The ʿAy rests, to the שְׁפֵלָה (*šᵉphēlāh*), or **western
foothills**, below, and flows out across the **entire coast**. No one is
ignorant. No one is unaffected. Familiar terms used to define the
land of promise in 1:4 appear again and remind the reader of the
original commission to Israel: "I will give you every place where you
set your foot" (1:3).

Naturally, those who stand in Israel's footpath oppose this kind
of an agenda. They include the standard litany of people groups,
representing distinct ethnic and language enclaves: **Hittites, Amorites, Canaanites, Perizzites, Hivites and Jebusites**.² These folk, who
have regularly and viciously clashed with each other over the course
of time, now close ranks in opposition to this mutual enemy.³ A
coordinated local response has been slow in coming, but if cement-
ed, will represent an enormous challenge to Israel's commission.⁴

---

²Cf. 12:8; Deut 20:17. Deut 7:1 adds Girgashites to the list. See also
Supplemental Study on Amorites in ch. 5, p. 130.

³The phrase פֶּה אֶחָד (*peh ʾeḥād*) is skipped over in the translation of the
NIV, depriving the original text of some strength. The folk of Canaan gather themselves together with "one mouth." Even though the inhabitants of
the land comprise many people groups and even many languages, on this
subject they can speak with singular agreement, or perhaps as the English
idiom suggests, "with one mind."

Butler, *Joshua*, p. 97, suggests that this "one mouth" of the Canaanites
contrasts the singularity of Israel expressed in 8:30-35.

⁴Woudstra points out how "the spirit of Psa 2 comes to expression here"
(*Joshua*, p. 153): "Why do the nations conspire and the peoples plot in vain?
The kings of the earth take their stand and the rulers gather together
against the LORD and against his Anointed One" (Ps 2:1-2).

2. The Gibeonite Exception (9:3-15)

[3]However, when the people of Gibeon heard what Joshua had done to Jericho and Ai, [4]they resorted to a ruse: They went as a delegation whose donkeys were loaded[a] with worn-out sacks and old wineskins, cracked and mended. [5]The men put worn and patched sandals on their feet and wore old clothes. All the bread of their food supply was dry and moldy. [6]Then they went to Joshua in the camp at Gilgal and said to him and the men of Israel, "We have come from a distant country; make a treaty with us."

[7]The men of Israel said to the Hivites, "But perhaps you live near us. How then can we make a treaty with you?"

[8]"We are your servants," they said to Joshua.

But Joshua asked, "Who are you and where do you come from?"

[9]They answered: "Your servants have come from a very distant country because of the fame of the LORD your God. For we have heard reports of him: all that he did in Egypt, [10]and all that he did to the two kings of the Amorites east of the Jordan—Sihon king of Heshbon, and Og king of Bashan, who reigned in Ashtaroth. [11]And our elders and all those living in our country said to us, 'Take provisions for your journey; go and meet them and say to them, "We are your servants; make a treaty with us."' [12]This bread of ours was warm when we packed it at home on the day we left to come to you. But now see how dry and moldy it is. [13]And these wineskins that we filled were new, but see how cracked they are. And our clothes and sandals are worn out by the very long journey."

[14]The men of Israel sampled their provisions but did not inquire of the LORD. [15]Then Joshua made a treaty of peace with them to let them live, and the leaders of the assembly ratified it by oath.

[a]4 Most Hebrew manuscripts; some Hebrew manuscripts, Vulgate and Syriac (see also Septuagint) *They prepared provisions and loaded their donkeys*

9:3-5 An exception to the coalition of opposition arises at the site of Gibeon (modern el-Jib),[5] identified as one of several Hivite sites

---

[5]Excavations in the late 1950s and early 1960s were conducted at el-Jib. Numerous jar handles stamped with the seal of Gibeon confirm the identity of the site in the Iron Age. Beyond these, the nature of the published

(Josh 9:7,17).[6] Located near The *'Ay* but straddling the primary north-south route, Gibeon represents a strategic Hill Country settlement. From here, the ruse begins with a flurry of activity. Verbs are dropped one after the other as **a delegation**[7] is prepared by the people[8] and dispatched, ostensibly to Gilgal in the Rift Valley, where Israel continues to camp.[9] The appearance of this delegation is crafted to communicate to audiences both near and far. The men load their donkeys with sacks that are worn out and wineskins that are split and mended. Likewise they don patched clothing and repaired

---

reports makes conclusive statements difficult. Finkelstein, *Archaeology of Israelite Settlement*, p. 60, fn. 6, suggests that a substantial city wall revealed on the mound dates to the MBA. Undoubtedly, it would have been reused, if possible, by later inhabitants. Burials demonstrate occupation at the site throughout the MBA and LBA.

[6]According to biblical testimony, the Hivites were distinguished from Canaanites (2 Sam 24:7). They were located in a cluster of villages around Gibeon and in the northern reaches (11:2) in Joshua's day, although previously, they were also found at Shechem (Gen 34:2). Their name suggests that these folk were "tent-dwellers" or "nomads" at one time. Archaeologically, however, the Hivites cannot be distinguished from their neighbors. For this claim, see Amihai Mazar, "Jerusalem and Its Vicinity in Iron Age I," in *From Nomadism to Monarchy: Archaeological and Historical Aspects of Early Israel*, ed. by Israel Finkelstein and Nadav Na'aman (Washington, DC: BAS, 1994), p. 91.

[7]The NIV squeezes a noun from an odd verb in order to produce this translation. The verb, וַיִּצְטַיָּרוּ (*wayyiṣṭayyārû*), appears only here in Scripture, and may be built on the root *ṣyr*. Elsewhere this root may be pointed as a noun and read as "messenger" or "envoy." If "verbalized" as a hitpael imperfect (which is the case here), it may suggest the act of "making a messenger (team)" or, as the NIV puts it, a "delegation."

These gyrations may be avoided if one letter of this questionable verbal form is swapped for another look-alike letter. The MT apparatus suggests replacing the odd *wayyiṣṭayyārû* with וַיִּצְטַיָּדוּ (*wayyiṣṭayyādû*), "they took provisions." While this form is not common either, it does appear a few verses later in 9:9. Accepting this textual emendation provides the following translation for the beginning of v. 4: "They thus designed a manipulation. They went and *prepared provisions*. . . ." For what it is worth, this emendation is consistent with the LXX reading.

[8]No chief of Gibeon is mentioned, an odd contrast in this context. Here the *chiefs* of the land prepare a war (9:1), but the *people* of Gibeon prepare a ruse (9:3-4). Later, the Gibeonite delegation refers to their leaders as "our elders," זְקֵנֵינוּ (*zᵊqênênû*) (9:11). Interestingly, in this way, the "mobile" Hivites appear more Israelite than Canaanite.

[9]The identification of Gilgal here is debated. Some suggest that this is a different Gilgal then that of 5:10. See Woudstra, *Joshua*, p. 156, for more.

sandals.[10] To complete this image of depletion, they pack crumbly and molded bread as provisions. As these preparations are described, three flashbacks occur. First, memories of the ill-fated campaign at The 'Ay come to mind: narrator and reader again share dangerous secrets and withhold the same from Israel. Second, the theme of hiddenness returns without a break. Unlike the last chapter, though, where Israel was the ambushers, Israel is now susceptible to being ambushed. Third, the reference to worn out sandals and patched clothing somehow twists back to the days of Sinai wandering. In that case, Israel's sandals remained sturdy on their feet, their clothing was patch-free, and, just to complete the scenario, they needed no provision-bread at all (Deut 29:5-6). In an odd sort of way, therefore, the Gibeonites appear like an Israel in need of Yahweh! Polzin takes this picture into account when he suggests that the link between Israel and the Gibeonites rests in the recognition that neither rightly deserves a covenant relationship.[11] If *torah* is strictly interpreted, both deserve obliteration; only by grace can they survive.

9:6 The Gibeonites arrive and bypass all polite conversation. As if time is against them, they crisply utter their request: "from a *distance* we have come; *so now*, make a treaty with us." Their voice emphasizes the space traveled, their mood emphasizes the imperative nature of their claim, and their words emphasize the urgency of the task. Such a gush is clearly suspicious (and likely accompanied by a trickle of sweat!). It also assumes knowledge of Deuteronomy 20:10-18, a key passage for interpreting the present text. *Torah* allows Israel to make treaties (or covenants) with distant cities and exempts the same from the prescribed Yahweh war (see Supplemental Study on Yahweh War in ch. 6, p. 151). The Gibeonites are somehow privy to this clause and seek to exploit it.

9:7-8 Israel balks. They inquire if the delegation is, in fact, what they claim. "Perhaps you live in our midst. **How then can we make a treaty with you?**" The narrator directs this question out of the

---

[10]In the economy of biblical narrative descriptions of clothing are rarely given. When some aspect of physical appearance is noted, it will likely become an element of the story. For more on this, see Shimon Bar-Efrat, *Narrative Art in the Bible*, 2nd ed. (Decatur: Almond, 1984), pp. 48-53; or David M. Gunn and Danna Nolan Fewell, *Narrative in the Hebrew Bible* (Oxford: Oxford University, 1993), pp. 57-59.

[11]Polzin, *Moses and the Deuteronomist*, p. 119.

mouth of Israel and specifically toward **the Hivites** as if to shrilly announce their true identity. Don't be fooled! They are *Hivites*! They are among those in the land who are to be annihilated (Deut 7:2; 20:17, etc.)! Moreover, the specific wording of Israel's question confirms the suspicion. Israel wonders if the Gibeonite delegation is "in our midst" (בְּקִרְבִּי, *bᵊqirbî*), an ironic barb given the presence of the same word used earlier to describe the position of Rahab — "she dwelled *in the midst* of Israel" (6:25) — as well as the aliens at Shechem — "who walked *in their midst*" (8:35).

Faced with this direct question, the Gibeonites do not blink: **"We are your servants."** Their answer is *no answer* at all! It continues the pattern of clipped speech previously noted and stresses a positive reason for Israel to agree to a treaty: it appeals to their own best interests. Curiously, as a kind of appeal voiced directly to Joshua and not to "the men of Israel," it serves a proleptic function (9:23,27).[12] Joshua assumes the lead and pushes for details: **"Who are you and where do you come from?"**

9:9-13 Forced out at last, the delegates recite their (well-rehearsed?) story. Elements of this story are reminiscent of Rahab's speech to the spies (2:9-13). Like Rahab, they have heard of Yahweh and know what He did in Egypt and Transjordan.[13] Also like Rahab, they speak glowingly of the **fame**, or "name," of Israel's God and of their draw to Him.[14] Unlike Rahab, however, certain elements of

---

[12]One senses a developing distinction between Joshua and "the men [lit., man] of Israel." Some commentators explain this distinction as compositional layering (e.g., Nelson, *Joshua*, p. 123). Others read the text more holistically, but seek to deconstruct it along these lines (e.g., Hawk, *Joshua*, p. 139).

While neither of these approaches is adopted here, it is apparent that the incident provokes a crisis of decision making on the part of the Israelites. While Joshua will have the last word (9:26), the "men of Israel" (9:6-7), the "men" (9:14), the "leaders of the assembly" (9:15,18), and the "assembly" (9:18) will offer various points of view. A careful reading of the text is necessary.

[13]Curiously, the Gibeonites fail to mention that they know what happened at Jericho and The *'Ay* as well, given that this news initiated their mission!

[14]The phrase, לְשֵׁם יהוה אֱלֹהֶיךָ (*lᵊšēm YHWH 'ĕlōhêkā*) of 9:9 may be translated in many ways. The NIV renders the preposition *lᵊ*- as a "lamed of interest" or a "benefactive dative," i.e., "*because* of the name of Yahweh" we have come (see Waltke and O'Connor, *Biblical Hebrew Syntax*, sec. 11.2.10). However, with verbs of motion — as in this case — the preposition *lᵊ*- is more commonly translated in an allative way (ibid., p. 205). This adjustment yields the fol-

their speech are clearly false, thus casting doubt upon the whole of their claim. The delegates continue to assert that they are from a distant place and seek to prove it to Joshua by means of three exhibits: depleted provisions, worn clothes, and tired sandals. As told, these items were fresh and new when their journey to Israel (and Yahweh) began. But the length of the journey has exhausted them. Their original request is neatly tucked in again through the voice of their dispatchers: "we have come a great distance; **make a treaty with us.**"[15] With imagination, one can almost feel their panting breath!

9:14-15 While long on exhibits, the Gibeonites are short on facts. Their vague answer does not identify the name of their homeland, home village(s), or paths taken to the meeting. Given the high stakes of this campaign (remember that blessing and curse are suspended overhead at all times), a careful investigation of the delegates' claim is in order. When this does not happen, it is not the Gibeonites, but the reader who is left gasping for air! How could Israel be snookered by such a transparent ruse? Did this exchange happen too quickly to be caught? How can Israel pledge allegiance to *torah* at one moment (8:30-35) and fail to earnestly apply it in the next (9:1-15)? Is there more to this story than meets the eye?

Faced by a rush of questions, the narrator drops an editorial opinion, rendered all the more important by its rarity.[16] Israel sampled the

---

lowing translation: we "have come *to* the name of the LORD." Could this be suggestive of some kindling of faith, what might be termed "a conversion experience" in today's language, or is it simply another piece of the rhetorical appeal, and therefore, nothing more than manufactured claptrap?

[15]These ideas of "swearing" and "treaties of peace" are familiar ones in the context of LBA Canaan. A key player in 14th-century Canaan is one Lab'ayu, a chief of Shechem. In a local conflict, he writes to the king of Egypt: "Now you have written to me, 'Guard the men who have seized the city!' How can I guard the men? By an act of aggression was the city seized, when I had taken the oath of peace! And when I swore, the officer swore with me. The city was taken and also my god! I have been slandered before the king." These words are recorded in Amarna Letter 252 and are found in Rainey and Notley, *Sacred Bridge*, p. 83.

[16]In most stretches of biblical narrative, the narrator is unobtrusive and self-effacing. Evaluation is produced through indirect tactics (such as characterization or material arrangement). Breakthroughs such as this one bespeak intentionality and demand that a specific interpretation not be left to chance. For more on this, see Alter's work on "Characterization and the Art of Reticence," in his *The Art of Biblical Narrative*, pp. 114-130.

provision-bread[17] — presumably by eating it with their own mouths — but they did "**not inquire** from the mouth of Yahweh." The contrast makes explicit the charge of self-reliance, a point already encountered in the mouths of The 'Ay scouts: "do not weary all the people, for only a few men are there" (7:3). Such a potent charge demands pause, and, in fact, may suggest a crisis running deeper than the Gibeonite issue at hand. At stake is Israel's own vocation — the reason it was called into being — namely, to partner with Yahweh in his work to bring blessing to the earth (Gen 12:3; Exod 19:5-6). While the direction of that effort may swivel from age to age or from place to place, the manner in which such a partnership is executed does not. Noun patterns drawn from Joshua's great commission are informative here and may be carried forward. Strength and courage (1:6) are qualities often associated with rugged independence, but care and meditation (1:8) provide important checks and balances. All are necessary. All are complementary. That Israel would plunge blindly ahead, independent, out of range, yet cocksure, resonates with the ego of the human spirit. Still, that same spirit intuitively knows that the formula has never been: "God's people lead — Yahweh follows"; it is the other way around. This message must be repeated again and again whenever theology becomes packaged and self-serving, ministry operates from too much strength, or God's people become too cozy with a triumphalist culture.

Hence, by means of this maneuver, the fast-talking Gibeonites extract שָׁלוֹם (šālôm), **peace** from Joshua, a notion that encompasses not just the absence of war, but wholeness, prosperity, and integration. This בְּרִית לְחַיּוֹתָם (bᵊrîth lᵊhayyôthām) or "covenant to preserve their lives" is ratified by **the leaders of the assembly** through an unstated oath. With the deal sworn and signed, the only thing that remains is the obvious question: what will Israel do now?

---

[17]Other readings of this passage are possible. The beginning of v. 14 states that "the men took from their provisions." The view adopted here is that of the NIV and the most logical, given the context: "the men" are "the men *of Israel.*" Another view, however, is that "the men" are the Gibeonites, who, at this point take (out) the described exhibits for display. A third view, intriguing, but imaginative, suggests that at this point *all the men* involved take provisions as some sort of concluding covenant meal.

SUPPLEMENTAL STUDY

SWEARING

No doubt, after the discovery of the Gibeonite maneuver, there were those in Israel who wanted to see heads roll. They had been snookered and did not like it. These feelings were widespread: "the whole assembly grumbled against the leaders" (9:18b). Given this ugly ferment, why was action not taken? The words of the leaders provide an answer: "we have given them [the Gibeonites] our oath by the Lord, the God of Israel, and we cannot touch them now" (9:19). Key to deciphering this passage is knowing what rests beneath the phrase אֲנַחְנוּ נִשְׁבַּעְנוּ (*'ănaḥnû nišba'nû*), "we have sworn."[18]

The act of "swearing" in our own culture is often synonymous with "cussing." While related at the core (the phrase "cuss," after all, is old slang for "curse"), the biblical speech-act of swearing — or oath uttering — is much heavier then the droppings of rude profanity.[19] Biblically, "to swear" is to add assurance to a stated intention by appealing to a witness.[20] Consider the oath, חַי־יהוה (*ḥay-YHWH*), or "as the Lord lives!" Appearing more than 40 times in the pages of the Old Testament, it frequently precedes a declaration of determination by appealing to the highest witness of all, e.g., "As the Lord lives, I will do such-and-such" (Judg 8:19; Ruth 3:13; 2 Sam 12:5, etc.). The appeal is a rhetorical one and should be considered in the

---

[18]It is also helpful for understanding other textual moments in the text of Joshua. Consider three. First, Yahweh "swears" to follow through with promises given to Israel's forefathers (1:6). Second, Rahab presses the scouts to "swear" by Yahweh to show her kindness (2:12), an oath that is modified (2:17-18), accepted (2:20), and honored (6:22). Finally, in his last words, Joshua instructs Israel not to "swear" by the names of Canaan's gods.

[19]Still, some modern speakers may coarsely, say, "By God . . ." and then offer some statement of intention. In form, these words edge in the direction of a biblical oath. In truth, such words are often uttered thoughtlessly. To reduce God to nothing or to refer to his presence glibly — as if it were nothing — would violate every point of the torah command, "Do not misuse the name of the Lord your God" (Exod 20:7).

Similarly, invoking damnation upon a thing in the name of God is a kind of curse or prayer, although few who use it do so in the context of earnest spiritual conversation!

[20]For a grammatical explanation of oath formulas, see Waltke and O'Connor, *Biblical Hebrew Syntax*, sec. 40.2.2.

context of persuasive speech. Interestingly, Yahweh may swear by himself, by his own name, or by his own holiness (e.g., Gen 22:16; Jer 51:14; Amos 4:2). Lesser witnesses include the life of another person or the life of the king (e.g., 1 Sam 1:26; 17:55; 2 Sam 14:19). Occasionally, the one who swears not only appeals to a witness as a guarantor, but invokes a curse upon himself should the promise be broken: "May the LORD do so to me and more, if . . ." (e.g. Ruth 1:17; 1 Sam 20:13).

Seizing upon this latter example of the self-curse, two points may be drawn; one veers in the direction of social analysis, and the other veers in the direction of theology. First, given the honor-shame code that seems so basic to the culture of Old Testament Israel, it is clear that the spoken word is not to be taken lightly.[21] Failure to follow-through with a stated intention damages one's status within the community and exposes inner weakness, cowardice, or foolishness. This kind of shame not only damages the name of the individual but his or her family as well. For most readers, understanding this honor-shame code is difficult and distant, as life in the modern West places little weight on the spoken word. In fact, its value is so diminished that recourse must be made to the written word in legal situations (contracts, deeds, signature cards, etc.). No so in ancient Israel. Once the leaders had given their word to the Gibeonites, it could not be taken back without incurring great shame.

Beyond this social observation is the theological perspective. Here, a return to Joshua 9:19 is needed. The leaders recall that their agreement with the Gibeonites has been offered in oath, "by Yahweh, God of Israel." To go back on their word would not just incur the shame of the community, it could possibly incur the wrath, or קֶצֶף (qeṣeph), of God (Josh 9:20).[22] The partners of this agreement have placed themselves under judgment should either fail to live up to their side of the bargain. It is worth noting that even here the holiness of God remains the operative or enforcing principle; to not follow through with a promise is to be placed outside a relationship of protection and grace. For the leaders of Israel, it is better to keep

---

[21]For an introduction to the honor-shame social code, see Pilch and Malina, *Handbook*, pp. 106-115.

[22]According to *TWOT* (s.v., קֶצֶף), this word is one of the strongest synonyms in the family of words related to anger.

this hasty oath than to accept the consequences of social shame and divine wrath.

One cannot contemplate this story from Joshua without thinking through the longer biblical view to the matter. Even in an honor-shame society, core values can be abused. The prophets condemn those who falsely swear by the "life of the LORD" (*ḥay-YHWH*) (e.g., Hos 4:15; Jer 5:2). Within Rabbinic Judaism, oath-making and oath-breaking were so widespread that efforts were made to curb the action. Rather than swearing by the name of God, roundabout tactics (the principle of circumlocution) were introduced; hence, one might instead swear in the name of *"heaven"* (the place of God) or by the *"throne* of God." Such hairsplitting overlooks the fact that Yahweh is still Lord over all places and pieces. It is likely in response to this kind of abuse that Jesus taught his followers to avoid the practice altogether. No appeals to an outside witness are necessary for the people of integrity. "Simply let your 'Yes' be 'Yes,' and your 'No,' 'No'" (Matt 5:33-37; cf. 23:16-22 and Jas 5:12). Spoken words do matter!

3. The Maneuver Discovered (9:16-21)

[16]Three days after they made the treaty with the Gibeonites, the Israelites heard that they were neighbors, living near them. [17]So the Israelites set out and on the third day came to their cities: Gibeon, Kephirah, Beeroth and Kiriath Jearim. [18]But the Israelites did not attack them, because the leaders of the assembly had sworn an oath to them by the LORD, the God of Israel.

The whole assembly grumbled against the leaders, [19]but all the leaders answered, "We have given them our oath by the LORD, the God of Israel, and we cannot touch them now. [20]This is what we will do to them: We will let them live, so that wrath will not fall on us for breaking the oath we swore to them." [21]They continued, "Let them live, but let them be woodcutters and water carriers for the entire community." So the leaders' promise to them was kept.

9:16-19 That this agreement was made in haste is demonstrated when the real story is discovered only a short time later (see Supplemental Study on "Three Days" in ch. 1, p. 72). The revelation is hardly a surprise to the reader but it is precisely what Israel feared: the visiting delegation represents a group that is "near," and indeed, "living in their midst" (cf. 9:7). Moreover, it is learned that the delegation not only represents a single village, Gibeon (cf. 9:3), but three other villages besides: **Kephirah,**[23] **Beeroth,**[24] **and Kiriath Jearim.**[25] If identified correctly, this settlement cluster rests in one of the most strategic crossroads in the region.[26] Far from distant, they are a federation fixed in the heart of the *Heartland.*

Although the means by which this revelation is received is not offered, the result is clear: grumbling![27] The decision of Israel's leaders creates a paralyzing dilemma that rocks the unity demonstrated at Shechem. On one hand, obedience to the *torah* of Yahweh and to the war of Yahweh demands that these shrewd locals be slain. On the other hand, an unbreakable oath has been sworn by Yahweh that this group should be preserved (cf. Num 30:2[3]; Ps 15:4). Undoubtedly, the debate swirled like glowing embers around every hearth, even as variations of it drift up to this very day. Must a promise be kept if wrongly obtained? Is there really a lesser of two evils? What is the value of a spoken agreement? When does a maneuver become

---

[23]Kephirah or Chephirah ("Lioness") has been identified with the ruins at Khirbet Kefire, about five miles southwest of el-Jib (Gibeon). See Rainey and Notley, *Sacred Bridge,* p. 126.

[24]Identification of Beeroth is uncertain. Sites less than a mile south of el-Jib (Gibeon) that have been proposed include el-Burj, Khirbet el-Biyar, and Nabi Samwel. Note also Josh 18:25 and 2 Sam 4:2. For a discussion of the problem of locating this site and other matters of Gibeonite/Hivite locations, see ibid.

[25]Kiriath Jearim is commonly associated with Deir el-Azar near Abu Ghosh. These ruins rest on an important ridge running downslope and due west of el-Jib (Gibeon).

[26]This settlement cluster spills over the western edge of a strategic area alternatively known as the Saddle of Benjamin (Baly, *Geography,* p. 177), Plateau of Benjamin (Finkelstein, *The Archaeology of the Israelite Settlement,* p. 56) or the Central Benjamin Plateau (James M. Monson, *The Land Between: A Regional Study Guide to the Land of the Bible.* [Jerusalem: Institute of Holy Land Studies, 1983], p. 115). Records demonstrate time and time again that control of this area is key to controlling approach to Jerusalem. See discussion in chapter 18 below.

[27]This is the same verbal root, לין (*lûn*), that is used of Israel's grumbling (or murmuring) in the wilderness. Just as an earlier generation grumbled at the leadership of Moses (Exod 15:24; Num 14:2; 16:41[H 17:6]), a later generation now grumbles against those who lead with Joshua.

a manipulation? What is the difference between a wise act and a cunning one?

9:20-21 Caught in a quandary of their own making and pressed by their own people, the leaders of Israel (notice how Joshua goes unnamed here) are forced to make a choice. In the end they choose to let the Gibeonites live. It must be noted that this compromise is not triggered by notions of mercy or compassion, but simply by a fear of divine reprisal. Worse may happen if Israel breaks their oath to Yahweh. Letting the Gibeonites live will satisfy one side of the dilemma, but how about the other? Can the *ḥāram*-order of Yahweh still be satisfied?

The answer is partially anticipated by the Gibeonites themselves.[28] When pressed by Israel as to how a covenant may be "cut" (v. 7), the Gibeonites replied, "we are your servants" (v. 8). Such words are the vocabulary of submission. Still, the role of servant is an all-too-familiar one for Israel; its explicit use here may be mulled over a moment longer. In a previous generation, Israel was abused in Egypt and forced to do the bidding of others (e.g., Exod 1:13; 14:12). Now arises an opportunity to force others to serve them. Would this be attractive? Would it be marked by hostility? Or, given the *ḥāram*-alternative, could it be justified as a merciful move? The leaders carefully weigh their options, and, in the end, repay cunning with cunning, **we will let them live . . . but let them be woodcutters and water carriers**. Menial and necessary jobs must be done on a daily basis. Why not let someone else do it? To announce that the Gibeonites will sweat on behalf of **the entire community** undoubtedly quashes the grumbling for the moment. Such a solution, however, leaves the reader feeling uneasy. Very uneasy.

4. Confrontation (9:22-27)

[22]Then Joshua summoned the Gibeonites and said, "Why did you deceive us by saying, 'We live a long way from you,' while actu-

---

[28]It is also anticipated in Deut 29:10-11: "All of you are standing today in the presence of the LORD your God—your leaders and chief men, your elders and officials, and all the other men of Israel, together with your children and your wives, and the *alien* [Heb. *gēr*] *who is in the midst* of your camps, from the one *who chops your wood* to the one *who carries your water*."

ally you live near us? ²³You are now under a curse: You will never cease to serve as woodcutters and water carriers for the house of my God."

²⁴They answered Joshua, "Your servants were clearly told how the LORD your God had commanded his servant Moses to give you the whole land and to wipe out all its inhabitants from before you. So we feared for our lives because of you, and that is why we did this. ²⁵We are now in your hands. Do to us whatever seems good and right to you."

²⁶So Joshua saved them from the Israelites, and they did not kill them. ²⁷That day he made the Gibeonites woodcutters and water carriers for the community and for the altar of the LORD at the place the LORD would choose. And that is what they are to this day.

9:22-23 Joshua reappears to inform the Gibeonites of their fate. **Why did you deceive us?** From Joshua's perspective, theirs is no clever maneuver. It is a deceptive manipulation. He begins with a probing of the conscience, a formulaic ploy that does not seek an answer as much as it seeks to inform all who listen that the Gibeonites have determined their own fate.[29] Joshua then moves to the sentencing: **You are now under a curse**. To be cursed is to be separated in some way from the community.[30] In the case of the

---

[29]Curse statements in the Old Testament regularly begin with a question about the past: "why have you done this?" or "because you have done this." Curse statements also contain some declaration about the present, bridging completed action with future action, hence, "and now. . . " (e.g., Gen 3:14; 4:10-11).

[30]Josef Scharbert observes that in the context of life in the ancient Near East, the purpose of a curse is "to prevent unjust harm; thus a person curses his enemy whom he cannot prosecute" (*TWOT*, s.v. אָרַר). As the Gibeonites have maneuvered themselves into a position of safety, there is a measure of truth here. Because of the Israelite oath, they cannot be touched.

However, this curse should not be read simply as personal retaliation. Joshua's words have a distinctly legal flavor (as seen in documents of public interest, ordinances, treaties, etc.), and may have even been some part of the covenant described in v. 15. As Scharbert goes on to point out, curses are well-known guarantors of agreement in legal contexts. They create space between the one who curses and the one who is cursed by signaling the end of a relationship and the expulsion from a community. On this point, see also Herbert Chanan Brichto, *The Problem of "Curse" in the Hebrew Bible* (Philadelphia: SBL, 1963), pp. 89-90, 101-102.

Gibeonites, their lives will indeed be spared but they will be separated from the community by means of a downgraded status, from vassal to underclass. Joshua communicates the conclusion that "they will certainly become slaves,"[31] hewing wood[32] and drawing water. This much is expected. What is unexpected — and jolting — is Joshua's final clause: the Gibeonites will work **for the house of my God.** What can this mean? Earlier, the leaders of Israel promised laborers "for the entire community" (9:21). Does Joshua's target, "the house of my God," intend the same thing, or does it represent a significant deviation from the opinion of the leaders?

It is possible that the phrase, "the house of my God," refers to a literal structure or institution, either the tabernacle (system) of Yahweh at Shiloh or the temple (system) of Yahweh in Jerusalem (1 Sam 3:3; Ps 42:4; Isa 2:3; Micah 4:2). The modifying phrase "the altar of Yahweh" lingers at the tail of the passage and points this direction (9:27). To get there from here, however, requires the passage of time and some compositional finagling; there is obviously no Yahweh temple in the Jerusalem of Joshua's day.

A more attractive route is the possibility of a double fulfillment. Those who would study and preserve the text at a later date may connect the Gibeonites to the Jerusalem temple, but in the immediate context it may be that the phrase "the *house* of my God" is code for "the *Israel* of God." The term בֵּית (*bêth*), "house" can communicate the sense of "household," "family," or "clan." Witness phrases such as "the house of Aaron" (e.g., Ps 115:12) or "the house of Judah" (e.g., 2 Sam 2:4). Closer to home is the conclusion of Rahab's story in the Jericho account. There, precious people and precious things are brought into "the treasury of the house of Yahweh" (6:19,24).

---

[31]Embedded in the idiom of לֹא־יִכָּרֵת (*lō' yikkārēth*) is the idea, "without fail," or "certainly," hence: "you will *most certainly* be a servant." See *HALOT*, s.v. *krth*.

[32]The work of "hewing wood" would have been laborious indeed. As iron implements would not have been readily available until some time after Joshua's day, possibly as late as the 10th century B.C., the felling of trees would have been accomplished using stone or bronze-headed axes. See Jane C. Waldbaum, "The First Archaeological Appearance of Iron and the Transition to the Iron Age," *The Coming of the Age of Iron*, ed. by Theodore A. Wertime and James D. Muhly (New Haven, CT: Yale University, 1980), pp. 86-87.

Three additional thoughts assist this double-fulfillment thinking. First, commuting the service of the Gibeonites from the community of Israel (at large) to the "house of God" specifically, in no way keeps them from serving "all Israel." Either way, this work is essential, public, and perhaps most appropriate for reasons offered below. Large amounts of water and wood would be used for the preparation and execution of sacrifice, not to mention the daily needs of those serving in this holy site. Second, assigning these locals to a particular task in a particular place (be it a tabernacle at Gilgal or a temple in Jerusalem) keeps the Gibeonites more focused than would distributing them throughout the entire community. The text suggests that early in the settlement period, Shiloh became a center for Yahweh worship. Later, of course, this center shifts to Jerusalem. The four Hivite villages are well-positioned to service either place. Third, and perhaps most provocatively, offering the Gibeonites to Yahweh may, in a sense, satisfy the *ḥāram* order. At the core of *ḥāram* is the notion of complete dedication, usually conceived in terms of death. Joshua's jolting clause takes the Gibeonites and *gives them over wholly to service* to Yahweh, not destroying them *per se*, but destroying their former identity and placing them in a new relationship with Israel and her God. It is a surprising move, but one that de-centers the definition of "Israel" yet one more time.[33]

9:24-25 The Gibeonites readily accept this sentencing, communicate what they know, and request fair treatment. Like Rahab, they display inside knowledge of Moses, Yahweh, and the *ḥāram* order. Interestingly, they even stitch together a reference to themselves as servants ("your servants were told") with a reference to Moses ("servant of Yahweh your God"). In their final plea, they choose words typically applied to those slated for destruction, "we are in your hands now" (e.g., 6:2; 8:1), but couple the usual words with a most unusual request, "Whatever is good and proper to do to us, do!" This declaration raises the question broached earlier. What is good and proper? What should be done to them? However the question is landed, one thing is certain: the Gibeonites will not blink!

---

[33]A later testimony should be kept in mind. In 2 Sam 21:2, the narrator's aside states: "Now the Gibeonites were *not a part of Israel* but were survivors of the Amorites." According to a testimony of life in David's day, the Gibeonites continued to live within Israel, but seemingly did not have the same rights as full citizens (cf. 2 Sam 21:4).

9:26-27 The narrator has the last word, another surprising one. Joshua does exactly as promised, and in the process, "snatches" the Gibeonites "out of the hands of Israel."[34] In this curious reversal, the text hints at a difference between the will of Joshua to save and the will of Israel to destroy. The Gibeonites become hewers of wood and drawers of water "for the community (of Israel) *and* for the altar of Yahweh" (note the final resolution that combines Joshua's clause with the conclusion of Israel's leaders). Like the stones of the Jordan (4:9), the name of Gilgal (5:9), the legacy of Rahab (6:25), and the rubble-cairn at The ʿAy, (8:28-29), the Gibeonite presence within Israel serves as a kind of memorial "to this day."

---

[34]The term translated in 9:26 as "saved" is נָצַל (nāṣal) in the hiphil. It is a common word used to refer to the rescue of cities, property, and people from death. It is even used of prey snatched from the mouths of wild animals (1 Sam 17:35).

JOSHUA 10

J. YAHWEH FIGHTS FOR ISRAEL (10:1-43)

Yahweh fights for Israel. This is the point that is eventually reached as the narrator tells a story of conflict, stops, backtracks, and covers the same ground again, this time peering in a new direction. As a result of several such trips . . . and vistas . . . the reader, like a passenger at the window, captures the thought. Such pedagogy is sand in the gears of the strict chronologist, historian, and text critic who prefer to travel roads only once, and even then, down the most direct path.

All of this suggests that what may appear convoluted to some is artful to others. This is true here.[1] Narratively, the connections between this chapter and the vision of Moses for the Canaanite conquest can hardly be viewed as accidental; aspects of the descriptions of Joshua 10 seem to be deliberately shaped in response to Deuteronomy 7. Common vocabulary, themes, and directions might even suggest that a subtitle for this campaign be drawn from the words of *torah* itself, וְנָתַן מַלְכֵיהֶם בְּיָדֶךָ (*wᵊnāthan malkêhem bᵊyādekā*), "And He will give their chiefs into your hand" (Deut 7:24a). This is *how* Yahweh fights for Israel. This is *how* the Israelite invasion of Canaan should appear. This is the *way* of miracles.

Structurally, the chapter falls into four parts that grow directly out of "The Gibeonite Maneuver" of chapter 9. In the first part (10:1-11), the chief of Jerusalem initiates a battle in the highlands that is eventually lost on the plain. The second part (10:12-15) retells one small aspect of that confrontation, emphasizing some celestial

---

[1]Could not the same be said of Josh 3:1–4:24? How many times does Israel cross the Jordan River? Once? Twice? Three times? This pattern of giving a brief, general picture and then following it up with a detailed story is a well-known tactic of biblical narrative. See comments at 3:17.

assistance along the way. The third part (10:16-27) continues this overlapping character: here the focus is on the capture and execution of enemy chiefs. Finally, the fourth part (10:28-43) follows the action into the territory of the defeated enemy and summarizes the Israelite raid of south Canaan.

1. Tricks and Stones (10:1-11)

[1]Now Adoni-Zedek king of Jerusalem heard that Joshua had taken Ai and totally destroyed[a] it, doing to Ai and its king as he had done to Jericho and its king, and that the people of Gibeon had made a treaty of peace with Israel and were living near them. [2]He and his people were very much alarmed at this, because Gibeon was an important city, like one of the royal cities; it was larger than Ai, and all its men were good fighters. [3]So Adoni-Zedek king of Jerusalem appealed to Hoham king of Hebron, Piram king of Jarmuth, Japhia king of Lachish and Debir king of Eglon. [4]"Come up and help me attack Gibeon," he said, "because it has made peace with Joshua and the Israelites."

[5]Then the five kings of the Amorites—the kings of Jerusalem, Hebron, Jarmuth, Lachish and Eglon—joined forces. They moved up with all their troops and took up positions against Gibeon and attacked it.

[6]The Gibeonites then sent word to Joshua in the camp at Gilgal: "Do not abandon your servants. Come up to us quickly and save us! Help us, because all the Amorite kings from the hill country have joined forces against us."

[7]So Joshua marched up from Gilgal with his entire army, including all the best fighting men. [8]The LORD said to Joshua, "Do not be afraid of them; I have given them into your hand. Not one of them will be able to withstand you."

[9]After an all-night march from Gilgal, Joshua took them by surprise. [10]The LORD threw them into confusion before Israel, who defeated them in a great victory at Gibeon. Israel pursued them along the road going up to Beth Horon and cut them down all the way to Azekah and Makkedah. [11]As they fled before Israel on the road down from Beth Horon to Azekah, the LORD hurled large hail-

stones down on them from the sky, and more of them died from the hailstones than were killed by the swords of the Israelites.

^a*1* **The Hebrew term refers to the irrevocable giving over of things or persons to the LORD, often by totally destroying them; also in verses 28, 35, 37, 39 and 40.**

10:1-2 The news that initiated action in the previous chapter (9:1) continues to provoke. This time, it is **Adoni-Zedek**,[2] chief of Jerusalem,[3] who springs to action. He not only hears what Israel has done to The *'Ay* and to Jericho, but specifically what happened to their chiefs; it is unnerving news for any sovereign! To make matters worse, he also hears that his northern neighbors, the Gibeonites, have **made a treaty of peace** with Israel, and have gone over "into the midst" of them.[4] This last statement, suggesting an assimilation

---

[2] אֲדֹנִי־צֶדֶק (*ʾĂdōnî-ṣedeq*) means literally, "My lord is righteous" or "My lord is *ṣedeq*," (possibly alluding to a divine name). The name is reminiscent of another chief from the same place named מַלְכִּי־צֶדֶק (*Malkî-ṣedeq* or Melchizedek), "My chief is righteous" (see Gen 14:18). The name is also similar to אֲדֹנִי־בֶזֶק (*ʾĂdōnî-bezeq*) of Judg 1:5-6. Confusion concerning this character of Judges 1 and the character of Joshua 10 arises because the LXX reads the latter as *Adonibezek*. It is unlikely that these two texts refer to the same person.

[3] This is the first explicit mention of Jerusalem by name in the Old Testament. Jerusalem is located on the crest of the Judean Ridge, approximately five miles southeast of el-Jib (Gibeon). Any change of status with respect to Gibeon would be immediately felt in Jerusalem.

Undoubtedly, the site's occupation goes back at least to the 19th century B.C. where the name appears in Egyptian execration texts. Literary appearances in the Amarna Letters show its importance in LBA Canaan. For these literary mentions, see Rainey and Notley, *Sacred Bridge*, pp. 52, 58, 85-86. Archaeological remains from Joshua's time (Area G, Level 16), however, are skimpy and debated. See, for example, Amihai Mazar, "Jerusalem and Its Vicinity in Iron Age I," pp. 72-73.

[4] The phrase literally reads, וַיִּהְיוּ בְּקִרְבָּם (*wayyihyû bᵉqirbām*), "they were in their midst." The interpretive question revolves around the antecedents of the pronouns "they" and "their." It is possible that he hears that Israel ("they") is/are in their ("the Canaanites") midst? The nearness of this threat could prompt his fear. See Supplemental Study on Ethnicity below.

However, the immediate context suggests that what he hears is that "they" (the Gibeonites) are in "their" (Israel's) midst, a frightening thought for Adoni-zedek due to their combined power. Significantly, this phrase comes on the heels of the statement that Israel has made peace (hiphil of *šlm*) with Gibeon. It suggests that this peace-making agreement resulted in a total assimilation; Israel and Gibeon are now one. The LXX supports this view

of these Hivites into Israel, contributes yet another piece to the larger discussion of Israel's identity. Such an alliance generates "great fear" or perhaps an "icy respect"[5] as Gibeon is a substantial place, a significant center,[6] like a city that has a chief.[7] It is populated with **good fighters**, and controls all northern approaches to Adoni-zedek's own chiefdom. That Israel could almost effortlessly drive a wedge right through the center of the *Heartland* — dividing north from south — does not bode well for his personal future. Anxiety runs high.

SUPPLEMENTAL STUDY

ETHNICITY

Seven specific people groups are identified as occupants of the *Heartland* in Joshua 3:10: Canaanites, Hittites, Hivites, Perizzites, Girgashites, Amorites, and Jebusites. This exact roster is detailed elsewhere (cf. Deut 7:1), while still other variations of this list exist (e.g., Gen 15:18-21). The interaction between these people groups and the tribes of Israel create tension and heartbreak in some of the best-known stories of the Old Testament.

Beyond this world of text, the task of identifying these groups is difficult. Part of that difficulty stems from the fact that stylistic diversity, an important concept in the materialist world of the archaeologist, is not clearly visible on the ground. Tool sets, pottery types,

---

emphasizing Adoni-zedek's perspective that the Gibeonites are "deserters" who now "reside in" Israel.

[5]Habit suggests "great fear" to be the reading. However, the previous occurrence of this verb in the text describes the way in which Israel regarded Joshua. In 4:14, the people "revere" ("fear"?) Joshua as they had previously "revered" ("feared"?) Moses. Since this fear of 10:2 is modified by מְאֹד (*mᵊ'ōd*), an adverb of magnitude, the idiom "icy respect" is generated. This is not the noun for "terror" (אֵימָה, *'êmāh*) appearing in 2:9.

[6]Gibeon is called an עִיר גְּדוֹלָה (*'îr gᵊdôlāh*), a "great city." This same phrase is used in later texts to describe capital cities like Jerusalem (Jer 22:8) or Nineveh (Jonah 1:2 and 3:2).

[7]There is no chief associated with Gibeon in the text. In 9:3, the ruse is concocted by "the people." Later in 9:11, reference is made to their leaders as "elders." Evidently, from Adoni-zedek's perspective, Gibeon is powerful and populated enough to have a chief. For whatever reason, however, they do not have one.

house design, and artistic representation are helpful in identifying cultural boundaries between groups. Such expressions, when identified in patterns and correlated with written records, can be used to color maps with lines and circles. However, as one moves from one end of Canaan to the other in the seam between the Bronze and Iron Ages (ca. 1200 B.C.), these expressions are remarkably uniform. To be sure, regional variations occur, but one wonders if they are more a product of locale (highlands versus lowlands) or lifeways issues (urban versus rural), and less an issue of ethnicity. This similarity raises many important questions of interest to the reader of Joshua. How does one distinguish a "Hivite" from a "Hittite" on the street? A "Girgashite" from a "Jebusite" in the field? A "Canaanite" from an "Israelite" in a battle? Can you tell them apart by the color of their skin? The style of their clothing? The cut of their hair? What aspects of these cultures are indigenous? What are imported? What are mixed?

If only there was a soundtrack from the ancient world! One wonders how much of the difference between these groups might be heard in their language. Would local accents flavor or hinder conversation? It is worth a moment's thought, but ultimately, the dialogue of the biblical text is both word-full and soundless at the same time. Therefore, the Canaanite Rahab chats amiably with the Israelite scouts. The delegation from Hivite Gibeon converses with the men of Israel. The chief of Hazor sends communications to a coalition of northern Canaanite leaders. No linguistic barriers seem to isolate these groups from one another. Could it really be any other way? The narrator will hardly wait for stuttering or slurring!

If it is a challenge to define ethnicity even within contemporary society, how much more difficult grows the task when dealing with a distant past that is selectively preserved? The outlook for landing on solid answers is bleak. Most contemporary archaeologists working in the *Heartland* are pessimistic about separating such folk on the basis of material culture alone.[8]

Sociology offers little assistance. Here the argument swirls between two poles.[9] One pole suggests that ethnicity is determined

---

[8]A recent assessment of the data may be found in Killebrew, *Archaeology of Ethnicity*.

[9]These poles are labeled "primordial" or "circumstantial" by Killebrew (ibid., p. 8).

genetically, that is, a person belongs to a group because his/her ancestors belonged to that same group. Their history is remembered through stories and perpetuated by maintaining strong "us" and "them" boundaries. The other pole suggests that ethnicity is ultimately an expression of "self-interest," and is therefore much more fluid. Here, the boundary between "us" and "them" is not as much genetic as it is a matter of choice. Those who argue this point suggest that true ethnicity flexes in response to economic and political realities. Undoubtedly, the truth lies somewhere between. Both genetics and choice play a part.

The book of Joshua is keenly interested in the gnawing question of Israelite definition. While genetics is typically the argument of default, in our own time as well as the distant past, Joshua challenges this hasty conclusion. Recognizing this "Israel of faith" pushes the reader to consider that the distinctiveness of Israel runs beyond questions of ethnicity or historical memory. Its distinctive character rests in a single-minded devotion to Yahweh and in the choice of ethical options consistent with his character. The former finds expression in passages (such as 2:11; 3:13; 4:24; or 22:22) where Yahweh is described as beyond compare. The latter finds expression in passages (such as 1:8; 7:11-13; 8:34; or 23:11-13) where faithful obedience is placed squarely upon the shoulders of those who choose Him. Identifying such "features of ethnicity" in the archaeological record will always be an impossible task. However, it may very well be the point of reading the text.

10:3-4 The coalition of opposition hinted at previously (9:2), comes together, at least in part. Adoni-zedek summons important allies from the south; the names of their cities are old, perhaps already legendary. These are **Hoham** chief of **Hebron**,[10] **Piram** chief of **Jarmuth**,[11] **Japhia** chief of **Lachish**,[12] and **Debir** chief of **Eglon**.[13] The

---

[10]Biblical Hebron is located at Jebel Rumeideh, approximately nineteen miles south-southeast of Jerusalem. It is attested historically and archaeologically in the LBA.

The name Hoham is not known outside of this passage. However, the LXX renders the name as *Ailam* or *Elam*. In this form, it is a familiar regional name from the southeastern Mesopotamian landscape.

[11]Jarmuth is identified with Khirbet el-Yarmuk and is located in the "lowlands" (שְׁפֵלָה, *šᵉphēlāh*) approximately sixteen miles southwest of Jerusalem.

appeal of Adoni-zedek is expected, the target of that appeal, however, is not. **Help me attack Gibeon**. One would expect Adoni-zedek to take aim at Joshua and the Israelite camp; after all, they are the *casus belli*. It is also difficult to imagine why Adoni-zedek would choose to confront Gibeon directly, given his previous assessment that it is sizable and well-manned. Nonetheless, the smell of sour grapes is in the air as Adoni-zedek snorts and spews. The point is important enough to be repeated: Gibeon has allied itself with Israel.

10:5 The coalition of opposition, collectively referred to as **Amorites,** musters, goes up, establishes their positions in the plain about Gibeon, and besieges the city (see Supplemental Study on Amorites, ch. 5, p. 130). The language used to describe troop movements, the number of chiefs present, and the hometowns they represent, all suggest that this is a coordinated show of force the likes of which have yet to be seen.

10:6 Choked by this force, the Gibeonites appeal to their new protectors for help. Word is sent to the Gilgal camp, **Do not abandon**, or more literally, "Do not relax your hand"[14] with respect to **your servants**. Given that the Gibeonite alliance was born in deception and is seemingly the best that Israel could whittle out of an awkward situation, doing nothing is one course of action for Joshua to consider. In fact, by *not* responding to the Gibeonite cry, the failure of Israel to destroy these people might even be easily emended; the coalition under the leadership of Adoni-zedek could do the destroy-

---

A LBA settlement has been partially excavated there. See *NEAEHL*, s.v. "Jarmuth, Tel." Nothing is known of its king, Piram, apart from this text.

[12]Tell ed-Duweir is commonly identified with biblical Lachish. It is also located in the foothills (*šᵊphēlāh*), approximately twenty-five miles southwest of Jerusalem and downslope from Hebron. This large settlement is well known in the Bronze Age and was repeatedly destroyed by fire: c. 1500 B.C., c. 1200 B.C., and c. 1150–1130 B.C. See discussion by David Merling Sr., *The Book of Joshua: Its Theme and Role in Archaeological Discussions*, Andrews University Doctoral Dissertaion Series 23 (Berrien Springs, MI: Andrews University, 1997), pp. 128-130.

[13]The location of Eglon is disputed. It appears here as well as the list of foothill (*šᵊphēlāh*) settlements in 15:39. Two possibilities include Tell 'Aitun and Tell el-Hesi. See discussion by Merling, *Joshua*, pp. 130-134.

Debir is well attested as a place name, but is unusual as a personal name.

[14]The root *rph* in the hiphil communicates the idea of a hand gone limp, a thing turned loose, a person left in the lurch. See BDB, s.v. רפה.

ing for them. It is possible that this thought is lurking behind the Hivite fear as the alarm is voiced three times over: "Help us! Come quick! Save us!" While not exactly the cry of the damsel in distress, it is shrill enough to suggest that this community of "good fighters," as described in verse 2, may not be prepared to live up to its billing. In fact, one even senses a bit of expansion in the Gibeonite appeal as the *five* chiefs of verse 3 become *all* the Amorite chiefs in verse 6. Some backpedaling is then attempted: it is not quite all the Amorites, but *all* the Amorite chiefs *of the hill country*. Truth-telling does not appear to be a part of the Gibeonite arsenal.

10:7-8 Joshua responds with warriors; Yahweh responds with familiar encouragement: **Do not be afraid . . . I have given them into your hand** (cf. 6:2; 8:1), **Not one of them will be able to withstand you.**[15] This encouragement is particularly significant on this occasion, as the coalition under Adoni-zedek, entrenched on the ridge above them, likely represents the finest forces of the region. They have the advantage of the high ground, familiar terrain, local support, technological superiority, and troop strength.

10:9-11 No plan of attack is announced in advance by the narrator, only a brief summary of the action. Joshua and his men make an all-night climb into the highlands and catch the coalition suddenly: unguarded, and apparently, unorganized.[16] This is Yahweh's doing, as is what follows.[17] Suddenly faced by Israel, the enemy is agitated,

---

[15]This is an echo of Deut 7:24, a Mosaic description of the conquest of Canaan: לֹא־יִתְיַצֵּב אִישׁ בְּפָנֶיךָ (*lō' yithyaṣṣēb 'îš bᵉphānêkā*), "a man will not take a stand before you." The difference between these two passages rests in a verbal choice. The *torah* passage uses the hithpael of יצב (*yṣb*), "to stand" or, in military terms, "to hold ground." The Josh 10:8 passage uses the much more common and generic form, עמד ('*md*), "to stand." It is difficult to sense the nuance between these word choices; although the LXX manages by rendering the former in the sense of "nonresistance" (from ἀνθίστημι, *anthistēmi*), and the latter in the sense of "nonduration" (from ὑπολείπω, *hypoleipō*).

[16]For more on the all-night climb, see Supplemental Study on "Three Days" in ch. 1, p. 72.

[17]In v. 10, Yahweh initiates the panic (qal imperfect, 3ms of המם). The root of this word in Hebrew, Hebrew cognates, and Egyptian parallels suggests the making of disturbing or possibly roaring noises. Such sounds either produce confusion — and even insanity — or are the result of it. See *TDOT*, s.v., המם. If such a roar is produced by Yahweh, it is truly a "holy terror"! Two other appearances of *hmm* are worth noting for the sake of the pres-

put to panic, or confused. In the mêlée that follows, a deadly blow[18] is inflicted. Words and phrases such as "Yahweh gives them over" or they are "put to panic" further connect the description here to Deuteronomy 7:22-24, a *torah* vision of the Canaanite conquest. This linkage should not be missed; even in the act of battle, Joshua interprets Moses! Those who escape the killing fields flee westward down the Beth Horon Ridge Route,[19] with Israel in hot pursuit. Men continue to fall as far as **Azekah**[20] **and Makkedah**,[21] sites distant from Gibeon. While odd sounding (and, incidentally, invisible in the NIV), the subject of the series of verbs throughout verses 10 and 11 in the Hebrew text is Yahweh. It is Yahweh the warrior who not just

---

ent text. In Exod 14:24 the same root describes Yahweh's work in confusing the Egyptian army as they pursue Israel through the sea. Here, part of that "confusing" work somehow involves the motion of the chariots: their wheels grow sluggish! The second appearance is in Deut 7:23, yet another link between this and the current chapter.

[18]The forces of Adoni-zedek suffer a great "defeat" or מַכָּה (*makkāh*). This word communicates the image of one person slugging another with a fist. When used in the context of a military engagement, especially used as a cognate accusative with form of the verb *nkh* (as is the case here), it emphasizes an action resembling a roundhouse punch!

[19]The Beth-horon Ridge Route follows a prominent ridge that drops westward from the Saddle of Benjamin to the Valley of Aijalon. It is one of a few, and therefore strategic, east-west routes that links the top of the Central Ridge above to the Coastal Plain below. The path may be followed on a Bible atlas by moving west from Gibeon, through Upper and Lower Beth-horon, Aijalon, and ending where the plain opens at Gezer. This route is later fortified by Solomon (1 Kgs 9:17). See the map in Rainey and Notley, *Sacred Bridge*, p. 126.

[20]Biblical Azekah is associated with Tell Zakariyeh, a distant journey of some twenty-five miles from *el-Jib* (Gibeon). The site dominates a western pass leading from the highlands to the coastal plain (Valley of Elah or Wadi es-Samt). No fighting is described here; it is simply a geographical "high watermark" for the battle.

[21]The identity of Makkedah is debated. The most likely candidate is Khirbet el-Qom, six miles east of Lachish. This hilltop site is currently occupied by an Arab village. Limited excavations were conducted within the village and downslope from it. No LBA remains from the time of Joshua were encountered, but ostraca (potsherds with writing on them) from the 4th century B.C. confirm the name Makkedah at this point in time (Rainey and Notley, *Sacred Bridge*, p. 127). Other proposals include Khirbet el-Heishum, Khirbet Beit Maqdûm, el-Mughar, and Tell Bornat. For more on this discussion, see Merling, *Joshua*, pp. 123-125.

initiates a panic, but pursues, smites, and hurls. As presented, Israel may give legs to the battle, but it is their God who does the real work that brings about a victory.

This observation is detailed in verse 11. After the Amorites are put to flight, Yahweh hurls great stones upon them from the sky." These are described as "stones of hail" (בָּרָד, *bārād*).[22] That this aerial attack is terrifically deadly is suggested by the phrase, **more of them died from the hailstones than were killed by the swords**. Hail as a miraculous act of Yahweh's judgment is known elsewhere.[23] Such natural phenomena are not outside the realm of possibility; hailstones up to two inches in diameter have been known to fall in spring storms in Palestine.[24] What may be more interesting — because it strikes so unexpectedly — is the observation that this action also continues the integration of Joshua 10 with Deuteronomy 7. In *torah*, the destruction of the names of the Canaanite chiefs comes "from under the heavens" or "sky" (מִתַּחַת הַשָּׁמָיִם, *mittaḥath haššāmāyim*) (Deut 7:24). Here, the hailstones are flung by Yahweh "from the heavens" or "sky" מִן־הַשָּׁמַיִם (*min-haššāmāyim*). Again, Yahweh fights for Israel. Amazing enough by itself, this claim will not exhaust the divine assistance on this day.

2. East o' the Sun and West o' the Moon (10:12-15)

[12]**On the day the LORD gave the Amorites over to Israel, Joshua said to the LORD in the presence of Israel:**

"O sun, stand still over Gibeon,
   O moon, over the Valley of Aijalon."
[13]**So the sun stood still,**

---

[22]That the Heb. בָּרָד (*bārād*) refers to something "cold" and not, for example flaming-hot meteorites, is conclusively demonstrated by cognates in Arabic and elsewhere. See BDB, s.v. ברד.

[23]See Exod 9:18; Ps 105:32; or Rev 8:7 for examples. One more is found in Isaiah 28 in the context of a woe delivered against Ephraim. The prophet musters an image of the Gibeonite story in order to warn Israel of the possibility that they will share the same fate as the Canaanites at "Buster Mountain" (28:17). On two occasions Isaiah raises the image of destructive hailstones (28:2,17).

[24]R.B.Y. Scott, "Meteorological Phenomena and Terminology in the Old Testament," *ZAW* 64 (1952): 19-20.

> and the moon stopped,
>   till the nation avenged itself on[a] its enemies,
>
> as it is written in the Book of Jashar.
>   The sun stopped in the middle of the sky and delayed going down about a full day. [14]There has never been a day like it before or since, a day when the LORD listened to a man. Surely the LORD was fighting for Israel!
>   [15]Then Joshua returned with all Israel to the camp at Gilgal.

[a]*13 Or nation triumphed over*

10:12 The description of the miracle of the hailstones is followed by the description of another supernatural intervention. In the telling, the narrator first reinforces Yahweh's role as victor: He gives **the Amorites over to Israel**. Then, the process by which this is accomplished is described and celebrated, beginning with the prayer of Joshua. This prayer is offered **in the presence of Israel**, thereby underlining eyewitnesses' testimony, an important element given the nature of the request: **O sun,** be stationed over Gibeon, **O moon,** (be stationed) over the Valley of Aijalon.[25] That this is a prayer directed to Yahweh and not to the sun or to the moon is obvious by the lead-in, Joshua says **to the LORD**.[26] But what exactly is his odd request of Yahweh, and how does it relate to this battle narrative? Many interpreters have wrestled over the meaning of this text. A popular interpretation views Joshua's prayer as a call for the sun and moon to be arrested of *motion*, i.e., that they temporarily freeze in their orbits (or alternatively, that the earth stop spinning!). Joshua's prayer at the end of the day then becomes a request for more *time* so that the enemy will not escape under cover of darkness. Additional evidence from the end of verse 13 seems to support this "longest day" view.[27] A second interpretation views Joshua's prayer

---

[25]Aijalon or Yalu is located six miles east of Gezer. The settlement carries the same name as the drainage system it occupies. For a linguistic discussion of mentions, see Elitzur, *Ancient Place Names,* pp. 170-171.

[26]Compare with Hab 3:11 where similar wording demonstrates that creator and creation are not to be confused. The structure of the phrase does present Joshua offering direct address to the sun and moon, but this is easily explained as poetic use, sometimes referred to as apostrophizing.

[27]Or does it? The text reads the "sun was positioned [יַעֲמֹד, *ya'ămōd*] in the middle of the sky, and it did not hurry to set like a regular [תָּמִים, *tāmîm*]

as a request that the sun and moon be arrested, not of motion, but of *action*. Seen in this way, the request is that these celestial bodies stop *shining* in some manner. This view — nearly the opposite of the first — views Joshua's words as an appeal for less light, not more. Less light, in the form of a solar eclipse will add to the panic of the enemy as they beat their hasty retreat. Alternatively, a request for less light ("ease up on the 'shine!'") might be understood as a prayer for less heat. Joshua and company, exhausted from their night march, might be overcome by a relentless afternoon sun. A reprieve from these rays will give them the energy they need to complete the rout. Key to each of these views is the imperative use of דמם (*dmm*) in verse 13, a term translated in the NIV as **stand still**.[28]

From the perspective of language and logic, however, none of these interpretations are wholly satisfactory. From the vantage point of the Beth Horon Ridge Route, a sun in the eastern sky over Gibeon suggests that Joshua's prayer arises in the morning. This could hardly be a request for more time. The pursuit only begins at sunrise; Joshua could not yet know how much time would be needed. Similarly, a request for less light or heat would offer equal, if not more, advantage to the pursued over the pursuer. They hope to be hidden. The solar eclipse theory is interesting, but impossible when the sun and moon are in opposite corners of the sky. If the text is regarded seriously, the sun and moon are perfectly balanced[29]: they

---

day" (v. 13). As Walton proposes, "When the full moon comes on the 14th, and the month has the proper number of days, then each of the days of the month is a 'full-length' day. This is what constitutes a good omen. In this text, the sun and moon do not act as they would on a 'full length' day" See John H. Walton, "Joshua 10:12-15 and Mesopotamian Celestial Omen Texts," in *Faith, Tradition and History: Old Testament Historiography in Its Near Eastern Context*, ed. by A.R. Millard, James K. Hoffmeier, and David W. Baker (Winona Lake, IN: Eisenbrauns, 1994), p. 189.

[28]The verbal root, *dmm*, often finds poetic use. Perhaps the most famous of these is in Ps 37:7, "*Be still* before the LORD and wait quietly for Him." Other similar uses are found in Lev 10:3; Lam 2:10; and in Ezek 24:17. For a discussion of this root, see *TWOT*, s.v. דמם.

[29]According to Walton, "Joshua 10:12-15 and Mesopotamian Celestial Omen Texts," p. 188, the sun and moon would occupy such a position on the 14th day of the month. If such a position were observed at any other moment in time, it would be interpreted as unnatural, and therefore a calamitous sign.

are like Gibeon and the Valley of Aijalon, on *opposite* horizons, aligned on an east-west axis. Given these difficulties, how else can this odd request by Joshua be read?

A study of second millennium omen texts by John Walton has demonstrated not only the widespread interest in astrological signs in the Ancient Near East, but the fact that these observations affected choices made in life, including military actions.[30] Most interesting is the discovery of language that finds parallel in the present text.[31] Walton raises the possibility that Joshua's words of 10:12 are a request for a particular alignment (or "standing") of sun and moon at dawn. The Canaanite leaders, acutely aware of celestial movements, would readily note this alignment. Read in this way, Joshua's request, therefore, is not for more time or less light, but that the Canaanite's own tool of divination be turned against them. When this interpretation is read back into the text resumptively (as was noted in the case of Israel's crossing and recrossing the Jordan in Joshua 3 and 4), the prayer, possibly offered in the grind of Israel's all-night climb, explains how the battle might be broken ("the LORD threw them into confusion," [v. 10]) with the rays of the dawn.

10:13 Yahweh answers Joshua's prayer. In language that matches the request, the sun and moon are observed to be standing in positions considered unnatural for that particular day. This sudden and awful realization — "by the dawn's early light" — that all "heaven" is against them, corresponds with the moment of the Israelite charge as well as the hail to come.[32] The coalition's advantage of high ground, familiar terrain, local support, technological superiority,

---

[30]Walton, "Joshua 10:12-15 and Mesopotamian Celestial Omen Texts," pp. 181-190. Walton's conclusions are similar to those drawn by other scholars including John Holliday, "Day(s) the Moon Stood Still," *JBL* 87 (1968): 166-178.

[31]Consider an example drawn from a description of Mars passing the constellation of Cancer: "In the midst it did not stand, it did not wait, and it did not rest, it went forth hurriedly" (Walton, "Joshua 10:12-15 and Mesopotamian Celestial Omen Texts," p. 186).

[32]Consider another Mesopotamian omen text: "When the Moon and Sun are seen with one another out of their expected time, a strong enemy will overcome the land; the king of Akkad will accomplish the defeat of his foe" (Holliday, "Day[s] the Moon Stood Still," p. 174).

and troop strength is shattered in a moment. Just as the Canaanites arise, they are knocked back down.[33]

Readers have the luxury of slowing down to contemplate the portents in the sky (hail, sun, or moon), but the narrator presents an altogether different reason for pause. The true marvel arises when an audacious prayer is coupled with a positive answer: "Yahweh *listens*" or possibly even "*obeys* the voice of a man."[34] As on the banks of the Jordan River, Yahweh exalts "Joshua in the sight of all Israel" (4:14). Recalling the corroboratory claim that accompanied Joshua's prayer ("in the presence of Israel," 10:12), it is not surprising that such an event would be recorded elsewhere as well, in this case, a long-lost composition called, "The book of the Righteous [One]."[35] Even without this particular testimony, lost to time, an inference may be drawn: Joshua is functioning as a new Moses. He speaks directly with God and God with him. It is a legitimate, unmediated partnership. As the text itself is a mediated presentation, it is difficult to plow this row in a straight line, but one cannot help but wonder if the relationship between Yahweh and Joshua might actually be plotted? More narrative transparency on the part of Joshua would be helpful. Still, even without this assistance, it is clear that there will not be any more mediating "captains" once Joshua passes his own "burning bush" experience near Jericho (5:13-15). He has come into his own.

10:15 Joshua and the Israelites return to Gilgal. It is presumed that this is the site of the original camp. Sequentially, the action clos-

---

[33]This reading is suggested as one way to deal with the odd use of יָקֹם (*yiqqōm*) here. See *TDOT*, s.v. נָקַם.

[34]In this, Joshua is like Moses who enjoyed an intimate relationship with God (Num 12:8).

[35]To suggest that Jashar is a proper name, "The book of Jashar," overlooks the presence of the definite article preceding the term יָשָׁר (*yāšār*, "righteous" or "righteousness"). The term הַיָּשָׁר (*hayyāšār*, "The righteous [one] . . .") may be the opening phrase of the book, as is the literary convention (e.g., אֵלֶּה הַדְּבָרִים, '*elleh hadd^ebārîm*, "These are the words . . ." is the Hebrew name of the book commonly known as Deuteronomy). Many questions about the nature of this lost book, its contents, and location may be asked but few answers are found. It cannot even be determined where in the text of Joshua the quote from this book precisely begins and ends. Obviously, no quotation marks are offered in the original text. What is certain is that the book is also mentioned in 2 Sam 1:18 and connected to a lament of David. No book by this name survives today.

COLLEGE PRESS NIV COMMENTARY

es the revealed detail of the day and corresponds to the closing offered in 10:43. Narratively, however, the day is still far from over. A rewind and play will bring out still more important angles.

3. On Chiefs and Caves (10:16-27)

[16]Now the five kings had fled and hidden in the cave at Makkedah. [17]When Joshua was told that the five kings had been found hiding in the cave at Makkedah, [18]he said, "Roll large rocks up to the mouth of the cave, and post some men there to guard it. [19]But don't stop! Pursue your enemies, attack them from the rear and don't let them reach their cities, for the LORD your God has given them into your hand."

[20]So Joshua and the Israelites destroyed them completely— almost to a man—but the few who were left reached their fortified cities. [21]The whole army then returned safely to Joshua in the camp at Makkedah, and no one uttered a word against the Israelites.

[22]Joshua said, "Open the mouth of the cave and bring those five kings out to me." [23]So they brought the five kings out of the cave— the kings of Jerusalem, Hebron, Jarmuth, Lachish and Eglon. [24]When they had brought these kings to Joshua, he summoned all the men of Israel and said to the army commanders who had come with him, "Come here and put your feet on the necks of these kings." So they came forward and placed their feet on their necks.

[25]Joshua said to them, "Do not be afraid; do not be discouraged. Be strong and courageous. This is what the LORD will do to all the enemies you are going to fight." [26]Then Joshua struck and killed the kings and hung them on five trees, and they were left hanging on the trees until evening.

[27]At sunset Joshua gave the order and they took them down from the trees and threw them into the cave where they had been hiding. At the mouth of the cave they placed large rocks, which are there to this day.

10:16-19 The third part of this chapter continues to detail events of this remarkable battle. Emphasis in the telling is not given to personal exploits, but to the obedience of Israel and the Moseslike encouragement of Joshua.

With the skirmishers put to flight, focus shifts to the enemy leaders. The five chiefs previously mentioned as part of the coalition of opposition (10:5), flee, and hide **in the cave at Makkedah**.[36] When apprised of their discovery, Joshua orders his men to seal the cave with stones, set a watch, and continue pursuing all stragglers. In this telling, wordplay abounds. The command to roll "large stones" (אֲבָנִים גְּדֹלֹת, 'ăbānîm gᵉdôlôth) here curiously parallels 10:11, where it was Yahweh who "hurled large stones" ('ăbānîm gᵉdôlôth). Similarly, Joshua orders the men not to "stand" (עָמַד, 'āmad) (10:19), explicitly contrasting the order given the sun and moon to do just that (10:13). The enemy is to be prevented from "entering" (לָבוֹא, lābô') their cities, just as the sun was to be prevented literally from "entering" (lābô'), or, in English, "setting." Finally, the enemies of Israel are destroyed "completely" (תָּמָם, tummām), echoing the complete (תָּמִים, tāmîm) day of 10:13. Such creativity argues for the continuity of the text. It may also suggest that the acts of Israel are an echo of the acts of Yahweh.

Caves are common in this limestone land and are often used as temporary dwellings, stables, latrines, tombs, and hiding places. For the five defeated chiefs, exhausted from their panicked flight, the cave at Makkedah may have appeared as an ideal stop. It is cool, offers respite from the light of this abnormal day, and, hopefully, escape from the eyes of the pursuing Israelites. For the reader, the attempt of the chiefs to "go underground" brings the stolen items of Achan to mind (7:21). As in Achan's story, that which is believed to be a safe hiding place becomes a trap, and eventually, a tomb.

10:20 A summary statement demonstrates how the Israelites were obedient to Joshua's command. The language here cannot be structured any more emphatically: Israel delivers a "show-stopping,"[37] "uppercut,"[38] "knock-out punch."[39] Those who do manage to escape

---

[36]See note on the location of Makkedah at 10:10.

[37]The modifying phrase is more literally translated, "unto their complete end," or עַד־תֻּמָּם ('ad-tummām). On the root tmm, it is said that the "situation entirely fulfills the speaker's expectations" (TDOT, s.v. תָּמַם). The coalition of opposition is permanently broken.

[38]Further modification here is hardly necessary, but the narrator is unrelenting. The knockout blow is "a very big (one)," גְּדוֹלָה־מְאֹד (gᵉdôlāh mᵉ'ōd).

[39]In Hebrew, לְהַכּוֹתָם מַכָּה (lᵉhakkôthām makkāh). The infinitive construct and the noun are built from the same root, nkh.

with their lives flee to fortified cities. This last clause may appear to stand in contrast with the summary statement; however, it is valuable for two reasons. First, it offers a realistic glimpse of the mopping-up operation. Survivors are inevitable in such an elongated battle. By this admission, hyperbole is minimized.[40] Second, it helps explain the presence of defenders at the fortified cities in 10:29-42.

10:21-27 With the pursuit completed, the Israelite fighters return to Joshua at Makkedah, now revealed to be an Israelite encampment. They return **safely**, "in peace, free of (enemy) threats."[41] In this *tongue-free* environment (no murmuring now!), Joshua calls for the *mouth* of the cave at Makkedah to be opened and the trapped chiefs brought forth. There before the assembly, the leaders of Israel place their feet upon the necks of the celebrity captives. This act is not some kind of macho move, but is a ceremony of public humiliation known in the ancient world, celebrated in word and image.[42]

Joshua uses this moment as an occasion to offer encouragement from his own mouth. He pulls forward a familiar phrase, **Be strong and courageous** (Deut 31:7; Josh 1:6,7,9,18) and emphasizes the superiority of Yahweh over all human threats. Following this, he kills the five chiefs and hangs each one on a tree in display. This display lasts until the evening — here meaningfully worded as "the entering of the sun." At this time, the bodies are taken down from the trees and *hurled* (cf. 10:11) back into their place of hiding.[43] The cave is again sealed with "large stones" (cf. 10:11), which **are there to this**

---

[40]When this statement of victory is compared with other statements drawn from the archives of the region in the LBA, it is actually fairly modest! Consider the rhetoric of Tutmosis III as mustered by Kitchen. *Reliability*, p. 174: "The numerous army of Mitanni was overthrown within the hour, annihilated totally, like those (now) non-existent."

[41]The NIV suggests this in the translation, "no one uttered a word against the Israelites." The clause is an expansion of the descriptive phrase, "in peace." After this stunning defeat, there are no tongue-waggers, enemy warriors, or critics to be found. Israel is free of such "trash talk."

[42]See the image of Assyrian king Tiglath Pileser III resting his foot on the neck of a defeated king. This is visible in a relief panel from Calah (Ninrud) reproduced in *ISBE*, s.v., "Gesture." This action corresponds to the biblical idea of putting one's enemies under one's feet." See 1 Kgs 5:3 (H 17); Ps 110:1.

[43]The king of The *'Ay* is treated in this same way, cf. 8:29. In all examples, obedience to *torah* is demonstrated; cf. Deut 21:22-23.

day (cf. 4:9; 5:9; 6:25; 7:26; 8:28-29; 9:27). It has been a busy day for hurling all sorts of things!

4. The Raid on South Canaan (10:28-43)

[28]That day Joshua took Makkedah. He put the city and its king to the sword and totally destroyed everyone in it. He left no survivors. And he did to the king of Makkedah as he had done to the king of Jericho.

[29]Then Joshua and all Israel with him moved on from Makkedah to Libnah and attacked it. [30]The LORD also gave that city and its king into Israel's hand. The city and everyone in it Joshua put to the sword. He left no survivors there. And he did to its king as he had done to the king of Jericho.

[31]Then Joshua and all Israel with him moved on from Libnah to Lachish; he took up positions against it and attacked it. [32]The LORD handed Lachish over to Israel, and Joshua took it on the second day. The city and everyone in it he put to the sword, just as he had done to Libnah. [33]Meanwhile, Horam king of Gezer had come up to help Lachish, but Joshua defeated him and his army—until no survivors were left.

[34]Then Joshua and all Israel with him moved on from Lachish to Eglon; they took up positions against it and attacked it. [35]They captured it that same day and put it to the sword and totally destroyed everyone in it, just as they had done to Lachish.

[36]Then Joshua and all Israel with him went up from Eglon to Hebron and attacked it. [37]They took the city and put it to the sword, together with its king, its villages and everyone in it. They left no survivors. Just as at Eglon, they totally destroyed it and everyone in it.

[38]Then Joshua and all Israel with him turned around and attacked Debir. [39]They took the city, its king and its villages, and put them to the sword. Everyone in it they totally destroyed. They left no survivors. They did to Debir and its king as they had done to Libnah and its king and to Hebron.

[40]So Joshua subdued the whole region, including the hill country, the Negev, the western foothills and the mountain slopes, together with all their kings. He left no survivors. He totally

destroyed all who breathed, just as the LORD, the God of Israel, had commanded. [41]Joshua subdued them from Kadesh Barnea to Gaza and from the whole region of Goshen to Gibeon. [42]All these kings and their lands Joshua conquered in one campaign, because the LORD, the God of Israel, fought for Israel.

[43]Then Joshua returned with all Israel to the camp at Gilgal.

The fourth and final part of this chapter shows how the battle to assist Gibeon provides the momentum to overrun southern Canaan. This section is an outgrowth of preceding verses and continues to demonstrate how Yahweh fought for Israel. One by one, sites are encountered and raided. Action is described in a rapid, staccato-style narrative that is consistent with military summaries of the time.[44] Still, communicating historical information is hardly the primary purpose of the text. More central is the effort to show fulfillment of the promised "pedestrian expedition" couched in the promise of Yahweh: "I will give you every place where you set your foot" (1:3).

10:28 Following the execution of the five chiefs at the cave at Makkedah, the local community is subdued. All living beings are killed, including the chief.

10:29-30 From Makkedah, the campaign turns to **Libnah**.[45] The specific location of Libnah is uncertain, although it is likely located near Lachish in the foothills. Here, too, the formulaic **put to the sword** appears (10:28,30,32), as does **he left no survivors** (10:28,30, 33,39,40).

10:31-33 The site of **Lachish** is the next target. For the first time in the campaign, Israel takes **up positions** or "encamps" against the city, suggestive of fortifications and besieging tactics.[46] However, the

---

[44]See Younger, *Ancient Conquest Accounts*, p. 199. Similarly, see James K. Hoffmeier, "The Structure of Joshua 1-11 and the Annals of Thutmose III," in *Faith, Tradition, and History. Old Testament Historiography in Its Near Eastern Context*, ed. by A.R. Millard, James K. Hoffmeier, and David W. Baker (Winona Lake, IN: Eisenbrauns, 1994), pp. 165-179. Finally, note Kitchen, *Reliability*, pp. 170-173.

[45]Proposals for biblical Libnah include Tell es-Safi and Tell Bornat (Tel Burna), and Tell Judeideh. See the discussion by Merling, *Joshua*, pp. 125-128; or Rainey and Notley, *Sacred Bridge*, p. 127.

[46]Besieging tactics are anticipated in *torah* (Deut 20:19) and well known in and out of the Bible. lf, however, at this early stage, Israel could conduct an

campaign does not bog down as, miraculously, Yahweh **handed Lachish over . . . on the second day**. As the chief of Lachish was among the five chiefs executed previously, defense of the site may have fallen to **Horam**, chief of **Gezer**.[47] He and his forces may have attempted to relieve the siege; these are also defeated.

10:34-35 From Lachish, the battle moves to **Eglon**.[48] Here too, an encampment is made that is immediately successful. As with Lachish, the chief of Eglon was among the five chiefs already killed at Makkedah.

10:36-37 Following the victory at Eglon, Israel ascends back into the Hill Country and attacks **Hebron**. Two details bear further comment. First, in connection with the capture of the city, the narrator claims that the chief is killed. However, the chief of Hebron is also among the five who are killed at the cave at Makkedah. Is this an error in fact or a textual corruption? Woudstra solves the difficulty by suggesting that this raid on south Canaan may have taken some time to complete; perhaps a new chief was appointed to replace the one executed by Israel.[49] Woudstra's thinking is helpful, but may be slightly adjusted. If the succession is established,[50] no time is required to set up the replacement; the campaign could still be a rapid one. Second, in the attack on Hebron, the text says that the settlement was captured along with **its villages**, a variation in the report not seen previously. Apparently, Hebron is a regional or "ranked" center, possibly like Gibeon, existing in some kind of political or economic relationship with its smaller neighbors. When Hebron is captured, this Hill Country system collapses.

10:38-39 Like Hebron, the site of **Debir**[51] is also a regional cen-

---

effective siege is questionable. Fortunately, according to the text, it was unnecessary.

[47]Gezer (Tell Jazari) was occupied at the time of Joshua, but appears to have been passed by. It is located some twenty miles north of Lachish (Tell ed-Duweir), a long march for Horam and his forces.

[48]If Eglon is identified with Tell 'Eton ('Airun), it rests approximately six miles southeast of Lachish (Tell ed-Duweir). See discussion in Rainey and Notley, *Sacred Bridge*, p. 128.

[49]Woudstra, *Joshua*, p. 183.

[50]As Robert Miller, *Chieftains of the Highland Clans*, p. 7, puts it, "the office of chief exists apart from the individual holding that office."

[51]Khirbet Rabud is the most likely candidate for biblical Debir. It is located on the road between Hebron and Beer-Sheba, approximately eight miles

ter in the Hill Country with a cast of supporting villages. However,
like Hebron, it too falls and is subjected to the *ḥāram*.

10:40-43 In summary, Israel overruns the region of southern
Canaan in a lightning raid. Areas affected rest between the central
ridge and the coastal plain and extend to the desert reaches of the
Negev. As none of the six sites explicitly named — Makkedah, Libnah,
Lachish, Eglon Hebron, and Debir — are located in the Negev, it is
possible that other forays go unmentioned. On the other hand,
Jerusalem and Gezer are mentioned as partners in the coalition of
opposition, but escape notice in the final tally. Emphasis throughout
is not placed on the military action itself, the extent of physical
destruction inflicted upon the sites,[52] nor the effort to occupy or garrison them. These last two points are significant in light of historical
reconstructions that overstate the nature of Israel's campaign of
Canaan. As described in this chapter, Israel conducts a single military raid, killing inhabitants when encountered, and disrupting an
already skittish political landscape. As told, emphasis is placed upon
the larger issues of divine promise and human obedience, particularly with respect to the *ḥāram*. The impact of this raid is felt as far
away as **Kadesh Barnea**,[53] in the deep south, **Gaza**,[54] on the coastal
plain, **Goshen**,[55] on the edge of the Negev, and **Gibeon**, in the Hill
Country.[56] All of this is made possible "in a single move"[57] because
Yahweh fights **for Israel**.

---

southwest from Hebron. Occupation has been demonstrated in the LBA
and in Early Iron I. See discussion by Merling, *Joshua*, pp. 134-139, and in
Rainey and Notley, *Sacred Bridge*, p. 128-129.

[52]It is possible, as 11:13-14 demonstrates, to "take a city," "put its citizen-
ry to the sword," and "utterly destroy it" without burning the place down
and subjecting it to wholesale destruction.

[53]Kadesh Barnea is associated with 'Ain el-Qudeirat, although settlement
occupation before the Iron Age is elusive.

[54]Modern Gaza is a heavily populated area. There is little chance at present for archaeological investigation.

[55]Goshen is tentatively identified with Tell Khuweilifeh (Tell Halif). It is
located approximately thirty miles southeast of Gaza.

[56]By this mention of Gibeon, the narrative that began in 9:1 comes full
circle.

[57]The idiom אֶחָת פַּעַם (*pa'am 'eḥāth*) suggests a single occurrence, move,
or blow. Within the text of Joshua (6:3,11,14), the same phrase is used to
describe how Israel circled Jericho, only *once* on each of six days. Even more

helpful is its use in 1 Sam 26:8: "Abishai said to David, 'Today God has delivered your enemy into your hands. Now let me pin him to the ground with
one thrust (*pa'am 'eḥāth*) of my spear; I won't strike him twice.'" Here,
southern Canaan is overrun in "one thrust." It is a single action. For more
see Jeffrey Niehaus, "*Pa'am 'Eḥāt* and the Israelite Conquest," *VT* 30 (1980):
236-238.

JOSHUA 11

K. OVERRUN COMPLETED (11:1–12:24)

If a raid in southern Canaan could crack local resistance, so too, a raid in northern Canaan. This is attempted in order to complete Israel's initial overrun of the land and prepare it for settlement. The account is narrated and contextualized in three moves. The first (11:1-15) describes a foray in the region of Hazor. The second (11:16-23) summarizes the larger campaigns of Joshua in terms of what is taken and why. The third (12:1-24) offers a list of defeated chiefs. Links between this section and the previous one come by way of narrative flow and word choice.

1. The Raid on North Canaan (11:1-15)

¹When Jabin king of Hazor heard of this, he sent word to Jobab king of Madon, to the kings of Shimron and Acshaph, ²and to the northern kings who were in the mountains, in the Arabah south of Kinnereth, in the western foothills and in Naphoth Dorᵃ on the west; ³to the Canaanites in the east and west; to the Amorites, Hittites, Perizzites and Jebusites in the hill country; and to the Hivites below Hermon in the region of Mizpah. ⁴They came out with all their troops and a large number of horses and chariots—a huge army, as numerous as the sand on the seashore. ⁵All these kings joined forces and made camp together at the Waters of Merom, to fight against Israel.

⁶The LORD said to Joshua, "Do not be afraid of them, because by this time tomorrow I will hand all of them over to Israel, slain. You are to hamstring their horses and burn their chariots."

⁷So Joshua and his whole army came against them suddenly at the Waters of Merom and attacked them, ⁸and the LORD gave them

into the hand of Israel. They defeated them and pursued them all
the way to Greater Sidon, to Misrephoth Maim, and to the Valley
of Mizpah on the east, until no survivors were left. ⁹Joshua did to
them as the LORD had directed: He hamstrung their horses and
burned their chariots.

¹⁰At that time Joshua turned back and captured Hazor and put
its king to the sword. (Hazor had been the head of all these kingdoms.) ¹¹Everyone in it they put to the sword. They totally
destroyed[b] them, not sparing anything that breathed, and he
burned up Hazor itself.

¹²Joshua took all these royal cities and their kings and put them
to the sword. He totally destroyed them, as Moses the servant of
the LORD had commanded. ¹³Yet Israel did not burn any of the
cities built on their mounds—except Hazor, which Joshua burned.
¹⁴The Israelites carried off for themselves all the plunder and livestock of these cities, but all the people they put to the sword until
they completely destroyed them, not sparing anyone that
breathed. ¹⁵As the LORD commanded his servant Moses, so Moses
commanded Joshua, and Joshua did it; he left nothing undone of
all that the LORD commanded Moses.

ᵃ2 Or *in the heights of Dor*   ᴮ*11* The Hebrew term refers to the irrevocable giving over of things or persons to the LORD, often by totally destroying them; also in verses 12, 20 and 21.

11:1-5 As previously, hearing is a prelude to action (cf. 5:1; 9:1;
10:1). The יָבִין (*Yābîn*),[1] chief of **Hazor**,[2] hears of Israel's accomplishments and summons others to join him in another coalition of oppo-

---

[1]If the name Jabin (*Yābîn*) is derived from the verbal root *bîn*, it may possibly mean "Intelligent One" or "Genius." The same name is also associated
with chief of Hazor in Judges 4. Some scholars attempt to connect these two
accounts through this personality, but such a move is unnecessary. It is possible that the term is a title rather than a personal name, and therefore
could have been adopted by many individuals. As a title, it may even have a
derogatory slant, coined by the narrator to smother a real name and communicate sarcasm, e.g., the chief of Hazor is a "Brainiac" or "Whiz-kid."

[2]The site of Hazor ("Enclosure") is located in the southwest corner of the
Hula Basin, approximately ten miles north of the Sea of Galilee. The mound
is known as Tell el-Qedah and, in its prime, measured some 200 acres, by
far the largest in the *Heartland*. Excavations have revealed no less than 21
superimposed cities upon the tell; habitation is consistent with the biblical
record. For details, see *NEAEHL*, s.v. "Hazor."

sition. This includes **Jobab** chief of **Madon**,[3] unnamed chiefs of **Shimron**[4] and **Acshaph**,[5] and other chiefs from the northern mountains, the Lower Jordan Valley,[6] Lower Galilee,[7] and the Plain of Dor.[8] These sites and regions together define north Canaan. It is vast, extending from the Mediterranean Sea on the west to the Great Rift Valley on the east, and from Upper Galilee on the north to the Jezreel Valley on the south. The narrator further defines the people groups included in the summons. It turns out to be the usual list of suspects, corresponding exactly with those engaged in the raid to the south (9:1): Canaanites, Amorites, Hittites, Perizzites, Jebusites, and Hivites.[9]

---

[3]The location of Madon is unknown, although the site of Khirbet Madin, five and one-half miles above modern Tiberias, is a good candidate. For a relatively recent argument, see Zvi Gal, "Iron I in Lower Galilee and the Margins of the Jezreel Valley," in *From Nomadism to Monarchy: Archaeological and Historical Aspects of Early Israel*, ed. by Israel Finkelstein and Nadav Na'aman (Washington: BAS, 1994), pp. 43-44.

[4]Like Madon, the location of Shimron is debated. Linguistic affiliations connect it with Khirbet Sammuniyeh, five miles west of Nazareth. See again the discussion by Merling, *Joshua*, p. 143.

[5]Acshaph has been linked with Tell Keisan or Tell Harbaj on the Plain of Acco. See ibid., pp. 143-145, or Rainey and Notley, *Sacred Bridge*, p. 129.

[6]The text reads literally in the עֲרָבָה (*'ărābāh*), south of כִּנְרוֹת (*Kinărôth*). The *'ărābāh* is a general reference to the Great Rift (or Jordan) Valley; the sea of *Kinnereth* ("Harp Lake") refers to what is known in the period of the New Testament as the Sea of Galilee.

[7]The term שְׁפֵלָה (*šᵊphēlāh*) or "lowlands" is often used to describe the foothills between the coastal plain and the central ridge of Judah. On this occasion, however, it refers to the chalky foothills of Lower Galilee, a region Baly calls the "Galilean Shephelah" (*Geography*, p. 162).

[8]Aharoni proposes that נָפוֹת דּוֹר (*nāphôth-dôr*) does not refer to the "heights of Dor, as is commonly thought, but "Dor of the Sharon," or "Dor of the wooded country." This etymology is based on an archaic Greek term (*Land of the Bible*, p. 313).

Dor is located along the Mediterranean coast, about thirteen miles south of modern Haifa. The excavations at the site known as Khirbet el-Burj have revealed continuous occupation from the MBA to the Roman period.

[9]Here, Hivites are said to dwell "below Hermon in the land of the Mizpah. Hivites are also encountered in Gibeon (9:7; 11:19) among other places (Judg 3:3). In this last reference, Hivites are described as living in the "Lebanon Mountains." This corresponds with Josh 11:3,8 as Mt. Hermon is the southernmost peak of the Anti-Lebanon Range. As the term Hivites may mean "tent-dweller," it seems to indicate a group practicing a nomadic, hence mobile, lifestyle. Cf. note at 9:3.   *More on next page*

The response to the call of the *Yābîn* is impressive.[10] The chiefs answer by producing campaign encampments and chariot teams. Recent study clarifies aspects of chariot warfare in the LBA and illuminates this passage.[11] For example, the heyday of this style of fighting appears to have come as a result of the combination of light, fast, chariots, with an equally impressive weapon, the composite bow. Effective chariot teams required training of horses, drivers, and archers. Construction of chariots, bows, and arrows was a time-consuming and expensive task, the luxury of political and economic monopolies. Similarly, those who drove the chariots and shot from them were typically drawn from elite classes. When called into action, chariots were literally carried to the field of battle (they were too delicate and valuable to be risked in the journey), assembled in a fixed camp, and dispatched in waves that attempted to outflank the enemy. These squadrons would circle in fixed formation, looping in and out of range, shooting until the arrows were exhausted, then returning to the fixed base to be resupplied. Lightly clad infantry were used to move and guard the camp and possibly to rescue chariot teams that became disabled on the field of battle.[12] Given this background, the text of 11:4 becomes more meaningful.

Many individual sites carry the name "Mizpah" ("Lookout"). Mizpah as a "land" or "valley" (11:8), however, is not known elsewhere. It appears to be located somewhere in the shadow of Hermon, possibly in the region of the *Beqa'a* Valley.

[10]To help explain why, see Supplemental Study on Playing Monopoly below.

[11]For more, see "The Chariot Warfare," in Drews, *The End of the Bronze Age*, pp. 104-134.

[12]Drews, *The End of the Bronze Age*, pp. 208-225, argues, in part, that when personal armor advanced to the point where these teams of infantry could adequately protect themselves from arrows, the heyday of chariot warfare came to and end, ca. 1200 B.C. Although this technological transition is relatively close, it is unlikely that personal armor was part of the kit of Joshua's irregulars. In the open and against "mechanized" units, Israel is extremely vulnerable.

SUPPLEMENTAL STUDY
PLAYING MONOPOLY

There are many reasons why the *Yābîn* and other Canaanite chiefs consider Israel to be a threat. Undoubtedly, Israel's track record of success, coupled with rumors of *ḥāram*-warfare, reach their ears and build tension. Biblically, the narrator of Joshua suggests still more. Select passages suggest that the Canaanite coalition is goaded into conflict by Yahweh for the purpose of their own destruction (e.g., Josh 11:20). This spiritual explanation is consistent with God's work described elsewhere (Exod 14:17; 1 Kgs 22:20-22).

Some contemporary scholars have suggested that the fuller explanation may involve some rather *earthly* factors as well. To follow this line of thinking, one must consider social models built upon a synthesis of textual and archaeological data. In these, Israel appears as a tribally organized, power-sharing, and ex-slave community. By contrast, the Canaanite centers appear as chiefdoms (local "monarchies"), where wealth is concentrated in the hands of a few at the expense of the many. When these two constructions are held side by side, one can immediately sense the threat that Israel poses and a possible reason why the *Yābîn* might seek to attack and eliminate it: Israel's arrival represents a destabilization of the region, or read more personally, a destabilization of *his* region. The *Yābîn's* world is challenged. Brueggemann gives voice to this challenge when he writes, "I regard 'Israel' as an egalitarian, peasant movement hostile to every concentration, surplus, and monopoly."[13] If this construction is near to the truth, the formula "Canaan vs. Israel" suggests more than a theological conflict over the question of "whose god(s) are real" or a moral conflict about whose actions are right or wrong. The formula "Canaan vs. Israel" suggests a social-economic collision where those who have the most resources, like the *Yābîn*, are those who have the most to lose.

While drawn from the edges and not the center of the text, this line of thinking wedges an interesting scenario into the discussion.

---

[13]Walter Brueggemann, *A Social Reading of the Old Testament: Prophetic Approaches to Israel's Communal Life*, ed. by Patrick D. Miller (Minneapolis: Fortress, 1994), p. 293.

Brueggemann — to use him as a spokesperson for this view — also
believes it helps explain some key pieces of the text, such as the
repeated mention in chapter 11 of "horses and chariots." Such military resources are the tools of wealth and empire. The Canaanites
have both aplenty (v. 4). Israel is ordered to sabotage these tools and
not take them into their own kit (v. 6). Joshua and company are
faithful in carrying out these orders (v. 9). However, as read here,
Brueggemann is quick to identify that the speech of Yahweh is
directed against weapons, but not against people. "It is not a summons to violence (though its practice might be construed so) but
only a permit that Joshua's community is entitled to dream, hope,
and imagine freedom and is entitled to act upon that dream, hope,
and imagination."[14]

Such talk is lofty, indeed. It is also loaded with many assumptions
about Israel's social structure, the nature of revelation, and even a
strategy for reading texts. In this, criticism follows complement. Was
the "liberation" of oppressed Canaanites truly a part of Israel's agenda or is this simply a by-product of it at least, or, a vivid imagination
at most? Is it fair to picture Israel as some kind of communal society harboring values such as freedom, equality, and justice? On the
other side, was there ever a broad band of Canaanites chafing
against greedy overlords, yearning for liberty and suffering under
the rule of those who would use weapons unjustly? How can one
seize upon one text and ignore others? In the end, while these interpretations are helpful, one senses that parts of this social-economic
model of Israel's arrival in Canaan are driven by modern agendas.

A Canaanite base is established at the **Waters of Merom**, the
"water of the heights,"[15] possibly located at the spring of Nebi Shu'eib
below Tel Qarnei Hittin.[16] Such a location guarded the ascent of the

---

[14]Ibid., pp. 295-296.

[15]This phrase appears nowhere else in Scripture. LXX suggests the
spelling *Marron* in the place of Merom. Rainey argues although the word
resembles the name of the modern village Meiron, the latter "hardly reflect
any early nomenclature. It is a modern invention" (*Sacred Bridge*, p. 129).
Aharoni notes the mention of the site of Merom in Egyptian sources from
the late second millennium B.C. (*Land of the Bible*, p. 225).

[16]This is suggested by Zvi Gal in his "Iron I in Lower Galilee," p. 44. Gal's
view regarding the location of Merom, however, is just one of many. Rainey

"Via Maris," a crucial choke point between the Galilee Basin (Sea of Galilee) and the plateaus of Lower Galilee. Here, the speed and mobility of the chariots could quickly destroy any lightly clad infantry units caught in the open. This shrewd choice of ground by the *Yābîn* puts every advantage into Canaanite hands (assuming Israel would be foolhardy enough to march into the trap of the "Genius"!).

By crafting the prelude at the start of the northern raid (11:1-5) in a deliberate imitation of the start of the southern raid (10:1-5), the narrator leads the reader to anticipate a similar conclusion. A chief hears a report of Israel, gathers fellow chiefs from specific groups of known enemies (cf. the list of seven nations, Deut 7:1; 20:17), and forges an alliance with a single purpose in mind: **to fight against Israel.** However, challenging the quick and easy conclusion — that this raid will end in victory just like the last — are tension-building variations. This time around, the coalition forces are enormous, **as numerous as the sand on the seashore.**[17] Moreover, they are not like the highland regulars in the south: they are explicitly a chariot force. Israel has neither the numbers nor the technology to compete on this field of battle. This is not a fight to be picked.

11:6 In the face of these staggering odds, Yahweh offers encouragement. The familiar "do not fear their presence" prefaces what is to happen. **By this time tomorrow,** i.e., in short order, this superior force will be "skewered"[18] and served.[19] The conclusion is inescapable: Yahweh continues to fight for Israel. To remember this fact in the face of conflict, however, is no easy task. This is especially true

---

suggests the site of Merom is Tell el-Khureibeh, two miles south of Marun er-Ras. The spring in question would then be located on the slopes of Jebel Jarmaq (*Sacred Bridge*, p. 129).

[17]The metaphor of sand (-grains) on the beach suggests that which is too numerous to count. It is used in the biblical text to describe vast quantities of descendants (e.g., Gen 22:17; 32:12[H 13]; Jer 33:22), cereal stores (Gen 41:49), deep knowledge (1 Kgs 4:29[H 5:9]), and enemies on a field of battle (e.g., Judg 7:12; 1 Sam 13:5).

[18]The verbal form, "pierced" or "shot-through" is drawn from the root חלל (*ḥll*), often used of those slain in battle. It is a technical term used of the battlefield according to *TDOT*, s.v. חלל II.

[19]"Served" is an admittedly loose, but appropriate reading, as Yahweh will present (lit., "give over") these pierced enemies, לִפְנֵי יִשְׂרָאֵל (*liphnê Yiśrā'ēl*), "to" or "in the presence of Israel."

when power presents itself with all the trappings of metal and muscle. Because such displays are so visibly overpowering, the temptation is to regard them as not just irresistible, but desirable as the
only true forms of power.[20] Anything else is either so inferior or so
distant as to be unhelpful.

The mandate of 11:6 is to keep the people of God from being
seduced by this kind of thinking. When captured, the chariot horses are to be hamstrung, the tendon of the leg cut to prevent them
from ever pulling chariots again.[21] As for the chariots themselves,
these sleek "fighter jets" of the day must be burned.[22] This hostile
attitude directed towards chariots and horses comes here for the
first time in Scripture. It will not be the last. On this point, Brueggemann musters four texts that discuss the practice of "chariotry" and
comments upon each in turn. Contrasted is a worldview that seeks
to acquire and employ the technology of war and a worldview that
disavows and ultimately triumphs over it. Without going into detail,
it is enough to share his eloquent conclusion.

> These factors together in the four narratives of 1 Kings 20:26-
> 30; 2 Kings 6:16-17; 2 Kings 7:6; and 2 Kings 18:19–19:37 are
> indeed revelatory. They disclose what had not been seen. They
> make known what had not been known. And when this alter-
> native is known and seen, the sure, managed world of royal

---

[20]Deut 20:1 is brought to mind: "When you go to war against you enemies
and see horses and chariots and an army greater than yours, do not be
afraid of them, because the LORD your God, who brought you up out of
Egypt, will be with you."

[21]In the text of the Old Testament, horses are always regarded as a beast
of battle. They are expensive to maintain, prideful in appearance, and find
little application in the lifestyle of agriculturalists. The disabling act of ham-
stringing further limits their value. For more on horses, see Oded Borowski,
Every Living Thing: Daily Use of Animals in Ancient Israel (Walnut Creek, CA:
AltaMira, 1998), pp. 99-108.

[22]Cf. 2 Sam 8:4; 1 Chr 18:4; Ps 20:7[H 8]. These texts make the point:
"Some trust in chariots and some in horses, but we trust in the name of
Yahweh our God."

A less "theological" reading of the destruction of the chariots is offered
by Victor Matthews. He suggests that the Israelites did not have the technology to maintain the chariots or any real need for them (in the rugged
highlands). Therefore, to simply keep them out of Canaanite hands, they
were burned. See his *Manners and Customs in the Bible*, rev. ed. (Peabody,
MA: Hendrickson, 1991), p. 62.

technique and certitude is stunningly dismantled. The rules of
this age are marvelously put to flight. Israel's life is rendered
in these narratives in an alternative rationality that has power,
substance, and reality, all rooted in and derived from this sub-
versive disclosure of Yahweh.[23]

11:7-9 Little of the ensuing battle is known, but the telling of it
parallels the telling of the southern raid, in part. The use of the term
suddenly, describing the Israelite approach, alludes to the panic of
10:9-10 and suggests that Joshua may have utilized some form of hiddenness. No stones are flung from the sky in this skirmish, but in
this case, Israel itself "falls" (יִפְּלוּ, *yippᵊlû*) upon the hapless camp
and strikes it. Credit for the victory is attributed to Yahweh who
gives the enemy into Israel's hand (cf. 10:12). Finally, the defeated
are pursued and killed over the course of some distance, in this case,
as far as **Greater Sidon, Misrephoth Maim,** and the **Valley of Mizpah.**[24]
Just as Yahweh delivers in his promise of victory, Joshua delivers by
destroying both the captives and the chariot technology.[25] Faith triumphs over metal and muscle.

11:10-15 Following the successful pursuit, Joshua returns (to the
original scene of the battle?), captures Hazor, burns it, and executes
all who live there, including Hazor's "Genius" chief. Again, how this
victory is accomplished (were the defenses penetrated?) is not in the
interests of the narrator, but is impressive nonetheless, given the
fact that Hazor was **formerly the head of all these kingdoms.**[26] More

---

[23]Brueggemann, *Social Reading of the Old Testament*, p. 310.

[24]Greater Sidon refers to the Phoenician port city located at Saida in modern Lebanon. Misrephoth Maim, or "Misrephoth of the Water," possibly
located at 'Ain Mesherifeh on the Plain of Acco. Both of these sites are located northwest of the proposed battlefield, in the case of the first, more than
fifty miles away, and in the case of the second, some thirty miles away.

The Valley of Mizpah, on the other hand, rests northeast of the proposed
battlefield, in the vicinity of Mt. Hermon. See Aharoni, *Land of the Bible*,
p. 217.

[25]Joshua fulfills the divine order to hamstring horses and burn chariots.
Butler suggests that the reason this line is repeated at the end of v. 9 may
be to explain the "surprising" means by which the forces of Joshua are able
to achieve victory (*Joshua*, p. 128). It is a thought, although it may be more
in keeping with the tenor of the text to see this repetition as a demonstration of how Joshua follows orders, e.g., mandate given, mandate followed.

[26]The excavations directed by Yigael Yadin at Tell el-Qedah recovered a

in keeping with the presentation is the emphasis on Joshua's faithfulness in keeping the commands of Moses (vv. 12 and 15). Communities in league with Hazor are also captured, plundered, and their
inhabitants annihilated, in accordance with the *ḥāram*-order issued
at The *'Ay* (but not like that at Jericho). Hazor alone is razed; a careful note however alerts the reader to the preservation of all other
sites. These may be appropriated by Israel according to the prescription of Deuteronomy 6:10-11.

2. The Overrun Summarized (11:16-23)

[16]**So Joshua took this entire land: the hill country, all the Negev,
the whole region of Goshen, the western foothills, the Arabah and
the mountains of Israel with their foothills,** [17]**from Mount Halak,
which rises toward Seir, to Baal Gad in the Valley of Lebanon
below Mount Hermon. He captured all their kings and struck
them down, putting them to death.** [18]**Joshua waged war against all
these kings for a long time.** [19]**Except for the Hivites living in
Gibeon, not one city made a treaty of peace with the Israelites,
who took them all in battle.** [20]**For it was the LORD himself who hardened their hearts to wage war against Israel, so that he might
destroy them totally, exterminating them without mercy, as the
LORD had commanded Moses.**

[21]**At that time Joshua went and destroyed the Anakites from the
hill country: from Hebron, Debir and Anab, from all the hill country of Judah, and from all the hill country of Israel. Joshua totally
destroyed them and their towns.** [22]**No Anakites were left in
Israelite territory; only in Gaza, Gath and Ashdod did any survive.**
[23]**So Joshua took the entire land, just as the LORD had directed
Moses, and he gave it as an inheritance to Israel according to their
tribal divisions.**

Then the land had rest from war.

---

destruction level that measured more than one meter thick in places.
Deliberate mutilation of cult objects were noted in areas C and H. Yadin
dated this destruction of Stratum XIII to the last quarter of the 13th century
B.C. and attributed it to the Israelites. For a recent summary, see A. Ben-
Tor, "Excavating Hazor, Part II: Did the Israelites Destroy the Canaanite
City?" *BAR* 25 (Mar./Apr. 1999): 22-39.

11:16-19 Pause is given to take stock of the situation. Adjustments will be needed, but for the moment, the statement **Joshua took this entire land** stands true (see Supplemental Study on "Mission Accomplished" in ch. 13, p. 259). The feet of Israel (cf. 1:3) have padded across **the hill country** or central highlands, into **the Negev**, or desert "southland," through **the whole region of Goshen, the lowlands**, or foothills, possibly adjacent to the hill country of Galilee, down into **the Arabah**, the Great Rift (or Jordan River) Valley, and throughout **the hill country of Israel and its lowland**. "A Great Commission" has been issued by Yahweh, distributed among his people, and used to induce courage, comfort, and above all else, obedience. The land is now ripe for settlement. It is staggering in size and diversity, stretching from the dry cap of **Mt. Halak**,[27] in the deep south, to the lush valley of **Baal-Gad**[28] in the far north. With the threat of local chiefs eliminated, Israel stands on a threshold of opportunity, ready to realize the dream of their landless ancestors.

This synopsis alerts the reader to an essential conclusion: the northern and southern raids are only the beginning of the much larger job of conquest and settlement. As presented, these raids consist of rapid, guerrilla-like operations, punctuated by overt displays of divine assistance. In each case, a contest of arms is followed by a mop-up pursuit. Israel repeatedly returns to a base camp in Gilgal, with no effort given to control, much less to occupy these overrun areas. This picture sits in contrast to the larger, untold story, quietly couched in the phrase, **Joshua waged war against all these kings for a long time**.[29] This, too, reports the situation honestly (and from a distance); but to accomplish the goals of the narrative, attention is given only to the initial overrun. What inevitably follows is long-term and bloody, as only the Hivites in Gibeon made peace with Israel. The narrative itself quietly ambushes any dullish optimism for a quick deal.

---

[27]Mt. Halak is associated with Jebel Halaq, located in the central Negev. *Halaq* means "bald." The location of this mountain corresponds in some way with Seir, i.e., Edom, on the far side of the Great Rift Valley.

[28]Baal Gad is located in "the Valley of Lebanon," "below Mt. Hermon" (13:5). Many suggestions for its location have been offered, from Baalbek, in modern Lebanon, to Banias, in occupied Syria. See MacDonald, *"East of the Jordan,"* p. 154, n. 10.

[29]An extended conquest has antecedent, e.g., Exod 23:29-30; Deut 7:22.

11:20 Beyond this sketch of the physical conflict, a deeper, spiritual conflict is also revealed. In this revelation, the "why" question is answered at last, explaining the mystifying choices (translate: blunders) made by the Canaanite chiefs. Perhaps a new reading is in order: "The hardening of their (Canaanite) hearts was Yahweh's doing — that is why they did battle with Israel — in order that he might destroy them all, not showing them mercy." This fascinating text raises no less than three points to ponder.

First, the Canaanite chiefs acted as they did because of "hard hearts." This idiom is formed from a combination of the verbal root, חָזַק (ḥzq, "to be strong," "to strengthen") with the noun לֵב (lēb, "heart"). As Hesse writes, "the entire person whose heart has grown 'hard' shows himself intractable, obdurate, hardened."[30] As might be expected, the same phrase is used to describe the pharaoh of the Exodus. Activating this rationale again helps clarify the why-did-it-happen-this-way question of Joshua chapters 2–11. In stubbornness, the chief of Jericho hid behind his enclosure walls while the chief of the 'Ay charged recklessly outside of his. Arrogantly, the chief of Jerusalem attacked Gibeon instead of Israel, was caught flatfooted and unprepared, and later, was trapped with his allies in a cave of doom. Impervious to wise counsel, the Yābîn of Hazor camped out in the open at the Waters of Merom and despite his own "genius," failed to anticipate an ambush. This list goes on and on; hubris is clearly lurking at the core of the Canaanite impotence, a hubris lightly nudged by the finger of God.[31]

Second, the immediate context suggests, for whatever reason, that the people of Gibeon were not subject to the same dynamics: they were exceptional. They made a covenant of peace with Israel because their hearts were not hardened. By so doing they saved their skins, and, as verse 20 suggests, they received the mercy (תְחִנָּה, tᵉḥinnāh) of Yahweh: the very salvation denied to others. This raises the age-old question of personal choice versus divine destiny (unsolvable here!) but is interesting to consider as one muses over the possibility of other

---

[30]F. Hesse, *TDOT*, s.v. חָזַק.

[31]Paul J. Kissling points out how this "hard-heartedness" of the Canaanites and that of the Pharaoh of the Exodus presses the theme of "implacable foes." See his *Reliable Characters in the Primary History: Profiles of Moses, Joshua, Elijah and Elisha.* JSOTSupp 224 (Sheffield: Sheffield, 1996), p. 80.

chiefs making the same choice. In the case of the pharaoh of the exodus, the text suggests that Yahweh hardened his heart (9:12; 10:1-2) but only after a pattern of obstinacy was clearly established (cf. Exod 4:21; 5:2,6-7,17; 7:13-14,22; 8:15,19[H 11,15]; 8:32[H 28]; 9:7). In the case of the Canaanite chiefs, was another scenario possible, and if so, how? An alternative reality can only be imagined.

Third and finally, the text of 11:20 demonstrates that the extermination of the Canaanites was intrinsically part of Yahweh's plan. Through obedience, Joshua and Israel became agents of radical change, indeed, agents of divine judgment. This notion is hardly new here; it is clearly anticipated in Genesis 15:12-21 and cast as legal code in Deuteronomy 20. The present text presents the conclusion that "the sin of the Amorite" *has now* reached "its full measure."

11:21-22 Further details of the campaign concern the **Anakites**. Remembered as the descendants of Anak and the Nephalim (Gen 6:4; Num 13:22,32-33), the Anakites may refer to a specific people group or to the Canaanites in general. The word עֲנָק ('ănāq) literally means "long-necked," hence, "tall" or "giant," akin to the Rephaim and Emim (Deut 2:10,20-21). People of great stature were encountered in Canaan by the scouts dispatched by Moses, prompting the original report of terror (Num 13:32-33). This text in Joshua, suitably placed, puts that bad memory to sleep, as Israel destroys the Anakites living in the highlands generally and in Hebron, Debir,[32] and Anab[33] specifically. Only in Gaza, Gath, and Ashdod, cities of the south coastal plain, do Anakites survive.

11:23 Again, the obedience factor is emphasized as it trickles down from Yahweh to Moses and on to Joshua. Familiar themes surface again, themes that unify the book: land is a gift (ch. 1–12); land is an inheritance (chapters 13–24). Similarly paradigmatic, obedience precedes reward: **then the land had rest from war.** While carrying forward the theme of rest from 1:12-15, this expression is constructed somewhat differently.[34] Rest here is that of a drooping head or hand, or in this case, the earth itself is personified. It droops and

---

[32]See comments at 10:38.

[33]Anab is identified with Khirbet 'Unnab es-Saghir, about eleven miles southwest of Hebron.

[34]The word translated into English as "rest" in 1:12-15 emerges from the verbal root of נוּחַ (nûaḥ), "to lie down" or "settle down." The "rest" of 11:23

slumps, ground down by war. Such a reprieve can only be temporary at best. Canaan's big chiefs may be gone, but many local folk remain entrenched. If the land can take a breather, God's people cannot; their task has only begun.

---

comes from the root *šqṭ*, suggestive of inactivity. Use of this root in inscriptions, Late Hebrew, and cognate languages suggest the idea of drooping head, neck, or hands. See BDB, s.v. שָׁקַט.

JOSHUA 12

3. The Defeated Chiefs (12:1-24)

[1]These are the kings of the land whom the Israelites had defeated and whose territory they took over east of the Jordan, from the Arnon Gorge to Mount Hermon, including all the eastern side of the Arabah:

[2]Sihon king of the Amorites,
> who reigned in Heshbon. He ruled from Aroer on the rim of the Arnon Gorge—from the middle of the gorge—to the Jabbok River, which is the border of the Ammonites. This included half of Gilead. [3]He also ruled over the eastern Arabah from the Sea of Kinnereth[a] to the Sea of the Arabah (the Salt Sea[b]), to Beth Jeshimoth, and then southward below the slopes of Pisgah.

[4]And the territory of Og king of Bashan,
> one of the last of the Rephaites, who reigned in Ashtaroth and Edrei. [5]He ruled over Mount Hermon, Salecah, all of Bashan to the border of the people of Geshur and Maacah, and half of Gilead to the border of Sihon king of Heshbon.

[6]Moses, the servant of the LORD, and the Israelites conquered them. And Moses the servant of the LORD gave their land to the Reubenites, the Gadites and the half-tribe of Manasseh to be their possession.

[7]These are the kings of the land that Joshua and the Israelites conquered on the west side of the Jordan, from Baal Gad in the Valley of Lebanon to Mount Halak, which rises toward Seir (their lands Joshua gave as an inheritance to the tribes of Israel according to their tribal divisions— [8]the hill country, the western foothills, the Arabah, the mountain slopes, the desert and the Negev—the

lands of the Hittites, Amorites, Canaanites, Perizzites, Hivites and
Jebusites):

[9]the king of Jericho	one
the king of Ai (near Bethel)	one
[10]the king of Jerusalem	one
the king of Hebron	one
[11]the king of Jarmuth	one
the king of Lachish	one
[12]the king of Eglon	one
the king of Gezer	one
[13]the king of Debir	one
the king of Geder	one
[14]the king of Hormah	one
the king of Arad	one
[15]the king of Libnah	one
the king of Adullam	one
[16]the king of Makkedah	one
the king of Bethel	one
[17]the king of Tappuah	one
the king of Hepher	one
[18]the king of Aphek	one
the king of Lasharon	one
[19]the king of Madon	one
the king of Hazor	one
[20]the king of Shimron Meron	one
the king of Acshaph	one
[21]the king of Taanach	one
the king of Megiddo	one
[22]the king of Kedesh	one
the king of Jokneam in Carmel	one
[23]the king of Dor (in Naphoth Dor[c])	one
the king of Goyim in Gilgal	one
[24]the king of Tirzah	one

thirty-one kings in all.

[a]*3* That is, Galilee   [b]*3* That is, the Dead Sea   [c]*23* Or *in the heights of Dor*

This chapter marks an important transition between the effort to
acquire land and the effort to distribute it. Control must be trans-

ferred from Canaanite hands into Israelite hands, a move made possible only by the defeat of local chiefs (see Supplemental Study on Canaanite Chiefs below). These defeated chiefs are inventoried and identified with their respective territories, beginning in Transjordan (12:1-6), then moving to Cisjordan (12:7-24).[1] As the final piece of the first part of the book, this list prompts a contemplative review of stories told and silent wonder over those that are not. As an introductory piece to that which follows, the list justifies territorial allotments: this is land "contractually" claimed as the spoils of war.

SUPPLEMENTAL STUDY

CANAANITE CHIEFS

Despite persistent use of the term "king" to describe a man like the community leader of Jericho, it may not be the best fit for this time and place. Late second millennium Canaan appears to have been sprinkled irregularly with homesteads, villages, and towns. These settlements were located mostly in the fertile lowlands and fluidly arranged in some fifteen to twenty (depending upon the period) self-governing groups of cooperative and competitive relationships. Leaders worked to control local resources, crouch over trade routes, chase off rogues, and curry favor with Egypt. Poverty and malnutrition were widespread in this universe of orbiting circles; wealth gravitated to old fortified centers and was conspicuously held in the hands of a privileged few. Those who had it lived well, ate well, sent their sons to Egypt, organized militias, attempted to subvert their neighbors, and enriched, mythologized, and defended

---

[1]Kitchen, *Reliability*, pp. 178-179, writes, "Such an arrangement is almost a verbal equivalent of the partly pictorial topographical lists of vanquished places and peoples that the pharaohs often set out on the great pylon towers and outside walls of their temples during mainly the New Kingdom, from Tuthmosis III (1479–1425) down to Rameses III (ca. 1184–1153) with one major successor, Shishak or Shoshenq I (ca. 945–924).

"Nobody should imagine that the young Joshua in Egypt gazed up awed at such reliefs, and that old Joshua in Canaan therefore did a verbal list to parody Egyptian triumphs. But what we do have is the same broad concept of setting out the scale of the victory at the end of the record, in each culture, and within the same epoch."

their positions. The rest bloodied their knuckles just to stay alive. Disparity within Canaanite society was appalling.[2]

Mud, sweat, and tears were mixed into a plaster and used to seal the adobe walls at sites like Jericho. This work was done more for fending off greedy neighbors than it was for repelling the firepower of a genuine kingdom like Egypt.[3] In fact, as the view from the banks of the Nile had it, the city-state leaders of Canaan were "mayors" or "governors" at best, "thugs" or "warlords" at worst. For Egypt, Canaan was an add-on: it was simply another jerry can bolted to the powerful vehicle of state.[4] As such, it represented a resource to be systematically exploited, harnessed, skinned, shorn, or ground to bits. It was a place from which wine and grain products could be extracted, taxes could be raked, slaves and soldiers could be hunted, and, of course, a place that could be rigged as a "trip wire" in case northern invaders grew restless and pressed their own appetites. As long as Egyptian interests were uninterrupted, bickering among the leaders of the Canaanite city-states — no matter what labels they took for themselves — was tolerated, if not ignored. When necessary, a teeth-flashing raid sent all parties scurrying back to their mudded strongholds.

To better understand the role of Jericho's "king" and his late second millennium B.C. counterparts, anthropologists appeal to the model[5]

---

[2]Consider the article by John M. Halligan, "The Role of the Peasant in the Amarna Period," in *Palestine in Transition: The Emergence of Ancient Israel*, ed. by David Noel Freedman and David Frank Graf (Sheffield: Almond, 1983), pp. 15-24.

[3]Some have even suggested that the Egyptians discouraged or forbade the building of heavy fortifications in LBA Canaan. See Wayne T. Pitard, "Before Israel: Syria-Palestine in the Bronze Age," in *The Oxford History of the Biblical World*, ed. by Michael D. Coogan (New York: Oxford, 1998), p. 66.

[4]This concept has been expressed in different terms using world-systems analysis. This view is helpful for understanding relations between societies over the course of time. In the late second millennium, Egypt represented an economic core while Canaan functioned as a periphery zone. Cf. Immanuel Wallerstein, *World Systems Analysis: An Introduction* (Durham, NC: Duke University, 2004).

[5]Social-scientific models are tools that, as Esler puts it, fire "the imagination to ask new questions of data." They help organize data and make comparisons possible. For more on how models may be employed by Bible students, see Philip F. Esler, "Social-Scientific Models in Biblical Interpretation," in *Ancient Israel: The Old Testament in Its Social Context*, ed. by Philip F. Esler (Minneapolis: Fortress, 2006), pp. 3-14.

of the complex chiefdom.[6] A chiefdom is usually viewed as the most developed category of human society within a family-based system. Within it, the chief is the highest ranking member, holding his position as a result of birth (ascribed rank). Chiefdoms differ from "Big Man" societies insofar as this highest position is not secured as a result of gritty displays of personal strength or great accomplishments (achieved rank). Instead, it is an inherited position. Chiefdoms differ from "states" in that they display no true specialized administration, hierarchy, or developed legal systems. There is simply the chief who makes decisions and families who follow his lead. Complex chiefdoms occupy a position somewhere between this simple two-tiered arrangement and a true state; a distinguishing factor of the complex chiefdom is a secondary level of "subchiefs" nestled in the midst of the societal strata. Late second millennium Canaan was organized in this three-tiered fashion: chief, subchiefs, families. Power flowed overtly from top to bottom; but there were other currents as well.

Study of contemporary societies classed in this way has shown that complex chiefdoms exhibit three characteristics. First, with respect to wealth: while it does certainly flow upward to the chief, it must inevitably flow downward too, albeit in a different form and for different reasons. This is due, in part, to the self-sufficient nature of a farming/herding community. Wealth, in the form of surplus foodstuff, comes to the chief as tribute. When redistributed, it descends as a sign of favor to ensure group loyalty (possibly as a feast in good times or as a dole-line in bad times), or it is transformed by means of trade into something else, like prestige or luxury items. These are given as gifts to secure future goodwill or to repay favors done in the past. Second, within observed complex chiefdoms, there are measurable cycles of control. A complete turnover of power — where one ruling family or dynasty gives way to another — occurs in regular rhythms that stretch out as long as a century. Other patterns of a less drastic nature, such as the cycling

---

[6]For more on this, see the chapter on "The Chief" in Victor H. Matthews and Don C. Benjamin's *Social World of Ancient Israel 1250–587 BCE* (Hendrickson, MA: Peabody, 1993), pp. 96-109, or the chapter on "The Complex Chiefdom Model" by Robert D. Miller in his *Chieftains of the Highland Clans*, pp. 6-14.

between two-tier and three-tier chiefdom models, occur more regularly. Third and finally, complex chiefdoms tend to legitimate the rule of the current chief and work toward legitimating the rule of the next by means of exploiting sacred connections. Each chief is pressed into the heritage line through an expressed intimate relationship to his predecessor. For this to happen, practically speaking, genealogies may have to be tweaked or even completely rewritten to place the chief legitimately in a position where the community's support is obligatory. If desperate, appeal to divine right could be made; the gods of Canaan, after all, were viewed as chiefs of chiefs.

12:1 The review begins in Transjordan with a list of chiefs "that Israel killed and possessed their land." Transjordan is defined in two ways: first, it stretches from **the Arnon Gorge**[7] in the south to **Mt. Hermon** in the north, and, second, it includes all territory east of the **Arabah** or Great Rift Valley.[8]

12:2-3 In Transjordan, Israel also lays claim to the territory of **Sihon** chief **of the Amorites**. This territory is carefully delineated. It composes the highlands between two streams, the **Arnon** in the south and the **Jabbok**[9] in the north. This area is also known, in part, as **Gilead**.[10] Beyond these highlands, Sihon also controlled a portion of the **Arabah**, or Great Rift Valley from **Sea of Kinnereth** to the **Sea of the Arabah, Salt Sea**, or Dead Sea.[11] Within this description, three sites of biblical significance also appear; these prompt memories of

---

[7]The Arnon Gorge (Wadi Mujib) is impressive, a kind of "Grand Canyon" on a smaller scale. It cuts through the broad tableland of Moab and empties into the east side of the Dead Sea. For more, see Baly, *Geography*, pp. 229-233.

[8]The measure not given is on the east side. This is not necessary, however, as the suffocating deserts of what is now East Jordan, Syria, and West Iraq quickly limit the possibilities for human settlement.

[9]The Arnon is identified today with the Wadi Mujib. It runs through a deep canyon that gashes the Madaba plateau (the *mishor*) and empties into the east shore of the Dead Sea. The Jabbok is identified with the Wadi az-Zarqa. It begins in a spring in modern-day Amman and meanders through Gilead before releasing into the Jordan River.

[10]The term Gilead is a clan name given to a region in central Transjordan. For the struggle to define it, see MacDonald, *"East of the Jordan,"* pp. 195-208.

[11]See notes at 11:2 for more on these terms.

Israel's initial entrance into the land. **Heshbon** was the residence of Sihon and a site of conflict (Num 21:21-31; Deut 2:24; Josh 2:10).[12] **Beth Jeshimoth** marked the camping area in Moab, the last stage of Israel's wilderness wanderings (Num 33:49),[13] and **Pisgah**, is identified with the massif from which Moses viewed the land of promise,[14] a strategically placed flashback, indeed.

12:4-5 Israel also lays claim to **the territory of Og**, chief of **Bashan**. Og is identified among the last of the **Rephaites**, a term used to define the legendary "great ones" of the land (Deut 2:10-11; 3:11). The territory of Og included **Mt Hermon** and **Salecah**[15] in the far north and **Bashan**, the rich plateau spread below. On the north, the tribal territories of **Geshur** and **Maacah**[16] formed a boundary with Og, while on the south, the land of Sihon limited his power.

12:6 Victories over Sihon and Og are celebrated "firsts" in the land, connected with the leadership of **Moses**. The phrase **servant of the LORD** is twice linked with the name of Moses (cf. comment at 8:31) and may serve in this text to underline the bequest of Transjordan by Moses to the two and one-half tribes (cf. Numbers 32; Josh 1:12-15).

12:7-8 Having completed the review of action in Transjordan, the region of Cisjordan swings into view. Just as Moses distributes land east of the Jordan, so Joshua distributes land west of the Jordan **according to their tribal divisions**. The move, again, laces the work of Joshua into the work of Moses (e.g., 1:17; 4:14). Geographical limits here extend from the **Valley of Lebanon** to **Mount Halak** (cf.

---

[12]See note at 9:10.

[13]It is associated with Tell el-'Azeimeh, located above the northeast corner of the Dead Sea. See MacDonald, *"East of the Jordan,"* pp. 89.

[14]The name Pisgah is problematic, cf. Josh 13:20. It is likely connected with the summit of Mt. Nebo on the basis of Deut 34:1.

[15]Salecah is identified with modern Salkhad, resting high on a cinder cone in the alpine reaches of the Anti-Lebanon Range. This connection is based upon linguistic analysis; the archaeological story has yet to be told. See MacDonald, *"East of the Jordan,"* p. 152, n. 4.

[16]The lands of Geshur and Maacah extend from the Great Rift Valley eastward to the edge of the desert and are bounded on the north by Mt. Hermon and on the south by the Yarmuk. For more details on these lands, see B. Mazar, "Geshur and Maachah" in *The Early Biblical Period: Historical Studies*, ed. by S. Ahituv and B.A. Levine (Jerusalem: Israel Exploration Society, 1986), pp. 113-125.

11:17). Within these limits, familiar geographical designations (the hill country, the western foothills, the *Arabah*, the mountain slopes, the desert, and the Negev) are juxtaposed against familiar people groups (Hittites, Amorites, Canaanites, Perizzites, Hivites, and Jebusites).[17] In these areas and from these people groups, a list of conquered chiefs is drawn.

12:9-24 The list is formulaic, consisting of three elements. In the first element, the construct form of מֶלֶךְ (*melek*, "chief of") appears. In the second element, a site name is inserted, with modifications as needed, e.g., The '*Ay* (v. 9), Jokneam (v. 22), Dor (v. 23), and the enigmatic *Goyim* (v. 23). In the third element is the cardinal numeral, אֶחָד (*'eḥād*), "one," standing like a tally marker used to keep score[18] (see Supplemental Study on Site Identification in ch. 18, p. 318). Little more needs to be said of the first and third elements; the site names, however, require additional comment.

Of the names drawn from the text of Joshua 1–11, they appear roughly in the order they were encountered: the central thrust, the southern raid, and the northern raid. However, other names not previously encountered appear; some clustered geographically, a few, not. What drifts throughout, as onomastic study reveals, is the rich smell of earth. This list does not portray a "never-never land" of whimsical invention, but an inventory of actual places with anchorage in the second millennium B.C.[19]

In verses 9-13a, place names already familiar to the reader of Joshua appear: **Jericho** (6:1 ff.), The '*Ay* (7:2 ff.), **Jerusalem** (10:3), **Hebron** (10:36), **Jarmuth** (10:3), **Lachish** (10:31), **Eglon** (10:34), **Gezer** (10:33), and **Debir** (10:38).

Next come three place names known elsewhere, but seen here

---

[17]See note at 9:1.

[18]Nelson, *Joshua*, p. 162, points out how this "recalls the custom known from the Arad ostraca of following names with tally marks or numbers." It should also be noted, however, that the presence of the numeral "one" throughout is missing in the LXX tradition.

[19]Contra the conclusion of those who reject the "essential history" of the list on the basis of archaeological evidence alone. One must be careful to note the difference in the text between the destruction of cities and the destruction of its citizens. The fact that extensive destruction levels are not present at all sites of mention at the same time is not reason enough to jettison the "historicity" of the story told.

for the first time: **Geder**, possibly emended as Gerar,[20] **Hormah** (Num 14:45; 21:3),[21] and **Arad** (Num 21:1).[22]

Additional sites in the center and south are given: **Libnah** (10:29), **Adullam** (not previously mentioned, but geographically centered here),[23] **Makkedah** (10:28), and **Bethel** (8:17); followed by sites making a first time appearance in this text: **Tappuah**,[24] **Hepher**,[25] **Aphek**,[26] and **Lasharon**.[27]

---

[20]The name Geder is associated with Khirbet Jedur where LB II and Iron I pottery have been recovered. Alternatively, Aharoni, *Land of the Bible*, pp. 231, 435, suggests a common orthographic error may have caused an original "Gerar" to be misspelled as "Geder" (these letters look very similar). The site of Gerar is clearly in the vicinity of the other sites mentioned here, although its specific identity continues to be debated. Most identify Gerar with Tell Abu Hureireh, near Beersheba.

[21]Hormah, literally "a devoted place," stands on the edge of the Negev. It appears in the list of settlements connected with Judah (15:30) and Simeon (19:4). Specific site identification has not been demonstrated conclusively, but Khirbet el-Meshash is a possibility.

[22]Tell Arad, located approximately twenty miles east of Beersheba, is commonly identified as the Arad of the Bible. However, this identification is problematic as the site was abandoned in the middle of the third millennium B.C. and not occupied again until after 1200 B.C. For a statement of the problem and proposed solutions, see Aharoni, *Land of the Bible*, pp. 215-217; or Kitchen, *Reliability*, pp. 192-193.

[23]Adullam has several mentions in the biblical text, but has yet to be firmly identified. Tell esh-Sheik Madkur, five miles south of Beth-Shemesh, is one candidate, but is, as yet, unexcavated. For a discussion of the site name, see Elitzur, *Ancient Place Names*, pp. 137-139.

[24]Tappuah appears to be a name taken by two (or possibly, three) different sites. One is located in the district of Judah (Josh 15:34). Another is in the district of Ephraim (Josh 16:8). A third is possible, if the text of 2 Kgs 15:16 is emended from Tiphsah to Tappuah. Which, if any, of these three sites is mentioned here is unknown.

[25]Hepher is known elsewhere in Solomon's administrative lists (1 Kgs 4:10). It was located in the tribal area of Manasseh and is linked to the ruins at Tell el-Muhaffar in the Valley of Dothan (Zertal, *Shechem Syncline*, pp. 71-72). Thus far, the site is unexcavated.

[26]Aphek is a site located at Tell Ras el-'Ayin, a critical junction in the coastal plain. Excavations in the 1970s and 1980s revealed a substantial LBA presence here, complete with several palaces, the last of which has been identified as an Egyptian fortified residency. See *OEANE*, s.v. "Aphek."

[27]*Lasharon* is literally "to the Sharon" and is not likely a site name (as MT), but instead, a clause modifying Aphek, e.g., "Aphek belonging to the Sharon." This is how the passage is read by the LXX.

Sites from the northern raid appear: **Madon** (11:1), **Hazor,** (11:1, 10-11), **Shimron Meron** (11:1),[28] **Acshaph** (11:1). These are followed by a handful of surprises, consisting of some of the best known and fortified sites in Canaan: **Taanach,**[29] **Megiddo,**[30] **Kedesh,**[31] **Jokneam in Carmel,**[32] **Dor in Naphoth Dor,**[33] **Goyim in Gilgal,**[34] and **Tirzeh.**[35]

Added together, the sites of Cisjordan yield **thirty-one** chiefs.[36] The cumulative effect of this presentation confirms the promise, "no one will be able to stand against you" (1:5).

How did Yahweh lead Israel into Canaan? The answer is simple: victoriously.

---

[28]It is assumed that Shimron Meron is a longer form of the site name that appears in 11:1 as simply Shimron. Some early Greek versions, however, separate Shimron Meron into two separate sites. See Nelson, *Joshua*, p. 158.

[29]Taanach is established at Tell Ta'annek on the south rim of the Jezreel Valley. It was a sizable site, occupied off and on throughout the Bronze Age. Fortifications were erected in the MBA and may have still been in use in Joshua's day. The site was dug for three seasons in the 1960s, but delays in final publication series have slowed the recognition of a significant MBA-LBA presence on the site. See *NEAEHL*, s.v. "Taanach."

[30]Megiddo, firmly located at Tell el-Mutesellim, is perhaps the best-known settlement of the Jezreel Valley. Like its neighbor, Taanach, Megiddo was almost continuously occupied throughout the Bronze Age. A destruction associated with Stratum VIIA is dated to the latter half of the 12th century B.C. Literary and archaeological finds illustrate the importance of this Canaanite center.

[31]The site of Tell Abu Qudeis, associated with Kadesh, is located between Megiddo and Taanach. Early settlement here is Iron I. Another possibility is Tell Qudeish, on the rim of the Hula Basin. Remains here span the Bronze Age.

[32]Jokneam in Carmel is situated at the head of a pass through the Carmel Ridge, about halfway between modern Haifa and the mound of Megiddo. Reference to the site is made in the topographical list of Thutmose III in the 15th century B.C. The LB II settlement (Stratum XIX) was destroyed in the 13th or 12th c. B.C.

[33]For Dor, see comment on 11:2.

[34]"Goyim in Gilgal" is a difficult nut to crack. *Goyim* simply means "gentiles," or "people," although it could reference a particular site. Help is offered by the LXX substitution of "Galilee" for the MT "Gilgal," producing the following construction: "the chief of Goyim (site name) in Galilee (regional name)," akin to "Jokneam (site name) in Carmel (regional name)."

[35]Tirzeh, identified with Tell el-Far'ah (north), is located approximately seven miles northeast of Shechem. Excavations in the last century revealed occupation here throughout the Bronze Age, including LB II (Period VI).

[36]The LXX lists twenty-nine.

JOSHUA 13

II. WHAT HAPPENED AFTER ISRAEL ARRIVED IN CANAAN (13:1–21:45)

The first part of the book of Joshua details how Yahweh led Israel into Canaan. This entrance is nothing short of miraculous: waters are parted at their approach (at the Jordan River), and the occupants of Canaan either shrink back in fear (as at Jericho), foolishly expose themselves (as at The 'Ay and Hazor), or fight each other (as at Gibeon). Setbacks are limited (The 'Ay) and divine assistance is great. This positive assessment culminates in the inventory of conquered chiefs offered in Joshua 12.

However, Israel's success in *entering* this land should not be confused with the effort to *settle* it. This distinction may be contemplated in military, theological, or literary terms. From a military perspective, the difference between running a *blitzkrieg* ("lightning war") over a region and truly achieving control within it is enormous.[1] "Shock and awe" tactics must eventually give way to patient efforts of a finer grind. Neither is pretty; the latter can be pretty personal and pretty risky. A *blitzkrieg* campaign, almost by definition, requires a speed and resolution that moves beyond the ability to support it. Hence, the features that make this tactic effective also render it vulnerable.[2]

---

[1] One need not dig very far for examples. The modern conflict involving United States forces in Iraq clearly reveals this difference. The effort to seize the larger region by immobilizing Iraq's standing army and seizing Iraq's leaders was accomplished in relatively short order. The effort to curb violence on local levels is an ongoing task. Although used by Townshend in a different context, his labels of "high intensity war" and "low intensity conflict" may be profitably brought into this discussion. See his "Introduction" in *The Oxford History of Modern War*, ed. by Charles Townshend, new ed. (Oxford: Oxford University Press, 2005), pp. 18-19.

[2] John Childs acknowledges this dangerous truth in discussing warfare in

From a theological perspective, the difference between *entering* this land and *settling* it may be reduced to what Peterson terms, "a long obedience in the same direction."[3] Unfortunately, capturing this idea in a way that generates traction and relevance in the present day is a real challenge for the expositor of Joshua 12–21. Boundary lists and village inventories hardly make for gripping narrative, unless, of course, the larger trajectory is kept in mind. Israel has been charged with "a great commission." To be successful in this, they must be strong, courageous, careful, and meditative — not just once — but over and over again. Site by site, boundary by boundary, region by region, tribe by tribe, as each name is pronounced, a new opportunity for faithfulness — or faithlessness — arises. Make no mistake: the narrative that follows will not be like that of Rahab and the scouts, a "three day" kind of journey; but rather, a long haul of obedient carry-through that has its beginning in the text of Joshua but goes well beyond it. Judges, Samuel, and Kings will continue the exercise, contemplation, and evaluation of Israel's obedience, each in their own way. And at last, when the end does finally swing round into view, while not exactly a happily-ever-after affair, it does provide an essential beginning point for the best kind of theology: theology with legs. It becomes possible to integrate issues including obedience, land, and the identity of God's people in practical ways that gain traction and movement in the present day.

Finally, briefly, when contemplating the difference between *entering* and *settling* land in literary terms, two issues may be brought forward. First, it must be remembered that *torah* has already given instructions for land division (Num 26:52-56; 33:50-54). Interpreting

---

the Late Middle Ages: "An alternative strategy was to mount a rapid and decisive campaign aimed at achieving political results without becoming involved in a long attritional war. Such thinking probably lay behind the intervention of Gustavus Adolphus of Sweden in Germany in 1630, as well as the French attacks on the Dutch republic in 1672 and Philippsburg in 1688. These 'blitzes' nearly always failed — William of Orange's assault on England in 1688 was about the only successful example — condemning to a long war the belligerent who could not secure a speedy peace." See his "The Military Revolution I," in *The Oxford History of Modern War*, ed. by Charles Townshend, new ed. (Oxford: Oxford University, 2005), pp. 22-23.

[3]Eugene Peterson, *A Long Obedience in the Same Direction: Discipleship in an Instant Society*, 2nd ed. (Downers Grove, IL: InterVarsity, 2000).

Moses on this score means following through with local tribal assignments. To etch these lines on the ground is to once again raise the themes of boundaries and self-identity. Second, as will be demonstrated, the text from here on out is cast as the last acts and words of Joshua. Through these actions and speeches, the incentives for not just settling land but living in it successfully are offered.

An outline for the portion of the text that follows may be suggested. First, a progress report is offered (13:1-7). Second, a glance backward is given to boundaries in Transjordan (13:8-33). Third, the boundaries of Cisjordan are prescribed (14:1–19:51). Finally, some special allowances are offered (20:1–21:45).

A. A PROGRESS REPORT: INCOMPLETE (13:1-7)

1. Future Work for Israel (13:1-5)

¹**When Joshua was old and well advanced in years, the LORD said to him, "You are very old, and there are still very large areas of land to be taken over.**

²**"This is the land that remains: all the regions of the Philistines and Geshurites: ³from the Shihor River on the east of Egypt to the territory of Ekron on the north, all of it counted as Canaanite (the territory of the five Philistine rulers in Gaza, Ashdod, Ashkelon, Gath and Ekron—that of the Avvites ⁴from the south, all the land of the Canaanites, from Arah of the Sidonians as far as Aphek, the region of the Amorites, ⁵the area of the Gebalites[a]; and all Lebanon to the east, from Baal Gad below Mount Hermon to Lebo[b] Hamath.**

ᵃ5 That is, the area of Byblos   ᵇ5 Or *to the entrance to*

13:1 The program for the second major unit of the book comes by way of a speech to Joshua. Within it is a progress report. The narrator gives voice to Yahweh himself, who begins with the juxtaposition of two critical facts. First, Joshua is approaching the end of his life. This announcement comes suddenly, but not unexpectedly, especially when it is remembered that Joshua emerged from the earliest days of the exodus experience. He served as the first military leader of Israel (Exod 17:9-10), participated in the wondrous events of Sinai (Exod 33:11), and helped Moses from his youth (Num 11:28). It is also remembered that he shared with Caleb the claim of "sole survivor": only the two of them outlived the long dry years of wilderness wanderings (Num 14:30).[4] Added to this résumé is notice of his extensive warring experience in Canaan (11:18). Hence, the conclusion grows: Joshua is **old and well advanced in years,** or, more literally, "aged by accumulating days."[5] This is repeated in 23:1-2, creating a specific context in which the intervening text of 13:2–22:34 may be read. This is deserving of further exploration.

The phrase used here of Joshua is also used to describe Abraham and David when they are advanced in age. In each case, this notice does not immediately precede a description of their quiet deaths, but quite the opposite. It introduces a flurry of action that will mark the final "chapter" of their respective lives. In the case of Abraham, *after* this notice of old age (Gen 24:1), he will secure a wife for his son, take a second wife, and, in short, do what he is supposed to do: be a father to many. In the case of David, *after* this notice of old age (1 Kgs 1:1), he will put his house in order, give Solomon some last instructions, and do what he is supposed to do: pass forward the baton of *messiah*-kingship. One wonders if this Joshua text ought not to be read in the same way? The fact that the narrator offers this observation (with half the text of the book still to come) may therefore not be viewed as a prelude to a death notice, but instead, viewed as an introduction to final important actions. It is time for Joshua to do what he is supposed to do. Joshua must put his house in order.

This condition gives urgency to the second critical fact of Yahweh's assessment. While the *Heartland* has been overrun and its inhabitants miraculously — but temporarily — put to flight, the task of possessing this land has barely begun. This announcement is perhaps more surprising than the flight of years: **there are still very large areas of land to be taken over.**[6] Israel's response to a great commission is incomplete. They have yet to get beyond Gilgal (14:6). (See Supplemental Study on "Mission Accomplished.")

---

[4]It is possible that Israel has been in the land of Canaan now for some five years. See the notes for 14:10 below.

[5]The text reads, זָקֵן בָּא בַּיָּמִים (*zāqēn bā' bayyāmîm*).

[6]The phrase here "to be taken over" is a translation of the Hebrew root יָרֵשׁ (*yrš*). In military terms, this term suggests the action of "driving out" or

SUPPLEMENTAL STUDY
"MISSION ACCOMPLISHED"

On War, by Carl von Clausewitz, is an influential work on the philosophy of armed conflict in the West. Within it is discovered an oft-discussed distinction between what Clausewitz terms "absolute war" and "real war." In the case of the former, victory can only be measured at the absolute end of the confrontation. As he writes, "until then, nothing is decided, nothing won, and nothing lost. In this form of war we must always keep in mind that it is the end that crowns the work."[7] On the other hand, "real war" seizes upon the truth that conflict is usually played out as a series of limited engagements. Clausewitz likens it to "match consisting of several games."[8] Emphasis upon this perspective may lead a military strategist to focus upon minor gains while leaving the rest to be concluded in the hands of others. The lesson here for the political state is one of "counting the cost." A war that cannot be won is a war that should not be started.

One wonders if this distinction between "absolute war" and "real war" has been lurking behind a debate in the U.S. "War on Terrorism." On May 1, 2003, President George Bush landed a Navy jet on the flight deck of the carrier, USS Abraham Lincoln. He then stepped to the podium aboard the ship to offer a speech. Behind him hung an enormous red, white, and blue banner proclaiming "Mission Accomplished."[9] This banner did not go unnoticed by the press and produced a vigorous debate as to who put the sign up and for whom. Did it represent the end of the mission for those from the carrier who had finished their tour of duty, or did it align with the point of Bush's speech that day that announced the end of major

---

"seizing." This suggests that the task of conquest is far from complete and that the work that remains is more than simply that of "distribution" or "allotment."

[7]Carl von Clausewitz, *On War,* trans by Michael Howard and Peter Paret (Oxford: Oxford University, 2007), p. 226.

[8]Ibid., p. 227.

[9]Kathleen T. Rhem, "Aboard Lincoln, President Bush Proclaims End to Major Combat Ops in Iraq," Navy News [newspaper on-line]; accessed 2 May, 2003; available from http://www.news.navy.mil/search/display.asp?story_id=7239.

combat operations in Iraq? The latter seems to have been the intention, although the fighting — including major combat operations — continues to this day, some five years after the announcement of "Mission Accomplished."

A similar debate may be raised in light of seemingly conflicting statements found within the text of Joshua. Toward the end of chapter 11 the reader is told that "Joshua took this entire land" and that "the land had rest from war" (11:16,23). Yet by the beginning of chapter 13 it is realized that "there are still very large areas of land to be taken over" (13:1). One way of reading these texts is to simply confess that this is a contradiction of fact, either brought about inadvertently as a result of poor logic and bumbly editing, or that the contradiction is in some way deliberate, intended to cultivate humor or irony. Neither option is very attractive. A second way of reading these texts is to soften their claims by appealing to hyperbole. This would seem to be a better way to go; rhetorical features like this are common to military reports from the late second millennium.[10] In fact, compared to some, the statements of Joshua are downright conservative! A third possibility may in some way seize upon Clausewitz's distinction between "absolute war" and "real war." Viewed in absolute terms, the statements of Joshua would seem to be false or contradictory, checked almost immediately by counterclaims within the text itself. Canaan has been overrun and is exhausted (another way of reading "had rest from") but is not occupied. On the other hand, when these statements are placed into Clausewitz's sense of "real war," or, better yet, as a series of limited engagements, some reconciliation is achieved. One stage of the conflict in Canaan is complete. However, there are many more engagements to come.

13:2-3 The land that remains to be seized is described in a series of two sweeping measures. The first finds focus on the south coastal plain resting between the Mediterranean Sea and the central ridge of Judah. This rich and open land is easy to enter but difficult to hold as alternating waves of occupants historically attest. The

---

[10]Consider the late 13th century B.C. Egyptian claims of the Merneptah Stela: the site of "Yano'am is made non-existent"; as for the people Israel, "its grain is not" (Hasel, *"Israel* in the Merneptah Stela," p. 53). Other examples may be found (Kitchen, *Reliability*, p. 174).

Philistines are perhaps the best known of these biblically, but not to be ignored are lesser-known groups such as the **Geshurites**[11] and the **Avvites**.[12] Measured differently, this untouched region extends from the **Sihor River**, likely the Wadi el-'Arish,[13] to the "border of" **Ekron**.[14] Between these rest the five cities of the Philistines (the so-called Philistine "Pentapolis").[15] Regardless of who occupies this land at the moment, the reminder is issued: it is **counted as Canaanite**, and is therefore a part of Israel's inheritance.

13:4-5 A second measure of the Canaanite "land that remains" seems to indicate the north coastal plain. Here, reference points offered include **Arah of the Sidonians**[16] and **Aphek**. Assuming the iden-

---

[11]Known elsewhere in this southern context in 1 Sam 27:8.

[12]The Avvites or Avites appear to have been the earlier inhabitants of the plain, cf. Deut 2:23.

[13]This system drains the desert wastes between the Negev and the Sinai Peninsula. It may also be called the "River of Egypt" (Josh 15:4). For a discussion, see *NBD*, s.v. "Egypt, River of."

[14]Excavations at Khirbet el-Muqanna' (Tel Miqne) have positively identified this site as biblical Ekron. Revealed settlement demonstrates occupation for more than a millennium, from the 17th through the early 6th centuries B.C. The site overlooks the major route connecting Egypt with Mesopotamia. For a linguistic discussion, see Elitzur, *Ancient Place Names*, pp. 119-121. As for the identities of the other Philistine cities (Gaza, Ashdod, Ashkelon, and Gath) and the results of their excavations, consult Trude Dothan, *The Philistines and Their Material Culture* (New Haven: Yale, 1982), pp. 25-93.

[15]It is alleged that this mention of the Philistines here is anachronistic since evidence for their intensive settlement in Palestine is not clear until the early Iron I period (12th century B.C). Two responses may be mustered. First, such a claim appears larger than the text, as a Philistine presence is not necessarily demanded here. The description of land may be in terms contemporary with the time of writing. Put differently, the narrator describes the land in terms of what it will become rather than what it is. Second, and perhaps more importantly (given the presence of "Philistines" in Genesis): it is possible that early Aegean traders and merchants were present in Palestine in advance of the better known 12th century invasions. The group known as the *Luka* in the Amarna letters (14th century B.C.) appears to be akin to the Sea Peoples. See *NBD*, s.v. "Philistines, Philistia," or Dothan, *Philistines and Their Material Culture*, p. 1.

[16]This place is unknown. The NIV reads the Hebrew, וּמְעָרָה (*ûmᵊ'ārāh*), as the *waw* conjunction "and" plus the preposition *min*, "from," plus a proper name, *'ārāh*. No town by this name is known. Other translations (ASV, NASB, NKJV, etc.) opt to include the *mem* as a part of the proper name, hence, "Mearah." This still does not relieve the difficulty as this name is not known elsewhere either.

tification of Aphek with Afqa in modern Lebanon, this region includes coastal stretches northward to Tyre and beyond. In terms of people groups this is the territory of the Sidonians, Gebalites (Byblians), or Phoenicians. Their land is remembered as "The Lebanon" and is marked on the ground by **Baal Gad**[17] and **Lebo Hamath**.[18]

2. Future Work for Yahweh (13:6-7)

[6]**"As for all the inhabitants of the mountain regions from Lebanon to Misrephoth Maim, that is, all the Sidonians, I myself will drive them out before the Israelites. Be sure to allocate this land to Israel for an inheritance, as I have instructed you, [7]and divide it as an inheritance among the nine tribes and half of the tribe of Manasseh."**

13:6-7 From a description of the Canaanite "land that remains," the progress report of Yahweh drifts back to the mandate. Those who occupy the inland northern highlands will be impoverished or dispossessed by Yahweh himself; Israel's responsibility is to allocate it as an inheritance. Hence, the final instruction here pertains to the whole of Cisjordan and reinforces themes of joint responsibility already introduced. Yahweh will lead and dispossess; Israel must follow faithfully and possess. The task of an aging Joshua to "put the house in order" involves dividing the land among the remaining tribal groups for conquest and settlement. These remaining groups number nine and a half tribes. Two and a half tribes have already been given land in Transjordan. The narrator turns to this latter group first.

B. THE DIVISION OF TRANSJORDAN REMEMBERED (13:8-33)

Following the orientation by Yahweh the narrator returns to work, describing land allotments previously given to the tribes of Reuben, Gad, and half of Manasseh.[19] This division of the "land

---

[17]See note at 11:17.

[18]For Lebo-hamath, see Benjamin Mazar, "Lebo-hamath and the Northern Border of Canaan," in *The Early Biblical Period Historical Studies*, ed. by Shmuel Aḥituv and Baruch A. Levine (Jerusalem: IES, 1986), pp. 189-202.

[19]Num 32:1-34:15; Deut 3:8-22.

toward the sunrise" (cf. 1:12-15; 12:1-6) comes as prelude to the division of Cisjordan. The larger limits are defined (13:8-14) and followed by specific tribal allotments to Reuben (13:15-23), Gad (13:24-28), and Manasseh (East) (13:29-32). Indelibly stamped throughout is the name of Moses (13:8,12,15,24,29,32,33). The likeness, again, is uncanny; just as Moses makes land assignments, so too, his successor. It is therefore appropriate to preface Joshua's work in Cisjordan by remembering Moses' work in Transjordan.

1. Transjordan Defined (13:8-14)

[8]The other half of Manasseh,[a] the Reubenites and the Gadites had received the inheritance that Moses had given them east of the Jordan, as he, the servant of the LORD, had assigned it to them.

[9]It extended from Aroer on the rim of the Arnon Gorge, and from the town in the middle of the gorge, and included the whole plateau of Medeba as far as Dibon, [10]and all the towns of Sihon king of the Amorites, who ruled in Heshbon, out to the border of the Ammonites. [11]It also included Gilead, the territory of the people of Geshur and Maacah, all of Mount Hermon and all Bashan as far as Salecah— [12]that is, the whole kingdom of Og in Bashan, who had reigned in Ashtaroth and Edrei and had survived as one of the last of the Rephaites. Moses had defeated them and taken over their land. [13]But the Israelites did not drive out the people of Geshur and Maacah, so they continue to live among the Israelites to this day.

[14]But to the tribe of Levi he gave no inheritance, since the offerings made by fire to the LORD, the God of Israel, are their inheritance, as he promised them.

[a]8 Hebrew *With it* (that is, with the other half of Manasseh)

13:8-12 The larger description of Transjordan begins in the south and sweeps northward in three strokes.[20] The first stroke begins at the

---

[20]For maps and verbal descriptions of the regions of Transjordan, see Baly, *Geography*, pp. 210-240; or G.A. Smith, *Historical Geography of the Holy Land*, pp. 335-397.

edge of wilderness where the border fortress of **Aroer**[21] guards the
rim of the yawning **Arnon Gorge.** North of this gorge the rich flatlands of **Medeba**[22] stretch out and are connected with **Dibon**[23] and
other Amorite sites. The second stroke begins with the rising folds of
Gilead and includes the people of **Geshur and Maacah.** The third
stroke completes the description, reaching as far as the dramatic highlands of **Bashan** and **Mt. Hermon** (the modern "Golan Heights").
Placed end to end, the regions covered in these three strokes encompass more than one hundred miles from south to north. Preserved
within these folds and flats are memories of past victories.

13:13 Juxtaposed against these victories, however, is an ominous
notice. Failure to remove the **people of Geshur and Maacah** from
Transjordan will result in their continued presence within Israel.
That the region of Transjordan is considered "Israel" should not be
missed. The question of defining "Israel" is kept alive; it will be contemplated yet again before the book concludes. The Jordan River
may divide the land in a physical way, but clearly, Israel is found on
both banks. More to the moment, the warning of 13:13 corresponds
with Yahweh's announcement of 13:1 and reminds the reader that
obedience to *torah* is the primary challenge for Israel (cf. 1:7-8).

13:14 In this immediate context, the **tribe of Levi** receives no
inheritance of land. Rather, "the fire of Yahweh, God of Israel" is to
be their legacy. This odd phrase signals Levi's unique role as the ten-
ders of the altar of sacrifice. While the comment may appear out of
place, the corresponding note in 13:33 indicates otherwise. Descriptions of the Transjordan inheritance are carefully framed by the conclusion that the tribe of Levi will not be involved with land grant
issues here. Their focus lies elsewhere.[24]

---

[21]Aroer is likely identified with Khirbet Arair. Bronze and Iron Age
remains have been recovered from this dramatic site. See the discussion by
MacDonald, *"East of the Jordan,"* pp. 96-97.

[22]Ancient Medaba is found in the center of a modern town by the same
name, located some 18 miles south of Amman. Archaeological work to
reveal this region is ongoing through the Madaba Plains Project and others.
For more, see Øystein LaBianca, *Sedentarization and Nomadization. Hesban 1*
(Berrien Springs, MI: Andrews University, 1990); or MacDonald, *"East of the
Jordan,"* pp. 108-110.

[23]The ancient name of Dibon is preserved in the modern Arab village of
Dhiban, immediately to the north of the Arnon gorge. For more, see
MacDonald, *"East of the Jordan,"* pp. 84-85.

[24]It may also be a concern of the narrator to keep the number of tribes of

2. Reuben's Land (13:15-23)

¹⁵**This is what Moses had given to the tribe of Reuben, clan by clan:**

¹⁶**The territory from Aroer on the rim of the Arnon Gorge, and from the town in the middle of the gorge, and the whole plateau past Medeba ¹⁷to Heshbon and all its towns on the plateau, including Dibon, Bamoth Baal, Beth Baal Meon, ¹⁸Jahaz, Kedemoth, Mephaath, ¹⁹Kiriathaim, Sibmah, Zereth Shahar on the hill in the valley, ²⁰Beth Peor, the slopes of Pisgah, and Beth Jeshimoth ²¹—all the towns on the plateau and the entire realm of Sihon king of the Amorites, who ruled at Heshbon. Moses had defeated him and the Midianite chiefs, Evi, Rekem, Zur, Hur and Reba—princes allied with Sihon—who lived in that country. ²²In addition to those slain in battle, the Israelites had put to the sword Balaam son of Beor, who practiced divination. ²³The boundary of the Reubenites was the bank of the Jordan. These towns and their villages were the inheritance of the Reubenites, clan by clan.**

13:15-23 Just as the larger definition of Transjordan moves from south to north, so too, does the allotment of tribal territory. Of the three descriptions offered, Reuben's land is the most detailed. Specific site-, feature-, and personal-names are sprinkled throughout this description of territory that corresponds to the narrow tableland immediately east of the Dead Sea.[25] This fertile steppe zone is transitional in many ways; the desert from the east and south seasonally presses it.[26] Survival strategies require water conservation

---

Israel at twelve. By counting the Joseph tribes of Ephraim and Manasseh separately, the count of Israel's tribes rises to thirteen. See 14:4 below.

[25]Sites mentioned by name that correspond to Heshbon (Tell Jalul?) include Dibon (Dhiban), Bamoth Baal (Jebel Atarus?), Beth Baal Meon (Main?), Jahaz (Libb?, Khirbet Iskander? Khirbet el Medeiyineh?), Kedemoth (Kasr ez-Za'feran or Khirbet er Remeil), Mephaath (Tell Jawa?), Kiriathaim, Sibmah (Khirbet al-Qibsh), Zereth Shahar (Khirbet Qurn el-Kibsh?, Khirbet el-Libb? or Zarat?), Beth Peor (Khirbet Uyun Musa?), and Beth Jeshimoth (Tell el-Azeme?). For a fairly recent discussion of this list, as well as sites appearing in the region of Gad and eastern Manasseh, see MacDonald, *"East of the Jordan,"* pp. 132-145.

[26]For a more thorough description, see Baly, *Geography*, pp. 226-228.

and a mixed approach of animal herding and cereal farming. Of the site- and feature-names mentioned, some are known elsewhere in the biblical text (e.g., Heshbon, Dibon, Beth Peor, Jahaz) but many are not. Similarly, some sites have been confidently identified as a result of archaeological excavation (e.g., Aroer, Dibon) but many continue to be debated. Personal names such as Sihon and Balaam recall the dangers posed by the inhabitants of the land and Israel's victories over them (cf. Numbers 21, 31).

3. Gad's Land (13:24-28)

[24]**This is what Moses had given to the tribe of Gad, clan by clan:**

[25]**The territory of Jazer, all the towns of Gilead and half the Ammonite country as far as Aroer, near Rabbah;** [26]**and from Heshbon to Ramath Mizpah and Betonim, and from Mahanaim to the territory of Debir;** [27]**and in the valley, Beth Haram, Beth Nimrah, Succoth and Zaphon with the rest of the realm of Sihon king of Heshbon (the east side of the Jordan, the territory up to the end of the Sea of Kinnereth[a]).** [28]**These towns and their villages were the inheritance of the Gadites, clan by clan.**

[a]**27 That is, Galilee**

13:24-28 Territory assigned to the tribe of Gad rests to the north of Reuben's assignment. It includes the **territory of Jazer,** possibly identified with the Wadi Shu'ayb system (cf. Num 32:1),[27] **all the towns of Gilead**, located along the mountainous highlands on either side of the Wadi Jabbok, and **half the Ammonite country**, resting at the upland end of the Wadi Jabbok system.[28] These three descriptors indicate a parcel of land running parallel to the (Lower) Jordan Valley, stretching from the southern end of the Sea of Galilee to the northern end of the Dead Sea. Excellent rainfall in the region provides moisture from above and from below (through

---

[27]Jazer appears as a site and a region. It appears to be preserved at Khirbet Jazzir in the *Wadi Shu'ayb*, located approximately 18 miles northeast of Jericho. See MacDonald, *"East of the Jordan,"* p. 112.

[28]Moses did not give the homeland of Ammon to Israel. It was off limits for the sake of Lot (Deut 2:19).

springs).[29] Thick forests here are famous (2 Sam 18:8) and cultivation is possible where clearings are made. Two lines of settlements are offered, the first running along the scarp above where the (Lower) Jordan Valley breaks off.[30] The second follows the Jordan Valley floor.[31]

4. Manasseh's (East) Land (13:29-31)

[29]This is what Moses had given to the half-tribe of Manasseh, that is, to half the family of the descendants of Manasseh, clan by clan:

[30]The territory extending from Mahanaim and including all of Bashan, the entire realm of Og king of Bashan—all the settlements of Jair in Bashan, sixty towns, [31]half of Gilead, and Ashtaroth and Edrei (the royal cities of Og in Bashan). This was for the descendants of Makir son of Manasseh—for half of the sons of Makir, clan by clan.

13:29-31 The third territory to be delineated is assigned to half of the tribe of Manasseh (a second parcel on the west side of the Jordan is offered in 17:1-18). Of the three Transjordan land descriptions, this is the least specific. It involves what was previously the realm of **Og of Bashan**, the campsites[32] **of Jair**, and half of Gilead. This collective description indicates a region north of the territory of Gad and centers on the Yarmuk basin. This is a brutal land.[33] Volcanic activity in the hoary past has scarred it with cinder cones and lava

---

[29]For a more thorough description, see Baly, *Geography*, pp. 219-225.

[30]This elevated line of settlement runs from Heshbon to Ramath Mizpah, Betonim (Khirbet el-Batne?), Mahanaim (Tell edh-Dhahab?), and Debir (Umm el-Dabar?). See MacDonald, *"East of the Jordan,"* for discussions of these sites.

[31]This lower line of settlement runs from Beth Haram (Tell er-Rameh or Tell Iktanu?) to Beth Nimrah (Tell Nimrin or Tell el-Bleibil?), Succoth (Tell Deir Allah?), and Zaphon (Tell el-Qos, Tell es-Sa'idiyyeh, or Tell el-Mazar?). See ibid. for discussions of these sites.

[32]"Campsite" or "tent-village" is suggested by the Hebrew חַוָּה (*ḥāwwāh*). Such language is indicative of the lifestyle of nomadic peoples. Later in 13:30, the term עִיר (*'îr*), "city," is used in apposition to *ḥāwwāh* suggesting that a modern understanding of "city" in this time and place must be seriously downgraded.

[33]For a more thorough description, see Baly, *Geography*, pp. 213-219.

flows. Winter weather is frigid, marked by heavy rain and snow. Only with coaxing can cereal grains be planted and harvested. Overlooking it all, the head of Mt. Hermon (Arabic, *Jebel es-Sheikh*, "old man mountain") rises like a frosty sentinel to an elevation of more than 9,000 feet.

The site of **Mahanaim** figures into the description of Gad's land (13:26); now it poses as a southern border to the land of Manasseh. Other sites mentioned by name include **Ashtaroth and Edrei**, sites previously controlled by Og.[34] These regions and sites are given specifically to the **descendants of Makir son of Manasseh**. It is hardly accidental that the progeny of this tough warrior (cf. 17:1) is given a tough land.

5. The Memory Summarized (13:32-33)

[32]**This is the inheritance Moses had given when he was in the plains of Moab across the Jordan east of Jericho. [33]But to the tribe of Levi, Moses had given no inheritance; the LORD, the God of Israel, is their inheritance, as he promised them.**

13:32-33 Two concluding statements summarize the description of the Transjordan allotment. First, the reader is reminded that these boundaries are not freshly invented, but are anticipated by the commands of Moses (cf. Num 32:33-42). Second, the reader is reminded that Levi will not receive a land grant (13:14). This declaration with regard to "the word" of **the LORD, the God of Israel**, laces together this description of inheritance with the authority behind the memory.

---

[34]Ashtaroth is elsewhere referred to as Ashtaroth-karnaim or "Ashtaroth of the (two) horns" (Gen 14:5). This name likely refers to the Canaanite goddess of fertility who is depicted, at times, with a set of horns on her head. It is possible that this site is represented today by the remains at Tel Ashtarah, some 20 miles east of the Sea of Galilee. See MacDonald, *"East of the Jordan,"* pp. 152-153, n. 5. The location of Edrei may tentatively be identified with the modern site of Dera'a in Syria (ibid., p. 151, n. 1).

JOSHUA 14

C. THE DIVISION OF CISJORDAN PRESCRIBED (14:1–19:51)

The allotment of land shifts from the area east of the Jordan (Transjordan) to the area west of the Jordan (Cisjordan). By way of prelude, additional reminders of obedience are pulled forward (14:1-5) and one vignette of obedience and success is offered (14:6-15). This is followed by a description of allotment given to three tribes: Judah (15:1-63), Ephraim (16:1-10), and Manasseh (West) (17:1-18). Following additional reconnaissance (18:1-10), the allotments given to the seven remaining tribes are detailed (18:11–19:51). The correlation between 14:1 and 19:51 creates a bracket for this section and establishes it as a distinct thought-block within the larger presentation.

1. Continuing Reminders (14:1-5)

¹Now these are the areas the Israelites received as an inheritance in the land of Canaan, which Eleazar the priest, Joshua son of Nun and the heads of the tribal clans of Israel allotted to them. ²Their inheritances were assigned by lot to the nine-and-a-half tribes, as the LORD had commanded through Moses. ³Moses had granted the two-and-a-half tribes their inheritance east of the Jordan but had not granted the Levites an inheritance among the rest, ⁴for the sons of Joseph had become two tribes—Manasseh and Ephraim. The Levites received no share of the land but only towns to live in, with pasturelands for their flocks and herds. ⁵So the Israelites divided the land, just as the LORD had commanded Moses.

14:1-5 The narrative leaves no doubt that this division of Canaan is in keeping with *torah*. As with the Transjordan allotments, the responsibility of land distribution is given by Moses to Eleazar,[1] Joshua, and the tribal heads. Specific reference to these three agents — even down to the detail of their order — follows the mandate of Numbers 32:28. Similarly, the sacred lot as the means of apportionment is specified, a reminder that personal or tribal agendas have no play here; such choices are the work of Yahweh alone. Additionally, just as in the previous chapter, the Levite legacy is noted,[2] the name of Moses surfaces repeatedly, and the note of Israelite compliance is raised. Such narrative circling (at risk of digression) clarifies the thrust of the text: God leads; Israel follows.

2. Caleb's Story as a Conquest Model (14:6-15)

[6]**Now the men of Judah approached Joshua at Gilgal, and Caleb son of Jephunneh the Kenizzite said to him, "You know what the LORD said to Moses the man of God at Kadesh Barnea about you and me. [7]I was forty years old when Moses the servant of the LORD sent me from Kadesh Barnea to explore the land. And I brought him back a report according to my convictions, [8]but my brothers who went up with me made the hearts of the people melt with fear. I, however, followed the LORD my God wholeheartedly. [9]So on that day Moses swore to me, 'The land on which your feet have walked will be your inheritance and that of your children forever, because you have followed the LORD my God wholeheartedly.'**[a]

[10]**"Now then, just as the LORD promised, he has kept me alive for forty-five years since the time he said this to Moses, while Israel moved about in the desert. So here I am today, eighty-five**

---

[1]Eleazar appears in 14:1 for the first time in the text of Joshua. *Torah* presents Eleazar as the third son of Aaron (Exod 6:23). After the death of his father, Eleazar served as High Priest of Israel. In this context it is significant that Eleazar is presented as the keeper of the Urim (Num 27:21) presumably the sacred "lot" (גּוֹרָל, *gôral*) referred to in Josh 14:2.

[2]The present context suggests that the narrative impulse is to maintain Israel as twelve tribes. In 14:4, the Joseph legacy is clearly divided between Manasseh and Ephraim. Each of these tribes will receive a land grant. However, Levi will not. This is not the first mention of this fact concerning Levi (cf. 13:14,33), but it is the first mention of it juxtaposed against the division of Joseph's legacy. In the end, even though Levi is excluded, 12 tribes will receive land grants.

years old! [11]I am still as strong today as the day Moses sent me out; I'm just as vigorous to go out to battle now as I was then. [12]Now give me this hill country that the LORD promised me that day. You yourself heard then that the Anakites were there and their cities were large and fortified, but, the LORD helping me, I will drive them out just as he said."

[13]Then Joshua blessed Caleb son of Jephunneh and gave him Hebron as his inheritance. [14]So Hebron has belonged to Caleb son of Jephunneh the Kenizzite ever since, because he followed the LORD, the God of Israel, wholeheartedly. [15](Hebron used to be called Kiriath Arba after Arba, who was the greatest man among the Anakites.)

Then the land had rest from war.

[a]9 Deut. 1:36

One vignette of obedience and success is identified in Caleb's story. It is rooted in Israel's loss of nerve experienced when the scouts returned to Kadesh Barnea from Canaan (Numbers 13–14). However, a closer correspondence in vocabulary is found when the text of Joshua 14:6-15 is compared to Moses' recollection of the event in Deuteronomy 1:19-46. In the present context, Caleb's story presses three points of interest. First, the discussion of *how* the people of God are to be defined is renewed. Second, faithful obedience to Moses and *torah* is emphasized. Third, as the first to receive a Cisjordan inheritance, Caleb's story is presented as a model for the rest of the tribes awaiting their parcels. In these three ways, this small but important narrative pulls at threads knotted elsewhere.

14:6-9 The speech of Caleb[3] comes as the **men of Judah** approach Joshua, presumably with a request. Their meeting occurs

---

[3]The name Caleb (כָּלֵב, *Kālēb*) is drawn from the root *klb*, literally meaning "dog." While it is possible to conclude that names taken from the animal world should be rendered generally as terms of endearment (in this case, possibly "Whelp"), it is a difficult leap with canines in this time and place. In the Near East, dogs appear as unclean scavengers, carrion eaters, blood-lickers, and churlish beasts. A name like Caleb can hardly be regarded as a blessing. At best, he is a slave or watchman. The study, however, does give a nuance to this character and reinforces the conclusion that he is an outsider. Like the character Rahab, he is truly the "Underdog"! See *TWOT*, s.v. כלב. For more on names, see Supplemental Study on Theophoric Names below.

in **Gilgal**, and, if taken in sequence with the book's presentation, demonstrates yet another return to this familiar base.[4] The specific identification of Caleb here cannot be overlooked; he is, yet isn't, Israel. He represents the tribe of Judah in word and deed (cf. Num 13:6), yet is still specifically numbered among **the son of Jephunneh the Kenizzite**.[5] Elsewhere it is clear that the Kenizzites trace their line of descent from Esau and are more properly identified as Edomite than Israelite (Gen 36:11). Furthermore, Kenizzites are listed among the nine people groups inhabiting Canaan at the time of Abraham, a people from whom this land of promise is clearly to be snatched away (Gen 15:19)! To label Caleb as a Kenizzite can hardly be reckoned as a narrative slip; it seems to be a deliberate move to push him — and the thoughtful reader — to the edge of the envelope of an ethnic definition of Israel.

Once this edge is felt, the memory that Caleb resurrects from Kadesh Barnea can be properly considered (cf. Num 13:30; 14:6-9, 38; Deut 1:36). Like the speech of Rahab (Josh 2:9-13), Caleb's recollected words outstrip those of the scouts and communicate confidence in the power and program of Yahweh. For this reason, Caleb was promised an inheritance by Moses, a promise Joshua is urged now to make good. Word choices initiate a rush of flashbacks: Caleb's commission is given at age **forty**, a familiar starting point (cf. Gen 25:20; 26:34), Moses is titled a **servant of the LORD** (e.g., Deut 34:5), Caleb's report is offered **according to my convictions** (lit. "from my heart"), whereas the report of the other scouts **made the hearts of the people melt with fear** (cf. Deut 1:28; Josh 2:11). Beyond these, the theme of the pedestrian expedition is recalled by the phrase, **the land**

---

[4]This is particularly surprising. The text of 13:1 suggests that considerable time had passed since Israel's initial entry into the land. If 14:10 is read straightforwardly, it is possible that this time measures five years. See note on 14:10 below.

[5]While Caleb is regularly described as "the son of Jephunneh" only here and in Num 32:12 is he also described as a Kenizzite. For more on Caleb's assimilation, see de Vaux, *Ancient Israel*, p. 6.

An alternative view to the one presented here reckons Caleb as a descendent of an unknown Judahite named Kenaz. This would resolve the presupposed tension raised by considering Caleb as an "outsider." There are two men named Kenaz in Caleb's genealogy, one is his brother, the other, his grandson (1 Chr 4:13,15). For this and other thoughts, see Woudstra, *Joshua*, p. 227, n. 1.

on which your feet have walked (cf. Josh 1:3), as is the power of human choice. Caleb may inherit because he **followed the LORD . . . wholeheartedly** (cf. Deut 1:36). The logical vortex has gravity: Caleb is pulled into the center of what Israel should look like and is elevated as the model of faithfulness in this "Great Commission" enterprise. How can Joshua — much less the reader — deny him?[6]

SUPPLEMENTAL STUDY

THEOPHORIC NAMES

In cultures where names carry meaning, theophoric (from the Greek θεός, *theos*, "God" and φέρω, *pherō*, "to bear or carry") elements are important markers. They communicate aspects of personal belief by conveying something about who/what God is, what God has done in the past, or what one hopes God will do in the future. There are many theophoric names in the text of the Old Testament, some connected to the name of the God of Israel, Yahweh (shortened to *Yah, Yaho,* or *Yahu*) including Hezekiah, חִזְקִיָּה (*Ḥizqiyyāh,* "*Yah* strengthens"), Jeremiah, יִרְמְיָהוּ (*Yirmᵊyahu,* "*Yahu* has loosed," possibly in reference to the womb?), or Jehoshaphat, יְהוֹשָׁפָט (*Yᵊhôšāphāṭ,* "Let *Yaho* judge"). Other theophoric names utilize the more generic word for God (אֱלֹהִים, *ᵓĕlōhîm,* or simply *ᵓēl*). The person of Ezekiel, יְחֶזְקֵאל (*Yᵊḥezqē'l,* "*El* makes strong") and the place name Jezreel, יִזְרְעֵאל (*Yizrᵊ'ē'l,* "*El* plants"), come quickly to mind. Finally some names found in the biblical text reflect the existence of other, non-Israelite, systems of belief. Gideon is also remembered as Jerub-Baal, יְרֻבַּעַל (*Yᵊrub-ba'al,* "Let Baal contend"), while one of Daniel's friends will be issued a new name in a new place, oddly, honoring a Babylonian deity, Abednego (עֲבֵד נְגוֹ, *'ăbed-nᵊgô,* "Servant of *Nego*"). Even the term Israel (יִשְׂרָאֵל, *Yiśrā'ēl*), is considered theophoric, although there is no agreement concerning its meaning ("God contends," "He contends with God," or even "God

---

[6]Our reading contrasts others who encounter this episode of Caleb and regard it as "surprising" (Harris, Brown, and Moore, *Joshua, Judges, Ruth,* p. 86) or a "digression" (Nelson, *Joshua,* p. 176). Rather than being awkwardly placed, Caleb's story is viewed as the paradigm to be imitated by all would-be inheritors.

heals"). Names like these display the depth of spiritual belief and experience felt across the world of the Old Testament.

In the text of Joshua, there are far more place names than people names, but theophoric elements are found amongst both categories. The site of Ashtaroth (עַשְׁתָּרוֹת, 'Aštārôth) (9:10), loosely, "Goddesses-city," is clearly derived from the pagan fertility figure, Astart or Ashtoreth. The same is true of Baal-gad (בַּעַל־גָּד, Baʿal-gād) (11:17), "Baal is lucky," as well as Beth-dagon (בֵּית־דָּגוֹן, Bêth-dāgôn) (15:41), "Dagon's place," village-names that incorporate Canaanite fertility gods in their labels. Less threatening, perhaps, are Bethel (בֵּית־אֵל, Bêth-'ēl) (7:2), "house of El," and the more prayerful, Jabneel (יַבְנְאֵל, Yabn'ʾēl) (15:11), "Let El build." These suggest either a generic term for God (ēl) or the high god of the Canaanite pantheon.

The pool of personal names in the text of Joshua is smaller, yet, theophoric elements are found here too. The marvelously repugnant name of Og (עוֹג, 'Ôg) given to the King of Bashan (2:10), lumbers down from the throne of some ancient pagan deity. The king of Jerusalem is called Adoni-Zedek (אֲדֹנִי־צֶדֶק, 'ădōnî-ṣedeq), "My master is ṣedeq," likely referring to a Canaanite god (10:1). Among named Israelites, familiar combinations using el and yah are encountered. The son-in-law of Caleb, Othniel (עָתְנִיאֵל, 'Othnî'ēl) ("God is powerful") (15:17), and the high priest and son of Aaron, Eleazar (אֶלְעָזָר, 'Elʿāzār) ("God has helped") (14:1) demonstrate use of El. Examples using an abbreviated form of the tetragrammaton, YHWH, include the tribal name Judah (יְהוּדָה, Y'hûdāh) ("Praise Yah!") (7:1), and the namesake of the book, Joshua (יְהוֹשֻׁעַ, Y'hôšûaʿ) ("Yah saves!" or "Let Yah save!").

14:10-12 The final basis for Caleb's claim leaps from the distant past to "this day." It has been forty-five years since he and Joshua issued their minority report at Kadesh Barnea, yet Caleb's gusto has not diminished.[7] **I am still as strong today as the day Moses sent me out.** To this he adds that "as my power was then, so it is now"[8] for

---

[7]As elsewhere, the interpretation of numbers in the book of Joshua is difficult. However, if read straightforwardly, it may be surmised that Israel has been in Canaan for five years. Caleb has aged forty years in the desert wanderings and now five more years in the land.

[8]This loosely translates כְּכֹחִי אָז וּכְכֹחִי עַתָּה (k'kōḥî 'āz ûk'kōḥî 'attāh), "as my

the purposes of battle.[9] Crediting Yahweh for his amazing preservation at age eighty-five, he presses his claim: **give me** this hill (country). The object of his request is grammatically definite but difficult to define on the basis of this phrase alone. Caleb refers to "this elevated peak" or "ridge," possibly gesturing toward the Central Ridge of Canaan. This long north-south watershed arches like a backbone to the land of promise, rising ever higher southwards until it tumbles down into the Negev. From the region of Gilgal, it casts a long shadow and is truly representative of the whole of Cisjordan. This last thought raises the possibility that the ambiguity of Caleb's claim, "give me this hill (country)," may be deliberate. While aged, his voice has become that of a new generation in Israel, indeed, a new *type* of Israel: those who remember Yahweh's promises from the past and are eager and ready to follow Yahweh's lead in the future.

Further confirmation that the whole of Cisjordan is within Caleb's purview comes by way of his recognition of the **Anakite** presence. These people live in "this hill (country)" in **large and fortified** settlements, but may be driven out only with Yahweh's help. This rare reference to a particular type of Canaanite takes its cue from Numbers 13:33 where the Anakites are described as the descendants of the נְפִלִים (Nᵉphilîm), the "fallen ones," or possibly, "giants."[10] It is this specific group that makes Israel look like grasshoppers and generates the fear that foils the original invasion. Caleb musters this

---

power (was) then, so my power (is) now." The word translated as "power" (כֹּחַ, kōaḥ) here in the second half of v. 11 is different than the word for "strong" (חָזָק, ḥāzāq) appearing in the first half of v. 11. The former term, kōaḥ, may refer to raw strength or working power; it is used of Samson (e.g., Judg 16:17), bulls (Prov 14:4), and rams (Dan 8:7). It may also denote mental acuity (Dan 1:4). The later word, ḥāzāq, also communicates strength and vigor; it is used of things that are secure or hardened, such as foreheads and hearts (e.g., Ezek 2:4; 3:8), swords and sword-hands (e.g., Isa 27:1; Ezek 30:21), and authorities and kingdoms (e.g., Num 13:18; Isa 40:10).

[9]The phrase "for coming in and going out" may be an idiom of military action, cf. 1 Sam 29:6. See Butler, *Joshua*, p. 168.

[10]The Anakites or "sons of Anak" appear also in Deut 1:28; 9:2; Num 13:22,28; Josh 11:22; 15:13,14; Judg 1:20. They appear in the text as the "ultimate Canaanite," fearsome warriors who are "larger than life." The LXX rendering of "the sons of Anak" in Deut 1:28 is υἱοὺς γιγάντων (huious gigantōn), or "sons of giants"! Nothing is known of this people group apart from the Bible.

image of "the ultimate Canaanite" in order to stress his own personal devotion certainly; but in a larger narrative sense, it sketches the limits of the possible. As in Kadesh Barnea, Caleb eloquently argues that even the largest threat imaginable cannot withstand Israel when empowered by Yahweh. Through his recollection, the goals of the narrative are nudged forward. Caleb becomes the poster-child of obedience and success in Cisjordan; his vignette provides an opportunity to compare and contrast all other examples (such as the Joseph tribes in 17:14-18). Less obviously, it again asks well-worn questions: Who exactly is Israel and what can or will Israel do? Finally, Caleb's story serves as a calculated prelude to the mechanical description of land division to follow. Will other individuals of his ilk rise to the challenge of giant-killing and stronghold-taking?

14:13-15 Joshua blesses Caleb and honors the promises given him by Yahweh through Moses. In the end, Caleb is given "this hill," or more specifically, the settlement of Hebron, resting on the last and highest point of the Central Ridge. While this point has been overrun previously as part of a regional raid (10:36-37), further action in securing and settling this highland site and its satellite villages will be necessary.

Three further notes of interest are offered to close the chapter. First, Caleb's willingness to follow Yahweh's lead wholeheartedly is repeated, emphasizing his role as a model conquistador. Second, further comment on Hebron's identification and heritage is given. Noted is Hebron's previous name, **Kiriath Arba,** or "city of Arba," named after the most hair-raising of all the "ultimate Canaanites"! Third and finally, closure is brought to the section, "then the land was exhausted by war." This reprieve from the action and dialogue signals, as elsewhere (11:23; 18:1), a lull rising off the heels of success. What follows may be developed without threat of interruption.

JOSHUA 15

3. Judah's Land (15:1-63)

[1]The allotment for the tribe of Judah, clan by clan, extended down to the territory of Edom, to the Desert of Zin in the extreme south.

[2]Their southern boundary started from the bay at the southern end of the Salt Sea,[a] [3]crossed south of Scorpion[b] Pass, continued on to Zin and went over to the south of Kadesh Barnea. Then it ran past Hezron up to Addar and curved around to Karka. [4]It then passed along to Azmon and joined the Wadi of Egypt, ending at the sea. This is their[c] southern boundary.

[5]The eastern boundary is the Salt Sea as far as the mouth of the Jordan.

The northern boundary started from the bay of the sea at the mouth of the Jordan, [6]went up to Beth Hoglah and continued north of Beth Arabah to the Stone of Bohan son of Reuben. [7]The boundary then went up to Debir from the Valley of Achor and turned north to Gilgal, which faces the Pass of Adummim south of the gorge. It continued along to the waters of En Shemesh and came out at En Rogel. [8]Then it ran up the Valley of Ben Hinnom along the southern slope of the Jebusite city (that is, Jerusalem). From there it climbed to the top of the hill west of the Hinnom Valley at the northern end of the Valley of Rephaim. [9]From the hilltop the boundary headed toward the spring of the waters of Nephtoah, came out at the towns of Mount Ephron and went down toward Baalah (that is, Kiriath Jearim). [10]Then it curved westward from Baalah to Mount Seir, ran along the northern slope of Mount Jearim (that is, Kesalon), contin-

ued down to Beth Shemesh and crossed to Timnah. [11]It went
to the northern slope of Ekron, turned toward Shikkeron,
passed along to Mount Baalah and reached Jabneel. The
boundary ended at the sea.

[12]The western boundary is the coastline of the Great Sea.[d]
These are the boundaries around the people of Judah by their
clans.

[13]In accordance with the LORD's command to him, Joshua gave to
Caleb son of Jephunneh a portion in Judah—Kiriath Arba, that is,
Hebron. (Arba was the forefather of Anak.) [14]From Hebron Caleb
drove out the three Anakites—Sheshai, Ahiman and Talmai—descen-
dants of Anak. [15]From there he marched against the people living in
Debir (formerly called Kiriath Sepher). [16]And Caleb said, "I will give
my daughter Acsah in marriage to the man who attacks and captures
Kiriath Sepher." [17]Othniel son of Kenaz, Caleb's brother, took it; so
Caleb gave his daughter Acsah to him in marriage.

[18]One day when she came to Othniel, she urged him[e] to ask her
father for a field. When she got off her donkey, Caleb asked her,
"What can I do for you?"

[19]She replied, "Do me a special favor. Since you have given me
land in the Negev, give me also springs of water." So Caleb gave
her the upper and lower springs.

[20]This is the inheritance of the tribe of Judah, clan by clan:

[21]The southernmost towns of the tribe of Judah in the Negev
toward the boundary of Edom were:

Kabzeel, Eder, Jagur, [22]Kinah, Dimonah, Adadah, [23]Kedesh,
Hazor, Ithnan, [24]Ziph, Telem, Bealoth, [25]Hazor Hadattah,
Kerioth Hezron (that is, Hazor), [26]Amam, Shema, Moladah,
[27]Hazar Gaddah, Heshmon, Beth Pelet, [28]Hazar Shual, Beersheba, Biziothiah, [29]Baalah, Iim, Ezem, [30]Eltolad, Kesil, Hormah, [31]Ziklag, Madmannah, Sansannah, [32]Lebaoth, Shilhim,
Ain and Rimmon—a total of twenty-nine towns and their
villages.

[33]In the western foothills:

Eshtaol, Zorah, Ashnah, [34]Zanoah, En Gannim, Tappuah,
Enam, [35]Jarmuth, Adullam, Socoh, Azekah, [36]Shaaraim,
Adithaim and Gederah (or Gederothaim)[f]—fourteen towns
and their villages.

[37]Zenan, Hadashah, Migdal Gad, [38]Dilean, Mizpah, Joktheel, [39]Lachish, Bozkath, Eglon, [40]Cabbon, Lahmas, Kitlish, [41]Gederoth, Beth Dagon, Naamah and Makkedah—sixteen towns and their villages.

[42]Libnah, Ether, Ashan, [43]Iphtah, Ashnah, Nezib, [44]Keilah, Aczib and Mareshah—nine towns and their villages.

[45]Ekron, with its surrounding settlements and villages; [46]west of Ekron, all that were in the vicinity of Ashdod, together with their villages; [47]Ashdod, its surrounding settlements and villages; and Gaza, its settlements and villages, as far as the Wadi of Egypt and the coastline of the Great Sea.

[48]In the hill country:

Shamir, Jattir, Socoh, [49]Dannah, Kiriath Sannah (that is, Debir), [50]Anab, Eshtemoh, Anim, [51]Goshen, Holon and Giloh—eleven towns and their villages.

[52]Arab, Dumah, Eshan, [53]Janim, Beth Tappuah, Aphekah, [54]Humtah, Kiriath Arba (that is, Hebron) and Zior—nine towns and their villages.

[55]Maon, Carmel, Ziph, Juttah, [56]Jezreel, Jokdeam, Zanoah, [57]Kain, Gibeah and Timnah—ten towns and their villages.

[58]Halhul, Beth Zur, Gedor, [59]Maarath, Beth Anoth and Eltekon—six towns and their villages.

[60]Kiriath Baal (that is, Kiriath Jearim) and Rabbah—two towns and their villages.

[61]In the desert:

Beth Arabah, Middin, Secacah, [62]Nibshan, the City of Salt and En Gedi—six towns and their villages.

[63]Judah could not dislodge the Jebusites, who were living in Jerusalem; to this day the Jebusites live there with the people of Judah.

[a]*2* That is, the Dead Sea; also in verse 5   [b]*3* Hebrew *Akrabbim*
[c]*4* Hebrew *your*   [d]*12* That is, the Mediterranean; also in verse 47
[e]*18* Hebrew and some Septuagint manuscripts; other Septuagint manuscripts (see also note at Judges 1:14) *Othniel, he urged her*   [f]*36* Or *Gederah and Gederothaim*

The goal of land tenure is suspended before the eyes of Israel and repeatedly couched in terms of "inheritance" and "gift." To realize this goal, a pedestrian conquest of raids temporarily ignites the people of God and panics the local inhabitants. But to possess the land truly, much more must be done. Cisjordan must be systematically carved into discrete parcels, fully controlled and thoroughly settled, hill by hill, village by village, house by house. As instructed by Yahweh, land assignments for the tribes are not directed by a human agency but by sacred lot (גּוֹרָל, *gôrāl*).[1]

The first of these parcels to be described in Cisjordan falls to the tribe of Judah. Boundaries are introduced (15:1-12), Caleb's story is infilled (15:13-19), and an inventory of settlements is offered (15:20-63). Through it all, the myriad of place names can become little more than static, a distant noise with little meaning (see Supplemental Study on Site Identification in ch. 18, p. 318). An attentive listener, however, recognizes that as each village name is pronounced, a specific site comes into focus, each pulsing with life, each offering unique opportunities, and each suggesting to the landless individual the promise of sitting without fear "under his own vine and under his own fig tree" (Micah 4:4). Similarly, the careful listener understands that boundaries have purpose. No doubt, they make for better neighbors, but this is only a part. Each bending line encloses yet another farm or field and may be shown to have strategic or demonstrable purpose: a grassy knob here, an eroded gully there. All told, site names and boundary lines collude to suggest this is no make-believe land. They are pebbles of promise that collectively give voice to a larger prayer: a prayer for a future kingdom where heaven and earth are one (cf. Matt 6:9-10).

15:1-4 By way of overview, Judah inherits the southernmost territory, extending as far as Edomite lands.[2] A **southern boundary** is delineated, running essentially from the south end of the Dead Sea westward through the desert to the Mediterranean shore. Sites and

---

[1]Scant clues are given to suggest the process by which land-tracts and tribes are connected. A participant list is prescribed in Num 34:16-29. Beyond this is the common verbal description of a "lot" (*gôral*) that "arises" (עָלָה, *ʿālāh*) or "comes out" (יָצָא, *yāṣāʾ*) to this tribe or that, cf. 16:1; 17:1; 18:11; 19:1,10,17,24,32,40. For more thoughts on this process, refer to the Supplemental Study on Lot Casting in ch. 16, p. 298.

[2]Edom is typically considered a Transjordan entity, but the evidence shows regular Edomite penetrations in the south deserts of Cisjordan. For the suggestion of an early Edomite presence there, see Num 20:16.

features encountered along the way include **Scorpion Pass**,[3] **Zin**,[4] **Kadesh Barnea**,[5] **Hezron, Addar**,[6] **Karka**,[7] **Azmon**,[8] and **the Wadi of Egypt**.[9] Correspondence between this southern boundary of Judah and the southern boundary for the land as a whole may be seen when this passage is compared with Numbers 34:3-5. It is also noted that the line formed by this boundary was possibly an ancient route across the southern desert, punctuated by important wells.

15:5-12 The eastern and western boundaries of the territory of Judah require little comment. Judah is defined by two lapping shores, the Dead Sea to the east and the Mediterranean Sea to the

---

[3]Scorpion Pass, lit., the "ascent of the scorpions" (מַעֲלֵה עַקְרַבִּים, *ma'ălēh 'aqrabbîm)*, has been regularly identified with modern Naqb es-Safa. The latter was a well-known passage in the 2nd century A.D. and used by the Roman army to make the precarious climb out of the Great Rift and into the Negev. Baly poetically describes the west face of the Great Rift here as a veritable "Niagara of rock" (*Geography*, p. 35).

[4]Zin (צִנָה, *ṣināh*) as a site is unknown; however, as a region, "the wilderness of Zin" seems to encompass a dry region to the southwest of the Dead Sea (eastern Negev). Rolling hills, shallow wadis, and some wells, make elevated portions of this land cultivable at times. In the main, though, it represents the extreme limits of settled life. For more see Baly, *Geography*, pp. 247-251.

[5]Kadesh Barnea is a well-known center for Israel during the time of the wilderness wanderings (Deut 1:46). The site of Tell el-Qudeirat is often associated with Kadesh Barnea, although excavations revealed the presence of a fort no earlier than the 10th century B.C. Aharoni suggests the immediate region surrounding 'Ain el-Qudeirat where several springs are located may be labeled "Kadesh Barnea" (*Land of the Bible*, p. 70). For a good overview of the problem, see Rainey anad Notley, *Sacred Bridge*, p. 121. See also the note on Josh 10:41.

[6]Num 34:4 identifies a single site as Hazar Addar ("enclosure of Addar/threshing floor"?), whereas the text of Joshua distinguishes between a Hezron ("Campsite" or "Reeds"?) and an Addar ("threshing floor"?). Neither site has been identified with certainty, although 'Ain Qudeis, a two-mile hike from 'Ain al-Qudeirat, is a likely suspect for one or both locations.

[7]Aharoni tentatively identifies "the Karka" (*haqqarqā'āh*, possibly, "the flat(s)"?) with 'Ain Qeseima. 'Ain Qeseima is a watering station about five miles west of 'Ain Qudeirat (*Land of the Bible*, p. 72).

[8]John Gray identifies Azmon with Quseima (*Joshua, Judges, and Ruth*. NCB, rev. ed. [Greenwood: Attic, 1977], p. 111). Aharoni and Rainey opt for the well at 'Ain Muweilih (Aharoni, *Land of the Bible*, p. 72; Rainey and Notley, *Sacred Bridge*, p. 35).

[9]See notes for 13:3.

west. These, too, mimic the larger boundaries of the land as a whole
(cf. Num 34:6,12).

The northern boundary of the territory of Judah represents a
more delicate situation. The line rises up from the mouth of the
Jordan at the Dead Sea, drapes over the Central Ridge (just south of
Jerusalem), and drops down to the Mediterranean.[10] The care given
to navigating its path anticipates future conflicts between Judah and
their northern neighbors.[11] It is also significant that Judah's boundary runs adjacent to the base of Jerusalem (Jebus), but does not
include it. This fact, too, has implications for future tribal relations.

Sites and features marking Judah's northern boundary include
Beth Hoglah,[12] **Beth Arabah,**[13] **Stone of Bohan son of Reuben,**[14]
Debir,[15] **Valley of Achor,**[16] **Gilgal which faces the pass of Adum-**

---

[10]Topographically, the boundary appears to run in a parallel course south
of the Wadi Qelt on the east side of the ridge and in a parallel course north
of the Wadi Sorek on the west side of the ridge. Both courses follow ridges
and represent real lines of travel.

[11]The detailed attention given to Judah's allotment (as opposed to the
brevity of other tribal parcel descriptions) raises the possibility that this particular allotment is offered in full, while others have been abbreviated in the
process of editing the text. While this is a thoughtful possibility, it remains
as speculation. For this, see Aharoni, *Land of the Bible*, pp. 83, 250.

[12]Beth Hoglah may be located near modern Jericho at 'Ain Hajlah. Iron I
remains have been identified there. For a linguistic discussion of the name
("house of the partridge" or "circular place") and some late traditions, see
Elitzur, *Ancient Place Names*, pp. 37-41.

[13]Beth Arabah may be located at 'Ain el-Gharbah, located about two and
a half miles east of modern Jericho. Iron I and II occupation has been identified here.

[14]The curious feature dubbed, the "Stone of Bohan son of Reuben" is
unknown. Some attention has been given to it, however, in the context of
multiple (and separate) tribal invasion theories. These assume a connection
between the heritage of Bohan (a personal name otherwise unknown) and
an earlier presence of the Reubenite tribe in Cisjordan. See Aharoni, *Land
of the Bible*, pp. 207-208. On a lighter note, the term בֹּהַן (*bōhan*) may refer
to the first digit of the hand or foot (cf. Judg 1:6). Hence, this feature might
be remembered as "Stone of the Big Toe" or very loosely, "Stub-toe Rock"!

[15]This Debir should not be confused with the Debir of Josh 10:38. The
Debir of the present context is located on the northern edge of Judean ter-
ritory, possibly commemorated by the modern Thoghret ed-Debr, ("Pass of
Debir") some ten miles east of Jerusalem.

[16]See comments at Josh 7:26.

mim,[17] the waters of En Shemesh,[18] En Rogel,[19] Valley of Ben Hinnom,[20] Valley of Rephaim,[21] the waters of Neptoah,[22] Mount Ephron,[23] Baalah or Kiriath Jearim,[24] Mount Seir,[25] Mount Jearim or Kesalon,[26] Beth Shemesh,[27] Timnah,[28] Ekron,[29] Shikkeron,[30] Mount Baalah,[31] and Jabneel.[32]

---

[17]Considerable confusion has plagued the study of the "Gilgals" of Joshua. The fact that the narrator feels constrained to modify this particular Gilgal with the phrase "which faces the Pass of Adummim" suggests that this Gilgal is not to be confused with the Israelite base near Jericho.

[18]The waters of En Shemesh may be located at Ein el-Hod, immediately to the east of Bethany. See Rainey and Notley, *Sacred Bridge*, p. 181.

[19]En Rogel rests immediately to the south of Jerusalem at the intersection of the Kidron and Hinnom Valleys. It is known elsewhere (2 Sam 17:17; 1 Kgs 1:9) in the Bible and is traditionally referred to today as Bir Ayyub, or "Job's Well."

[20]The Valley of Ben Hinnom is also remembered simply as the Hinnom Valley. This valley skirts the southern and western edges of the old city of Jerusalem.

[21]The exact identity of the Valley of Rephaim is unknown. Logic points toward the upper Sorek system, possibly in the vicinity of Jerusalem. Gray boldly suggests the tract of land around the modern railway station (the *Biq'a*) in West Jerusalem (*Joshua, Judges, Ruth*, p. 112).

[22]The "Waters of Neptoah" are unknown. Efforts to locate them at 'Ain en-Natuf, located about three and a half miles south of Bethlehem seem too distant from the established border trajectory. More likely is some association with Lifta, a village located immediately to the northwest of modern Jerusalem.

[23]Mount Ephron or "Dusty Mountain" may be located at el-Qastel (near Mozah).

[24]See comment at Josh 9:17.

[25]The identity of a Mount Seir or "Thicket Mountain" in Cisjordan is unknown.

[26]Mount Jearim or Kesalon is possibly remembered at modern Kasla, about ten miles west of Jerusalem. Iron I remains assist in this identification.

[27]The ruins at Tell er-Rumeilah are identified as biblical Beth Shemesh. This site is located about 16 miles southwest of Jerusalem. Occupation here spans the period of the Old Testament.

[28]Timnah is likely to be found about four miles downslope of Beth Shemesh on the Wadi Sorek. Remains at Tell el-Batashi date to the Bronze and Iron ages.

[29]See comments at 13:3.

[30]The location of Shikkeron is debated. Tell el-Ful, located about four miles down slope of Tell Miqne along the Wadi Sorek, is one possibility.

[31]The identity of Mount Baalah is unknown.

[32]The name of Jabneel is likely preserved in the coastal town of Yebna/ Yavne, near where the Wadi Sorek releases into the Mediterranean Sea.

The land enclosed by these boundaries is dominated by the Central Ridge, a vertical challenge of nearly 3,000 feet that offers protection, but also divides Judah's inheritance into two distinct halves. To the west of the ridge, rich valleys reap the benefit of prevailing winds off of the Mediterranean, absorbing moisture and folding gently to the coastal plain below. This littoral zone is open, friendly, fertile — and for the exact same reasons — is difficult to control. By contrast, land east of the ridge is situated in a rain-shadow. It is rugged, torn, bereft of settlement, and may be exploited only seasonally by shepherds (hence, the "Wilderness of Judea"). Such a division of Judah's allotment is striking; it is a "bipolar" inheritance straddling a boundary between life and death.

15:13-20 Following this description of Judah, the Caleb story is revisited.[33] Previously, (14:6-15), the narrative focus was upon Caleb as a model for the faithful, a man who requested an inheritance promised by Yahweh. Now the action is picked up again and carried forward; Caleb clears out Hebron and dispossess the Anakites. No surprises here. However, following this point, attention is redirected by the narrator. A new site is brought into play along with two new characters. The site shifts from Hebron to nearby Debir/Kiriath Sepher,[34] presumably as Caleb extends his personal campaign of the region. One new character, Acsah ("Anklet"), is introduced as a battle prize to the man who takes Debir. A second new character, Othniel ("God is my protection"), is introduced as the one who captures Debir and receives his prize.[35] With all eyes on Othniel, however, Acsah displaces him (through seduction, enticement, or incitement?[36]) and demonstrates that she is truly her father's daughter. Like Caleb, Acsah forcefully makes a request, and like Caleb, Acsah receives more than expected (cf. 14:13 with 15:19[37]).

---

[33]A further expansion of this story is told in Judg 1:10-15. Othniel appears again as Israel's first judge in Judg 3:9-11.

[34]Note the comments at 10:38-39. As in the case of Hebron, the original description of the attack on this place may be regarded as trustworthy. Israel killed all the inhabitants who were found. This, however, does not account for those who were not found; some — perhaps many — refugees fled the site and subsequently returned.

[35]Compare this with David's incentive offered to the one leading the attack in the siege of Jerusalem (1 Chr 11:6).

[36]The verbal package, וַתְּסִיתֵהוּ (wat³sîthēhû), is built from the root, סוּת (sûth), and may suggest any of the above options.

[37]The term for "blessing" is translated by the NIV as "a special favor."

A host of translation and interpretive issues crop up in this short text. On a larger level, it is difficult to discern the narrator's intent in inserting Caleb's story between listing of Judah's boundaries and villages. More narrowly, it is difficult to discern Acsah's actions in verse 18. How and why does the scene so abruptly change from her manipulating her husband to her leaping from a donkey?[38] Why does Acsah initially press Othniel to request a "field" of her father and then when the request is finally made from her own mouth, it is for a גֻּלָּה (gullāh) of water?[39] Finally, what exactly is a gullāh?

In the case of the last question, the NIV translates gullāh as a "spring," although there is little to commend the word choice. Certainly, the land Acsah has received is dry (הַנֶּגֶב, hannegeb) and somehow her request aims to amend that fact. Less strained is a reading of gullāh as a "pool" or "pond," or even possibly a "(water) jar or bowl."[40] Interestingly, the LXX manages to dodge the entire issue by simply transliterating gullāh into Greek, and, by so doing, creating place names, viz., "And Caleb gave to her Upper Golathmain and "Lower Golathmain."[41] Despite these difficulties, the certainty of success on the part of Caleb's clan is clear. Perhaps this positive col-

---

[38]Even the verb used to describe Acsah's "dismount" is odd. The Hebrew root צנח (ṣnḥ) may simply suggest "to go down," although it may be suggested on the basis of Arabic parallels, that she "clapped (her hands)," possibly to get Caleb's attention. Besides appearing in this story (Josh 15:18 and Judg 1:14), the other place where this verb appears is in Judg 4:21 where it describes the tent peg of Jael that "pierces" the ground (and Sisera's head!). If this text nuances Acsah's actions in some way, perhaps she "drives" or "thunders" down from her donkey, like a tent peg struck by a hammer. Such bursting energy would explain Caleb's (incredulous?) response, מַה־לָּךְ (mah-lāk), or "What's up with you?" or less kindly, "What's your problem?" However read, one thing is clear: like Jael, Acsah is a woman of force.

[39]Perhaps a less literal reading here would help. If Acsah is truly a "country girl," maybe she is unhappy with the gift of "urban" Hebron; she requests a שָׂדֶה (śādeh), "field" or "rural village" (cf. 1 Sam 27:5 where "field villages" appear). An even simpler solution would be to read śādeh here as general term for "territory," "plot," or even "inheritance." In this way, an additional parcel — such as a pool or spring — would be congruent with her request.

[40]The term gullāh is not the common word for spring, well, or cistern (Heb. עַיִן ['ayin], בְּאֵר [bᵉ'ēr], or בּוֹר [bôr]). This rare form elsewhere represents a bowl or basin (cf. 1 Kgs 7:41-42; Eccl 12:6; Zech 4:3). However, see the comment below at 15:50.

[41]This should give the modern student reason for caution. If those responsible for the LXX balked at providing a translation, perhaps we should too!

oring of the use of force explains why this vignette is inserted *here*. Distributing, negotiating, and settling this land will require effort, even for models like Caleb and Acsah.

Having introduced Judah's boundaries and infilled the story of Judah's most celebrated conquistador, the remainder of the chapter is devoted to an inventory of villages that constitute Judah's inheritance. Four larger sets of villages emerge: the settlements on the extremities (vv. 21-32), the settlements in the Lowlands (vv. 33-47), the settlements in the Highlands (vv. 48-60), and the settlements in the (Judean) wilderness (vv. 61-62). These may be further subdivided into eleven subsets or "districts," a scheme followed here for the sake of convenience (see Supplemental Study on Mapping the Land below). Stock phrases that indicate settlement counts and suggest settlement hinterlands, e.g., "and their villages" unite the narrative. Against all of this, however, is the final pitch concerning Jerusalem (v. 63).

SUPPLEMENTAL STUDY

MAPPING THE LAND

Many modern study Bibles include a section of color maps. These are often found in the back of the volume and are helpful in understanding geographically sensitive materials such as the world of the patriarchs, the kingdoms of Israel and Judah, and the journeys of the Apostle Paul. Beyond this resource, more detailed information is available in Bible atlases,[42] in road maps,[43] and in archaeological studies.[44]

For the reader of Joshua, access to *Heartland* through maps is critical. This is especially true when contemplating the tribal allot-

---

[42]In the preparation of this manuscript, regular reference was made to the Bible Atlases of Rainey and Notley, *Sacred Bridges*, and Monson, *Student Map Manual*. Other helpful reference works include; Richard Cleave et al., *The Holy Land Satellite Atlas*, Vol. 1 *Terrain Recognition*, and Vol. 2 *The Regions* (Nicosia: Røhr Productions, 1999); Barry Beitzel, ed., *Biblica: The Bible Atlas: A Social and Historical Journey through the Lands of the Bible* (Lane Cove: Global, 2006), and, John J. Bimson et al., eds. *New Bible Atlas* (Downers Grove, IL: InterVarsity, 1994).

[43]Elena Belinki, *Israel Road Atlas* (Tel Aviv: Mapa, 2006).

[44]For example, Zertal, *Shechem Syncline* and *Eastern Valleys*.

ments, the Levitical cities, and the cities of refuge. What must be kept in mind, however, is the difference between prescription and follow-through, or, to put it differently, the difference between land given and land settled. The combined testimony of Joshua and Judges suggests that the tribal boundaries as assigned by Joshua were never fully realized. As the most obvious example, the tribe of Dan is given a relatively narrow parcel of ground extending from the summit of the central ridge to the Mediterranean coast (Joshua 19:40-48). This inheritance is outlined on every "Twelve Tribe" map, curling round from Gibeon to Joppa, with a bold-faced label "Dan" written over the top of it. Despite the confidence that these bold lines inspire, this ground did not become the inheritance of Dan, and, in the end, is exchanged for a single city in the north (Judges 18). It is not until much later, the time of David and Solomon, that Israel would wrest control of this parcel out of the Philistine grip; and even then, it is doubtful if but a few of the family of Dan ever settled there (recall, however, that Samson is exceptional in many ways; according to Judges 13:2 he was a Danite from Zorah). Hence, for reasons such as these, the map in the back of many Bibles titled, "The Twelve Tribes" is an *optimistic* presentation at best.[45]

Modern scholarship tends to be less than optimistic about such mapped presentations. A common view is that Joshua 13–19 is an imagined memory, a construct projected from the later period of the monarchy and used to justify the contemporary situation. This skepticism has been summarily addressed by Richard Hess who draws six points of interest from his own work and from the work of others.[46]

---

[45]While subject to interpretation, an interesting map exercise would be to place this standard "Twelve Tribe" map showing allotted boundaries against a map projecting early Israel sites. Aharoni tried this early on (*Land of the Bible*, p. 213), but much has been learned since his day. What is clear is that the presence of early Israel is seen most densely in the Lower Jordan Valley and in the Central Ridge north of Jerusalem. Less dense settlement is observed on the Central Ridge south of Jerusalem, on the western face of the central ridge extending to the Shephelah, and in Lower Galilee. If the tribal allotments projected in the book of Joshua were, in fact, pursued by the tribal groups who received the allotments, it would suggest that Benjamin, Ephraim, and Manasseh experienced the most success in settlement, while Judah, Issachar, Zebulun, and Naphtali were only moderately successful.

[46]Richard Hess, "Asking Historical Questions of Joshua 13–19: Recent Discussion concerning the Date of the Boundary Lists," in *Faith, Tradition*

Three of these bear repeating here. First, it is suggested that the borders offered in Joshua 13–19 may be partially present in literature of the late second millennium B.C. Texts recovered and remembered as the Amarna tablets describe the quarreling that took place among the city-states of LBA Canaan. In this context, sites are mentioned, claims of control (or noncontrol) are offered, and physical geography is described. Hess goes so far as to write, "it is significant that at no other time in the history of Old Testament Israel were regions demarcated in a way that so closely resembles the tribal allotments in Joshua."[47] Second, literary parallels in the wider Mediterranean world suggest that the pattern of "land conquest" (Joshua 1–12) followed by "land allotment" (Joshua 13–21) is not unique to the biblical text. While these parallels are drawn from later, classical models, it can be demonstrated that this arrangement of materials is hardly illogical or accidental. Third, the discovery of text tablets from the late second millennium sites such as Ugarit, Mari, and Alalakh demonstrate more extensive documentation of city lists and administrative duties than that which has been discovered in the centuries that follow. Admittedly this could be the accident of discovery, but it does poke a hole in the argument that detailed administrative lists must be a product of later times. What makes this line of thinking even more interesting is the fact that this genre of "border-listing" appears in treaty documents that regulate relationships, guarantee responsibilities, and provide recourse in matters of disputes. As the context of Joshua 24 has often been described as containing treaty or "covenant" language, this parallel is given additional traction.

15:21-32 The first set of villages constitutes those located on the extreme edge of the inheritance parcel. Some assistance in interpreting these site names and spellings is gained by comparing this list with the description of Simeon's inheritance offered in 19:2-8 and in 1 Chronicles 4:24-43. The sites of this first district border Edomite land in the south (*Negev*) and include **Kabzeel**,[48] **Eder**,[49] **Jagur**,[50]

---

and History: Old Testament Historiography in Its Near Eastern Context, ed. by A.R. Millard, James K. Hoffmeier, and David W. Baker (Winona Lake, IN: Eisenbrauns, 1994), pp. 196-205.

[47]Ibid., p. 197.

[48]A possible identification for Kabzeel is at Khirbet el-Gharrah, located eight miles east of modern Beersheba.   *Notes 49, 50, opposite.*

Kinah,[51] Dimonah,[52] Adadah,[53] Kedesh,[54] Hazor,[55] Ithnan, Ziph,[56]
Telem, Bealoth,[57] Hazor Hadattah,[58] Kerioth Hezron,[59] Amam,
Shema,[60] Moladah,[61] Hazar Gaddah, Heshmon,[62] Beth Pelet,[63] Hazar

---

[49]Aharoni, *Land of the Bible*, p. 117, suggests that Eder may be located at
the site of (Tell) Arad. He argues this on the basis of geographical context
and the possibility of a text emendation. A simple reversal of two consonants (very similar looking in an Iron Age script) turns עדר (*'dr*) into ערד
(*'rd*). Interestingly, some LXX manuscripts replace Eder with Arad in this
verse. If this reading is not accepted, it is difficult to understand why Arad
is not listed in this set.

[50]The ruins at el-Jura (adjacent to Ashkelon) have been suggested as the
identification of Jagur. This, however, seems unlikely given the distance from
el-Jura to other sites in this district more securely identified. Another possibility is Khirbet el-Gharrah, previously suggested as the location of Kabzeel.

[51]Aharoni, *Land of the Bible*, p. 406, suggests Khirbet Taiyib, located about
three and a half miles north of Arad, as Kinah.

[52]The location of Dimonah is unknown.

[53]Aharoni, *Land of the Bible*, p. 117, identifies the site with Khirbet
'Ar'arah, 12 miles southeast of modern Beersheba.

[54]Kedesh is a common part of bifid names, e.g., Kadesh Barnea. It is possible that the second part of this name is lost or simply unknown.

[55]This Hazor cannot be identified with the city of 11:1ff. Mixed readings
are given by the LXX and raise the possibility that this site and the following be read as a single entry, Hazor Ithnan.

[56]This Ziph of the Negev (v. 24) is different from the Ziph of the hill country (v. 55). The Ziph of the Negev may be located at Khirbet ez-Zeifeh,
southwest of Kurnub. Outside the Bible — in the Shishak inscription — a
northern and a southern Ziph are also noted (Elitzur, *Ancient Place Names*,
p. 48, n. 1).

[57]The location of Telem is unknown. So is that of Bealoth. However, some
suggest that it is the same as Baalath Beer of 19:8.

[58]Hazor Hadattah may tentatively be associated with modern el-Hudeira,
near the south end of the Dead Sea.

[59]As elsewhere, the choice to read bifid names here is difficult to judge.
The LXX identifies Kerioth Hezron as a single entry. Khirbet el-Qarytein,
five miles north of Arad, has been offered as a possibility (Woudstra, *Joshua*,
p. 244).

[60]The locations of Amam and Shema are unknown.

[61]Many sites in the vicinity of Beersheba have been proposed as the identification of Moladah. Khirbet el-Waten, five miles east of Beersheba, is one
possibility, as is Khirbet Kuseifeh, 12 miles east of Beersheba. Finally, Tell
el-Milh, often pondered as the Arad of Joshua's day, may possibly be
Moladah. Tell el-Milh is 11 miles southeast of Beersheba.

[62]The locations of Hazar Gaddah and Heshmon are unknown.

[63]Aharoni, *Land of the Bible*, p. 410, posits Tell es-Saqati as biblical Beth
Pelet.

Shual,[64] **Beersheba,**[65] **Biziothiah,**[66] **Baalah,**[67] **Iim,**[68] **Ezem,**[69] **Eltolad,**[70] **Kesil,**[71] **Hormah,**[72] **Ziklag,**[73] **Madmannah,**[74] **Sansannah,**[75] **Lebaoth,**[76] **Shilhim,**[77] **Ain,** and **Rimmon.**[78] Taken as a whole, the sites of this first set seem to be concentrated in the drainage system variously referred to as the Wadi Ghazzeh, Wadi Milh, or Nahal Beersheba. The calculated sum of twenty-nine settlements cannot be arrived at without manipulation, even after certain combinations are made. However, when it is understood that this list represents not just the settlements, but a supporting cast of dependent hamlets as well, the count becomes irrelevant.

---

[64]The identity of Hazar Shual is unknown.

[65]Tell es-Seba' is located on the eastern outskirts of the modern city of Beersheba. It is the location of the settlement from the biblical period.

[66]The term Biziothiah (בְּזִיוֹתְיָה, *bizyôthyāh*) could be a reference to an otherwise unknown settlement. If respelled, however, as בְּנוֹתֶיהָ (*bᵊnôthêhā*), it may modify Beersheba with the phrase "and her villages," cf. 17:11,16.

[67]The identity of Baalah in this context is unknown.

[68]The site of עִיִּים (*'îyîm*) is unknown. It is possible that it is a text error, the eye of the copyist drifting from Ezem. *'Îyîm* does not appear in 19:3.

[69]Ezem may be identified with Umm el-azam, situated some 15 miles south of Beersheba.

[70]The location of Eltolad or Tolad (1 Chr 4:29) is unknown; however, it is attested on an ostracon found at Beersheba (Aharoni, *Land of the Bible*, p. 260).

[71]Kesil appears as Bethul in 19:4.

[72]Tell Masos is often associated with biblical Hormah. This is not certain, though, and other possibilities, such as Tell el-Milh and Tell el-Meshash are also candidates. All three of these sites are located in the drainage basin of the Wadi Beersheba between modern Arad and modern Beersheba.

[73]Ziklag is usually identified with Tell esh-Shari'ah, nine miles northwest of Beersheba. Another candidate is Tell-Khuweilfeh, ten miles northeast of Beersheba (Woudstra, *Joshua*, p. 245).

[74]Khirbet umm Demneh and Khirbet Tatrit are possible locations for Madmannah. Both are northeast of Beersheba.

[75]Sansannah may be found at Khirbet esh-Shamshaniyat, nine miles northwest of Beersheba.

[76]Lebaoth appears as Beth Labaoth in 19:6. It is unidentified on the ground.

[77]Shilhim is likely to be the Sharuhen of 19:6.

[78]Ain and Rimmon are separated by a conjunction here, indicating two separate sites. In 19:7, no conjunction is found suggesting one site Ain Rimmon or "Spring of Rimmon." Khirbet Umm er-Ramamin, located about nine miles northeast of Beersheba is attractive on linguistic grounds, but may be difficult to establish archaeologically.

15:33-47 The second set of villages offered are those located in the Lowlands (*šᵉphēlāh*). These are further broken down into four districts and enumerated by geographical clusters.

In the first of four Lowland districts are **Eshtaol**,[79] **Zorah**,[80] **Ashnah**,[81] **Zanoah**,[82] **En Gannim**,[83] **Tappuah**,[84] **Enam**,[85] **Jarmuth, Adullam**,[86] **Socoh**,[87] **Azekah**,[88] **Shaaraim**,[89] **Adithaim**[90] and **Gederah (or Gederothaim)**.[91] The sites of this district appear to lie between the Sorek and Elah drainage systems at the point where they open from the highlands upon the coastal plain. Here as elsewhere, a close reading makes the count of **fourteen towns and their villages** difficult.

---

[79]Eshtaol is usually located at Ishwa, seven miles northeast of Socoh. However, this identification places the site outside the northern boundary of Judah's allotment (north of Beth Shemesh). The same is true of the identification of Zorah.

[80]Zorah is often identified with Sar'ah, six miles north of Socoh.

[81]Speculation over the location of Ashnah must include Khirbet el-Assalin and Khirbet Ashainah. Both are located near Sar'ah (Zorah). A second Ashnah, also in the tribal territory of Judah, is mentioned in 15:43.

[82]Khirbet Zanu', three miles northeast of Socoh, is identified as Zanoah. This site should not be confused with Zanoah of the Highlands (15:56).

[83]Two proposals for En Gannim may be considered. The first is at modern Beit Jemal, about two miles north of Socoh. The second is 'Umm Jinne, about three miles north of Socoh. This En Gannim of the "Lowlands" should not be confused with the Levitical city by the same name in the territory of Issachar (19:21).

[84]The location of Tappuah of the "Lowlands" is unknown. Regardless, it is distinct from the Highlands site bearing the same name (v. 53).

[85]The location of Enam is unknown.

[86]See comments at 10:23 and 12:15.

[87]This Socoh is identified with Khirbet 'Abbad, located about 13 miles west of Bethlehem. It should not be confused with a second Socoh (of the "Highlands") in 15:48.

[88]See comments at Josh 10:10.

[89]It is possible to link Shaaraim with Khirbet esh-Sharia, located approximately two miles northwest of Socoh. This is a different site from that identified with Ziklag.

[90]The location of Adithaim is unknown.

[91]If Gederah is intended to be a site (translated it means, "The Wall"), it may be located at Tell el-Judeireh, opposite Socoh in the Valley of Elah.

The NIV simply transliterates the following entry as "Gederothaim." The original text package, וּגְדֵרֹתָיִם (*ûgᵉdērōthāyim*), translates as, "and two walls." Is this truly another site name, or did the translators of the LXX get it right? The LXX renders the term as "and her villages," where "villages" is suggested by the dual form of "walls."

In the second district of the Lowlands are sixteen settlements: **Zenan**,[92] **Hadashah**,[93] **Migdal Gad**,[94] **Dilean**,[95] **Mizpah, Joktheel**,[96] **Lachish**,[97] **Bozkath**,[98] **Eglon**,[99] **Cabbon**,[100] **Lahmas**,[101] **Kitlish, Gederoth, Beth Dagon**,[102] **Naamah**,[103] and **Makkedah**.[104] Like the previous cluster to the north, this "district" appears to stretch from Highland to Lowland and straddles strategic drainage systems, notably the Wadis Qubeibah and Suweilit.

In the third district of Lowland sites are **Libnah**,[105] **Ether**,[106] **Ashan**,[107] **Iphtah**,[108] **Ashnah**,[109] **Nezib**,[110] **Keilah**,[111] **Aczib**,[112] and **Mareshah**.[113] These

---

[92]Zenan may be located at 'Araq el-Kharba, near Lachish. See Woudstra, *Joshua*, p. 248.

[93]The location of Hadashah is unknown.

[94]Migdal Gad may be located at Khirbet el-Mejdeleh, three and a half miles southeast of Lachish. The name Gad is curious here, leading to speculation that this site has some relation to the Transjordan tribe of Gad.

[95]Dilean, possibly located at Tell en-Najileh, southwest of Tell el-Hesi. See Woudstra, *Joshua*, p. 248.

[96]The locations of Mizpah and Joktheel are unknown.

[97]See comments at 10:3.

[98]Baly, *Geography*, p. 142, suggests ad-Duwaiyima as the location of biblical Bozkath. Ad-Duwaiyima is located approximately four miles up the Wadi Qubeibah from Lachish.

[99]See comments at 10:3

[100]The location of Cabbon is unknown.

[101]Lahmas may be identified with Khirbet el-Lahm, located about three miles east of Lachish.

[102]The locations of Kitlish, Gederoth, and Beth Dagan are unknown.

[103]Naamah may be located at Khirbet Farad near Timnah, or at Ni'amah or at Na'neh, six miles south of Lydda.

[104]See comments at 10:10.

[105]See comments at 10:29-30.

[106]Biblical Ether may be located at Khirbet el-Ata, two miles northwest of Tell Sandahana (Maresha).

[107]Aharoni, *Land of the Bible*, p. 354, identifies Ashan with Tell Beit Mirsim, ten miles south of Tell Sandahanna (Maresha).

[108]Baly, *Geography*, p. 142, identifies Iptah with the modern village of Tarqumiyeh, eight miles east of Tell Sandahanna (Maresha). Archaeological evidence for this claim is slim.

[109]Ashnah, possibly modern Idnah, five miles southeast of Tell Sandahanna (Maresha). Compare with a second mention of a village by this name in 15:33.

[110]Nezib corresponds with the ruins at Beit Nesib, eight miles east of Tell Sandahanna (Maresha).

[111]Keilah is identified with Khirbet Qeila, seven miles northeast of Tell Sandahanna (Maresha).   *Notes 112,113 opposite.*
Similarly other notes on these pages.

nine sites compose a settlement cluster situated in the center of the Lowlands. They cover strategic passes that culminate in an ascent into the Highlands at Hebron.

The fourth and final Lowland district includes three named sites: **Ekron, Ashdod**, and **Gaza**.[114] Unlike the previous sets that were tightly clustered and adhered to the highland flanks, this set is widely scattered upon the coastal plain. A hinterland is also offered: each site possesses **surrounding settlements and villages**.

15:48-60 The third set of sites are located in the Highlands and may be further subdivided into five districts. These are presented roughly from south to north.

In the first district are eleven sites situated along the southernmost edge of the Highlands. These cover the southern flank and include **Shamir**,[115] **Jattir**,[116] **Socoh**,[117] **Dannah**,[118] **Kiriath Sannah (that is, Debir)**,[119] **Anab**,[120] **Eshtemoh**,[121] **Anim**,[122] **Goshen**,[123] **Holon** and **Giloh**.[124]

---

[112]Aczib, possibly located at Tel el-Beida, four and a half miles northeast of Tell Sandahanna (Maresha) (Aharoni, *Land of the Bible*, p. 429).

[113]The large tell known as Sandahannah is identified with Maresha. It is central to this lowland "district."

[114]See comments at 13:3.

[115]Shamir, possibly located at modern el-Bireh (Woudstra, *Joshua*, p. 251) or at Khirbet es-Sumara, 12 miles west-southwest of Hebron (*EDB*, s.v. "Shamir").

[116]Jattir is likely identified with Khirbet 'Attir, located about four miles southwest of the modern village of es-Samu'a.

[117]Aharoni, *Land of the Bible*, p. 354, prefers Khirbet Shuweikeh as the location of this Socoh (of the Highlands). Khirbet Shuweikeh is located about four miles west of es-Samu'a. For another Socoh (of the Lowlands), see 15:35.

[118]The location of Dannah is unknown.

[119]Kiriath Sannah is offered as a second name for Debir. A third name, Kiriath Sepher, is offered in 15:15-16. These three names are believed to refer to the site at Khirbet Rabud, located about four miles northwest of es-Samu'a. See comments at 10:38.

[120]See comments at 11:21.

[121]Eshtemoh, may be located at modern es-Samu'a, about eight miles southwest of Hebron.

[122]Two neighboring sites carried the name *Anim* ("springs") in antiquity. According to inscriptions found at Arad, an "Upper" Anim and a "Lower" Anim were located in the region (Aharoni, *Land of the Bible*, pp. 354, 399-400). Possible identifications for these sites are Khirbet Ghuwein at-Tahta and Khirbet Guwein el-Foqa. Both are located about three miles south of es-

In the second district of the Highlands are **Arab**,[125] **Dumah**,[126] **Eshan**,[127] **Janim**,[128] **Beth Tappuah**,[129] **Aphekah, Humtah**,[130] **Kiriath Arba (that is, Hebron)**,[131] and **Zior**.[132] These nine sites appear to cluster in the immediate vicinity of Hebron.

In the third district of the Highlands are **Maon**,[133] **Carmel**,[134] **Ziph**,[135] **Juttah**,[136] **Jezreel**,[137] **Jokdeam, Zanoah**,[138] **Kain**,[139] **Gibeah**,[140] and **Timnah**.[141] These ten sites cluster on the southeastern flank of the Highland between Hebron and Arad.

In the fourth district of the Highlands are **Halhul**,[142] **Beth Zur**,[143] **Gedor**,[144] **Maarath**,[145] **Beth Anoth**,[146] and **Eltekon**.[147] These six sites

---

Samu'a. The impulse to link these twin sites with the request of Acsah in 15:19 is powerful.

[123]See comments at 10:41.

[124]The locations of Holon and Giloh are unknown.

[125]Arab, possibly located at er-Rabiyeh, near Hebron. However for Arab, Dumah, and Eshan, see Elitzur, *Ancient Place Names*, p. 385.

[126]Dumah may be located at Khirbet Domeh ed-Deir (Duma), about nine miles southwest of Hebron.

[127]Eshan, some have located at Khirbet Hallat Sama on etymological connection between Sama and the LXX spelling of the site as *Soma*.

[128]The location of Janim is unknown.

[129]Beth Tappuah is usually identified with modern Taffah (Tafuh), about four miles west of Hebron.

[130]The identities of Aphekah and Humtah are unknown.

[131]See comments at 10:3.

[132]The identity of Zior is unknown.

[133]Possibly Tell Ma'in, located about nine miles south of Hebron.

[134]Not to be confused with the mount of the same name located along the north coast of the *Heartland*. This village is usually identified with modern Khirbet el-Kirmil, seven miles south of Hebron.

[135]Likely at Tell Zif, about four miles southeast of Hebron.

[136]Identified with the modern village of Yatta, five miles south of Hebron.

[137]Not to be confused with the valley and site by the same name located in the north. The identity of this Jezreel of Judah is unknown.

[138]The locations of Jokdeam and Zanoah are uncertain. The latter should not be confused with the Zanoah of the Lowlands (15:34).

[139]Aharoni identifies this site with en-Nebi Yaqin, located about two miles southeast of Hebron (*Land of the Bible*, p. 438).

[140]The location of this Gibeah is uncertain. It should not be confused with Gibeah of Benjamin.

[141]See comments at 15:10.

[142]Preserved at modern Halhul, four miles north of Hebron.

[143]Possibly located at Khirbet et-Tubeiqeh, adjacent to Halhul.

[144]Khirbet Judur, seven miles north of Hebron, is a good candidate.

are situated along the heights of the central ridge between Hebron and Bethlehem.

In the fifth district of the Highland, only two sites are named in the MT: **Kiriath Baal (that is, Kiriath Jearim)** and **Rabbah.**[148]

15:61-62 Finally, the fourth set of sites is offered. These are located in the wilderness and include **Beth Arabah,**[149] **Middin,**[150] **Seca-cah,**[151] **Nibshan, the City of Salt**[152] and **En Gedi.**[153]

15:63 Despite the glowing promise of a territorial inheritance and the success of Caleb, the last line is a portent of things to come. The narrator returns to announce that the inhabitants of Jerusalem will not be driven from their home; instead, they will dwell among Judah.[154] Such notice links this conclusion with similar failures by Ephraim (16:10), Manasseh (17:12-13), and others (18:3).

---

[145]Khirbet Qufin may conceal the remains of biblical Maarath. Khirbet Qufin is located two miles north of Khirbet et-Tubeiqeh (Beth-zur?).

[146]Khirbet Beit 'Anun, located on the northeast edge of modern Hebron, is a possible location for this site.

[147]The location of Eltekon is unknown.

[148]The appearance of these two sites is somewhat awkward. It is an oddly placed description. It follows the general descriptive trend that moves from south to north; however, site identifications of Kiriath Jearim (with Deir al-Azar) and Rabbah (with Khirbet Bir el-Hilu) are more Lowland oriented (compare with the first Lowland district, 15:33-36). In the case of the latter site, it is also north of Judah's boundary described in 15:5-11. Additional complications arise when the MT presentation and LXX presentation of this list are compared. In the LXX, verse 59 is extended to offer an additional eleven sites missing in the MT. These additional sites center around Bethlehem, which, by itself, is a curious omission from a list of Judahite villages.

[149]See 15:6.

[150]Possibly located at Khirbet Abu Tabaq, nine miles south of Jericho.

[151]Secacah has been associated with the ruins at Khirbet es-Samrah, 11 miles south of Jericho. Still, the site of Qumran is possible. See H. Eshel, "A Note on Joshua 15:61-62 and the Identification of the City of Salt," *IEJ* 45 (1995): 37-40.

[152]The location of Nibshan and the City of Salt are unknown. The name of the latter obviously suggests a location near the shore of the Dead Sea.

[153]Ein Jedi (Gedi), located some 30 miles south of Jericho, is an oasis on the edge of the Dead Sea.

[154]Or less literally, "they will regularly interact with Judah," given the awkward reality that the tribal boundary for Judah described in 15:8 runs south of Jerusalem and does not include it. Jerusalem is in Benjamite territory proper (18:28).

JOSHUA 16

4. Joseph's Land (16:1–17:18)

[1]The allotment for Joseph began at the Jordan of Jericho,[a] east of the waters of Jericho, and went up from there through the desert into the hill country of Bethel. [2]It went on from Bethel (that is, Luz),[b] crossed over to the territory of the Arkites in Ataroth, [3]descended westward to the territory of the Japhletites as far as the region of Lower Beth Horon and on to Gezer, ending at the sea.

[4]So Manasseh and Ephraim, the descendants of Joseph, received their inheritance.

[5]This was the territory of Ephraim, clan by clan:

The boundary of their inheritance went from Ataroth Addar in the east to Upper Beth Horon [6]and continued to the sea. From Micmethath on the north it curved eastward to Taanath Shiloh, passing by it to Janoah on the east. [7]Then it went down from Janoah to Ataroth and Naarah, touched Jericho and came out at the Jordan. [8]From Tappuah the border went west to the Kanah Ravine and ended at the sea. This was the inheritance of the tribe of the Ephraimites, clan by clan. [9]It also included all the towns and their villages that were set aside for the Ephraimites within the inheritance of the Manassites.

[10]They did not dislodge the Canaanites living in Gezer; to this day the Canaanites live among the people of Ephraim but are required to do forced labor.

[a]1 *Jordan of Jericho* was possibly an ancient name for the Jordan River.
[b]2 Septuagint; Hebrew *Bethel to Luz*

Following the description of land allotments to the descendants of Judah, attention shifts to a description of allotments to the des-

297

cendants of Joseph. At a glance, these appear similar. Presentations of boundaries are offered (cf. 15:2-12; 16:1-9; 17:7-10), hero/heroine stories are inserted (cf. 15:13-19; 17:1-6), city lists are detailed (cf. 15:21-61; 17:11), and intonations of failure are voiced (cf. 15:63; 16:10; 17:12-18). A closer read, however, reveals how such structural similarities only accentuate deeper differences. That which is coherent, organized, and worthy of imitation in the case of Judah is piecemeal, uncertain, and strained in the case of Joseph.[1] Two silhouettes invite contrast; two portraits demand comparison.

In keeping with a Genesis perspective (46:20; 48:1-22; 49:22-26), two tribal groups are connected to Joseph and distinguished: Ephraim and Manasseh. Like blind old Jacob, the narrator crosses his arms, "puts Ephraim ahead of Manasseh" (Gen 48:20), and gives priority to the legacy of the younger brother (16:1-10). The legacy of Manasseh is subordinated (17:1-18); but both follow Judah (Gen 49:8-12).

16:1-3 As previously (15:1), the description begins with the formulaic וַיֵּצֵא הַגּוֹרָל (*wayyēṣēʾ haggôrāl*), "and the lot came out." (See Supplemental Study on Lot-Casting below.) Here it comes out to Joseph and initiates the etching of a single boundary. This line runs from east to west, beginning at the Jordan River and ending on the Mediterranean shore. On the way, familiar sites are recognized: from **Jericho**[2] it ascends the central ridge to **Bethel**, descends past **Beth Horon** and lands on the costal plain at **Gezer**.

SUPPLEMENTAL STUDY

LOT-CASTING

The search for a God's-eye view has long been a quest of the believing heart. It grows from a series of convictions beginning with the existence of God. From here it moves to the assumption that this

---

[1]This section poses many difficulties to the translator and interpreter. Some students have attempted to emend the text, others opt for wholesale rearrangement. The attempt here will try to deal with the text as it stands. See the introduction for additional comments on this point.

[2]The "waters of Jericho" likely refers to ʿAin es-Sultan, a perennial spring on the eastern edge of the tell.

existing God is a loving being who cares deeply for his creation. In fact, it is because of this deep care that a will takes shape, a will understood as a set of desires that are specific to, and discoverable by, humans. That these convictions are more than wishful thinking is a product of the biblical text; collectively, it offers an affirmative nod: God does indeed speak. Still, pause is needed at the end of this thought-string; how does one go about listening?

Prophetic thunder is hard to miss, as is Mosaic *torah* or large apostolic letter. But beyond these lines is another venue of communication. It is like Gideon's fleece (Judg 6:36-40), nonverbal, symbolic, and somewhat woolly. In the end, oddly enough, it prompts more questions than it answers. What does it mean to "cast lots"? How do these "lots" work? Is the practice genuine or manipulative? How is it different from the methods of Israel's neighbors? Is it an act to be imitated today? A quick survey of biblical words and mentions is in order, followed by some brief interpretive thoughts about lot-casting specifically and seeking God's will generally.[3]

Within the biblical story there are several instances of the practice. The language of lot-casting is easily searched. The "lot" is the גּוֹרָל (*gôral*) or the κλῆρος (*klēros*) in Greek. Both terms have at their core the idea of a bit of wood, pottery, or stone. These tokens may be marked in some way (1 Chr 26:13-16) and then "arise," "are given," "shaken," "cast," "go out," or, most frequently, "are caused to fall" by one who seeks specific knowledge. What this looks like up close is difficult to ascertain, although some help is gained from passages such as Proverbs 16:33: "the lot is cast in the lap, but its every decision is from the LORD." Key to their use, obviously, is the assumption that such tokens do not "tumble out" by chance or by the will of man. Instead, they are directed by the will of God. Such an idea can hardly be viewed as "primitive" but is simply a natural extension of the belief that God is at work in all things.

Seemingly connected to this lot-casting practice is the use of "The Urim"[4] and "The Thummim"[5] (הָאוּרִים, *hā'ûrîm* and הַתֻּמִּים, *hat-*

---

[3]An important article on this subject is J. Lindblom, "Lot-Casting in the Old Testament," *VT* 12 (Apr. 1962): 164-178.

[4]Possibly having something to do with light, e.g. a "shining (thing)" or an item of "enlightenment" (BDB, s.v. אוּר)?

[5]Possibly having to do with the perfect end of a thing, or a completed thing, e.g., the "finisher" (BDB, s.v. תָּמַם)?

tummîm), the unique property of the high priest. These small objects were worn "over the heart" in a "decision-making breastplate" (Exod 28:15,30) and may have been drawn out to answer a simple yes-no question. It is possible that one was white (made of limestone) and the other was black (made of basalt). Interestingly, a helpful passage that illustrates the use of "The Urim" and "The Thummim" is concerned with the transition of power between Moses and Joshua (Num 27:12-23).

Elsewhere, lots are used to help render decisions in many contexts. Israel's first king seems to have been publicly determined by lot (1 Sam 10:20-24). Saul's son, Jonathan, was identified as a "transgressor" in this way (1 Sam 14:36,40-42). Service in the Jerusalem temple was determined by lot (1 Chr 24:5-19), a practice still used in NT times (Luke 1:9). Lots were cast by the eleven to choose an apostle to replace Judas (Acts 1:26).

Outside of Israel, this method of decision making is also found. Booty and captives could be divided by lot (Joel 3:3[H 4:3]). Pagan sailors used some kind of small pieces to identify Jonah as the source of their problem (Jonah 1:7) and Haman used the lot (or, in Akkadian, the *pur* or *pûru* > *Purim*) to help him pick what he believed to be the right day for a massacre (Esth 3:7).[6] Finally, soldiers used lots at the foot of the cross as a way to determine who received Jesus' garments (Matt 27:35; see also Ps 22:18[H 19]).

Such passages help contextualize the use of lots in the book of Joshua: determining the guilt of Achan (7:10-15) and in dividing the land among the tribes (15:1; 16:1; 17:1; etc.). Significant in the case of the latter is the idea that just as Yahweh led Israel into the land, so too will he divide it. One idea suggests that the division was practically accomplished by drawing lots from two containers.[7] In one were markers with tribal names written on them; in the other, were tokens for specific land parcels.

If all this seems difficult to sort, one must consult passages such as Deuteronomy 18:9-14 or Ezekiel 21:21-23[H 26-28] where the Old Testament specifically condemns pagan superstition and the practice of magic. Absent from this list is recourse to the lot, and, for

---

[6]W.W. Hallo, "The First Purim," *BA* (1983): 19-29.

[7]*TDOT*, s.v. גּוֹרָל.

what it is worth, the interpretation of dreams. Neither are explicitly condemned, and both find use by the people of God.[8]

In light of this last observation, the final question arises: should lot-casting be practiced today? Interestingly, beyond the selection of Matthias in Acts 1:26, the practice of lot-casting does not appear again in the pages of the New Testament.[9] Of course many more decisions would be required of the early church, but these would be carefully weighed on the basis of Scripture, prayer, and common sense. As John Stott observes, these three "constitute a wholesome combination through which God may be trusted to guide us today."[10]

Three convergences of this line require further comment. First, while it nearly meets the northern boundary of Judah at Jericho in the east, it more typically runs between five and ten miles north of Judah in the center and western reaches of the land. This path effectively creates a buffer zone between the tribe of Judah and the tribes of Joseph, a parcel that will later be identified with Benjamin (18:11-28) and Dan (19:40-48). The strategic nature of this buffer zone is borne out later in Israel's history when the country is divided into two independent states, north (Israel) and south (Judah). Benjamin, with Jerusalem, rides between.[11]

A second convergence is the intersection between the southern line of the Joseph tribes and the boundary of the **Arkites at Ataroth**. Ataroth is identified as a Highland village,[12] but the Arkites are more

---

[8]Or nonuse. When faced by a Philistine dilemma, Saul sought a divine word. None came, however, either through dreams, through the Urim, or through the prophets (1 Sam 28:6). All channels were shut down.

[9]According to early Jewish tradition (Mishnah *Soṭa* ix.12), use of the lot-oracle ceased at the time of Solomon (*TDOT*, s.v. גּוֹרָל). Later uses of "lot" in the Old Testament seem to be more figurative than literal, with the "lot" of a man being the same as his "fate."

[10]John Stott, *The Spirit, The Church, and the World: The Message of Acts* (Downers Grove, IL: InterVarsity, 1990), p. 59.

[11]While one would imagine the southern boundary of the Joseph tribes and the northern boundary of the tribe of Benjamin to be identical, efforts to align these boundaries is difficult (cp. 16:1-3; 18:12-13).

[12]Possibly Khirbet Radannah (see Aharoni, *Land of the Bible*, p. 256), located about 11 miles southwest of Shiloh. For problems, see Elitzur, *Ancient Place Names*, pp. 157-158.

difficult to discern. Grammar suggests this is a proper name modified as a "place of origin" reference.[13] Unfortunately, no breadth of
use may be discerned within the biblical text. Other mentions of this
word are confined to descriptions of Hushai, the Arkite, a counselor
of David (2 Sam 15:32; 16:16; 17:5,14; 1 Chr 27:33). It is not known
whether these Arkites are a clan in or out of Israel.

The same may be said of the **Japhletites**. This mention falls with-
in the context of a third convergence between the boundary of the
Joseph tribes and the boundary of another. Unfortunately,
Japhletites are not known apart from this reference.[14]

16:4 With this southern boundary in place, the narrator pushes
forward to detail the allotment of the Joseph tribes, Ephraim and
Manasseh. Introduced together (16:1-4), they will be handled separately (16:5–17:13), and then reunited in conclusion (17:14-18). The
formulaic lead of 16:4 prepares the reader to consider first the borders of Ephraim.

16:5-8 Boundaries describing the allotment of Ephraim are
described in a series of three segments that awkwardly alternate
from south to north and from west to east. The first segment is a
part of the southern line previously established. It begins on top of
the central ridge at **Ataroth Addar**[15] and moves downhill past **Upper
Beth Horon**[16] and into the Mediterranean. A second thrust begins
again high on the ridge at "the **Micmethath**,"[17] but this time curves

---

[13]Grammatically, a gentilic (see Waltke and O'Connor, *Biblical Hebrew Syntax*, sec. 5.7c).

[14]The proper name Japhlet appears in a genealogical list of Asher (1 Chr 7:30, 32-33), but it is difficult to connect this mention with the text under discussion.

[15]It is here assumed that Ataroth Addar ("Big Ataroth") of v. 5 is the same as the Ataroth of v. 2, but different from the Ataroth of v. 7. This knotted problem is part of the reason why it is difficult to establish Ephraim's boundaries with certainty.

[16]Upper Beth Horon (cf. 10:10-11) is identified with Beit 'Ur al-Foqa and is separated from Lower Beth Horon (Beit 'Ur al-Tahta) by about a mile and a half. Both sites are located less than 16 miles southwest of Shiloh.

[17]The text reads literally, "the Micmethath," the article raising the possi-
bility that this is a feature or landmark rather than a settlement. Those who seek ruins have connected the site to Khirbet Makhna el-Fauqa, located about nine miles north of Shiloh.

southeastward past **Taanath Shiloh**,[18] **Janoah**,[19] **Ataroth**, and **Naarah**.[20] Ultimately it emerges from the Highlands at **Jericho** and concludes on the banks of the Jordan River. Strikingly, the area of Jericho thus becomes a hub from which lines of three tribal territories converge: Judah, Benjamin, and Ephraim. A third segment of Ephraim's allotment border returns the reader again to the Central Ridge at **Tappuah**[21] and follows the **Kanah Ravine**[22] eastward to the Mediterranean.

Despite the difficulty in tracing these line segments, the enclosed land is easily characterized. Like the allotment of Judah, Ephraim is dominated by the Central Ridge. Elevations in the vicinity of Baalhazor rise regularly above 3,000 feet, but tumble sharply into deep ravines on both the east and west faces. As in Judah, this vertical challenge limits travel to narrow ridges and spurs and makes for a defendable center.[23] It also efficiently bestows Ephraim with two very different characters: the dry "badlands" on the east contrast sharply with the verdant forests on the west. How much of the coastal plain below is included in the parcel is difficult to determine; any portion of the flat, fertile reaches between Aphek and Gezer would be valuable agricultural land.

16:9 A final note makes it clear that Ephraimites will not only have an allotment of their own, but they will also settle within territory allotted to Manasseh. Oddly, not all Ephraimites villages are even in Ephraim!

---

[18]Taanath Shiloh ("the fig tree of Shiloh") may also be a known landmark rather than a settlement. The site of Khirbet Tana el-Fauqa, located approximately ten miles northeast of Shiloh, is typically identified as Taanath Shiloh.

[19]Janoah may be identified with Khirbet Yanun, immediately west of Khirbet Tana el-Fauqa.

[20]Naarah is linked to the village of Niran (Tell el-Jisr), located on the northern outskirts of modern Jericho.

[21]Possibly Sheik Abu Zarad, located approximately four and a half miles northwest of Shiloh.

[22]The Kanah Ravine, or Wadi Qana, is a significant drainage system shared by Ephraim and Manasseh. See Baly's discussion (*Geography*, pp. 165-166).

[23]Such geographical constraints help explain why Shiloh became a focal point for early Israel (e.g., 1 Sam 1:24). It is centered along the ridge and difficult to approach from east or west.

16:10 Just as Ephraim will exist within Manasseh, a somber conclusion points out that the Canaanites will exist among Ephraim (cf. Judg 1:29). The parallel between this concluding comment regarding Ephraim's allotment and the concluding comment regarding Jerusalem in Judah's allotment (15:63) cannot be missed. Here, attention is given specifically to the stronghold of Gezer, previously noted in the central campaign (10:33).[24] Rather than dislodging these Canaanites as instructed, this indigenous population is permitted to remain in the land and **do forced labor**.[25] While the vocabulary is different, the Gibeonite deception and curse (9:22-27) are quickly drawn to mind; it is difficult to see this concession as positive.

---

[24]Nelson, *Joshua*, p. 197, suggests the tension standing between 10:33 and 16:10. The former passage states that there were no survivors among those who fought for the king of Gezer. The latter passage describes the fate of the surviving Gezerites. An additional point to be considered is the notable absence of Gezer in the final tally of captured kings (12:9-24) and the possibility that the forces of Gezer were defeated far from home while attempting to lift the siege of Lachish (see comments at 10:31-33). The Joshua 10 text says nothing about what may have happened to the site of Gezer or to those left behind to protect it.

[25]The term, מַס (*mas*), translated "forced labor" or *corvée* is used elsewhere in describing the Egyptian taskmasters (שָׂרֵי מִסִּים, *śārê missîm*, lit., "chiefs of the gangs") who directed Israel during the years of bondage (Exod 1:11). The noun also collectively describes those conscripted by Solomon in his building projects (1 Kgs 5:15). A later occurrence in 1 Kings describes non-Israelites who were put to work in slave gangs (9:21). These non-Israelites appear to be locals who survived the conquest of land, a connection linking this passage to Josh 16:10. For other mentions of "forced labor" see Deut 20:11; Judg 1:30,33,35.

JOSHUA 17

4. Joseph's Land, Continued (16:1–17:18)

¹This was the allotment for the tribe of Manasseh as Joseph's firstborn, that is, for Makir, Manasseh's firstborn. Makir was the ancestor of the Gileadites, who had received Gilead and Bashan because the Makirites were great soldiers. ²So this allotment was for the rest of the people of Manasseh—the clans of Abiezer, Helek, Asriel, Shechem, Hepher and Shemida. These are the other male descendants of Manasseh son of Joseph by their clans.

³Now Zelophehad son of Hepher, the son of Gilead, the son of Makir, the son of Manasseh, had no sons but only daughters, whose names were Mahlah, Noah, Hoglah, Milcah and Tirzah. ⁴They went to Eleazar the priest, Joshua son of Nun, and the leaders and said, "The LORD commanded Moses to give us an inheritance among our brothers." So Joshua gave them an inheritance along with the brothers of their father, according to the LORD's command. ⁵Manasseh's share consisted of ten tracts of land besides Gilead and Bashan east of the Jordan, ⁶because the daughters of the tribe of Manasseh received an inheritance among the sons. The land of Gilead belonged to the rest of the descendants of Manasseh.

⁷The territory of Manasseh extended from Asher to Micmethath east of Shechem. The boundary ran southward from there to include the people living at En Tappuah. ⁸(Manasseh had the land of Tappuah, but Tappuah itself, on the boundary of Manasseh, belonged to the Ephraimites.) ⁹Then the boundary continued south to the Kanah Ravine. There were towns belonging to Ephraim lying among the towns of Manasseh, but the boundary of Manasseh was the northern side of the ravine and ended at the sea. ¹⁰On the

south the land belonged to Ephraim, on the north to
Manasseh. The territory of Manasseh reached the sea and
bordered Asher on the north and Issachar on the east.

[11]Within Issachar and Asher, Manasseh also had Beth
Shan, Ibleam and the people of Dor, Endor, Taanach and
Megiddo, together with their surrounding settlements (the
third in the list is Naphoth[a]).

[12]Yet the Manassites were not able to occupy these towns, for the
Canaanites were determined to live in that region. [13]However,
when the Israelites grew stronger, they subjected the Canaanites to
forced labor but did not drive them out completely.

[14]The people of Joseph said to Joshua, "Why have you given us
only one allotment and one portion for an inheritance? We are a
numerous people and the LORD has blessed us abundantly."

[15]"If you are so numerous," Joshua answered, "and if the hill
country of Ephraim is too small for you, go up into the forest and
clear land for yourselves there in the land of the Perizzites and
Rephaites."

[16]The people of Joseph replied, "The hill country is not enough
for us, and all the Canaanites who live in the plain have iron chariots, both those in Beth Shan and its settlements and those in the
Valley of Jezreel."

[17]But Joshua said to the house of Joseph—to Ephraim and
Manasseh—"You are numerous and very powerful. You will have
not only one allotment [18]but the forested hill country as well. Clear
it, and its farthest limits will be yours; though the Canaanites have
iron chariots and though they are strong, you can drive them out."

[a]*11* That is, Naphoth Dor

Focus on the descendants of Joseph and their territorial allotment continues. Only now, attention shifts from the tribe of Ephraim
to the tribe of Manasseh. Manasseh is composed of warriors, fathers,
and daughters (17:1-6). This tribal identification is followed by a
review of boundaries and settlements (17:7-11). Finally, sentiments
of failure, dissatisfaction, and encouragement are offered (17:12-
18). (See Supplemental Study on the Survey of Manasseh.)

SUPPLEMENTAL STUDY
THE SURVEY OF MANASSEH

Archaeological reconnaissance in the core of the *Heartland* has revealed data of interest to the reader of Joshua. Unfortunately, due to a number of impediments, it has been slow in making its way into the community of biblical interpreters. For this reason, publication of the Manasseh Hill Country Survey is a welcome arrival. The field-work that it represents was conducted over a fourteen-year period between 1980 and 1994 under the direction of Adam Zertal of the University of Haifa, Israel. The work involved systematically walking across more than 2,000 square kilometers of ground, looking for archaeological sites and subjecting them to surface analysis. The geographical focus was the tribal territory of Manasseh, roughly centered around the modern city of Nablus (biblical Shechem). Some results of that survey were available early on in popular form from the hands of the director[1] or from those assessing his work,[2] while the hard data of the final report emerged later in stages, first in Hebrew, then in English.[3] While not without its critics,[4] the survey must be numbered among the most significant archaeological pub-

---

[1] Zertal, "Joshua's Altar," pp. 26-43; and "Israel Enters Canaan," pp. 28-49, 75; see also *NEAEHL*, s.v. "The Mount Manasseh (Northern Samarian Hills) Survey."

[2] Finkelstein, *Archaeology of the Israelite Settlement*, pp. 89-91; Aharon Kempinski, "Joshua's Altar—An Iron Age Watch Tower," *BAR* 12 (Jan./Feb. 1986): 43, 49-53.

[3] Two of a projected five-volume series of this important report are now available in English: Zertal, *The Manasseh Hill Country Survey, Vol. 1: The Shechem Syncline*, and *Vol. 2: The Eastern Valleys and the Fringes of the Desert*.

[4] William G. Dever either completely ignores the work of Zertal, as in *Who Were the Early Israelites and Where Did They Come From?* or speaks dismissively of it. See his essay, "How to Tell a Canaanite from an Israelite" in *The Rise of Ancient Israel*, Symposium at the Smithsonian Institution, October 26, 1991 (Washington D.C.: BAS, 1992). Ironically in the former work he claims that "Surface surveys . . . have been shown to give fairly reliable relative statistics—especially on period-by-period changes in settlement distribution" (*Who Were the Early Israelites?* pp. 94-95). In the latter work, however, he claims "Statistics based on that kind of sample are worse than meaningless. You can't really prove much of anything on the basis of surface surveys alone" ("How to Tell a Canaanite," p. 51). One wonders where Dever really stands with respect to surface survey?

lications to date in the context of studying Israel's arrival in Canaan. Given the limitations of the present effort, just three highlights of the survey are noted in passing.

First, the Manasseh Hill Country Survey offers details concerning the timing of Israel's initial settlement in the *Heartland's* core. More than 200 sites of relevance were discovered, mapped, and analyzed by the Survey. As indicated already, consensus suggests that the seam between the Bronze and Iron Ages, linked in hard numbers to the 13th century B.C., may be correlated with the moment of time when the Israelites began to settle into village life. If this is the case, it is possible the humble cooking pot may be a key piece of the puzzle. A distinctively shaped and decorated cooking pot is found in the earliest Iron I sites in the Jordan Valley. It then creeps into the *Heartland* from east to west, climbing into the central hills, but decreasing in percentage at site after site. It is possible that the trail of this pot marks the initial movement of Israel into the land, a process that required some time to develop as the text of Joshua suggests. Other corresponding features of the region, such as a shift in economy from herding to farming, are noted on the ground. It is difficult to ignore the possibility that these facts are related to Israel's arrival.

Second, the Manasseh Hill Country Survey offers details concerning settlement density and distribution. Here, too, numbers are important. As the Bronze Age dragged towards its sorry end in the *Heartland*, the total number of sites dwindled. In the Survey region, 116 MBA sites fade to just 39 LBA sites. Then in the Iron I period, the region is invigorated again; the total number of sites rises to 136. Zertal terms it "a population explosion."[5] Additionally, it is discovered that the newcomers located themselves in new places and used the land in new ways. Instead of concentrating themselves on the rich valley floors with easy access to water sources, the Iron Age folk preferred to settle higher up in the ridges and hills overlooking the valleys. Reasons for this may be imagined, but local security and a lifeway style based upon herding come quickly to mind. It is also noted that some chronological overlap exists between the older communities and the newer communities. For a time, they lived side by side.

---

[5]Zertal, "Israel Enters Canaan," p. 33.

Third, the Manasseh Hill Country Survey reveals site-specific discoveries that may impact the interpretation of the text of Joshua. Two examples of this have generated controversy, the second far more than the first. Zertal's identification of the site of el-'Unuq as biblical Gilgal is of considerable interest, given the failure of other proposals.[6] The elliptical or "sandal shape" of the site's perimeter wall (recall *gilgal* = "Wheel") and the fortunate position that it occupies in the Wadi Far'ah (as access point to "Canaan Central") demand further attention. If Zertal's identification of this "northern Gilgal" is accepted, or if there is more than one Gilgal, some rethinking will be required; this "Gilgal" is a long hike (more than 20 miles) from Jericho.

The second site-specific discovery of the Manasseh Hill Country Survey concerns a fieldstone structure found at the site of el-Burnat near the summit of Mt. Ebal.[7] This discovery continues to generate controversy given claims and counterclaims about its function.[8] An enclosure wall isolates an area of almost five acres. Within the closed space is a structure described as "a large sacrificial altar (9×4 m and 4 m high)." A double ramp of stone gives access to the altar itself. That it had a cultic function is part of the debate: a "layer of ash and bones" was found "all over." Egyptian scarab seals suggest that the structure was used in the 13th or 12th century B.C. The excavator concludes that this possibly is the very altar described in Joshua 8:30-35, the first cultic structure built by Israel![9] Kitchen is more guarded when he concludes, "Zertal's view is feasible, but absolute certainty eludes us."[10]

[6]Zertal, *Eastern Valleys*, pp. 433-435.

[7]For a description in the final report, see Zertal, *Shechem Syncline*, pp. 532-537. For still more, see Machlin, *Joshua's Altar*.

[8]E.g., Finkelstein, *Archaeology of Israelite Settlements*, pp. 82-85; Kempinski, "Joshua's Altar," pp. 43, 49-53; Dever, *Who Were the Israelites?* pp. 89-90; Kitchen, *Reliability*, pp. 232-234.

[9]Zertal, *Eastern Valleys*, p. 434.

[10]Kitchen, *Reliability*, p. 234.

17:1-6 Focus on Manasseh is introduced by the lot (*gôrāl*) and the acknowledgment that Manasseh is **Joseph's firstborn**. This tacit recognition of Jacob's reversal, giving priority to younger Ephraim, gives the narrator pause to explain how it is that Manasseh's legacy will be granted territory both east and west of the Jordan River. **Makir, Manasseh's firstborn** was a tough warrior who subdued and received a tough land (cf. Num 32:39-42; Josh 1:12; 13:8,29-31). Acknowledging this conquest action clears the way for a long-awaited explanation as to why the tribe of Manasseh will uniquely receive two inheritance parcels, one in Transjordan and one in Cisjordan.

A list of **male descendants** establishes the contrast for what follows. A fellow named **Zelophehad**, living three generations beyond Makir, had no male heirs, only daughters (cf. Num 26:29-34). From these daughters arises a petition: **give us an inheritance among our brothers**. This unusual request coming from the mouths of women is likely to be ignored in a patriarchal society; surprise is kindled when it is not. Joshua accedes to their request and gives them **ten tracts of land besides** their previous grant in Transjordan.

This prose account, offered without comment, exerts an irresistible pull for at least three reasons. First, the passage has pull due to the rarity of direct speech in this stretch of territorial presentation. That anyone is given the privilege of voice, here and now, invites further investigation. Second, the passage has pull when the similarity between this presentation of Joseph's inheritance is compared with the presentation of Judah's inheritance. The careful reader must place the demand of Zelophehad's daughters beside the similarly positioned demand of Caleb's daughter, Acsah (15:13-19). Finally, the passage has pull due to the striking observation that the request for inheritance emerges from the mouths of women. As in the case of Rahab at Jericho, the "alien" at Shechem or Gibeon, or even Caleb the Kenizzite, the narrator continues to challenge social boundaries of identity, power, and gender drawn by, between, and among the people of God.

Key to the request of Zelophehad's daughters is their appeal to the command of Yahweh. From their perspective, the demand is not exceptional, it is in keeping with *torah*. A rereading of Numbers 27:1-11 and 36:1-12 bears this out, as does the action that follows their request. Ten portions (of the lot) fall to territory of Manasseh. This verbal sequence of drawing near, requesting, and falling validates the claim of the daughters and results in their receiving land grants. An additional point gained underlines how Joshua is again presented as the legitimate successor and faithful interpreter of Moses.[11]

17:7-11 The edges of the **territory of Manasseh** are principally established in relation to other territories. The southern boundary is the only line traced on the ground. It connects **Asher**,[12] to **Micmethath, En Tappuah** and the **Kanah Ravine**,[13] to the Mediterranean **Sea**. The area north of this line belongs to Manasseh, while the area south of this line belongs to Ephraim. No other specifics for Manasseh's boundaries are given. The land of **Asher** rests to the north, the land of **Issachar** rests to **the east**.

Settlements within Manasseh are randomly presented and include **Beth Shan**,[14] **Ibleam**,[15] **Dor**,[16] **Endor**,[17] **Taanach**.[18] **Megiddo**,[19] and **Naphoth**.[20] As in other lists, daughter villages or hinterlands surround each of these sites. However, unlike previous lists, every site here will remain Canaanite; they are supposed to be, but will not become, "Manasseh."

---

[11]In Num 27:2, Zelophehad's daughters appear before "Moses, Eleazar the priest, the leaders, and the whole assembly." In Josh 17:4 the same appear before "Eleazar the priest, Joshua son of Nun, and the leaders." Note the substitution of Joshua for Moses. See the Supplemental Study on the Family in Ancient Israel in ch. 8, p. 186.

[12]Zertal, *Eastern Valleys*, pp. 107, 110, proposes Khirbet Yarzah for biblical Asher.

[13]For possible identifications of these places, see comments at 16:5-8.

[14]Beth Shan is identified with Tell el-Husn, located some 21 miles east of Megiddo in the Lower Jordan Valley.

[15]The ruins of Ibleam are likely to be found at Tell el-Balama, 11 miles southeast of Megiddo.

[16]Dor is identified with the ruins at Khirbet el-Burj (Tel Dor), resting on the coast approximately 16 miles west of Megiddo.

[17]It is difficult to understand how Khirbet es-Safsafa, typically identified as Endor, could be the same site referenced here. Khirbet es-Safsafa rests on the extreme northern edge of the Jezreel Valley, clearly in territory belonging to Issachar. The Endor of this reference is most likely unknown.

[18]The impressive mound of Tell Taannek is the location of Ta'anach. It rests about four and a half miles southeast of Megiddo.

[19]Megiddo is identified with the remains of Tell el-Mutasallim. The site rests on the southwestern rim of the Jezreel Valley.

[20]Naphoth appears in a difficult phrase, שְׁלֹשֶׁת הַנָּפֶת (šᵃlōšeth hannāpeth). The NIV renders it "the third in the list is Naphoth," although to what list this clause appeals is not known. The phrase could possibly modify the villages surrounding Megiddo in some way, "and its surrounding villages, *three levels (out)*."

Taken together, these borders and settlements suggest a geographical region focused on the northern end of the Central Ridge and spilling onto the surrounding plains. Unlike the southern (Judah) and central (Ephraim) allotments, however, the land of Manasseh is much more open, penetrated by wide valleys, and less elevated. Rain shadow dynamics create rich agricultural zones in the west that favor the farmer and more marginal zones in the east that favor the herder.

17:12-18 Sentiments of failure, dissatisfaction, and encouragement close the description of the tribal allotment for Manasseh. Failure here **to occupy these towns** parallels similar statements previously offered with respect to Judah (15:63) and Ephraim (16:10). Here, this failure prompts an exchange between the people of Joseph (both Ephraim and Manasseh) and Joshua. This exchange formally concludes the section (16:1–17:18) and appears as a negative complement to Caleb's request for more land (14:6-15).

It begins with a dissatisfied whine, **"Why have you given us only one allotment?"** What follows must be freshly translated. The Joseph tribes kvetch: "I am still a great people, and until now,[21] I have been blessed by Yahweh." This claim, set in first person, is both troubling and revealing. It is troubling because it asserts that even with good numbers and past blessing, the Joseph tribes are either unable or unwilling to subdue the parcel given them. Rather than facing their assigned duty, they ironically clamor for more, requesting an additional — or possibly an easier — assignment. This can't-do attitude stands in sharp contrast with the can-do attitude previously encountered in Judah's allotment story (15:13-19). But the claim here is more than troubling, it is downright revealing. It betrays a perspective that not only challenges the allotment system (and hence the power behind it), it communicates lost hope. Put more darkly, the Joseph tribes blame God for the current failure. The campaign has stalled because his blessing has expired.

Joshua solemnly counters such grousing: rise now for the purpose of shaping[22] land and confronting its inhabitants. Mention here

---

[21]For a temporal reading of the prepositional phrase, עַד־כֹּה (*'ad-kōh*), "until now," compare this use with Exod 7:16.

[22]The verbal root used here is בָּרָא (*bārā'*), the same form as that of Gen 1:1. It alludes to the act of creating, shaping, or as here, in the case of wild things, taming.

of the **Perizzites and Rephaites** brings to mind the ancient and formidable inhabitants of Canaan's highlands specifically targeted for
expulsion (Gen 15:20; Exod 3:8; Deut 7:1, etc.). Action is needed to
relieve oppression.[23]

His bold call receives a bald answer. With regard to the rugged
heights above, the Joseph tribes respond that they do not find it to
their liking or cannot secure it.[24] With regard to the flatlands below, the
Joseph tribes point out the ever-present danger of chariot patrols.[25]
Chariot centers from the Late Bronze Age are well known both in the
Lower Jordan Valley (Beth-shan, Tell el-Husn) and in the Jezreel Valley
(at sites such as Megiddo and Taannach). Hence, in their view,
progress is stymied by heights and depths. The reader casts about in
vain for a Caleb figure; none surfaces in Ephraim or Manasseh. All that
is heard are voices of timidity and unfaithfulness.

Joshua again attempts to cast the vision. To frame it, he takes the
vocabulary out of the mouths of the Joseph tribes, retools it in positive terms, and returns it *con brio*. "You are a great people" (עַם־רָב,
'am rab), he argues, affirming the "great people" statement of verse
14. Even more creatively, Joshua challenges the grouse of verse 14
that the blessing of Yahweh has limits (עַד־כֹּה, *'ad-kōh*), and puns,

---

[23]Joshua assumes the point of the Joseph tribes in a conditional clause,
namely, *if* you are so great and *if* the land confines or presses אָץ (*'āṣ*) you,
then act. According to the census of Numbers 26, however, it appears that
the Joseph tribes are quite average (Manasseh) or even below average
(Ephraim) in size, suggesting that their words are either a flat-out exaggera-
tion or a claim of arrogance, e.g., "we are simply superior"! Either way, suspicion is aroused, adding irony to the passage.

[24]More literally, v. 16 reads "the hill country is not found (לֹא־יִמָּצֵא, *lō'-
yimmāṣē'*) by/for us." It is either "not found" *to their liking* either for reasons
of shape or sufficiency (cf. Num 11:22; Zech 10:10), or "not found" by them
in the sense of possession, i.e., it is beyond our abilities (cf. Gen 19:11).

[25]Much is known of chariot design and tactics of the late second millennium B.C. It is a mistake to believe that the reference here to "iron chariots" (רֶכֶב בַּרְזֶל, *rekeb barzel*) describes an entire chariot made of iron. Such
a vehicle would be impossible to pull! Rather, the phrase "iron chariots"
refers to a chariot with select metal parts, e.g., hubs, bearings, or possibly
scythed wheels. Using state-of-the-art metalwork for these important elements would give the chariot strength and speed, and produce a stable fir-
ing platform for archers. Caught on flat and open ground, a group of lightly armed footmen could be systematically cut down by chariot squadrons
swooping in and out of bowshot range. See R. Drews, "The 'Chariots of
Iron' of Joshua and Judges," *JSOT* 45 (1989): 15-23.

"you have great power" (כֹּחַ גָּדוֹל, *kōaḥ gādôl*). Finally, he expansive-ly offers that which is requested: **"You will have not only one allot-ment."** But for this to be true, the Joseph tribes must act. They must shape the hill country and its strategic passes. They must recognize that they already have all the blessing that is necessary to confront the state-of-the-art technology of the plains. They must remember the words of Moses: "When you go to war against your enemies and see horses and chariots and an army greater than yours, do not be afraid of them, because the LORD your God, who brought you up out of Egypt, will be with you" (Deut 20:1).

In the end, Joshua's appeal suggests to the reader of Scripture that Israel's failure to follow through with the program of conquest may not simply be relegated to the book of Judges. Despite calls to courage, accumulating signs signal that this "great commission" is in serious trouble. The administrative task of dividing the land into manageable sections for settlement is complete for the major tribes of Judah and Joseph. More will come. Still, Judah's compromise in the case of one city (Jerusalem), Ephraim's casual satisfaction in allowing the Canaanites to remain as forced labor, and now Manasseh's balk in the face of the conquest mandate, reveals a dete-riorating trend. Israel's future in a "land of promise" appears less and less promising.

JOSHUA 18

The text has given considerable attention to the tribes of Judah and Joseph. This attention to detail wanes, however, as the remainder of the tribal lands are assigned and described. These are taken as a group of seven and are ordered as follows: Benjamin (18:11-28), Simeon (19:1-9), Zebulun (19:10-16), Issachar (19:17-23), Asher (19:24-31), Naphtali (19:32-39), and Dan (19:40-48). Beyond Benjamin — whose complete presentation resembles Judah — there is uniformity to the presentation that communicates a steady but superficial, feel. From Simeon to Dan, the order progresses roughly from south to north. Boundaries are sketched; settlements are tallied. As elsewhere, the lot moves with almost supernatural force: it "arises" (עָלָה, 'ālāh) or "goes out" (יָצָא, yāṣā'). It attaches itself to a particular tribe and works through it, "clan by clan."[1]

Narratively, the action of 18:1-10 fixes the context for the allotments that follow (18:11–19:48), and, when coupled with 19:49-51, frames the section. Hence, from beginning to end the reader realizes that the division of the remaining land is not a deal done in a corner, but is a conjoint agreement witnessed by Yahweh and the people. After all, the shape of the land is everybody's business. To make sure of it, Joshua continues to stand between the will of Yahweh and the obedience of the people.

---

[1]The NIV translation "clan by clan" renders the Hebrew phrase, לְמִשְׁפְּחֹתָם (lᵊmišpᵊḥōthām), "according to their extended family." The preposition lᵊ- renders the goal of the verbal action more specific and may even have a quasi-distributive sense, i.e., "the lot came out to the tribe of x, *specifically* to all its clans." Tribal groups are composed of a number of such related mišpāḥôth or "clans." The point of the text is that no group may be excluded. See Supplemental Study on the Family in Ancient Israel in ch. 8, p. 186.

5. Additional Encouragements (18:1-10)

[1]The whole assembly of the Israelites gathered at Shiloh and set up the Tent of Meeting there. The country was brought under their control, [2]but there were still seven Israelite tribes who had not yet received their inheritance.

[3]So Joshua said to the Israelites: "How long will you wait before you begin to take possession of the land that the LORD, the God of your fathers, has given you? [4]Appoint three men from each tribe. I will send them out to make a survey of the land and to write a description of it, according to the inheritance of each. Then they will return to me. [5]You are to divide the land into seven parts. Judah is to remain in its territory on the south and the house of Joseph in its territory on the north. [6]After you have written descriptions of the seven parts of the land, bring them here to me and I will cast lots for you in the presence of the LORD our God. [7]The Levites, however, do not get a portion among you, because the priestly service of the LORD is their inheritance. And Gad, Reuben and the half-tribe of Manasseh have already received their inheritance on the east side of the Jordan. Moses the servant of the LORD gave it to them."

[8]As the men started on their way to map out the land, Joshua instructed them, "Go and make a survey of the land and write a description of it. Then return to me, and I will cast lots for you here at Shiloh in the presence of the LORD." [9]So the men left and went through the land. They wrote its description on a scroll, town by town, in seven parts, and returned to Joshua in the camp at Shiloh. [10]Joshua then cast lots for them in Shiloh in the presence of the LORD, and there he distributed the land to the Israelites according to their tribal divisions.

18:1-2 A meeting is convened to deal with the remainder of the land assignments. Present is **the whole assembly of the Israelites**, a common *torah* phrase used to describe the larger collective of people (e.g., Exod 16:1-2; 35:1,4,20; Lev 19:2; Num 1:2; 13:26). In this case, they gather as one at the centrally located site of Shiloh,[2] where

---

[2]The site of Shiloh has been identified with Khirbet Seilun, located approximately ten miles south of modern Nablus (Shechem). Remains there

the **Tent of Meeting** appears in the text for the first time since the period of wandering. It is unpacked, strung, hung, and made functional. Notice that the land, for the moment, under Israelite control, sends four signals. First, it signals a lull in the action (the root from which the word Shiloh is derived appropriately suggests the name "Relaxation"[3]) that gives space for the present narrative to develop (cf. 11:23; 14:15). Second, it signals a sense of order, given the fact that Shiloh is located in the tribal territory of Ephraim; control must be established upon the ground (16:5-10) before the tabernacle pegs are driven into it. Third, it signals a sense of movement. Prior to this point, Israel's center has been Gilgal; with the hill country established, that center seemingly now moves.[4] Fourth and finally, it signals a sense of fulfillment.[5] Moses proclaimed that Yahweh would choose a place of dwelling after some measure of security is gained (Deut 12:10-11). It may be inferred that Shiloh is this place, perhaps even the first true Israelite settlement in the land,[6] although the narrator offers no explicit statement of divine selection here.

18:3-7 In this assembly Joshua challenges the initiative of the group. The question **how long?** is reminiscent of words previously voiced by Yahweh himself concerning the people (Exod 16:28; Num 14:11). Now, their slack-handedness[7] is made manifest again with regard to the possessing of the land gift. To invigorate the settle-

---

clearly go back to the MBA, but extensive occupation in later periods has made it difficult to assess the earlier materials.

[3]The verbal root used to create the name Shiloh communicates a sense of "quietness," "ease," or "rest." See BDB s.v., שלה.

[4]On the basis of 8:30-34 and 24:1 one could argue for the priority of Shechem over Shiloh as a "hill country" center. However, there is never explicit mention of Israelite settlement at Shechem (in fact, it goes unnamed in Joshua 8).

[5]As tangential to the present work, word choices in 18:1 and 19:49,51 also signal linkage to the creation account of Genesis 1 and 2. Gershon Hepner has recently outlined the thesis that the Genesis account is worded in such a way as to suggest that the *Heartland* is created to be subdued and settled. See his "Israelites Should Conquer Israel: The Hidden Polemic of the First Creation Narrative," in *RB* 113 (Apr. 2006): 161-180.

[6]As argued by Merling, *Joshua*, p. 206.

[7]The verb רָפָה (rāphāh) is often used with respect to the hands, as in relaxing one's grip or in letting loose of an object so that the hands fall to one's sides. As a metaphor, the phrase may suggest a loss of courage (e.g., 2 Sam 4:1; Isa 13:7) or just laziness (Prov 18:9).

ment process, Joshua calls upon each tribe to provide three repre-sentatives[8] for the purpose of a special commissioning. This group is to "rise up," "walk around in the land" (a.k.a. the "pedestrian expe-dition"), describe and inventory what land remains, and report back to Joshua. Excluding parcels previously assigned to the Judah and Joseph tribes and parcels previously assigned to the Transjordan tribes, seven tracts are to be created. These will be assigned by lot to the seven tribes that remain landless, excluding Levi (cf. Num 18:20; Josh 13:33). As previously, the narrator resorts to "tribal math" to carefully preserve the twelve-tribe scheme.[9]

18:8-10 The special commissioning is repeated by Joshua. Then, obediently, these men "cross over"[10] the land, commit to writing a settlement-by-settlement description, and return to Shiloh (see Supplemental Study on Site Identification below). There Joshua flings the lots and makes final assignments. The presence of the tent of meeting at Shiloh and the use of lots "before Yahweh" underline the divine role in the process. Theologically, Yahweh goes before the reunited congregation, offering direction, assistance, and focus.

SUPPLEMENTAL STUDY

SITE IDENTIFICATION[11]

Many place names appear in the text of Joshua. Some of these are labels for regions, geographical features, or settlements. "Grounding" the text in the real world is a difficult job and requires knowledge in many diverse areas including topography, toponymy, archaeology, and philology.

---

[8]Are these three representatives drawn from each of the seven tribes that remain or from each and every tribe in Israel? The text does not commit to a position.

[9]The phrase "tribal math" is used by Davis, *No Falling Words*, p. 141.

[10]In 18:9 the men "go (וַיֵּלְכוּ, *wayyēlkû*) and cross over (וַיַּעַבְרוּ, *wayya'abrû*) the land," a phrase that harkens back to Israel's original commission to the pedestrian expedition (cf. 1:2-3).

[11]The essence of this essay appeared originally as a part of the article "Bible Lands and Lifeways," in *A Humble Defense: Evidence for the Christian Faith. A Special Tribute Honoring Dr. Lynn Gardner*, ed. by Mark Scott and Mark Moore (Joplin, MO: College Press, 2004), pp. 89-106.

To the extent that ancient names are preserved within modern ones, the task appears relatively easy. Complicating this, however, are false analogies, lost sites, moving targets, and literary issues. Some of these complications are illustrated by a look at two places: Jericho and Beth-shan.

The modern village known as *(Tariq) er-Riha* (Arabic, lit. "way of fragrance") may be a preservation of the older Hebrew "Jericho" *(Yerihu)*. Approximately one mile northwest of the Arabic town is a ruin-mound (Tell es-Sultan) identified with the Old Testament city. Approximately one mile to the west are the low ruins *(Tulul Abu el'Alayiq)* identified with a New Testament period palace. Hence, three sites on three different locations have been connected with the name Jericho. Pilgrim traditions tend to migrate to the most convenient site, a factor that may explain why "Zacchaeus's sycamore tree," visited by many tourists, is absurdly located in the middle of the Palestinian village. Fortunately, in this case, pilgrim lore and philological observation have given way to archaeological analysis. In the end, while the archaeology of Jericho is not without problems, the task of site separation and identification appears complete.

As for Beth-shan, the name has also been connected with more than one place. Egyptian records discovered on-site confirm that Tell el-Husn is the location of Old Testament Beth-shan. However, by the New Testament period, the settlement moved off the *tell* and onto the surrounding plain. In this period, the older name was lost, and the Hellenistic village was called Nysa or Scythopolis. Finally, in the Early Islamic period, a third site on a nearby ridge was settled and given the Arabic name Beisan. While carrying essentially the same name, the original Beth-shan and the later Beisan (note how similarly they sound) are separated significantly in time and place. One can only wonder how many other examples of moving targets have confounded the task of site association and thrown the investigator off the trail.

A final example of the challenge of place names comes from uses that may be labeled "literary" for lack of a better term. It is well known that Hebrew names have intrinsic meanings; many personal names suggest some characteristic or major event in the life of that person. A real challenge for Bible translators is choosing whether to translate a name or leave it alone in transliteration. Without a doubt, after Cain killed Abel he was doomed to be a wanderer by

God (Gen 4:12). However, one verse later it says he settled down, ironically, in the "land of wanderers" (*Nod*). This example is only one of many. Job lived in Uz; he was a wise man living in the land of "counsel" (Job 1:1). When entering Sinai, the Israelites could not drink the water at Marah ("Bitterness") because it was bitter (Exod 15:23-24). Joshua and company destroyed *ha-Ai* ("the ruin") and made it into one (Josh 8:28). The place where the dueling men stabbed each other was called *Helkath hazzurim* (*ḥelqath haṣṣurîm*), "a field of daggers." This field is explicitly located "in Gibeon" (2 Sam 2:16). Elijah fled from Jezebel but found refuge and strength at *Horeb* ("a desolate place"), also called "the mountain of God" (1 Kgs 19:8).

As these examples suggest, some places undoubtedly had other names, but the biblical writer chose instead to use a local referent, a pun, or an explanation that was a better fit for the literary purpose at hand. In this, one begins to sense the complex links that exist between a real event, the artistry of the written description, and a tradition that kept the memory of a place alive. A recognized parallel from our own culture might be the "Dead Man's Curve" found just outside of many towns in America. Such a label will never appear on a map but is a well-known element of the local landscape, vocabulary, and memory for a very real reason. David hid from Saul in *Ṣûrê hayyᵉ'ēlîm*, the "Rocks of the Wild Goats" (1 Sam 24:2[H 3]) and escaped from Saul at *Selaʿ hammaḥlᵉqôth*, the "Rock of Escape" (1 Sam 23:28). After thousands of years it is doubtful that such places could be identified, much less excavated.

In the end, according to one count, out of the approximately 475 unique place names in the Old Testament, about 262 have been identified "with any degrees of certainty, viz., 55 percent."[12] Of the 262 identified sites, 190 come as a result of the preservation of the ancient name in the modern one. This leaves 72 sites identified on the basis of other evidence, such as archaeological finds or historical description. With 45 percent of all Old Testament place names not yet on the map, there is certainly room for future work.

---

[12]Anson Rainey, "Historical Geography," in *Benchmarks in Time and Culture: Essays in Honor of Joseph A. Callaway*, ed. by J.F. Drinkard Jr., G.L. Mattingly, and J.M. Miller (Atlanta: Scholars, 1988), p. 359.

6. Benjamin's Land (18:11-28)

[11]The lot came up for the tribe of Benjamin, clan by clan. Their allotted territory lay between the tribes of Judah and Joseph:

[12]On the north side their boundary began at the Jordan, passed the northern slope of Jericho and headed west into the hill country, coming out at the desert of Beth Aven. [13]From there it crossed to the south slope of Luz (that is, Bethel) and went down to Ataroth Addar on the hill south of Lower Beth Horon.

[14]From the hill facing Beth Horon on the south the boundary turned south along the western side and came out at Kiriath Baal (that is, Kiriath Jearim), a town of the people of Judah. This was the western side.

[15]The southern side began at the outskirts of Kiriath Jearim on the west, and the boundary came out at the spring of the waters of Nephtoah. [16]The boundary went down to the foot of the hill facing the Valley of Ben Hinnom, north of the Valley of Rephaim. It continued down the Hinnom Valley along the southern slope of the Jebusite city and so to En Rogel. [17]It then curved north, went to En Shemesh, continued to Geliloth, which faces the Pass of Adummim, and ran down to the Stone of Bohan son of Reuben. [18]It continued to the northern slope of Beth Arabah[a] and on down into the Arabah. [19]It then went to the northern slope of Beth Hoglah and came out at the northern bay of the Salt Sea,[b] at the mouth of the Jordan in the south. This was the southern boundary.

[20]The Jordan formed the boundary on the eastern side.

These were the boundaries that marked out the inheritance of the clans of Benjamin on all sides.

[21]The tribe of Benjamin, clan by clan, had the following cities:

Jericho, Beth Hoglah, Emek Keziz, [22]Beth Arabah, Zemaraim, Bethel, [23]Avvim, Parah, Ophrah, [24]Kephar Ammoni, Ophni and Geba—twelve towns and their villages.

[25]Gibeon, Ramah, Beeroth, [26]Mizpah, Kephirah, Mozah, [27]Rekem, Irpeel, Taralah, [28]Zelah, Haeleph, the Jebusite city

**(that is, Jerusalem), Gibeah and Kiriath—fourteen towns
and their villages.**
This was the inheritance of Benjamin for its clans.

18 Septuagint; Hebrew *slope facing the Arabah*   *19* That is, the Dead
Sea

18:11-28 The first of the remaining tribes to receive an allotment
is Benjamin. Here, the lot "arises" and the border "goes out" to fix
a place resting strategically **between the tribes of Judah and Joseph**.
The northern border is described first and is contiguous with the
southern border of Ephraim (16:5-8). It begins on the east side, at
the Jordan River, passing by the "shoulder" of Jericho.[13] From there,
it ascends the Central Ridge, through the hilly steppes of **Beth Aven**[14]
to **Luz** or **Bethel**.[15] The corresponding descent on the west face of
the Central Ridge is more loosely defined: it passes by the site of
Ataroth Addar[16] and somehow angles south, ending abruptly at the
border with Judah at **Kiriath Baal** (**Kiriath Jearim**),[17] about half the
distance between the Central Ridge above and the coastal plain
below. The southern border is clear, sharing points of description
with Judah that require no further comment here (cf. 15:5-9).
Finally, the Jordan River forms the eastern boundary.

Sites included in the inheritance of Benjamin are outlined in two
districts or sets. The first set totals twelve settlements and includes
Jericho, Beth Hoglah,[18] **Emek Keziz,**[19] **Beth Arabah,**[20] **Zemaraim,**[21]
Bethel,[22] **Avvim,**[23] **Parah,**[24] **Ophrah,**[25] **Kephar Ammoni, Ophni,**[26] and

---

[13]The "shoulder" (כֶּתֶף, *ketheph*) here may not refer to the mound of
Jericho itself, but to the steep cliffs of the Great Rift Valley that form a natural boundary towering above it. See Elitzur, *Ancient Place Names*, p. 37, n. 2.

[14]For Beth Aven, see the note at 7:2.

[15]Luz is identified as the former name of Bethel in Gen 28:19.

[16]For Ataroth Addar, see the note at 16:5.

[17]For Kiriath Baal, see the note at 16:50.

[18]Beth Hoglah also appears in the border list of Judah; see 15:6.

[19]Emek Keziz, or "Keziz Valley" is unknown. Context suggests a location
on the wilderness side of Benjamin.

[20]Beth Arabah also appears in the list of cities given to Judah, cf. 15:61.

[21]Zemaraim may be located at Ras et-Tahuna in modern Ramallah/el-
Bireh (Aharoni, *Land of the Bible*, p. 443); 2 Chr 13:4 refers to a Mount
Zemaraim in the hill country of Ephraim.

[22]Cf. comments at 7:2.

[23]The location of Avvim is unknown.   *More opposite*

Geba.[27] Satellite settlements in the surrounding countryside are not named, but included by the phrase, **and their villages**.

The second set totals fourteen settlements and includes **Gibeon**,[28] **Ramah**,[29] **Beeroth**,[30] **Mizpah**,[31] **Kephirah**,[32] **Mozah**,[33] **Rekem**,[34] **Irpeel**, **Taralah**,[35] **Zelah**,[36] **Haeleph**,[37] **Jerusalem**,[38] **Gibeah**,[39] and **Kiriath**.[40] Here, too, acknowledgment is made of satellite sites.

---

[24]Parah is associated with Khirbet Abu Musarrah (or Khirbet el-Farah), located about six miles east of el-Jib.

[25]The modern village of et-Taiyibeh is often associated with Ophrah. It is located approximately ten miles northeast of el-Jib, and fairly north of the cluster of other Benjamite sites. For linguistic issues here, see Aharoni, *Land of the Bible*, p. 121, or Elitzur, *Ancient Place Names*, pp. 268-290.

[26]The locations of Kephar Ammoni and of Ophni are unknown.

[27]The location of Geba is disputed. Many students place it at Jeba', four miles east of el-Jib. Others place it at Khirbet et-Tell (not to be confused with the et-Tell of The *'Ai* discussion). Khirbet et-Tell is located some 12 miles northeast of el-Jib. The identity of Geba is fraught with difficulties as the site names of Gibeon, Gibeah, and more than one site called Geba (meaning simply "hill") are intertwined in the biblical text.

[28]For Gibeon, see Josh 9:3.

[29]The ancient name Ramah may be sensed in the modern village of er-Ram, located three miles east of el-Jib. Due to contemporary occupation, the site is unexcavated.

[30]For Beeroth, see Josh 10:17.

[31]Mizpah has long been associated with Tell en-Nasbe, located three miles northeast of el Jib.

[32]For Kephirah, see Josh 9:17.

[33]Mozah may be located at Khirbet Beit Mizzam, three and a half miles southwest of el-Jib.

[34]The identification of Rekem in this context is unknown. It should not be confused with the defeated chief by this same name (Josh 13:21).

[35]The identifications of Irpeel and of Taralah are unknown.

[36]The identification of Zelah (meaning "Rib" or "Plank") is unknown. It marks the final burial place of Saul and is possibly his hometown, cf. 2 Sam 21:14.

[37]The identification of Haeleph as an independent site is unknown. Against the opinion of the NIV text, הָאֶלֶף (hā'eleph) may modify Zelah (note the missing conjunction in the MT). However, this would throw off the count of fourteen settlements. A comparison between the MT and the LXX reveals several textual difficulties with this list.

[38]Jerusalem is also known as "the Jebusite city" after the clan of pre-Israelite residents of the site. At this time it was known as Jebus. It is possible that these residents were Hurrian, rather that Semites. Compare with 15:8.

[39]Gibeah is usually associated with Tell el-Ful, three miles southeast of el-Jib.

The land defined by these borders and settlements is not large, but it is strategic. Two factors account for this. First, the dominating Central Ridge dips in elevation at this point, and second, correspondingly, well-defined ascents emerge on both the east and west faces of the ridge. These dynamics render Benjamin a natural saddle, and, from a human perspective, an important crossroads. As such, it is a rare intersection for east-west travel in a land dominated by north-south trends. It also suggests that Benjamin will be vulnerable to outside forces and therefore must become a focus of internal fortifications. Some of this may already be sensed through a close reading of land and text. The setting for The 'Ay (Joshua 7–8) campaign is the eastern ascent to the Saddle of Benjamin between Jericho and Bethel. Similarly the battle of the Beth Horon Ridge (Joshua 10) is played out on the western descent from the Saddle of Benjamin between Gibeon and Gezer. Other biblical texts, recent history, and modern construction continue to underline this strategic recognition. Later in Israel's history, the Saddle of Benjamin will become the fortified crease separating the Divided Monarchy. Judah will be established south of this crease, while the Joseph tribes will be established north of this crease. Before it is over, tiny Benjamin will be claimed by both and lost in the fray.

---

[40]The Kiriath mentioned here may be a shortened form of Kiriath Jearim, a border site between Benjamin and Judah. See 9:17; 15:9,60; and 18:14.

JOSHUA 19

7. Simeon's Land (19:1-9)

[1]The second lot came out for the tribe of Simeon, clan by clan. Their inheritance lay within the territory of Judah. [2]It included: Beersheba (or Sheba),[a] Moladah, [3]Hazar Shual, Balah, Ezem, [4]Eltolad, Bethul, Hormah, [5]Ziklag, Beth Marcaboth, Hazar Susah, [6]Beth Lebaoth and Sharuhen—thirteen towns and their villages;

[7]Ain, Rimmon, Ether and Ashan—four towns and their villages— [8]and all the villages around these towns as far as Baalath Beer (Ramah in the Negev).

This was the inheritance of the tribe of the Simeonites, clan by clan. [9]The inheritance of the Simeonites was taken from the share of Judah, because Judah's portion was more than they needed. So the Simeonites received their inheritance within the territory of Judah.

[a]2 Or Beersheba, Sheba; 1 Chron. 4:28 does not have Sheba.

19:1, 9 The land allotted to Simeon is not defined as a single parcel, but as scattered settlements **within the territory of Judah**. This fulfills the prophetic utterance of Jacob who predicted in the case of both Simeon and Levi that, because of their killing spree at Shechem (Gen 34:25-31), they would be dispersed in Israel (Gen 49:7). It also finds explanation in the fact that Judah's portion was **more than they needed.**[1]

19:2-8 Settlements assigned to the clan of Simeon are presented in two sets or districts. In the first district are thirteen settlements:

---

[1]This frank admission comes courtesy of the comparative marker, מִן (min), in the translation of כִּי־הָיָה חֵלֶק בְּנֵי־יְהוּדָה רַב מֵהֶם (kî-hāyāh ḥēleq bᵊnê-yᵊhûdāh rab mēhem), "for the (land)-tract of Judah's descendants was too much (either in physical size or challenge) for them" (v. 9).

Beersheba,[2] **Moladah**,[3] **Hazar Shual**,[4] **Balah**,[5] **Ezem**, **Eltolad**,[6] **Bethul**,[7] **Hormah**, **Ziklag**,[8] **Beth Marcaboth**,[9] **Hazar Susah**,[10] **Beth Lebaoth**,[11] and **Sharuhen**.[12] Most of the identified sites in this district rest in the southern reaches of the land (the Negev) and correspond with settlements in Judah's first district. Comparison with the description of that allotment in Joshua 15:21-32 give assistance with site names and identifications.

In the second set are four sites: **Ain**, **Rimmon**,[13] **Ether**, and **Ashan**.[14]

This collection of 17 sites scattered throughout Judah (and in most cases, also assigned to Judah) raises questions of definition. How can tribal identity be maintained, organized, connected in such a setup? Most significantly, how can an "inheritance within an inheritance" be sustained over time? Simeon's subordination to Judah is clear as the campaign conquest continues (Judg 1:3,17) yet continues to find memory in the time of David's reign (1 Chr 4:24-43, but consider 4:27). Such notices are scant, however, and by the time of the exile, Simeon disappears altogether.

---

[2]Beersheba is also a settlement assigned to Judah; see Josh 15:28.

[3]Moladah is also a settlement assigned to Judah; see Josh 15:26.

[4]Hazar Shual is also a settlement assigned to Judah; see Josh 15:28.

[5]Balah appears as Baalah in Josh 15:29 and as Bilhah in 1 Chr 4:29.

[6]Ezem and Eltolad are also assigned to Judah; see Josh 15:29 and 30 respectively.

[7]Bethul is uniquely connected to Simeon; cf. 1 Chr 4:30. It may be associated with Khirbet el-Qarjeten.

[8]Hormah and Ziklag are also assigned to Judah; see Josh 15:30 and 31 respectively.

[9]Beth Marcaboth also appears in 1 Chr 4:31. It is unidentified on the ground.

[10]Hazar Susah may be the same settlement called Sansannah in Josh 15:31. In 1 Chr 4:31 it is remembered as Hazar Susim.

[11]Beth Lebaoth may be the same settlement as Laboth in Josh 15:32.

[12]Sharuhen is likely the same settlement as Shilhim in Josh 15:32. In 1 Chr 4:31 it appears as Shaaraim. Tell el Ajjul is the best candidate for Sharuhen, although Tell el Far'ah (south) is a possibility.

[13]Ain is also a settlement assigned to Judah. Here, the LXX views Ain and Rimmon as a single place, hence Erimmon (reflecting Ain Rimmon) and adds another site, Thalcha to achieve the necessary "four towns." See comments at Josh 15:32.

[14]Ether and Ashan are also assigned to Judah; see Josh 15:42.

8. Zebulun's Land (19:10-16)

[10]The third lot came up for Zebulun, clan by clan:
   The boundary of their inheritance went as far as Sarid.
[11]Going west it ran to Maralah, touched Dabbesheth, and
extended to the ravine near Jokneam. [12]It turned east from
Sarid toward the sunrise to the territory of Kisloth Tabor
and went on to Daberath and up to Japhia. [13]Then it continued eastward to Gath Hepher and Eth Kazin; it came out at
Rimmon and turned toward Neah. [14]There the boundary
went around on the north to Hannathon and ended at the
Valley of Iphtah El. [15]Included were Kattath, Nahalal,
Shimron, Idalah and Bethlehem. There were twelve towns
and their villages.
[16]These towns and their villages were the inheritance of Zebulun,
clan by clan.

19:10-16 The allotment for Zebulun is suggested by the sketch-
ing of three lines. The first line begins at **Sarid**[15] and proceeds west
following the Kishon brook past **Maralah**[16] and **Dabbesheth**,[17] before
ending near **Jokneam**.[18] The second line begins afresh at Sarid, but
this time stutters eastward, passing **Kisloth Tabor**,[19] **Daberath**,[20] but

---

[15]Sarid is identified with Tell Shadud on the basis of the LXX reading of
Sedoud. See Elitzur, *Ancient Place Names*, p. 110, n. 17. Tell Shadud is located four miles southwest from the center of Nazareth.

[16]It is possible that Tell Thorah represents biblical Maralah. Tell Thorah
rests in the Kishon drainage basin, eight miles west of the center of
Nazareth.

[17]Dabbesheth is associated with Tell esh-Shammam, located nine miles
west of the center of Nazareth, also on the banks of the Kishon.

[18]The border here reaches (lit. "touches") to the watercourse (נַחַל, *naḥal*)
that is in front of Jokneam (Tell Qeimun). This "watercourse" likely refers
either to the Kishon itself or to the Wadi Musrarah which empties into the
Kishon. Either way, this point is both convenient and recognizable; hills
close in on the Jezreel Valley from both sides constricting it to a tiny narrows before releasing it upon the coastal plain.

[19]In the site name, Kisloth Tabor (or the "flanks of Tabor"), the modifier
Tabor distinguishes this Kisloth from another, possibly Kesalon of Judah
(Josh 15:10). To link this site name with modern Iskal, see Elitzur, *Ancient
Place Names*, pp. 160-163. Iskal is located two miles southeast and below the
center of Nazareth.

backtracking to pick up **Japhia**.[21] The third and final line extends the second, looping back around toward **Gath Hepher**,[22] **Eth Kazin**,[23] **Rimmon**,[24] **Neah**,[25] and **Hannathon**,[26] and trailing off into the **Valley of Ipthtah El**.[27] While these lines are both segmented and convoluted, the resulting parcel emerges; it is well-defined on three sides, but is open to the west. Other features rescue the description, however, as the essence of Zebulun's land is the east-west ridge running between the Turan Valley and the Jezreel Valley. In modern times, the city of Nazareth crowns this ridge.[28] Here, along the elevated folds, soils and climate support the cultivation of vegetables, olives, and grapes. Cereals may be sown in the rich valleys on all sides. However, the value of the western descents (the Galilean *Shephelah* or Allonim hills) decreases for human occupation as a chalky crust (*nari*) encourages agriculturalists to work elsewhere. In antiquity, the oak forests of this wild side of Zebulun faced the Mediterranean Sea alone.[29]

---

[20]The site known as Daberath (Dabburiya) covers the western flank of Mt. Tabor, approximately four miles east of the center of Nazareth. For linguistic matters, see Elitzur, *Ancient Place Names*, pp. 222-231.

[21]Japhia is identified with Yafa and located a mile and one half west of the center of Nazareth. This identity, however, is awkward from the perspective of presentation. One would expect Yafa to be the most easterly of the three sites it is presented with; instead it is the most westerly.

[22]Gath Hepher (Khirbet ez-Zurraa) rests approximately three miles northeast of the center of Nazareth.

[23]The identity of Eth Kazin is unknown.

[24]Rimmon is identified with modern Rummana, resting at the mouth of the Tiran Valley. It lies six miles north of the center of Nazareth.

[25]The identity of Neah (as a settlement or landmark) is unknown.

[26]Biblical Hannathon corresponds to the ruins at Tell el-Badawiyah, six miles northwest of the center of Nazareth.

[27]The Valley of Ipthtah El runs between and therefore separates the Tiran and Nazareth ridges. It corresponds to the Arabic Wadi el-Malik.

[28]In this context it is difficult to pass by the prophetic word of Isaiah who speaks of a coming Messiah: "there will be no more gloom for those who were in distress. In the past he humbled the land of Zebulun and the land of Naphtali, but in the future he will honor Galilee of the Gentiles (9:1). And later in that same passage, "For to us a child is born, to us a son is given, and the government will be on his shoulders" (see 9:6ff.).

[29]Zebulun's territory is, therefore, by the seashore and will profit from it. This point is significant in light of the blessing of Gen 49:13 which states that "Zebulun will live by the seashore and become a haven for ships; his border will extend toward Sidon."

Settlements of mention in this parcel include **Kattath, Nahalal, Shimron,**[30] **Idalah,**[31] and **Bethlehem.**[32] The statement that **there were twelve towns** here must take into account settlements included in the boundary list (of which there are at least eleven) or unmentioned sites to augment the short catalogue of five.[34]

9. Issachar's Land (19:17-23)

[17]**The fourth lot came out for Issachar, clan by clan.** [18]**Their territory included:**

Jezreel, Kesulloth, Shunem, [19]**Hapharaim, Shion, Anaharath,** [20]**Rabbith, Kishion, Ebez,** [21]**Remeth, En Gannim, En Haddah and Beth Pazzez.** [22]**The boundary touched Tabor, Shahazumah and Beth Shemesh, and ended at the Jordan. There were sixteen towns and their villages.**
[23]**These towns and their villages were the inheritance of the tribe of Issachar, clan by clan.**

19:17-23 The allotment for Issachar is defined by a catalogue of sites and a single boundary line. The catalogue includes: **Jezreel,**[35] **Kesulloth,**[36] **Shunem,**[37] **Hapharaim,**[38] **Shion,**[39] **Anaharath,**[40] **Rabbith,**[41]

---

[30]The locations of Kattath and Nahalal are unknown.

[31]Shimron may be identified with Khirbet Sammuniya, located on the western edge of the Galilean Shephelah. It is about five miles from the center of Nazareth.

[32]The identity of Idalah is unknown.

[33]Bethlehem of Lower Galilee should not be confused with Bethlehem of Judah. This Bethlehem, fixed at the site of Beit Lahm, is located about seven miles northwest of the center of Nazareth.

[34]The LXX alleviates the difficulty by not mentioning this tally at all!

[35]Jezreel is identified with the ruins at Zirin (or Yizreel), located on the eastern end of the Jezreel Valley where the Harod begins to descend into the Lower Jordan Valley.

[36]For Kesulloth, see comments at 19:12.

[37]Shunem or Sulam is located three miles north of the site of Jezreel on the outskirts of modern Affula.

[38]Hapharaim may be located seven and a half miles northeast of the site of Jezreel at the site of et Taiyibe.

[39]The identity of Shion is unknown.

[40]Tell el Mukharkhash is a proposed location for biblical Anaharath. It rests ten and a half miles northeast of the site of Jezreel.

Kishion,[42] **Ebez**,[43] **Remeth**,[44] **En Gannim**,[45] **En Haddah**,[46] and **Beth Pazzez**.[47] This scatter of thirteen sites appears to fit inside a triangular area of land cornered by Mt. Tabor on the west, the southern end of the Sea of Galilee on the northeast, and the edge of the Beth Shan plain on the southeast. This area is an upland of open plateaus and windy ridges known as eastern Lower Galilee. A tortured past is visible at a glance, jagged basalt flows render this area difficult to farm; deficient rainfall only confirms it.

A single boundary line is offered: the northern line of the triangle. It touches three sites, **Tabor**,[48] **Shahazumah**,[49] and **Beth Shemesh**,[50] and ends at the Jordan River. Those grasping for some sense of closure may seize upon the larger context: Manasseh lies somehow to the west (Josh 17:10) and south, Zebulun lies northwest, Naphtali is north, and the Jordan River slips away on the east. A quest of a different order might wonder if this less-than-satisfactory description of a less-than-satisfactory land is not the result of a text gone bad, but is actually some kind of deliberate tactic. Could the narrative itself somehow be testimony to Israel's less-than-satisfactory future here?

---

[41]The identity of Rabbith is unknown. However, see Zertal, *Eastern Valleys*, pp. 105-106.

[42]Kishion may be found at el-Khirba, eight miles northeast of the site of Jezreel.

[43]The identity of Ebez is unknown.

[44]Remeth has been identified with the ruins at Kaukab el-Hawa, 12 miles east of the site of Jezreel.

[45]The site of Khirbet Beit Jann has been proposed for the location of En Gannim. Khirbet Beit Jann is located approximately 15 miles northeast of the site of Jezreel. However, for the possibility that the site may be located at Genin (Jenin) in the Samaritan hills, see Elitzur, *Ancient Place Names*, p. 287, n. 70, and pp. 377-378. It is curious that Joshua 17:11 identifies Ibleam (Tell Balama) — located just one mile south of modern Genin — as a site of Manasseh that is located "in Issachar."

[46]En Haddah is associated with the ruins at el Hadatha, a site approximately 13 miles northeast of the site of Jezreel.

[47]The identity of Beth Pazzez is unknown.

[48]It is assumed that Tabor in this context refers to Mt. Tabor (Jebel et Tur).

[49]The identity of biblical Shahazumah is unknown.

[50]This Beth Shemesh should not be confused with a site with the same name in the Judean Shephelah. This Galilean Beth Shemesh may be found at Khirbet Sheik esh-Shamsawi, 15 miles northeast of the site of Jezreel.

10. Asher's Land (19:24-31)

²⁴The fifth lot came out for the tribe of Asher, clan by clan. ²⁵Their
territory included:

Helkath, Hali, Beten, Acshaph, ²⁶Allammelech, Amad
and Mishal. On the west the boundary touched Carmel and
Shihor Libnath. ²⁷It then turned east toward Beth Dagon,
touched Zebulun and the Valley of Iphtah El, and went
north to Beth Emek and Neiel, passing Cabul on the left. ²⁸It
went to Abdon,^a Rehob, Hammon and Kanah, as far as
Greater Sidon. ²⁹The boundary then turned back toward
Ramah and went to the fortified city of Tyre, turned toward
Hosah and came out at the sea in the region of Aczib,
³⁰Ummah, Aphek and Rehob. There were twenty-two towns
and their villages.

³¹These towns and their villages were the inheritance of the tribe
of Asher, clan by clan.

^a*28* Some Hebrew manuscripts (see also Joshua 21:30 most Hebrew man-
uscripts *Ebron*

19:24-31 The allotment for Asher appears as a brief catalogue of
seven sites followed by a border description. The seven sites are
Helkath,[51] **Hali**,[52] **Beten**,[53] **Acshaph**,[54] **Allammelech, Amad**,[55] **Mishal**.[56]
No governing order is evident.

The border description of Asher is much more complete than the
three previous tribal allotments. Beginning with the headland of
Carmel[57] on the Mediterranean Sea, it encloses a coastal district that

---

[51]Helkath is commonly associated with Tell el-Qassis (Qashish), a site
strategically situated in the narrow passage between the coastal plain and
the Valley of Jezreel. It is less than two miles north of Jokneam.

[52]Khirbet Ras Ali may be biblical Hali. This site is in the midst of the
Galilean "Lowlands," 11 miles southeast of Acco.

[53]If Beten is located at Khirbet Ibtin, it is approximately 11 miles south of
Acco.

[54]Khirbet el-Harbaj has been tentatively connected with Acshaph. It lies in
the drainage basin of the Kishon, 11½ miles due south of Acco.

[55]The sites of Allammelech and Amad are unidentified.

[56]Mishal may rest at the sizeable tell known as Keisan. It rests about five
miles southeast of Acco.

[57]Mt. Carmel is the most easily recognized feature of the *Heartland* map.
The ridge of Carmel reaches westward into the Mediterranean Sea and
appears as a "bump" in an otherwise straight coastline.

331

reaches as far north as **Greater Sidon**.[58] Sites or features that appear to be on the southernmost end of the circuit include **Shihor Libnath**[59] and **Beth Dagon**.[60] Sites that appear on the eastern side of the circuit, and thus on the flanks of Zebulun's land, include **Beth Emek**,[61] **Neiel**,[62] **Cabul**,[63] **Abdon**,[64] and possibly an unidentified **Rehob**. Sites that appear on the northernmost end of the circuit with Sidon include **Hammon**,[65] **Kanah**,[66] **Ramah**,[67] **Tyre**,[68] and **Hosah**.[69] Sites that edge the sea on the west and close the circuit include **Aczib**,[70] **Ummah**,[71] **Aphek**,[72] and

---

[58]There is little question that the site of Saida in Lebanon is biblical Sidon. Inquiry here must shift to the meaning of the modifier. Is צִידוֹן רַבָּה (ṣîdôn rabbāh) to be rendered as "Big Sidon" (contrasting a small one) or "Sidon the Great," or possibly some reference to the fact that Asher's land extended to the edge of the territory controlled by Sidon? This is the inference made by the NIV, namely "Greater Sidon."

[59]Shihor Libnath may mean the "swamp of Libnath." It has been identified with the marshy area at the mouth of the Kishon and may possibly indicate the harbor of the ancient site at Tell Abu Hawam (Aharoni, *Land of the Bible*, p. 258.

[60]The location of Beth Dagon is unknown.

[61]Beth Emek may be located at Tell Mimas, approximately five miles northeast of Acco.

[62]Khirbet Yanin has been identified as biblical Neiel. It is about eight miles east of Acco.

[63]Cabul or Kabul is located two miles south of Khirbet Yanin.

[64]Abdon or Ebron has been associated with Khirbet Abdah. The site rests approximately ten miles northeast of Acco.

[65]Hammon may be located at Umm el-Awamid. It rests directly on the coastline, just beyond Ras an-Naqura, some 15 miles north of Acco.

[66]Kanah or Qana is located in the hills above Tyre, approximately 23 miles northeast of Acco.

[67]The location of a Ramah in this region is not known.

[68]Tyre, or es-Sur, faces the Mediterranean Sea approximately 25 miles north of Acco.

[69]Hosah may be identified with Tell Rashidiya, immediately south of Tyre.

[70]Aczib is identified with ez-Zib, nine miles north of Acco. See Elitzur, *Ancient Place Names*, pp. 167-170.

[71]Acco, historically one of the most significant cities of the region is notably missing from this list in the MT. However, in the LXX, it is substituted for Ummah at this point. The mound of ancient Acco is known as Tell el-Fukhkhar and is located about one mile east of the much later port at Ptolemais or Acre.

[72]The ruins of Aphek, or Tell Kurdana, are located about five and a half miles southeast of Acco. It should not be confused with a southern Aphek, identified at Ras el-'Ain near Tel Aviv.

Rehob.[73] Thus, twenty-two settlements are offered on behalf of Asher; connecting this tally to those explicitly named is impossible.

Asher's land, then, is a littoral, or coastal plain, characterized by a narrow strip of alluvial soils bordered by highlands to the east and the sea to the west. Ridges of petrified sand dunes (locally known as *kurkar*) often hinder runoff from reaching the sea, regularly creating brackish marshes. If these are managed, the agricultural potential here is enormous. Illustration comes by way of a promise: "Asher's fare will be robust, it shall yield dainties fit for a king" (Gen 49:20).

11. Naphtali's Land (19:32-39)

[32]**The sixth lot came out for Naphtali, clan by clan:**
    [33]**Their boundary went from Heleph and the large tree in Zaanannim, passing Adami Nekeb and Jabneel to Lakkum and ending at the Jordan. **[34]**The boundary ran west through Aznoth Tabor and came out at Hukkok. It touched Zebulun on the south, Asher on the west and the Jordan**[a] **on the east. **[35]**The fortified cities were Ziddim, Zer, Hammath, Rakkath, Kinnereth, **[36]**Adamah, Ramah, Hazor, **[37]**Kedesh, Edrei, En Hazor, **[38]**Iron, Migdal El, Horem, Beth Anath and Beth Shemesh. There were nineteen towns and their villages.**
[39]**These towns and their villages were the inheritance of the tribe of Naphtali, clan by clan.**

[a]*34* **Septuagint; Hebrew** *west, and Judah, the Jordan,*

19:32-39 The allotment for Naphtali is indicated by two lines. The first begins at **Heleph**,[74] possibly at the oak of **Zaanannim**.[75] From

---

[73]This Rehob of Asher is possibly located at Tell Bir el-Gharbi, approximately five miles east of Acco.

[74]Biblical Heleph may be located at Khirbet Irbada, six miles southwest of the Horns of Hattin.

[75]The syntax of the NIV suggests that the oak tree in Zaanannim may be within Heleph. It reads the second min clause as an adjectival modifier. It may also be read in a more ablative sense, i.e., "the border (ran) from Heleph to the tree in Zaannanim, and (from there to). . . " See Waltke and O'Connor, *Biblical Hebrew Syntax*, sec. 11.2.11. Regardless, the more precise meaning or location of this tree is unknown, although the fact that it is remembered here and later (Judg 4:11) suggests it is a landmark of signifi-

there it passes three sites, **Adami Nekeb,**[76] **Jabneel,**[77] and **Lakkum,**[78] apparently following the natural fall of the Wadi Fajjas (Nahal Yavne'el) into the Jordan River. A second line begins near the starting point of the first, at **Aznoth Tabor,**[79] and runs a few miles north to **Hukkok.**[80] The remainder of the allotment must be inferred from the relationship of Naphtali's land to its neighbors. This is suggested with Zebulun on the south side, Asher on the west side, and the Jordan on the east side.[81]

Specific sites connected to this inheritance appear to be concentrated on the western side of the Sea of Galilee. These include **Ziddim, Zer,**[82] **Hammath,**[83] **Rakkath,**[84] **Kinnereth,**[85] **Adamah,**[86] and **Ramah.**[87] Other sites are either unknown or are located still further north. These include **Hazor**[88] **Kadesh,**[89] **Edrei, En Haron,**[90] **Iron,**[91] **Migdal El,**

---

cance. Perhaps the tree was a sizable specimen or, more darkly, a "sacred tree." The location of Zaanannim is unknown.

[76]Adami Nekeb is identified with Khirbet et-Tell, a site in the upper fingers of the Wadi Fajjas, three and one half miles south of the Horns of Hattin.

[77]Tell en-Naam has been proposed as the site of Jabneel. The ruins are located four miles downslope from Khirbet et Tell (Adami Nekeb) in the Wadi Fajjas.

[78]Khirbet el-Mansurah is one proposal for biblical Lakkum. The site is found at the opening of the Wadi Fajjas into the Lower Jordan Valley.

[79]Aznoth Tabor or the "ears of Tabor" is identified with Khirbet Umm Jubeil, three miles north of Mt. Tabor.

[80]Hukkok may be found at Huqoq or Jaquq, six miles north of the Horns of Hattin.

[81]Invisible in the NIV (and in the LXX) is the difficult MT clause that reads וּבִיהוּדָה הַיַּרְדֵּן מִזְרַח הַשָּׁמֶשׁ (ûbîhûdāh hayyardēn mizraḥ haššāmēš), or "and Judah of the Jordan (on the side of) the sunrise." This surprising mention of Judah so far north, has prompted numerous interpretations. For a discussion of these, see Woudstra, *Joshua,* pp. 291-292.

[82]The sites of Ziddim and Zer are unidentified.

[83]The ruins of Hammath are associated with Hammam Tabariya, immediately south of modern Tiberias on the Sea of Galilee.

[84]Within modern Tiberias is the ruin of Khirbet el-Quneitira, a candidate for biblical Rakkath.

[85]Kinnereth may be identified with Khirbet el-Ureima (Tel Kinrot) on the northwest shore of the Sea of Galilee.

[86]Two possibilities for Adamah may be considered. The first is at Qarn Hattin or the Horns of Hattin. The second is three miles further south at Khirbet ed-Damiya.

[87]Ramah may be found at Khirbet Zaitun er-Rama, nine and a half miles northwest of the Horns of Hattin.

[88]For Hazor, see the discussion at 11:1. As an aside, Aharoni, *Land of the*

Horem,[92] **Beth Anath,**[93] and **Beth Shemesh.**[94] Here, as elsewhere, the total site count is independent of the sites named.

The land allotted to the tribe of Naphtali is marked by contrasts. From the cool highlands of Upper Galilee to the tropical shores of the Sea of Galilee elevations jump, temperatures swing, and soils differ. Such diversity creates remarkable pockets of plant and animal life, and correspondingly, offers remarkable opportunities for human subsistence. Rugged terrain also renders Galilee aloof and defensible, a constraint not lost on future generations of settlers, bandits, and rebels.

12. Dan's Land (19:40-48)

[40]**The seventh lot came out for the tribe of Dan, clan by clan.** [41]**The territory of their inheritance included:**

Zorah, Eshtaol, Ir Shemesh, [42]**Shaalabbin, Aijalon, Ithlah,** [43]**Elon, Timnah, Ekron,** [44]**Eltekeh, Gibbethon, Baalath,** [45]**Jehud, Bene Berak, Gath Rimmon,** [46]**Me Jarkon and Rakkon, with the area facing Joppa.**

Bible, p. 88, uses this mention of Hazor in Naphtali's land list as demonstration that this text is no earlier than the Solomonic period. He argues that Hazor was not rebuilt until the Solomonic period according to texts (1 Kgs 9:15) and archaeological finds. One wonders, however, why a site must be occupied to be used in this present context? Particularly in the case of Hazor, the largest and possibly best known tell in the land, it would function as a secure landmark whether it was occupied or not.

[89]Kadesh of Naphtali is often associated with Tell Kidish, high on the west rim above the Huleh Basin. Another candidate for consideration, however, is Khirbet el Kidish, located above the southern end of the Sea of Galilee, seven miles southeast of the Horns of Hattin. See Aharoni, *Land of the Bible,* p. 224.

[90]The locations of Edrei and En Haron are unknown

[91]Iron or Yiron (Yarun) is located 20 miles north of the Horns of Hittin.

[92]The locations of Migdal El and Horem are unknown.

[93]Beth Anath is possibly located at Safed el Battikh, some 28 miles north of the Horns of Hattin in the folds of Upper Galilee.

[94]Assuming a general trend of describing sites from south to north, Beth Shemesh may likely be located in Upper Galilee. The proposal that places it at Tell er-Ruweisi (five miles northwest of the Horns of Hattin) is preferred to a view that places it at Khirbet Sheik esh-Shamsawi (approximately eight miles southeast of the Horns of Hattin). See Aharoni, *Land of the Bible,* pp. 235-236.

⁴⁷**(But the Danites had difficulty taking possession of their territory, so they went up and attacked Leshem, took it, put it to the sword and occupied it. They settled in Leshem and named it Dan after their forefather.)**
⁴⁸**These towns and their villages were the inheritance of the tribe of Dan, clan by clan.**

19:40-48 The final allotment goes to the tribe of Dan.⁹⁵ No attempt is made to trace any kind of boundary line here, a notion smoothed by the NIV translation of גְּבוּל (g°bûl) as "territory." Instead, a scatter of site names is cast. Included in the scatter are **Zorah, Eshtaol,**⁹⁶ **Ir Shemesh,**⁹⁷ **Shaalabbin,**⁹⁸ **Aijalon,**⁹⁹ **Ithlah, Elon,**¹⁰⁰ **Timnah,**¹⁰¹ **Ekron,**¹⁰² **Eltekeh,**¹⁰³ **Gibbethon,**¹⁰⁴ **Baalath,**¹⁰⁵ **Jehud,**¹⁰⁶ **Bene Berak,**¹⁰⁷ **Gath Rimmon,**¹⁰⁸ **Me Jarkon,**¹⁰⁹ and **Rakkon.**¹¹⁰ As a group,

---

⁹⁵On this, see Aaron Demsky, "The Boundary of the Tribe of Dan (Joshua 19:41-46)," in *Sefer Moshe: The Moshe Weinfeld Jubilee Volume: Studies in the Bible and the Ancient Near East, Qumran, and Post-Biblical Judaism,* ed. by Chaim Cohen, Avi Hurvitz, and Shalom M. Paul (Winona Lake, IN: Eisenbrauns, 2004), pp. 261-284.

⁹⁶Zorah and Eshtaol are also included in Judah's allotment; see 15:33.

⁹⁷Ir Shemesh ("city of Shemesh") may refer to the place known elsewhere as Beth Shemesh ("House of Shemesh"). See 15:10.

⁹⁸Shaalabbin or Shaalabim (cf. Judg 1:35) may be modern Selbit, located four miles east of Gezer in the Aijalon system.

⁹⁹For Aijalon, see Josh 10:12.

¹⁰⁰Ithlah and Elon are unknown.

¹⁰¹For Timnah, see Josh 15:10.

¹⁰²The border site of Ekron is assigned to Judah as well as Dan. See notes at 13:3; 15:11,45-46.

¹⁰³The location of Eltekeh is uncertain. One possibility is Tell esh-Shallaf located in the lower Sorek Valley, about nine miles west of Gezer (Aharoni, *Land of the Bible,* pp. 49, 434).

¹⁰⁴Gibbethon is identified with Tell el-Malat, three miles west of Gezer (Aharoni, *Land of the Bible,* p. 435).

¹⁰⁵Baalath may be another name for the unknown site of Baalah. See 15:10.

¹⁰⁶Jehud or el-Yahudiya is located about 12 miles northwest of Gezer.

¹⁰⁷The settlement of Bene Berak may be located at Kheiriyah, a site located in what was once the lower marsh of the Aijalon Valley. Kheiriyah is about 13½ miles northwest of Gezer.

¹⁰⁸Tell Jarisha may be biblical Gath Rimmon. Tell Jarisha is located four miles northwest of Kheiriyah along the banks of the Yarkon.

¹⁰⁹Me Jarkon or the "waters of the Yarkon" refers to the river that runs through the coastal area of modern Tel Aviv.   *110 across page*

these sites suggest a territory that is focused on the coastal plain between the Yarkon and Sorek drainage systems. Much of this space is occupied by the sprawl of greater Tel Aviv today.

Following this discourse the narrator states that the border (or territory) allotted to the tribe of Dan "fled from them," or more figuratively, "escaped them." Irony may be recognized here on two counts. First, the statement is ironic due to placement: as soon as the last word of the allotment to Dan drops, notice of failure begins (was the effort of giving this description an exercise in vanity?). Second, irony grows from the narrator's choice of words. Time and time again, borders have been described as writhing or living things; they "go out" and "twist" from this place to that. Here again, the border "goes out," only this time instead of leaving a particular landmark, it wiggles away from the hands of a people. Like the elusive snake in the flowerbed, it flees and defies capture.

For this reason, the Danites abandon the land given to them by lot (and hence, by Yahweh, as presented) in order to seek an inheritance of their own choosing. Such is found at the site of **Leshem**.[111] In a rush of initiative that imitates the vocabulary of the conquest program, the descendants of Dan fight, seize, kill, possess, squat upon, and rename this place. Through this series of word choices, the narrator forces the reader to confront the wrongheadedness of both impulse and target. The resulting conclusion is bitter: an illegitimate "conquest" has been substituted for the real thing (cf. Judg 18:1-31)! Obedience has been obscured by pragmatism and Dan's land has dwindled down to Dan's town. The contrast between the vignette of Caleb and the men of Judah (14:6-15) as a lead-in to the first tribal allotment and this vignette of the men of Dan, offered at the conclusion of the final tribal allotment, cannot be more strategically placed or boldly drawn. Something is terribly wrong and the careful reader knows it.

---

[110]The text reads, הָרַקּוֹן (hāraqqôn), "the Raqqon," and, if derived from the Hebrew root rqq, may mean something like "the straight" or "the narrows." Like the entry that precedes it, Me Jarkon, it may refer to a geographical landmark rather than a settlement. "The Raqqon" is further described as "the area facing (but not including?) Joppa." Joppa is most definitely a site of human occupation along the Mediterranean Sea.

[111]The site of Leshem is elsewhere called Laish (Judg 18:7,29). Today, it is known as Tell el-Qadi. For a discussion of the site name and mentions, see Elitzur, *Ancient Place Names*, pp. 201-209.

13. Concluding Comments (19:49-51)

⁴⁹When they had finished dividing the land into its allotted portions, the Israelites gave Joshua son of Nun an inheritance among them, ⁵⁰as the LORD had commanded. They gave him the town he asked for—Timnath Serah[a] in the hill country of Ephraim. And he built up the town and settled there.

⁵¹These are the territories that Eleazar the priest, Joshua son of Nun and the heads of the tribal clans of Israel assigned by lot at Shiloh in the presence of the LORD at the entrance to the Tent of Meeting. And so they finished dividing the land.

ᵃ*50* Also known as *Timnath Heres* (see Judges 2:9)

19:49-51 While special grants must still be prescribed (chapters 20–21), the comments offered here begin to close the presentation of the division of Cisjordan opened in 14:1. Reminders of how these divisions were achieved as well as the role of Yahweh, Joshua, and Israel's leaders are given. More narrowly, the comments also close the section opened in 18:1. Mention of Shiloh, the Tent of Meeting, and the completion of that which was incomplete, signal a conclusion.

Beyond these structural requirements, the section also notes a special allotment for Joshua. This honors the request of Joshua and the commandment of Yahweh. Joshua receives a settlement of his own, Timnath Serah,[112] located within Ephraim, the land of Joshua's kinsman. Notice that he "built" and "settled" the site suggests his personal obedience to the conquest mandate, a faithfulness demonstrated many years before as a scout in Canaan (Numbers 13–14).

---

[112]Timnath Serah or Temnath Heres is often identified with Khirbet Tibneh, located some 11 miles west of Shiloh. It will be the place of Joshua's burial (24:30; Judg 2:9). See Finkelstein, *The Archaeology of the Israelite Settlement*, p. 121.

JOSHUA 20

D. SPECIAL GRANTS PRESCRIBED (20:1–21:45)

According to *torah*, special space in the land must be granted to two groups: fugitives seeking justice and members of the tribe of Levi. Issues raised by the recognition and maintenance of these two groups differ in many ways, yet are united in the need for dedicated land parcels. Without them, the viability of the justice system, the present and future practice of Yahweh worship, the sustaining of social order — in short, the full application of *torah* — will not be possible. Accordingly, the allotment of special lands follows the allotment of tribal lands. As an essential background to this section, the text of Numbers 35:1-34 is remembered, as is the role of Joshua, who continues to interpret and apply *torah*. He faithfully facilitates the granting of special space for fugitives (20:1-9) and to Levites (21:1-45).

1. Space for Fugitives (20:1-9)

¹Then the LORD said to Joshua: ²"Tell the Israelites to designate the cities of refuge, as I instructed you through Moses, ³so that anyone who kills a person accidentally and unintentionally may flee there and find protection from the avenger of blood.

⁴"When he flees to one of these cities, he is to stand in the entrance of the city gate and state his case before the elders of that city. Then they are to admit him into their city and give him a place to live with them. ⁵If the avenger of blood pursues him, they must not surrender the one accused, because he killed his neighbor unintentionally and without malice aforethought. ⁶He is to stay in that city until he has stood trial before the assembly and until the death of the high priest who is serving at that time. Then he may go back to his own home in the town from which he fled."

⁷So they set apart Kedesh in Galilee in the hill country of Naphtali, Shechem in the hill country of Ephraim, and Kiriath Arba (that is, Hebron) in the hill country of Judah. ⁸On the east side of the Jordan of Jericho[a] they designated Bezer in the desert on the plateau in the tribe of Reuben, Ramoth in Gilead in the tribe of Gad, and Golan in Bashan in the tribe of Manasseh. ⁹Any of the Israelites or any alien living among them who killed someone accidentally could flee to these designated cities and not be killed by the avenger of blood prior to standing trial before the assembly.

[a]*8 Jordan of Jericho* **was possibly an ancient name for the Jordan River.**

20:1-3 Yahweh instructs Joshua to activate **the cities of refuge.**[1] Prescribed more fully in *torah* (Num 35:9-34; Deut 4:41-43; 19:1-13) as a response to rough justice, this system guards the sanctity of human life in a world where accidents happen, where fault is difficult to determine, or where fault takes time to determine. The principle of *lex talionis* demands "a life for a life," "an eye for an eye," "a tooth for a tooth" (Exod 21:23-24; Lev 24:20; Deut 19:21; Matt 5:38). In such an environment, one who takes a life forfeits his own and is immediately marginalized as רֹצֵחַ (*rōṣēaḥ*[2]) and fugitive (cf. Gen 4:14). Here, temporary allowance is made on behalf of a *rōṣēaḥ* whose actions are dubbed accidental or unintentional (e.g., a man is chopping wood when the head of his ax flies off the handle, strikes another man, and kills him). For such a killer, a city of refuge offers a temporary reprieve, a place of safety from those who may attempt immediate retribution, and the opportunity for due process.

One who would kill a killer to satisfy the blood vengeance principle is termed an **avenger of blood**, literally, a גֹּאֵל הַדָּם (*gō'ēl had-dām*). Elsewhere, the *gō'ēl* or "kinsman-redeemer" is described in less violent terms of inheritance and property (see Gen 38:8; Deut 25:5-10; and Ruth 3:9-12). The redeeming action of the *gō'ēl* in this con-

---

[1]The essence of "refuge" is drawn from the verbal root meaning "to take in" or "to accept." For more, see *TWOT*, s.v. קלט.

[2]The term *rōṣēaḥ*, "killer," arises from a family of words attached to the root *rṣḥ*. This base sense of the word may be applied in cases of premeditated murder (Exod 20:13), political assassination (2 Kgs 6:32), execution (Num 35:27), as well as accidental manslaughter (Josh 20:3). It is typically used of man-on-man killing; however, see Prov 22:13.

text is to take a life in exchange for a life taken. This act is not viewed as criminal, but rather as a way of avoiding the bloodguilt that defiles or "pollutes" the land (Deut 19:10; Num 35:33). Therefore, the avenger must be understood within a larger social context of creating purity for all rather than in the context of personally "getting even" (for another example, see the story told to David in 2 Sam 14:4-11).

20:4-6 To illustrate the "city of refuge" concept, a hypothetical *rōṣēaḥ* is pictured fleeing to the designated place. There, he states his case before the elders in the city gate and is granted the privilege of entering the community, presumably on the strength of his claim. Once admitted, the *rōṣēaḥ* receives a place to stay and is protected from would-be avengers. However, in order for his safety to be ensured, he must remain within the city walls until one of two things happens: either he is cleared of the charge of willful murder **before the assembly**, or, the person serving in the office of **high priest** dies. The former demonstrates that the "city of refuge" concept is a temporary measure at best, designed to ensure the survival of the accused until a fair hearing may be held. The latter suggests that even in the case of an unintentional killing, a life-for-life exchange is still at work. The death of the high priest is regarded vicariously, a curious antecedent of the work of "our merciful and faithful high priest" (Heb 2:17).[3] Thus, those who wait for their own redemption remain under a kind of "house arrest." Fault notwithstanding, a life that is sacred has been lost; there are always consequences. For this reason, the "city of refuge" is a type of both sanctuary and prison.

20:7-9 A total of six locations are set apart as "cities of refuge." Three are located in Cisjordan and are described from north to south: **Kadesh**,[4] **Shechem**,[5] and **Kiriath Arba**.[6] Three are located in

---

[3]Nuances of this idea are presented by several Christian interpreters including Davis (*No Falling Words*, p. 152), Woudstra (*Joshua*, pp. 300-301), and Wenham (*Numbers: An Introduction and Commentary*, TOTC [Downers Grove, IL: InterVarsity, 1981], p. 238).

[4]Kadesh is first mentioned in 12:22 as part of the conquest inventory. It may be the same site as Kadesh of Naphtali (Tell Qudeish), given a tribal association in 19:37. Finally, Kadesh of Naphtali is designated as a city of refuge (20:7) and a Levitical city (21:32). It rests on the northern edge of Cisjordan, overlooking the Hulah Basin.

[5]For Shechem, see comments at 8:30-31. Shechem rests in the center of Cisjordan, some 80 miles south of Kadesh of Naphtali (Tell Qudeish).

Transjordan and are described from south to north: **Bezer**,[7] **Ramoth Gilead**,[8] and **Golan**.[9] All six settlements will be assigned to the Levites, hinting at their role in the process. All six settlements are evenly distributed throughout the land and thereby reduce the challenge of distance for the refugee fleeing for his life. Finally, all six settlements are open to those to come from within or without the ranks of Israel. This last point may be contemplated in light of *ḥāram* warfare previously described in chapters 1–12. The ethics in play for subduing the land and the ethics in play for managing it are not to be confused.

---

[6]Kiriath Arba is also known as Hebron. See comments at 10:3; 14:13-15; and 15:54. It is a city of refuge (20:7) and a Levitical city (21:11). It rests on the southern edge of Cisjordan, approximately 63 miles south of Shechem.

[7]Good guesses for Bezer place it either at Umm al-'Amad, eight miles northeast of Madaba or at Tell Jalul, two miles east of Madaba. See MacDonald (*"East of the Jordan,"* pp. 177-178).

[8]Ramoth Gilead may be located at either Tell ar-Rumeith or at Ar-Ramtha. Both of these sites are located in the middle of the Transjordan region near the modern border between Jordan and Syria. For a discussion of location, see ibid., pp. 201-202.

[9]Golan is tentatively located at Saham al-Jaulan in modern Syria. See ibid., p. 155.

JOSHUA 21

2. Space for Levites (21:1-42)

[1]Now the family heads of the Levites approached Eleazar the priest, Joshua son of Nun, and the heads of the other tribal families of Israel [2]at Shiloh in Canaan and said to them, "The LORD commanded through Moses that you give us towns to live in, with pasturelands for our livestock." [3]So, as the LORD had commanded, the Israelites gave the Levites the following towns and pasturelands out of their own inheritance:

[4]The first lot came out for the Kohathites, clan by clan. The Levites who were descendants of Aaron the priest were allotted thirteen towns from the tribes of Judah, Simeon and Benjamin. [5]The rest of Kohath's descendants were allotted ten towns from the clans of the tribes of Ephraim, Dan and half of Manasseh.

[6]The descendants of Gershon were allotted thirteen towns from the clans of the tribes of Issachar, Asher, Naphtali and the half-tribe of Manasseh in Bashan.

[7]The descendants of Merari, clan by clan, received twelve towns from the tribes of Reuben, Gad and Zebulun.

[8]So the Israelites allotted to the Levites these towns and their pasturelands, as the LORD had commanded through Moses.

[9]From the tribes of Judah and Simeon they allotted the following towns by name [10](these towns were assigned to the descendants of Aaron who were from the Kohathite clans of the Levites, because the first lot fell to them):

[11]They gave them Kiriath Arba (that is, Hebron), with its surrounding pastureland, in the hill country of Judah. (Arba was the forefather of Anak.) [12]But the fields and villages around the city they had given to Caleb son of Jephunneh as his possession.

[13]So to the descendants of Aaron the priest they gave Hebron (a city of refuge for one accused of murder), Libnah, [14]Jattir, Eshtemoa, [15]Holon, Debir, [16]Ain, Juttah and Beth Shemesh, together with their pasturelands—nine towns from these two tribes.

[17]And from the tribe of Benjamin they gave them Gibeon, Geba, [18]Anathoth and Almon, together with their pasturelands—four towns.

[19]All the towns for the priests, the descendants of Aaron, were thirteen, together with their pasturelands.

[20]The rest of the Kohathite clans of the Levites were allotted towns from the tribe of Ephraim:

[21]In the hill country of Ephraim they were given Shechem (a city of refuge for one accused of murder) and Gezer, [22]Kibzaim and Beth Horon, together with their pasturelands—four towns.

[23]Also from the tribe of Dan they received Eltekeh, Gibbethon, [24]Aijalon and Gath Rimmon, together with their pasturelands—four towns.

[25]From half the tribe of Manasseh they received Taanach and Gath Rimmon, together with their pasturelands—two towns.

[26]All these ten towns and their pasturelands were given to the rest of the Kohathite clans.

[27]The Levite clans of the Gershonites were given:

from the half-tribe of Manasseh,

Golan in Bashan (a city of refuge for one accused of murder) and Be Eshtarah, together with their pasturelands—two towns;

[28]from the tribe of Issachar,

Kishion, Daberath, [29]Jarmuth and En Gannim, together with their pasturelands—four towns;

[30]from the tribe of Asher,

Mishal, Abdon, [31]Helkath and Rehob, together with their pasturelands—four towns;

[32]from the tribe of Naphtali,

Kedesh in Galilee (a city of refuge for one accused of murder), Hammoth Dor and Kartan, together with their pasturelands—three towns.

³³**All the towns of the Gershonite clans were thirteen, together with their pasturelands.**

³⁴**The Merarite clans (the rest of the Levites) were given:**
   from the tribe of Zebulun,
      Jokneam, Kartah, ³⁵Dimnah and Nahalal, together with their pasturelands—four towns;
³⁶**from the tribe of Reuben,**
      Bezer, Jahaz, ³⁷Kedemoth and Mephaath, together with their pasturelands—four towns;
³⁸**from the tribe of Gad,**
      Ramoth in Gilead (a city of refuge for one accused of murder), Mahanaim, ³⁹Heshbon and Jazer, together with their pasturelands—four towns in all.
⁴⁰**All the towns allotted to the Merarite clans, who were the rest of the Levites, were twelve.**

⁴¹**The towns of the Levites in the territory held by the Israelites were forty-eight in all, together with their pasturelands. ⁴²Each of these towns had pasturelands surrounding it; this was true for all these towns.**

21:1-3 As an introduction to the section, the leaders of the tribe of Levi request their land inheritance as promised by Moses (cf. Num 35:1-8). This request takes place at Shiloh and is directed to Joshua, Eleazar, and the heads of the tribes of Israel. Such mentions fix the passage within the context of inheritance administration (14:1; 17:4; and 19:51), stories of request initiatives (like that of Caleb or Zelophehad's daughters), and the larger theme of *torah* fulfillment.

The Levite request has two objects: settlements (עָרִים, *'ārîm*) for people and pastures (מִגְרָשׁוֹת, *migrōšôth*) for animals. Both terms describe space that is needed for life; both terms sound as motifs in what follows, e.g., "ten towns," "two towns," or "and their pasturelands." At a glance, this Levite request may appear to fly in the face of other statements that suggest that this tribe will not have a land inheritance (e.g., 13:14). However, a more holistic view clarifies the conclusion that land inheritance is not so much a hitch as it is a key difference between Levi and the other tribes (see Num 18:20-24 or Deut 18:1-8). Hence, no real tension exists. The place of the Levites in the land will be unique. It will not be limited to a single patch, field, or region, but rather, will be a scatter, akin to Simeon's land, drawn in bits and pieces from here and there. But unlike even Simeon's land — located within the inheritance of Judah alone — the real estate of Levi will be drawn from the whole of the land. In this, the narrator clearly eyes the dispersion predicted by blind old Jacob (Gen 49:5-7) as well as the larger view that the Levites are sojourners to be supported by all the tribes.[1] Yahweh has distributed land to Israel; Israel must exercise a similar generosity and assist those who are completely dedicated to Yahweh's service. Expositors may find antecedent here for a view of ministerial support voiced in 1 Corinthians 9. Beyond this introduction, the structure of the presentation moves from an overview (vv. 4-8), to a catalog of settlements (vv. 9-42),[2] to statements of conclusion (vv. 43-45).[3]

21:4-8 The Levites are identified by clans corresponding to the three sons of Levi: Kohath, Gershon, and Merari. As in the case of other land distributions, lots "come out," imbuing the process with divine sanction (see Supplemental Study on Lot Casting in ch. 16, p. 298). While this process itself is not detailed, it is possible that clusters of settlements were agreed to by the tribal leaders (or "given," as in v. 3) and the practice of lot casting was used to connect them to the Levite clans. Clan names direct the presentation: Kohathites, Gershonites, and Merarites. A "priest-first" ideal, rather than a birth order pattern is followed (Gershon, not Kohath is first-born. See Gen 46:11; Exod 6:16).

---

[1]Deut 18:6 describes the Levite life as that of a גֵּר (gār) or "sojourner." Sojourners move lightly and regularly over the ground.

Since these Levitical cities are also mentioned as allotments to other tribal groups, it may be concluded that they are not exclusively Levite, but are settlements to be shared by members of the local tribe and by the Levites who live among them. Specific ordinances govern the management of Levitical property (Lev 25:32-34).

[2]It may be noted that most sites in this catalog have previously been mentioned within the text. Many appear within the tribal inventories of chapters 15–19. All the cities of refuge (ch. 20) are also among the Levitical allotment. For this reason, most references within this section will simply direct the reader elsewhere in the commentary.

[3]This presentation may be compared with 1 Chr 6:54-81. To comment on the differences between these two lists, however, goes beyond the present task. See the discussion by Aharoni, *Land of the Bible*, pp. 301-305.

The descendants of Kohath are the first to be addressed.[4] Thir-teen settlements are drawn from the southern territories, while ten more come from territories in the north. The descendants of Gershon follow; they receive thirteen settlements in the region of Galilee. Bringing up the rear are the descendants of Merari. They receive twelve settlements located mostly in Transjordan, but some in Cisjordan. One wonders if even this randomness is significant: it douses the presentation with a sense of reality and counters the view that this catalog is some kind of a late, idealized list. Still, it must be remembered that receiving a land grant is a different matter than controlling it. Even this deep into the text, the conquest proposition must remain an open question: will Israel be strong, courageous, careful, meditative or not?[5] Framed by these larger issues, the cata-log of forty-eight sites is offered.

21:9-26 The Levite clan of Kohath is recognized as special, not only because of the priority of the lot, but also because of the pres-ence of Israel's priestly family within its ranks.[6] Both points are emphasized by means of repetition. Nine settlements from within the tribal area of Judah (and Simeon) are to be shared with the **Kohathite clans** who trace their descent from Aaron. These include **Kiriath Arba** or **Hebron, Libnah, Jattir, Eshtemoa, Holon, Debir, Ain, Juttah,** and **Beth Shemesh.**[7] Four more sites from the tribe of

---

[4]For the responsibilities of the Kohathite clan in the wilderness, see Num 3:27-32.

[5]This point flies in the face of the conclusion that requires Israel to con-trol sites before they can be allotted. Such thinking is presumed by the view that this list originates in the time of the United Monarchy (or later) and serves the administrative needs of the kingdom.

[6]All priests of Yahweh are Levites, but not all Levites are priests of Yahweh. This distinction goes back to the book of Exodus (28:1,4,41,43, etc.) where the family of Aaron is ordained for special duties. Some debate exists concerning the overlap between priestly and Levitical responsibilities, but it appears consistent with most texts to view the Levites as assistants to the priests, who do not offer sacrifices (e.g., see Exod 32:25-29; Lev 8:1–10:20; Num 3:11-13).

[7]For Kiriath Arba or Hebron, see 10:36-37; 12:10; 14:15; 15:13-14,54; 20:7. For Libnah, see 10:29-30; 15:42. For Jattir, see 15:48. For Eshtemoa, see 15:50. For Holon, see 15:51. For Debir, see 10:3,38; 11:21; 12:13; 15:15,49. For Ain, see 15:32; 19:7. For Juttah, see 15:55. For Beth Shemesh, see 15:10.

Benjamin are added to lengthen the list of "first family" sites to thirteen: **Gibeon**, **Geba**,[8] **Anathoth**,[9] and **Almon**.[10]

Other Kohathites who do not trace their ancestry to the priestly family of Aaron are the subject of the remainder of the list. Sites from the tribe of **Ephraim** to be shared with these folk include **Shechem**, **Gezer**,[11] **Kibzaim**,[12] and **Beth Horon**.[13] Sites to be shared from the tribe of **Dan** include **Eltekeh**, **Gibbethon**, **Aijalon**,[14] and **Gath Rimmon**.[15] Finally, two settlements from **the half the tribe of Manasseh** that fit into this context are **Taanach**[16] and **Gath Rimmon**.[17] All told, twenty-three sites are designated as the conjoint property of various tribe members and Levites from the clan of Kohath.

21:27-33 Attention shifts to the second clan of Levites, **the Gershonites**. Members of this clan trace their ancestry back to the oldest son of Levi.[18] A total of thirteen settlements from the lands of Manasseh, Issachar, Asher, and Naphtali are identified here as shared places. These include **Golan**,[19] **Be Eshtarah**,[20] **Kishion**,[21] **Dab-**

---

[8]For Gibeon, see 9:3ff. For Geba, see 18:24.

[9]Anathoth appears here in the text for the first time. It is often associated with Ras el Kharruba in the Arab village of Anata, located about two miles northeast of Jerusalem. See Elitzur, *Ancient Place Names*, pp. 159-160.

[10]Almon also is mentioned here for this first time. It may be located at Khirbet Alamit, just beyond Anata, northeast of Jerusalem. See Elitzur, *Ancient Place Names*, p. 57.

[11]For Shechem, see 8:30-35. For Gezer, see 10:33; 16:3,10.

[12]Kibzaim appears for the first time here. Curiously, in the parallel list of 1 Chr 6:67[H 53], the name Jokmeam appears in its place. Kibzaim is unidentified on the ground.

[13]For Beth Horon, see 10:10; 16:3,5; 18:13-14.

[14]For Eltekeh and Gibbethon, see 19:44. For Aijalon, see 10:12; 19:42.

[15]Gath Rimmon appears twice in this list. The first Gath Rimmon is considered a part of Dan, while the Gath Rimmon of 21:25 is considered a part of Manasseh. It is possible that the second appearance (of 21:25) is a scribal error, given the LXX mention here of Ibleam. For Gath Rimmon of Dan, see 19:45.

[16]For Taanach, see 12:21 and 17:11.

[17]See comment at fn. 15 above.

[18]For the responsibilities of the Gershonite clan in the wilderness, see Num 3:21-26.

[19]For Golan, see 20:8.

[20]This is the only appearance of Be Eshtarah (lit. "in Asherah"). In the parallel list in 1 Chr 6:71[H 56], it appears as Ashtaroth.

[21]Kishion appears only here. In the parallel list in 1 Chr 6:72[H 57], it appears as Kedesh.

erath,[22] Jarmuth,[23] En Gannim,[24] Mishal,[25] Abdon,[26] Helkath,[27] Rehob, Kadesh,[28] Hammoth Dor,[29] and Kartan.[30]

21:34-40 The third and final clan of Levites to receive settlements are those from the **Merarite clans**.[31] Of the named settlements offered, the first four, **Jokneam, Kartah,**[32] **Dimnath,**[33] and **Nahalal**[34] are located within the tribal lands of Zebulun in Cisjordan. The remaining eight sites are in Transjordan and include **Bezer, Jahaz, Kedemoth Mephaath, Ramoth, Mahanaim, Heshbon,** and **Jazer**.[35]

21:41-42 The total number of settlements allotted to the Levites is forty-eight. These are fairly evenly drawn from twelve tribes in a pattern that moves roughly from south to north to east.[36] As requested, the Levites receive settlements for people and pastures for animals.

3. Concluding Comments (21:43-45)

43So the LORD gave Israel all the land he had sworn to give their forefathers, and they took possession of it and settled there. 44The

---

[22]For Daberath, see 19:12.

[23]In 1 Chr 6:73[H 58], Jarmuth appears as Ramoth.

[24]For En Gannim in Issachar, see 19:21. An alternate spelling (?) of Anem appears in 1 Chr 6:73[H 58].

[25]For Mishal, see 19:26.

[26]Abdon appears here for the first time. It may be identified with Khirbet Abdeh, located on the coast between Tyre and Acco.

[27]For Helkath, see 19:25; 1 Chr 6:75[H 60] identifies it as Hukok.

[28]For Rehob, see 19:28,30. For Kadesh in Naphtali, see 12:22; 19:37.

[29]For Hammoth Dor, see 19:35; 1 Chr 6:76[H 61] identifies it as Hammon.

[30]Kartan is identified as Kiriathaim in 1 Chr 6:76[H 61]. It may be located at Khirbet el-Quneitireh (Aharoni, *Land of the Bible*, p. 441).

[31]For the responsibilities of the Merarite clan in the wilderness, see Num 3:33-37.

[32]For Jokneam, see 19:11. The location of Kartah is unknown.

[33]Dimnath appears in 1 Chr 6:75[H 62] as Rimmon. A site known as Rimmon appears in the Zebulun boundary description of 19:13.

[34]For Nahalal, see 19:15.

[35]For Bezer, see 20:8. For Jahaz, see 13:18. For Kedemoth, see 13:18. For Mephaath, see 13:18. For Ramoth, see 20:8. For Mahanaim, see 13:26,30. For Heshbon, see 13:27. For Jazer, see 13:25.

[36]Each tribe offers four sites, except Naphtali, that offers three. Offsetting this is the Judah/Simeon block that offers nine sites.

**LORD gave them rest on every side, just as he had sworn to their fore-
fathers. Not one of their enemies withstood them; the LORD handed
all their enemies over to them. [45]Not one of all the LORD's good promises to the house of Israel failed; every one was fulfilled.**

With the land assignments fully distributed, the narrator draws
back from his catalog to offer an assessment. It is directed to
Yahweh, but not limited to him. Yahweh's work in the conquest is
characterized here by "swearing," "giving," "causing rest," and
"speaking." Each is a powerful verb tugging at lines running through
the text of Joshua, but ultimately anchored in *torah*. Who can forget
that the promise of land has been sworn by an oath in the dim past?
Who can forget that land for the landless is a gift to be claimed by
the obedient act of walking upon it? Who can forget that the byprod-
uct of obedience is rest, a pure and exhilarating freedom? And finally, who can forget that all this has been the issue of a reliable source,
the very mouth of God? As if to underline this case for consistency,
a ringing appeal is made through the word "all" (כֹּל, *kol*): "*all* the
land," "*all* that he swore," "*all* their enemies," "*all* the good promises," "it *all* came to pass." The power of the verbs and the largeness
of the embrace are staggering. Yahweh is elevated as a faithful participant in the enterprise. His "word does not drop" but aligns perfectly with promises offered in the distant past.

This assessment, however, places the reader in a bind. Few would
hesitate to seize upon a view of Yahweh that recognizes his participation and celebrates his steadiness. However, a larger question asks how
can such a positive assessment be offered on the heels of a conquest
campaign marred by disobedience, ineffectiveness, laxity, and failure?
How can the statement of 13:1, "there are still very large areas of land
to be taken over" be comfortably tucked in beside the conclusion of
21:44, **"the LORD handed all their [Israel's] enemies over to them"**?
One or the other of these two statements may be true, but how is it
possible to hold both simultaneously? Which is true? Which is real?
Which is first? Does the narrator expect his readers to simply amble on
without protest?

Polzin, among others, does not believe so. In his view, this assessment is not meant to be taken literally: "the book of Joshua is scarce-
ly intelligible if 21:41-43 is not read in an *ironic* sense."[37] As he sees

---

[37]Polzin, *Moses and the Deuteronomist*, p. 132 (emphasis ours).

it, the voice of "authoritarian dogmatism" clearly surfaces here, a kind of shrill assertion that "all is right in the world" when all is really not. For Polzin, this assertion is so over-the-top that it begs rejection. It is part of a complex narrative designed to provoke the reader to seek meaning in contradiction.[38] In this way, he attempts to tie the second major section of the book (chapters 13–21) to the first major section of the book (chapters 1–12). Both, in his view, demonstrate how Israel only partially "occupies" both law and land. In the first section, that which is "legally" outside Israel (Rahab, Gibeon, the alien, etc.) is brought inside Israel as examples of God's mercy, and, in the process, become metaphors of Israel itself. In the second half, similar examples surface (e.g., Caleb, Jebusites, accidental killers), but here the emphasis is "spatially" oriented: outsiders obtain a place inside the land. None of this "legal" or "spatial" instability is expected; some of it may be invented by scholarship, but all of it forces the reader to confront again the question of Israel's identity.

While aspects of Polzin's view are attractive, another way through the immediate dilemma is possible. An understanding of 21:43-45 begins with the observation previously offered, namely, that this is an assessment specifically directed toward Yahweh. Here is an affirmation of the belief that the *leadership of Yahweh* has not flagged or failed. Throughout this campaign, he has consistently given Israel the opportunity to possess, settle, and rest. With this in mind, the viewpoint that concludes this second major block of the book ought not be evaluated according to how Israel responded to a great commission; this is a different matter altogether. Instead, it should be evaluated within the question of how Yahweh divided the land for conquest. Seen from this end, the conclusion fits, not perfectly enough to relieve every tension, I admit that, but well enough for the proposition to be mustered this way: for his part, Yahweh has been faithful in swearing, giving, offering rest, and speaking. Failure to follow this good lead is not necessarily the fault of the leader. It may be the choice of the follower. Any other lingering discomfort may very well be as a result of Polzin's pinch. The fact that the book does not — and, indeed, cannot — satisfactorily end here is telling. One suspects that when the last word falls, it will land somewhere short of positive.

---

[38]Ibid., pp. 128-134.

JOSHUA 22

III. HOW TO BE ISRAEL (22:1-24:35)

Just as Moses approached the end of his life with speeches in his mouth (Deuteronomy 33), so too, Joshua. Unlike a man, however, such exhortations are indifferent, if not downright immune to the slow grind of time, skipping lightly between done deals, contemporary struggles, and unfinished business. Narratively, such speeches have the power to stitch a book together, using shared memories as a tool for shaping the future. This is certainly the case here as the text of Joshua gathers itself for a rush to closure. Themes raised in the opening charge of the book (1:1-9) surface again, demonstrating continuity, but not necessarily an "all-holes-are-now-plugged" resolution. At the very least, the open-endedness of this "great commission" enterprise is sensed afresh. Joshua will not guarantee a successful outcome to Israel in its assigned task, only consequences that hinge upon future choices. Recognition of this perspective allows the interpreter to tap into an application that transcends both the moment of delivery and the situation of the original audience; it sets the challenge of choice before every reader.

With the people of God now established in the *Heartland*, questions of subsistence and survival give way to reflections concerning national identity. Three speeches grace the forum of this discussion. The first speech challenges definitions of Israel drawn up on the basis of land-lines alone (22:1-34). The second speech considers the notion of *torah* loyalty as the tool for uniting the community and distinguishing it from others (23:1-16). The third and final speech uses both invitation and provocation to induce Israel to honestly choose and serve Yahweh (24:1-35). Initial assessments of the "great commission" flow from each of these three speeches, and when taken together, knit a summary for the book.

A. WHO IS IN? WHO IS OUT? (22:1-34)

Geologically, the *Heartland* is torn apart by forces deep within the earth. These forces continue to wrench apart the peninsula of Arabia (Transjordan) from the continent of Africa (Cisjordan). The most visible result of this action is the Great Rift Valley and its associated systems; the Sea of Galilee, the Jordan River, and the Dead Sea function as a regional sump.

Likewise, division also characterizes the human history of the *Heartland*. As Smith observes:

> Palestine has never belonged to one nation, and probably never will. As her fauna and flora represent many geological ages, and are related to the animals and plants of other lands, so varieties of the human race, culture and religion, the most extreme, preserve themselves side by side on those different shelves and coigns of her surface, under those different conditions of her climate. Thus when history first lights up within Palestine, what we see is a confused medley of clans—that crowd of Canaanites, Amorites, Perizzites, Kenizzites, Hivites, Girgashites, Hittites, sons of Anak and Zamzummim—which perplexes the student, but is yet in such harmony with the natural conditions of the country and with the rest of the history.[1]

Understanding the fragmented nature of the land itself is a first point to remember in contemplating this section.

A second point to remember is that two and a half tribes received land allotments in Transjordan: Reuben, Gad, and half of Manasseh. Control of these allotments is achieved early on as described in *torah* (Num 32:1-42; Deut 3:12-20). As such, the conquest of Transjordan is already a given in the book of Joshua; it is treated as an assumed reality, rather than a story in its own right. What is relevant to the narrator are the orders given to the fighting men from these tribes to continue the campaign effort in Cisjordan until a similar end point is within the reach of all the tribes.

Third and finally, it should be noted that the biblical text regards the region of Transjordan ambiguously. There is a sense in which Transjordan is a part of whispered promises from antiquity, yet a

---

[1]G.A. Smith, *Historical Geography*, p. 61.

sense in which it is not. While two-and-a-half tribes are clearly given land by Moses on the east bank, the boundary list of Numbers 34 does not enclose this area or label it as "your land" (v. 12). That said, Transjordan is within the purview of the boundary sketch offered in Joshua 1:4. The geographer is left scratching: is Transjordan in or out? That the land on either side of the river is considered a united whole grows from the fact that the "cities of refuge" are distributed evenly from north to south *and* from east to west (Josh 20:8). That said; Moses dies in Transjordan, seemingly unable to enter the Promised Land. Add to this the significance of the Jordan crossing, as recorded in Joshua 3:1–4:24, celebrating the end of one kind of journey and the beginning of another. Taken together, these mixed signals raise the possibility that land-lines make for a poor measure of Israel. Could this ambiguity play into the developing theme of the book?

As early as 1:12-18, the reader is alerted to the unique role of the two-and-a-half Transjordan tribes. It is worth a second look. Their sturdy response of faith and encouragement to Joshua on the front end of the book has been held in abeyance, awaiting the balance of the story. The textual moment of chapter 22 swings that balance into view, and helps frame the message of the book.

1. The Release of the Transjordan Tribes (22:1-12)

¹**Then Joshua summoned the Reubenites, the Gadites and the half-tribe of Manasseh ²and said to them, "You have done all that Moses the servant of the LORD commanded, and you have obeyed me in everything I commanded. ³For a long time now—to this very day—you have not deserted your brothers but have carried out the mission the LORD your God gave you. ⁴Now that the LORD your God has given your brothers rest as he promised, return to your homes in the land that Moses the servant of the LORD gave you on the other side of the Jordan. ⁵But be very careful to keep the commandment and the law that Moses the servant of the LORD gave you: to love the LORD your God, to walk in all his ways, to obey his commands, to hold fast to him and to serve him with all your heart and all your soul."**

⁶**Then Joshua blessed them and sent them away, and they went to their homes. ⁷(To the half-tribe of Manasseh Moses had given**

land in Bashan, and to the other half of the tribe Joshua gave land on the west side of the Jordan with their brothers.) When Joshua sent them home, he blessed them, [8]saying, "Return to your homes with your great wealth—with large herds of livestock, with silver, gold, bronze and iron, and a great quantity of clothing—and divide with your brothers the plunder from your enemies."

[9]So the Reubenites, the Gadites and the half-tribe of Manasseh left the Israelites at Shiloh in Canaan to return to Gilead, their own land, which they had acquired in accordance with the command of the LORD through Moses.

[10]When they came to Geliloth near the Jordan in the land of Canaan, the Reubenites, the Gadites and the half-tribe of Manasseh built an imposing altar there by the Jordan. [11]And when the Israelites heard that they had built the altar on the border of Canaan at Geliloth near the Jordan on the Israelite side, [12]the whole assembly of Israel gathered at Shiloh to go to war against them.

22:1-6 While the gracious words of release to the Transjordan tribes come out of the mouth of Joshua, it is the speech of his mentor in many ways. Acknowledgment that the Transjordan tribes have not just listened to the commands of Joshua, but have "kept" (NIV, "done") the commands of Moses speaks to the fidelity of the response as well as to the Mosaic-like authority of Joshua. In fact, the visage of Moses is revived through the repetition of name and title, **the servant of the LORD** (three times in four short verses). The commendable acts shown to Moses, to Joshua, and to the rest of Israel on the part of the Transjordan tribes undergirds the developing story; from the start, narrator and reader share the inside knowledge of their faithfulness. Any tension that arises must mount from without.

The speech of Joshua formally recognizes what 21:44 anticipated, namely, that the moment of "rest" (נוּחַ, *nûaḥ*) for the Cisjordan tribes has arrived: Yahweh, **your God has given your brothers rest**. Such legal talk binds the moment of commission to the moment of release (cf. Deut 3:20; Josh 1:15). The pronouncement of rest is the signal; the Transjordan fighters are free of Cisjordan responsibility. They may now return to their "tents" (NIV, "homes") on the other side of the Jordan River and pursue their own interests.

As they go, however, Joshua reminds them to remember *torah*. Already, they have demonstrated the ability to "keep" all that Moses ordered (22:2). This must be continued in the future with intensity, **be very careful to keep** on doing *torah* (see Supplemental Study on The Nature of *Torah* below). To illustrate, Joshua shows just how *torah* life looks on the ground. The threefold command to love God, walk his paths, and follow his orders is standard Mosaic fare (e.g., Deut 30:15-16), an epitome of the *torah* life (Micah 6:8; Matt 22:36-37), and reminiscent of earlier admonitions (1:7). Two additional charges are rich in biblical meaning: **hold fast to him**, or "stick to him" and **serve him with all your heart and all your soul.** Such appeals will be repeated to the rest of the crowd in chapters 22 and 23.

SUPPLEMENTAL STUDY

THE NATURE OF *TORAH*

The image of Moses coming down from Sinai with stone tablets in hand is a familiar one. It is also a convenient point to begin a discussion of *torah*, or "law." The term appears more than 200 times in the text of the Old Testament and brings to mind thoughts of the Ten Commandments, the five books of Moses, the traditions of the elders, and a system of belief often contrasted with a system of grace. All of these ideas, and more, grow from mention of *torah*.

Students of language debate the meaning of the term. Some believe it is connected to the verbal idea of throwing or casting a thing, possibly as pointer, in a particular direction.[2] In this sense, *torah* shows the way. Others believe it comes from the verbal idea of giving orders or instruction.[3] In this sense, *torah* is connected to instruction or education. Whatever the etymology, a biblical context presents it as authoritative. It is the תּוֹרַת־יהוה (*tōrath-YHWH*, "teaching of Yahweh"), תּוֹרַת־אֱלֹהִים (*tōrath-ĕlōhîm*, "teaching of God"), or תּוֹרַת־מֹשֶׁה (*tōrath-mōšeh*, "teaching of Moses"). Only when carried into a Greek context does it become νόμος (*nomos*, "law"). Because *torah* represents a firm word in an ever-fluctuating world, it must be read, contemplated, and applied to life regularly, e.g., Exodus 18:20; Deuteronomy 1:5; Psalm 1:3; Nehemiah 8:8.

---

[2]From the verbal root in Hebrew, ירה (*yrh),* "to throw, hurl."
[3]From an Akkadian term *têrtu,* "to bring, lead."

From a traditional Jewish perspective, the *torah* of contemplation has two forms: one written, the other, oral. Both were given by God at Sinai and subsequently transmitted from Moses to Joshua, and from Joshua to other reliable intermediaries.[4] The written *torah* is familiar to Christian interpreters as the first five books of the Old Testament or the Pentateuch (הַתּוֹרָה סֵפֶר, *sēpher hattôrāh*). By contrast, the Oral *torah* is unfamiliar to many Christian interpreters. It is made up of stories and teachings that were committed to memory and preserved mouth to mouth until the Rabbinic period (beginning in the 3rd century A.D.), when these were finally written down in works known as the Mishnah and Talmud. By means of this Oral *torah*, Rabbinic Judaism claims a direct connection to biblical Judaism and finds the elasticity necessary for responding to the ever-changing challenges of life (including the destruction of the Jerusalem temple and its associated sacrificial system in A.D. 70, a crisis that brought biblical Judaism to an end).[5]

While traditional Christianity does not recognize the Jewish notion of an Oral *torah*, it does recognize the principle of implicit and explicit interpretations. Certainly, overt and covert readings are recognized in many Christian "theologies." Catholic tradition honors a "plain reading" as well as a "fuller sense." The principle is harder to find within Protestant thinking, although in some circles the "textual moment" is augmented by the "preaching moment," each packaged with its own brand of "inspiration" and interpretive value.

For most Christians, understanding the role of *torah* in the lives and teaching of those who lived in the Old Testament period is a difficult task. This is due, in part, to the distance in time and place between the Old Testament world and the present. It is also due to the human tendency to reduce *torah* to a wooden code or a tool of manipulation that establishes and maintains the power of some at

---

[4]This "Chain of Tradition" is described in the opening of a tractate from the Mishnah known as *Pirke Avoth* (or simply *Avoth*): "Moses received the Law from Sinai and committed it to Joshua, and Joshua to the Elders, and the Elders to the Prophets, and the Prophets committed it to the Men of the Great Synagogue." See *The Mishnah*, trans. by Herbert Danby (London: Oxford University, 1933), p. 446.

[5]For a sympathetic perspective on Oral Law, its nature and development, see Adin Steinsaltz, *The Essential Talmud*, 13th Anniversary ed. (New York: Basic, 2006), pp. 36-48.

the expense of others. Excesses are common and do not do justice to a God who is both the author of *torah* and consistent in character (Num 23:19).

In an effort to recast *torah* for fresh thinking, four points may be briefly considered.

First, as already mentioned, *torah* is authoritative. It is communicated by Yahweh to Moses at Sinai and is subsequently written down for the sake of the community.

Second, *torah* is radically monotheistic. Key to understanding the purpose of *torah* is recognizing how it explains the origins of Israel and the world in the past, how it prescribes coping strategies for holy living in the present, and how it sketches the possibility of resolutions engineered in the future. *Torah* makes this clear, both positively and negatively. It declares who Yahweh is and how that realization undermines all other worldviews.

Third, *torah* is covenantal. It defines a strategic partnership between Yahweh and Israel. Historical introductions to the parties involved come by way of Genesis, whereas legal materials are offered at the center of *torah*, Exodus through Numbers. These have moral and ceremonial components. Finally, Deuteronomy restates the terms of the partnership and the role of personal choice for maintaining or shattering it.

Fourth, *torah* is applicable. To be activated, *torah* must be freshly interpreted by each generation. This essential truth must be kept in mind while reading the text of Joshua. The challenge for the generation exiting the wilderness and entering Canaan is to apply *torah* in their present situation. Is Yahweh to be trusted in this grand pedestrian expedition? *Torah* provides an answer. How do I relate to my neighbors? *Torah* provides an answer. What happens if Yahweh's leadership is ignored? *Torah* provides an answer. What does it mean to be Israel in this time and place? *Torah* provides an answer. Hence, the text of Joshua provides a critical snapshot of what happens when *torah* is read, contemplated, and applied.

22:7-9 Additional details are mustered by means of a synoptic/ resumptive tactic.[6] The narrator further stretches out the telling of

---

[6]See comments and note at 3:17 and in the introduction to Joshua 10.

the departure to remind the reader of the place of blessing (Shiloh), the identity of the Transjordan tribes (Reuben, Gad, and half-Manasseh), and the lands to which they are returning (Bashan, Gilead). This old information will be brought into play again. New information comes with the acknowledgment that those who depart do so with **great wealth**, including **large herds of livestock, with silver, gold, bronze, and iron, and great quantity of clothing**. This booty is a result of the Canaanite campaign.[7] Joshua commands that it be shared with **your brothers**, presumably with those back "home" that did not participate in the Cisjordan raids.

22:10-12 The possibility of a "happily ever after" ending evaporates quickly. Two moves are described, both abrupt enough to be unbalancing. The first move is that of the departing Transjordan fighters. When they arrive at the Jordan River, they pause to build **an imposing altar**. No rationale for this project is offered; no action at the altar is explicitly described. For the alert reader, however, the story has a familiar ring. In chapters 3 and 4, all Israel crossed the Jordan *into* Canaan. The waters parted by divine miracle and the people walked across on dry land. When finished, stones were "set up" as "memorials." Flashbacks to that scene are engineered here, though this is definitely a crossing of a different order. It is an eastbound, not a westbound journey, out of, not into, *Heartland* central. Here, no river course is split, although the crosser-overs enter the "banks (גְּלִילוֹת, gᵉlîlôth[8]) of the Jordan," akin to the Ark-box company who entered the "edge (קְצֵה, qāṣēh) of the Jordan" (3:15-16). Most curious are the assembly of stones used to build an altar (מִזְבֵּחַ, mizbēaḥ). No miracle looms large; only a stony structure that "looks big." Is this altar for the purpose of sacrifice? Etymology alone might suggest so, but the flashback invites the conclusion that this is a Joshua-like "memorial" (זִכָּרוֹן, zikkārôn) (4:7). Like a wide-eyed child, the reader is prompted to question: "What do these stones mean?" (4:6,22).

---

[7]This acknowledgment of booty may be placed within the context of Num 31:27 and Deut 20:10-18. In the latter passage, allowance for booty from distant settlements is clear; allowance for booty from near settlements is not so clear.

[8]The NIV reads this word as a proper name (Geliloth). It is a possible reading (cf. 18:17), although elsewhere in and out of the book of Joshua it is also interpreted as a "border" or a "region," or "circuit" (13:2; Joel 3:4[H 4:4]).

One possible meaning is provided by the second abrupt and unbalancing move of the passage. In response to rumors of the stony structure, the Cisjordan tribes rally **to go to war against them**. The discontinuity almost explodes off the page! War against the Transjordan tribes? For what reason? To what end? Texts from 13:1 on have made it clear that Israel is struggling to fully occupy the land by driving out its inhabitants. A civil war would only imitate the foolish divisiveness of the Canaanites at Gibeon (10:1-5). Moreover, for Israel to choose war after Yahweh has granted "rest" (22:4) is beyond counterintuitive; it approaches direct disobedience. How can this turn of events be explained?

With this tension rushing through the gaps, the narrator drops two clues that may help unpack this surprising sequence. Both concern location. First, in the report of what the Cisjordan tribes "heard" (v. 11), the site of the altar is not just on the riverbank, it "fronts the land of Canaan" and is "towards the side of the children of Israel."[9] "Fronting" Canaan suggests that this "very visible" altar is located in a "very visible" place.[10] This bit of information deepens the mystery. Seen by *whom*?"[11] Canaanites? Cisjordanites? Transjordanites? Yahweh? The other clause is even more interesting, especially in this specific context. In verse 11, those who hear about this altar — and are enraged by the rumor alone — are specifically named the בְּנֵי־יִשְׂרָאֵל (*bᵊnê Yiśrā'ēl*), "the children of Israel." It is difficult to believe that the use of this phrase to describe Cisjordan folk over and against Transjordan folk is accidental. Are not *both* groups equally *bᵊnê Yiśrā'ēl*? The repeating of the division of Manasseh in

---

[9]Three coordinated phrases locate the altar in the Hebrew text of v. 11. Each is directed by the preposition *el*, "to" or "toward." It is located אֶל־מוּל אֶרֶץ כְּנַעַן (*'el-mûl 'ereṣ Kᵊna'an*), or "towards the forefront of Canaan." It is located אֶל־גְּלִילוֹת הַיַּרְדֵּן (*'el-gᵊlîlôth hayyardēn*), or "towards the boundary-banks of the Jordan." And finally, it is located אֶל־עֵבֶר בְּנֵי יִשְׂרָאֵל (*'el-'ēber bᵊnê Yiśrā'ēl*), or "towards the side of the children of Israel."

[10]An alternative reading of *'el-mûl 'ereṣ Kᵊna'an* is "toward the opposite (side) of the land of Canaan." The particle in question, *mûl*, may be read as "forefront" or as "opposite." What is at stake in this situation is the location of the altar. Is it on Canaan's front or opposite Canaan's front? Put differently, is it in Cisjordan or in Transjordan? No consensus among translators or commentators emerges. As an example, the NIV chooses the Cisjordan option while the KJV goes with a Transjordan location.

[11]Hawk, *Joshua*, p. 236.

verse 7, with half of the tribe in Cisjordan and half of the tribe in Transjordan, begins to take on even more significance. Is the division of Manasseh (east and west) merely a representative of the whole? Is this a surfacing division between Cisjordan and Transjordan folk, another kind of "great rift" that hinges upon the question of who is an insider in the community of Israel and who is on the margins of it?[12] Many questions swirl, but what is clear is that the departing Transjordan fighters leave behind a visible altar, likely on the Cisjordan side of the river. It is constructed outside of their own territorial inheritance and could be interpreted as a warning, a declaration of independence, or an unsettling testimony of discord.[13] So "all Israel" gathers "against them" (22:12), oddly, with "all Israel" in one corner and the Transjordan "them" in the other.

The narrator drops a second clue of a geographical nature. This concerns notice that the rally point for those advocating war is in Shiloh. This, by itself, is hardly surprising. Shiloh is the spot where final inheritance issues were sorted (18:1-2; 19:51; 21:2). It is the site where Joshua commended and encouraged the Transjordan fighters, and the place from which they departed to go home (22:9). It clearly functions as an administrative center for early Israel. However, recalling the establishment of the tabernacle at Shiloh adds yet another element, perhaps even the key element, to understanding this dispute. Deuteronomy 12:1-11 states that when Israel enters the land, Yahweh will choose a place to set his name or dwell. No other worship spot may coexist. No other sacred stones may be tolerated; no competing altar can stand (Deut 12:3). If the Cisjordan tribes believe that Shiloh is truly Yahweh's site of choice, this act of

---

[12]This approach to the text is pioneered by Polzin (*Moses and the Deuteronomist*, pp. 134-141) and followed by others. However, if this reading is valid, it seems odd that the "insiders" (Cisjordan people), rather than the "outsiders" (Transjordan people) would be the ones to initiate the conflict. One would expect the marginalized segment to attempt to take the center (or at least disturb the status quo) in order to obtain a voice, gain power, etc., not the other way around.

[13]Some have argued that the eastern tribes may not have recognized the Jordan River as a boundary, and therefore the altar represents a boundary violation (e.g., Robert G. Boling, *Joshua: A New Translation with Notes and Commentary*, AB [Garden City, NY: Doubleday, 1982], pp. 511-512). This is difficult to accept if 22:25 is taken at face value.

altar building by the Transjordan tribes may be viewed, at best, as confusion. At worst, it is apostasy.

Along this line, the narrative appears uncommitted, save for crumbs already dropped. Joshua's words of commendation to the departing members of the Transjordan tribes stressed their faithfulness and integrity. To this must be added the bold commitment initially offered in 1:16-18. Both texts encourage the reader to side with those recognized as obedient towards Yahweh, honest with themselves, and dependable with respect to their brothers. But therein lies the quandary. How can such folk build this kind of résumé *and* that looming altar? The text contracts into a binding position as the threat of violence draws near.

2. The Accusation of the Cisjordan Tribes (22:13-20)

[13]So the Israelites sent Phinehas son of Eleazar, the priest, to the land of Gilead—to Reuben, Gad and the half-tribe of Manasseh. [14]With him they sent ten of the chief men, one for each of the tribes of Israel, each the head of a family division among the Israelite clans.

[15]When they went to Gilead—to Reuben, Gad and the half-tribe of Manasseh—they said to them: [16]"The whole assembly of the LORD says: 'How could you break faith with the God of Israel like this? How could you turn away from the LORD and build yourselves an altar in rebellion against him now? [17]Was not the sin of Peor enough for us? Up to this very day we have not cleansed ourselves from that sin, even though a plague fell on the community of the LORD! [18]And are you now turning away from the LORD ?

"'If you rebel against the LORD today, tomorrow he will be angry with the whole community of Israel. [19]If the land you possess is defiled, come over to the LORD's land, where the LORD's tabernacle stands, and share the land with us. But do not rebel against the LORD or against us by building an altar for yourselves, other than the altar of the LORD our God. [20]When Achan son of Zerah acted unfaithfully regarding the devoted things,[a] did not wrath come upon the whole community of Israel? He was not the only one who died for his sin.'"

[a]*20* The Hebrew term refers to the irrevocable giving over of things or persons to the LORD, often by totally destroying them.

22:13-14 It is twice noted that the phrase *bᵊnê Yiśrā'ēl*, "sons of Israel," corresponds to those gathered at Shiloh. This is the "Israel" that dispatches **Phinehas son of Eleazar the priest** to Transjordan, along with **ten of the chief men.**[14] The mission represents the tribes of Cisjordan and is led by the grandson of Aaron and son of Eleazar. The replacing of Eleazar, who has been Joshua's coleader, with Phinehas is significant. His presence, together with these ten warlords, anticipates bloody conflict.[15] The absence of Joshua may be a matter of Moseslike delegation;[16] on the other hand, the goal of the narrative may be to create space between him from what follows. Space can preserve many things!

22:15-20 The words of the representatives are caustic and loaded. Insider-outsider language creeps in as the Cisjordan group identifies itself as "all the congregation of Yahweh." On the other hand, they identify the Transjordan folk as "unfaithful" and acting "against the God of Israel." They invoke the image of **the sin of Peor**, where Israel sacrificed to foreign gods, engaged in sexual immorality, but were preserved by Phinehas's own bloody action (Num 25:1-16). They also invoke the image of Achan from The '*Ay* fiasco (Josh 7:1-26). Both examples demonstrate how judgment fell not just

---

[14]The description of these ten men is significant for understanding the use of the Hebrew term אֶלֶף (*'eleph*) in the book of Joshua. Each of the men clearly represents one Cisjordan tribe. But the last clause of 22:14 reads: וְאִישׁ רֹאשׁ בֵּית־אֲבוֹתָם הֵמָּה לְאַלְפֵי יִשְׂרָאֵל (*wᵊ'îš rō'š bêth-'ăbôthām hēmmāh lᵊ'alphê yiśrā'ēl*). In this case, the NIV translates: "each (man was) the head of a family division among the Israelite clans." The term "clans" here is rendered elsewhere in the NIV as "thousands." Clearly, to conclude that *'eleph* must represent a whole number is not a foregone conclusion; even the inconsistency of the NIV points this way.

Perhaps a fresh translation is helpful: "each one represented his father's house; they corresponded to the military units of Israel." The introduction of *'eleph* here may be deliberate: it gives the text a military nuance. These ten men represent more than just ancestry. They are heavyweights chosen, in part, for the purpose of intimidation.

[15]As a leader, Phinehas does not conjure up the image of a subtle negotiator. Consider how he checked a plague by skewering both a man and a woman in an embrace. This zealous act resulted in his receiving a "covenant of peace" (Num 25:8,10-13).

[16]In Num 31:1-6 Moses dispatches a representative army (of one *'eleph* per tribe) from Israel to go to war against Midian. Here too, Phinehas enters the battlefield as the priestly leader.

upon those directly involved in sin, but upon the entire congregation. It is clear that this *delegation of intimidation* views the altar of the
Transjordan residents as a related signal of apostasy. Confronting
and eliminating this impurity by means of force is in everyone's best
interests, or so it seems.

Significant are the words of verse 19: **If the land you possess is
defiled, come over to the LORD's land, where the LORD's tabernacle
stands and share the land with us.** This text may be emphasized in
one of two ways. The first way latches upon the insider-outsider line
of thinking. In this case, the Cisjordan tribes assert that they live in
God's country (lit. "land seized by Yahweh") whereas the region of
Transjordan is obviously not (it is טְמֵאָה, *ṭᵊmēʾāh*, or "ritually unclean").
Encouragement is offered to the two and a half tribes to abandon
their place and move across the river to *God's country*.[17] There, they
can reenlist in the effort to continue subjugating Canaanites.

A second way to read the text seizes upon an explanation for the
altar. To paraphrase: if the altar was really built as a means of purification, such action is out-of-bounds in Transjordan. Purification is
the job of the Shiloh tabernacle and the Shiloh tabernacle alone.
Hence, one angle of reading disparages the land; the second angle
disparages the altar. Both angles may be challenged. Are the words
of this delegation of intimidation to be regarded as reliable?

3. The Response of the Transjordan Tribes (22:21-29)

[21]**Then Reuben, Gad and the half-tribe of Manasseh replied to
the heads of the clans of Israel:** [22]**"The Mighty One, God, the LORD!
The Mighty One, God, the LORD! He knows! And let Israel know!
If this has been in rebellion or disobedience to the LORD, do not
spare us this day.** [23]**If we have built our own altar to turn away from
the LORD and to offer burnt offerings and grain offerings, or to
sacrifice fellowship offerings[a] on it, may the LORD himself call us
to account.**

[24]**"No! We did it for fear that some day your descendants might
say to ours, 'What do you have to do with the LORD, the God of**

---

[17]The term translated as tabernacle is מִשְׁכָּן (*miškan*), "a dwelling-place." In
this case, the "dwelling place of Yahweh."

Israel? [25]The LORD has made the Jordan a boundary between us and you—you Reubenites and Gadites! You have no share in the LORD.' So your descendants might cause ours to stop fearing the LORD.

[26]"That is why we said, 'Let us get ready and build an altar—but not for burnt offerings or sacrifices.' [27]On the contrary, it is to be a witness between us and you and the generations that follow, that we will worship the LORD at his sanctuary with our burnt offerings, sacrifices and fellowship offerings. Then in the future your descendants will not be able to say to ours, 'You have no share in the LORD.'

[28]"And we said, 'If they ever say this to us, or to our descendants, we will answer: Look at the replica of the LORD's altar, which our fathers built, not for burnt offerings and sacrifices, but as a witness between us and you.'

[29]"Far be it from us to rebel against the LORD and turn away from him today by building an altar for burnt offerings, grain offerings and sacrifices, other than the altar of the LORD our God that stands before his tabernacle."

a23 Traditionally *peace offerings*; also in verse 27

22:21-23 Thus far into the controversy, the Transjordan tribes have offered no response. They have quietly listened to the Cisjordan delegation as speculation has given way to accusation and accusation has given way to the threat of force. A civil war hangs in the balance. At long last the silence is broken in an appeal that begins as a trickle. It grows in velocity, streaming, before finally releasing in a thunderous roar: אֵל אֱלֹהִים יהוה אֵל אֱלֹהִים יהוה הוּא יֹדֵעַ " *'ēl 'ĕlōhîm, YHWH 'ēl, 'ĕlōhîm, YHWH,* himself knows!" Syllable upon syllable, word upon word accumulates in a dramatic oath that is without peer in the prose of Scripture. The Transjordan fighters are supremely confident that Yahweh knows the truth of the matter and they will be vindicated. **Let Israel know!** If it is otherwise, they continue in oath formula, **do not spare us this day**. Connection between this oath and the words of the same group offered at the beginning of the book cannot be missed: "Whoever rebels against your word . . . will be put to death!" (1:18). Relief comes in the revealing. Rebellion plays no role in the building of the stony structure. It does not compete with the Shiloh establishment.

22:24-25 Instead, the altar was built with a view to what might happen in the future. The fear in Transjordan is that they will eventually be pushed out of *Israel*, and more importantly, cut off from Yahweh. Someday, the reasoning goes, the Cisjordan folk may say to them, **"What do you have to do with the LORD, the God of Israel? The LORD has made the Jordan a boundary between us and you. . . . You have no share in the LORD."** The explanation emerges slowly, but ironically. The fear in Transjordan is no future whimsy. It recognizes the erosion already at work. The discriminatory language of the delegation reveals contemporary thinking about who is and who is not "Israel." Despite possessing an outstanding résumé of faithfulness, those who are distant from the center of power are easily misunderstood and readily regarded with cool suspicion. Expositors seeking to teach this text may explore many modern examples of this principle.

22:26-29 The rationale of the Transjordan builders continues to be given. The stony structure was erected to counter spiritual suspicion and geographical discrimination. It serves as **a witness between us and you and the generations that follow**. Witnesses in the biblical text may be people; they may also be inanimate objects such as a song (Deut 31:19), scroll (Deut 31:26), or the moon (Ps 89:37[H 38]). Linking ideas to visible objects renders that object a reminder of truth.[18] Here, the symbolic reminder was patterned after the altar of Yahweh and meant to be **a replica**.[19] That it would create so much controversy speaks possibly to the accuracy of the model, to the reality of the problem, and to the dangers of listening to rumors and failing to communicate. The Transjordan defense argues for a third time that the structure was not meant to be a substitute for the Shiloh altar.

---

[18]The notion of a "witness" (עֵד, *ʿēd*) grows from a verbal idea "to return" or "do again." By means of a repeated report, a witness can affirm the truth of a thing. See BDB, s.v. עוּד.

Some similarity may be drawn between this account and the account of Gen 31:46-47 where a heap of stones serve as witness to an agreement between Jacob and Laban.

[19]The altar is literally a תַּבְנִית מִזְבַּח יהוה (*tabnîth mizbaḥ YHWH*), "a pattern" or "an image of the altar of Yahweh."

4. The Rescue of Israel (22:30-34)

[30]**When Phinehas the priest and the leaders of the community—the heads of the clans of the Israelites—heard what Reuben, Gad and Manasseh had to say, they were pleased.** [31]**And Phinehas son of Eleazar, the priest, said to Reuben, Gad and Manasseh, "Today we know that the LORD is with us, because you have not acted unfaithfully toward the LORD in this matter. Now you have rescued the Israelites from the LORD's hand."**

[32]**Then Phinehas son of Eleazar, the priest, and the leaders returned to Canaan from their meeting with the Reubenites and Gadites in Gilead and reported to the Israelites.** [33]**They were glad to hear the report and praised God. And they talked no more about going to war against them to devastate the country where the Reubenites and the Gadites lived.**

[34]**And the Reubenites and the Gadites gave the altar this name: A Witness Between Us that the LORD is God.**

22:30-31 The Transjordan reply is pleasing to the delegation, although the continued use of "us" and "you" terminology is disturbing. When Phinehas responds, **Today we know that the LORD is with us**, does the "us" refer only to the Cisjordan delegation or to all involved? What follows makes this clear: **because you have not acted unfaithfully**. Phinehas views the resolution as a signal that Yahweh is with the Cisjordan folk since the actions of the Transjordan folk are not treacherous. What is more, he too, credits the Transjordan folk for engineering a rescue. In a powerful statement, Phinehas declares, "In this case, you have delivered the children of Israel from the hand of Yahweh." By his mouth, an odd reversal is pronounced. Those who were accused of bringing down the wrath of Yahweh upon Israel have actually averted it and thereby saved Israel. Still, even in the words of Phinehas the question is not lost: who is really *Israel* here?

22:32-34 With the situation in stand-down mode, the delegation of intimidation returns back across the Jordan and reports **to the Israelites**. There, the report is judged to be good and God is blessed. The civil war is averted and talk of a conflict that would have spoiled **the country where the Reubenites and the Gadites lived** disappears. Again, an uncanny reversal presents itself. Previously (v. 19), the delegation suggested the possibility that the land of Transjordan may be "unclean," likely because of the influence of "outsiders." In conclusion, the narrator shrewdly points out that a true destruction of the land comes as a result of needless bickering, in this case, from the very center of Israel. Like Rahab and Caleb, the two-and-a-half tribes of Transjordan are of questionable status and limited power. Yet by their *words and actions* they demonstrate that true Israel cannot be defined by land-lines alone. "God's country" cannot be plotted on a map, on this side or that side of the Jordan. Oddly, the Israel that the reader expects is not the Israel that the reader gets.

JOSHUA 23

B. THE *TORAH* CENTER (23:1-16)

[1]After a long time had passed and the LORD had given Israel rest from all their enemies around them, Joshua, by then old and well advanced in years, [2]summoned all Israel—their elders, leaders, judges and officials—and said to them: "I am old and well advanced in years. [3]You yourselves have seen everything the LORD your God has done to all these nations for your sake; it was the LORD your God who fought for you. [4]Remember how I have allotted as an inheritance for your tribes all the land of the nations that remain—the nations I conquered—between the Jordan and the Great Sea[a] in the west. [5]The LORD your God himself will drive them out of your way. He will push them out before you, and you will take possession of their land, as the LORD your God promised you.

[6]"Be very strong; be careful to obey all that is written in the Book of the Law of Moses, without turning aside to the right or to the left. [7]Do not associate with these nations that remain among you; do not invoke the names of their gods or swear by them. You must not serve them or bow down to them. [8]But you are to hold fast to the LORD your God, as you have until now.

[9]"The LORD has driven out before you great and powerful nations; to this day no one has been able to withstand you. [10]One of you routs a thousand, because the LORD your God fights for you, just as he promised. [11]So be very careful to love the LORD your God.

[12]"But if you turn away and ally yourselves with the survivors of these nations that remain among you and if you intermarry with them and associate with them, [13]then you may be sure that the LORD your God will no longer drive out these nations before you. Instead, they will become snares and traps for you, whips on your

backs and thorns in your eyes, until you perish from this good
land, which the LORD your God has given you.
[14]"Now I am about to go the way of all the earth. You know with
all your heart and soul that not one of all the good promises the
LORD your God gave you has failed. Every promise has been fulfilled; not one has failed. [15]But just as every good promise of the
LORD your God has come true, so the LORD will bring on you all the
evil he has threatened, until he has destroyed you from this good
land he has given you. [16]If you violate the covenant of the LORD your
God, which he commanded you, and go and serve other gods and
bow down to them, the LORD's anger will burn against you, and you
will quickly perish from the good land he has given you."

[a]4 That is, the Mediterranean

The primer for this plot of conquest is "a great commission"
issued by Yahweh, distributed among his people, and used to induce
courage, comfort, and, above all else, obedience. Just as speeches
introduced values critical for the success of the mission, speeches
will also carry the book to its conclusion.

The speech of the previous chapter challenged definitions of
Israel drawn up on the basis of land-lines alone. Geographical Israel
is not necessarily true Israel. This insider-outsider critique is appropriately followed now by a second speech that presents the notion
of *torah* loyalty as the tool for uniting the community of true Israel
and distinguishing it from all others (23:1-16).

The structure of chapter 23 is difficult to discern. For those interested in sourcing, its meandering lines may suggest an authentic oral
setting. More helpful is the identification of three poles in the
ground, repeatedly circled: recollection of past deeds, encouragement for present action, and warnings concerning the future. Taken
together, the message these poles communicate is that the way to
maintain the identity of the community is by keeping *torah*. To the
very end, Joshua will serve Moses.

23:1-2 That **a long time had passed** (lit. "many days") suggests no
specifics with respect to a beginning point, end point, or exact duration of time. It does, however, condense many cycles of activity into
a single imaginable moment: children are born, fields are planted
and harvested, settlements are remodeled, founded, constructed; in
short, life rolls on. In the midst of these etching patterns of life the

notice arises that Yahweh has **given Israel rest**. This realization links
with other narrative lulls, opportunities ripe for handling important
matters (e.g., 11:23; 14:15; 22:4). That Joshua is **old and well advanced in years** has already been said (13:1), but is repeated here
(vv. 1-2), now, ostensibly for the purpose of stumping some last
words.[1] On the other hand, could it be that little progress has been
made since the narrative moment of 13:1? Does the house that needed to be set in order still need to be set in order?

As in the past, the people solemnly gather[2] — together with the
reader — around the gray visage of the departing Patriarch. There
we listen, learn, and are blessed.[3] By virtue of this familiar motif,
Joshua is supremely positioned. He rests somewhere between heav-
en and earth, between God and the people. With a finger on each,
he can muster empathy, plead earnestly, or prophesy darkly, as
needs be.

23:3-5 The assembled ones are called to witness to Yahweh's activity. Grammatically, the text flows from Joshua's "I" of verse 2 to the
audience's "you" of verse 3. Both Joshua, who is old, and **you yourselves,** who have encountered Israel's story thus far, have gained perspective as a result of the ride. Not only has Yahweh waged war, he
has done so specifically on Israel's behalf. Armed with this shared
memory, Joshua urges Israel to recognize that the **nations that
remain** in the breadth of Cisjordan can muster no collective power.
They are limp. Yahweh has flung the גּוֹיִם (gôyim) like an axehead
loosed from its handle[4] in order to open wide the land as an inheritance. The danger that remains is not the threat of their resistance;
it is the threat of their presence. And present they are. The gôyim,

---

[1]It may also be repeated because little has changed since 13:1. Put differently, the house is still "not yet set in order." See comments on 13:1.

[2]In v. 2 the assembly is described as "all Israel," but is immediately followed by "the elders, leaders, judges and officials." Grammatically, the
appositional use of the *lamed* in each case qualifies who "all Israel" is on this
occasion. It appears that the audience of Joshua's speech in chapter 23 is
more limited than the audience of his speech in chapter 24.

[3]The motif of the "Departing Patriarch" is as old as Genesis. Like Isaac
(Genesis 27), Jacob (Genesis 49), and Moses (Deuteronomy 33) before him,
Joshua settles into this familiar position; the book-closing genre is remem-
bered. See Sternberg for a discussion of old age within the text of Genesis
(*Poetics of Biblical Narrative*, pp. 349-354).

[4]For this figure of speech, see Deut 7:22.

"nations," or "non-Israel," arise no less than seven times in this brief speech and are the focus of concern.[5] Even defanged and no longer a military threat, what they pack in terms of ideology and values may be as fatal as the blow of any weapon. This realization is key to the conclusion of the book. The final appeals of Joshua escalate the continuing conflict in spiritual, rather than in military, terms.

23:6-8 Given Yahweh's gracious acts, the appropriate response surfaces again, **be very strong; be careful.**[6] This should not be confused with saber rattling. Man-on-man contests of strength or wits are not the true measure of faithfulness. Rather, as outlined in the opening charge of the book (1:1-9), Joshua encourages God's people to continue keeping and doing *torah*. It is *to this end*, that their strength and care must be used. Application comes in contrasting *torah* influence with other influences. To waver either **to the right or to the left** is to lapse and lose, to become entangled (lit., or "enter," v. 7) in a worldview tagged for destruction. Crooked company is to be shunned; foreign ideas of deity excised. A din of compromising activity reveals the razor's edge of this admonition: do not "commemorate,"[7] "swear by," "serve," or "bow down to" these gods. Such winding paths are anathema. By contrast, the straight road leads to embracing Yahweh.[8]

23:9-10 Assessment of the pedestrian campaign reveals that this has never been a contest of arms. In keeping with the developing

---

[5]The term *gôyim* is often translated as "nations" in the NIV. It may represent Israel on occasion, but more often represents "other peoples" in general and sometimes the inhabitants of Canaan, particularly (cf. Deut 19:1; 31:3).

[6]The challenge to "be strong and courageous" (cf. 1:6,7,9,18) has been variously voiced, using imperatives of חֲזַק (*ḥāzaq*), אָמַץ (*'āmaṣ*), and שָׁמַר (*šāmar*). This is yet another variation of this theme, narratively linking the end of this book to its beginning.

[7]Commemoration may be done either by mentioning a name (as NIV translates, "invoke") or by erecting some sort of stone or structure. The Hebrew root זכר (*zkr*) in the Hiphil suggests the activity of "remembering," "praising," or "memorializing." It appears that in the ancient world, to simply vocalize the name of a deity is to acknowledge his/her reality. Cf. Deut 6:13-14.

[8]The clause in v. 8 holds off the verb for as long as it is possible, כִּי אִם־בַּיהוה אֱלֹהֵיכֶם תִּדְבָּקוּ (*kî 'im-baYHWH 'ĕlōhêkem, tidbāqû*). "Only to the LORD your God . . . cling!" The root *dbq* communicates the idea of physical proximity, e.g., "cling," "cleave," "stay close." It is famously used of the relationship between a man and his wife (Gen 2:24).

theme, Joshua returns to the true source of power: as for Yahweh, he makes war; as for you, not a man will confront you. **One of you routs a thousand.** This is an allusion to Leviticus 26:8: "Five of you will chase a hundred, and a hundred of you will chase ten thousand!" Joshua teaches that victory is achieved not by troop strength or superior tactics, but through *torah* loyalty.

23:11 Because Yahweh is true to his promises, a two-part conclusion arises. The first part concerns personal diligence. The NIV renders it as "be very careful." More loosely, it may be read as "check yourself to the core." Unmonitored, one's core, soul, appetite or נֶפֶשׁ (*nepheš*), may veer out of control and be wasted on bitter ends. A better alternative is offered in the second part of the verse, **love the LORD your God.** This is the principle that unites true Israel and distinguishes it from all other communities. So which will it be? Will Israel choose bitter or better?

23:12-13 Following this conclusion, a warning is offered. Grammatically, this is offered in an if-then, or conditional, clause. If Israel "clings to the surviving *gôyim*" or "nations" by making allies, marriage partners, or associates of those destined for expulsion, then consequences will follow. These include the cessation of Yahweh's support and the jeopardizing of Israel's future in the land. Local inhabitants who would not be a problem because of Yahweh's action may become a problem due to Israel's choices. How can Yahweh drive them out if geographical Israel is clinging to them? The graphic imagery of snares, traps, whips, and thorns make this clear (cf. Num 33:55; Deut 7:16). An ominous line of thinking emerges: if Israel fails to "check itself to the core" and gives free reign to its own desire, it **will perish from this good land.** Permanent occupation of the *Heartland* is not an unconditional promise. Expositors may probe this point from two directions.

First, when probed theologically, the text raises the question of human choice within the larger frame of God's sovereignty. Is grace truly gracious if forced? In an open system, the freedom to choose God must also include the freedom to reject him. Rejecting God may lead to a forfeiture of promises. Hard teachings such as this never come easily, but come they must!

A second direction worth probing shifts the emphasis from theology to history. Joshua's point here may be explored within the larger trajectory of Israel's story. Joshua clearly anticipates Israel's future exile at the hands of the Babylonians and the end of the Old Testament story. This anticipation is early, but not unique (e.g., like Moses, Deut 4:26-27), and, is a key element of Joshua's closing speeches (cf. 23:16; 24:19-22). Centuries after the fact, the prophet Jeremiah gives voice to the reality: "It was because of the LORD's anger that all this happened to Jerusalem and Judah, and in the end he thrust them from his presence" (Jer 52:3).

23:14 As this speech draws to a close, an appeal is made to the past for the sake of the future. Joshua is near death, in biblical terminology, going **the way of all the earth**. He reminds the leaders of what they instinctively (heart and soul) know, namely, that unlike people who die and depart, **not one of all the good promises the Lord your God gave you** will go away (cf. 21:45). Humans eventually grow frail and fail, but God's word does not.

23:15-16 Stunningly, it is not on this positive note that the address ends. As surely as good words and good land have come to Israel, likewise comes disaster. The leaders are left to ponder the possibility that the devastation directed at the inhabitants of the *Heartland* may be turned toward Israel as well. Just as God "destroyed" the Canaanites, so too, announces Joshua, will he **destroy you from this good land**.[9] The NIV attempts to soften this pronouncement by sneaking an if-then conditional clause into verse 16. However, the original text is not so squeamish. It comes as a cut block aimed straight at the knees, vicious, foreboding, and inevitable: "*When* you violate the covenant . . . **then the LORD's anger will burn against you, and you will quickly perish.** Hawk reads it this way, "As Joshua looks into the future, he watches Israel vanish from the land."[10] Sadly, the speech that begins with rest ends in agitation.

---

[9]The same verbal root (שׁמד, *šmd*) used in Deut 7:23 to describe the annihilation of the inhabitants of Canaan. Here it describes the annihilation of Israel.

[10]Hawk, *Joshua*, p. 258.

JOSHUA 24

C. CHOOSE ME IF YOU CAN (24:1-33)

In this final chapter, the observer (or for us, the reader) must render judgment in, what Fielding terms "the court of conscience."[1] It is naive to assume that the goal of the narrator is simply to tell a story; all along the way the presentation has sought to instill a value system, undermine another value system, or perhaps do a little of each. Offered is a way of seeing the world and one's self in it. The end, therefore, ushers all observers to stand in the threshold of choice. On the face of it, the thrust is simple enough: choose Yahweh. No surprises here. Strategically, of course, the path to this choice is as irresistible as gravity. The ground has been beaten down toward this end through twenty-three chapters. Argued from such a secure base, the real question is not, will Israel choose Yahweh? Rather, it is this: why would one choose otherwise? For expositors seeking to sustain contemporary interest in a world of simplistic answers, the problem is an all-too-familiar one. Choices, after all, must be genuinely choosable! It is all the more surprising, therefore, that even under the weight of this lumbering predictability, the narrator manages to lithely exit the book with a twist.

Three texts are pulled forward and engaged in closing. The first two of these, Deuteronomy 27:1-28:68 and Joshua 8:30-35, prescribe and describe, respectively, the enactment of covenant on Mt. Ebal and Mt. Gerizim. The setting for this ceremony establishes an environment of commitment for "the court of conscience" and the last speech of Joshua. The third text emerges from Genesis 35, an even earlier episode of Yahweh-choosing.[2]

---

[1]Henry Fielding, as quoted by Sternberg, *Poetics of Biblical Narrative*, p. 441.

[2]In addition to these three biblical texts, students of the text have also

By way of overview, Joshua 24 records the final speech and death of Joshua. Within the final speech are challenges from Joshua to the people, and challenges from the people to Joshua. The presentation may be ordered into three sections, verses 1-15, verses 16-27, and verses 28-33. Just as the book opens with a series of speeches, it closes in the same way. Through the presentation of testimony, an assessment of the "great commission" mandate is offered and closure is achieved.

1. One Renewal at Shechem (24:1-15)

[1]Then Joshua assembled all the tribes of Israel at Shechem. He summoned the elders, leaders, judges and officials of Israel, and they presented themselves before God.

[2]Joshua said to all the people, "This is what the LORD, the God of Israel, says: 'Long ago your forefathers, including Terah the father of Abraham and Nahor, lived beyond the River[a] and worshiped other gods. [3]But I took your father Abraham from the land beyond the River and led him throughout Canaan and gave him many descendants. I gave him Isaac, [4]and to Isaac I gave Jacob and Esau. I assigned the hill country of Seir to Esau, but Jacob and his sons went down to Egypt.

[5]"'Then I sent Moses and Aaron, and I afflicted the Egyptians by what I did there, and I brought you out. [6]When I brought your fathers out of Egypt, you came to the sea, and the Egyptians pursued them with chariots and horsemen[b] as far as the Red Sea.[c] [7]But they cried to the LORD for help, and he put darkness between you and the Egyptians; he brought the sea over them and covered them. You saw with your own eyes what I did to the Egyptians. Then you lived in the desert for a long time.

[8]"'I brought you to the land of the Amorites who lived east of the Jordan. They fought against you, but I gave them into your

---

pondered the possibility that Joshua 24 resembles the form of second millennium treaties from the Ancient Near East. These treaties, particularly known in Hittite culture, express the relationship between monarchs and their vassals. The monarchs promise protection while the vassals promise loyalty. For more on this see Kitchen, *Reliability*, pp. 283-307.

hands. I destroyed them from before you, and you took possession of their land. [9]When Balak son of Zippor, the king of Moab, prepared to fight against Israel, he sent for Balaam son of Beor to put a curse on you. [10]But I would not listen to Balaam, so he blessed you again and again, and I delivered you out of his hand.

[11]"Then you crossed the Jordan and came to Jericho. The citizens of Jericho fought against you, as did also the Amorites, Perizzites, Canaanites, Hittites, Girgashites, Hivites and Jebusites, but I gave them into your hands. [12]I sent the hornet ahead of you, which drove them out before you—also the two Amorite kings. You did not do it with your own sword and bow. [13]So I gave you a land on which you did not toil and cities you did not build; and you live in them and eat from vineyards and olive groves that you did not plant.'

[14]"Now fear the LORD and serve him with all faithfulness. Throw away the gods your forefathers worshiped beyond the River and in Egypt, and serve the LORD. [15]But if serving the LORD seems undesirable to you, then choose for yourselves this day whom you will serve, whether the gods your forefathers served beyond the River, or the gods of the Amorites, in whose land you are living. But as for me and my household, we will serve the LORD."

[a]2 That is, the Euphrates; also in verses 3, 14 and 15   [b]6 Or *charioteers*
[c]6 Hebrew *Yam Suph*; that is, Sea of Reeds

24:1 Following a meeting that may have been restricted to Israel's leaders (23:1-16), a second, more inclusive, meeting is convened by Joshua. This assembly takes place at Shechem, a centrally located and tradition-rich site.[3] A familiar roster of leaders is present (cf. 23:2), as are "all the tribes of Israel." Those who gather do so before Joshua, but with anticipation of an even larger bench: they meet to "present themselves before God." Word choice suggests a mood of quietism or an at-the-ready attitude among the people.[4]

---

[3]The LXX places this event at Shiloh, possibly because the phrase, "before the LORD" was thought to require the presence of the Ark of the Covenant. The weakness of this argument is transparent (e.g., Yahweh is omnipresent, or, the ark is portable), and, for reasons seen below, Shechem is a better reading.

[4]These nuances are carried by the use of *yāṣab* in the hithpael. See BDB, s.v. יצב.

24:2-13 Before this open assembly, Joshua speaks. Select comments concerning this speech may be directed toward matters of rhetoric and subject content. First, rhetorically, it must be noted that Joshua's opening line will become a prophetic favorite, כֹּה־אָמַר יהוה אֱלֹהֵי יִשְׂרָאֵל (kōh-'āmar YHWH 'ĕlōhê Yiśrā'ēl), or "thus saith the LORD God of Israel."[5] Such a mustering transcends the mouth and mind of the speaker and invests the content with ultimate authority.[6] Textually realized, the described sound may be recognized as the utterance of Joshua, but what is really heard is the voice of Yahweh. To test this weight, the following discourse thunders across the landscape as a series of active verbs repeatedly fired in first person: "I took," "I led," "I gave," "I assigned," "I sent," "I afflicted," "I brought," "I destroyed," "I delivered." Boom! Boom! BOOM! There is no ambiguity here; Joshua is the agent of Yahweh and Yahweh has been busy! Such a strategy renders the text far more than the memoirs of a wrinkled man; it elevates it into a grand rehearsal of Israel's story, told from the perspective of the Divine.

The flip side of this, grammatically, is the telescoping of repeating second person forms "your" and "you" to describe Israel. The distant "your forefathers" of verse 2 is reduced to simply "you" of verse 6. This is even more crisply illustrated by the example: **I brought *your fathers* out of Egypt, *you* came to the sea** [emphasis added]. By this strategy, the contemporary audience (now centuries removed in time from the described event) is dragged back to feel the sea spray. Contemplatively, there is no difference between God's work with generations past and God's work with generations present. Rhetorically speaking, "you" were there — in Egypt, at the sea, in the desert — experiencing it all. **You saw with your own eyes**. This sense of immediacy is not unique to Joshua's speech, but is a common focusing technique of biblical narrative elsewhere.[7]

---

[5]Numerous examples of formulas like this can be found. See e.g., 1 Kgs 11:31; Isa 45:1; Jer 2:2; Amos 1:3; Micah 2:3; Nahum 1:12; Hag 1:2; Zech 1:3; Mal 1:4. What is most interesting here is the use of the phrase "God of Israel" at Shechem (cf. Gen 33:20).

[6]The serialization of such an appeal is found in the showdown between Moses and Pharaoh over the release of the Hebrew slaves (Exod 5:1; 7:17,26[H 8:1]; 8:20[H 16]; 9:1,13; 10:3; 11:4).

[7]This "principle of contemporization" is discussed by Sailhamer, *Pentateuch as Narrative*, p. 31.

Moving to issues of subject content, little commentary is needed here. The story line springs lightly and involves the usual cast: Abraham, Isaac, Jacob, Moses. What may be highlighted is the shaping of the story to fit the present context. The active presentation of Yahweh and the passive presentation of Yahweh's followers seems deliberate, and even counterintuitive in a speech that concludes with an appeal to human choice. Israel's ancestors are polytheists, slaves, and refugees, hardly the stock of great achievers. Yet, they are pursued, rescued, attacked, cursed, and blessed. Through each of these crises they survive and continue to be the object of Yahweh's effort. The narrative of verses 11-13 clearly alludes to the whole of the Joshua text, incorporating it as the latest installment into Israel's ongoing drama.[8]

Setting this bigger picture aside for a moment, note is made of **the hornet** dispatched in advance of Israel's entry into the land (v. 12). While many proposals have been offered to explain this "instrument of God" (it appears in Exod 23:28 and Deut 7:20 as well), a simple solution may be to connect it to an "irrational terror" or "panic."[9] This may have been the dynamic at work in Canaan immediately before Israel's arrival. In this vein, Rahab's observation that "a great *fear* of you has fallen on us so that all who live in this country are melting" (Josh 2:9) finds ready explanation. Still, no matter how this "advance campaign" is understood — literally, metaphorically, or somewhere in between — the important point is that Israel is not responsible for it. Their role is passive yet pedestrian. **You did not do it with your own sword and bow.**

---

[8]Students of the text have also pondered the absence of certain aspects of Israel's story in this retelling. Obviously, there is little wiggle room, but it does seem odd that neither Sinai nor the giving of *torah* appear here. Could this be simply a matter of perspective? Hawk suggests that the Sinai experience may be more appropriately identified as Israel's response to God, rather than a story about who Israel is. Because it would "unnecessarily complicate the picture and diffuse the episode's linking of covenant with response," it is left out (*Joshua*, p. 268).

[9]Other options include reading צִרְעָה (*sir'āh*) as "downcast," "depression," or "discouragement." Of course, it could also refer to a literal insect, i.e., some kind of "hornet" or "bee" that entered Canaan as some kind of plague. The "bee" was sometimes used as a symbol for pharaoh; it could be understood as referring to an Egyptian campaign. See Woudstra, *Joshua*, p. 349.

In this same vein, it is noted that when Israel enters Canaan, they take advantage of the work of others: they settle into the developed land of others and even occupy whole villages of others. Those who would approach the archaeological evidence in search of early Israel must be prepared to confront this reality. When moving from Canaanite to Israelite (or even back again!), cultural *continuity*, rather than cultural *discontinuity* should be expected; this is exactly what has been found. Naturally, with so much potential for the blending of material culture, the question arises as to religious practice or worldview. Where, if any, is the overlap in this case? This is addressed directly.

24:14-15 The final part of Joshua's speech moves from a summary of past events to a call for a present response. The adverb of time, עַתָּה ('attāh), **now**, signals a break. Being objects of choice, Joshua implores his listeners (in Mosaic fashion, cf. Deut 6:10-15) to now exercise the gift of choice. "Fear Yahweh" and "serve him."[10] The "fear" that the text projects may also include reverence and honor.[11] The kind of service[12] the text envisions is doused with integrity, as captured in the NIV phrase, **with all faithfulness**.[13] Honest devotion requires that Joshua's listeners **throw away the gods your forefathers worshiped** and take Yahweh seriously. In this, no overlap is possible. Abraham was led out of the polytheistic culture of Mesopotamia; Yahweh trumped the power, magic, and ritual of Egypt and rescued Israel from slavery. The more distant worldviews of Mesopotamia and Egypt, therefore, are not viable

---

[10]The admonition to "fear the LORD" and "serve him" is a common phrase in the language of Moses. See for example, Deut 6:13 and 10:20. Even in this last speech of his life, Joshua continues to function as an interpreter of Moses.

[11]It is the same word used in 4:14 to describe the attitude of the people toward Moses and Joshua. Occasionally in Joshua it is used with reference to God, e.g., 4:24, but more often than not, it is used in contexts of encouragement, i.e., "do not fear" (8:1; 10:8,25; 11:6).

[12]The root עָבַד ('ābad), "to work" or "serve," is a key term in the three closing speeches of Joshua. Previously in the text of Joshua, it is used almost exclusively as a noun, e.g., "your servant," "servant of Yahweh." It gains verbal force, beginning in 22:5 and by chapter 24, is used 16 times, clearly a *leitwort* of status.

[13]The text reads וְעִבְדוּ אֹתוֹ בְּתָמִים וּבָאֱמֶת (wᵉ'ibdû 'ōthô bᵉthāmîm ûbe'ĕmeth), "and serve him in complete integrity and honesty."

choices (been there; done that); besides, Yahweh has paralyzed them by his acts. This is true of local attractions in Canaan as well, including those of **the Amorites in whose land you are living.**[14] Hence, this walkabout demonstrates that as far as choices go, both far and near, there is really only one good option. It flows naturally out of the speech of chapter 23 urging Israel to keep a life of *torah* observance as a way of maintaining community. Now, Joshua chooses it, leading with his familial clan: **as for me and my household, we will serve the LORD.** Person by person, family by family, the decision must be made. This kind of growth happens from the roots up.

Joshua's challenge cements the case that those who *become* Israel are those who are chosen and rescued by Yahweh. Those who *remain* Israel are those who choose and serve Yahweh. While not without some measure of paradox, this proposition may be used to back cut the text with profit. Suddenly, Rahab, Achan, Caleb, the two-and-a-half tribes of Transjordan (and how many others?) fall into place. Were they chosen and rescued? Did they choose and serve?

As indicated above, this particular text must be read in conjunction with Jacob's experiences at Shechem. A pause to reconsider the story told by Genesis 35 is in order. After returning from Mesopotamia with his family, Jacob settles in the land of Canaan. There, Jacob purifies his household. This reordering begins with the command, "get rid of the foreign gods you have with you" (Gen 35:2).[15] In response, the people "gave Jacob all the foreign gods they had and the rings in their ears and Jacob buried them under the oak at Shechem" (Gen 35:4). Finally, Jacob's clan pulls up stakes to move, and in a curious parallel, "the terror of God fell upon the towns all around them" (Gen 35:5). Purifying the household, burying foreign gods, and experiencing success in the land are three points of the

---

[14]Rahab's speech of 2:9-13 may be remembered here. She clearly voices the conviction that local faith choices will not sustain. Moreover, her description of the "melting hearts" and "failing courage" among her Canaanite countrymen reveals that this realization was not hers alone.

[15]Looking closer, Jacob orders, הָסִרוּ אֶת־אֱלֹהֵי הַנֵּכָר (*hāsirû 'eth-'ĕlōhê hannēkār*), "reject the foreign gods" whereas Joshua here orders הָסִרוּ אֶת־אֱלֹהִים אֲשֶׁר עָבְדוּ אֲבוֹתֵיכֶם (*hāsîrû 'eth-'ĕlōhîm 'ăšer 'ābdû 'ăbôthêkem*), "reject the gods which your fathers served." Both phrases share the *hiphil* imperative use of the verbal root *sûr*, "to turn aside" and the direct object "gods."

Jacob story connected to Shechem. In light of these, the text of Joshua 24 is hardly accidental. The present narrative deliberately weaves the Patriarchal past into Israel's present. Accepting this point leads to a remarkable discovery. The one element missing from Joshua's experience at Shechem is the "burial" of the foreign gods. This notable absence fuels the exchange that follows.

2. Two Witnesses at Large (24:16-28)

[16]Then the people answered, "Far be it from us to forsake the LORD to serve other gods! [17]It was the LORD our God himself who brought us and our fathers up out of Egypt, from that land of slavery, and performed those great signs before our eyes. He protected us on our entire journey and among all the nations through which we traveled. [18]And the LORD drove out before us all the nations, including the Amorites, who lived in the land. We too will serve the LORD, because he is our God."

[19]Joshua said to the people, "You are not able to serve the LORD. He is a holy God; he is a jealous God. He will not forgive your rebellion and your sins. [20]If you forsake the LORD and serve foreign gods, he will turn and bring disaster on you and make an end of you, after he has been good to you."

[21]But the people said to Joshua, "No! We will serve the LORD."

[22]Then Joshua said, "You are witnesses against yourselves that you have chosen to serve the LORD."

"Yes, we are witnesses," they replied.

[23]"Now then," said Joshua, "throw away the foreign gods that are among you and yield your hearts to the LORD, the God of Israel."

[24]And the people said to Joshua, "We will serve the LORD our God and obey him."

[25]On that day Joshua made a covenant for the people, and there at Shechem he drew up for them decrees and laws. [26]And Joshua recorded these things in the Book of the Law of God. Then he took a large stone and set it up there under the oak near the holy place of the LORD.

[27]"See!" he said to all the people. "This stone will be a witness against us. It has heard all the words the LORD has said to us. It will be a witness against you if you are untrue to your God."

[28]Then Joshua sent the people away, each to his own inheritance.

24:16-19 The people respond with enthusiasm to Joshua's charge and example. They recognize that their release from Egypt is the work of Yahweh, as are the protection and assistance that has secured their place in Canaan. **We too will serve the LORD, because he is our God.** That they would voice this choice is expected. What is unexpected — unless the Jacob parallels are deliberately remembered — is Joshua's hard return: **You are not able to serve the LORD.** This challenge careens like a boxcar down two rails. On the first rail rides a challenge offered on the basis of what Joshua knows about the people. On the second rail rides a challenge offered on the basis of what Joshua knows about God. Yahweh is both holy and zealous. People are not. That this divine-human compound will eventually destabilize into something lethal is demonstrated by the statement that follows in the last half of verse 19. Loosely translated, God "will not put up[16] with your broken relationships or your grievous sin."[17]

24:20 Just as in the previous speech (23:12-13), Joshua now declares a specific future.[18] This future is softened by attempts to cast it into an "if-then" conditional way.[19] Translating verse 20 afresh reveals a harder edge. "For *when* you abandon Yahweh and serve foreign gods,[20] he will stop regarding you positively; instead he will regard you negatively and be done with you." Here, in Joshua's assessment is the ultimate tension, the final twist to the book. It is not a warning, but a prediction. It is not a matter of *if*, but rather a

---

[16]"Put up" is our reading of נָשָׂא (*nāśā'*, "to lift up," "carry," or "be responsible for").

[17]"Your broken relationships" is a translation of פִּשְׁעֲכֶם (*piš'ăkem*). This word is used in other contexts to describe rebellion against authority or the breaking of contracts. See *TWOT*, s.v. פָּשַׁע. "Your grievous sin" is derived from חַטֹּאותֵיכֶם (*ḥaṭṭō'wthêkem*), a common word denoting a mark missed or a way lost. See *TWOT*, s.v. חָטָא.

[18]Compare this passage with what is found in Deut 31:14-22, on the eve of Moses' death.

[19]Woudstra's theology is destabilized again. Normally, as an interpreter he regards the text very literally. However, this text forces his eschatological views regarding Israel into a corner. He writes of these very words, "although their seriousness should not be minimized, they should nevertheless not be taken in an absolute sense" (*Joshua*, p. 353).

[20]Here, "foreign gods" is the language of Jacob (Gen 35:2).

matter of *when*. A pause for thought is required. For Israel, even the *right* choice is an *impossible* one. You will not choose Yahweh because you cannot choose Yahweh! The impact of this realization is staggering to the point of disorientation. Should this be regarded as a truth, the bottom line for not just the whole "great commission enterprise," but for a relationship with God at any level? Or is this merely the rhetoric of sly persuasion? In considering the latter, imagine the following halftime speech in the locker room:

> Coach Joshua: "I knew these guys were too tough for us. Let's go home."
> The People: "No they are not. We can do it in the second half!"
> Coach Joshua: "*Really?*"
> The People: "Really!"
> Coach Joshua (aside): "I know they can. But they need to know it too!"

The narrator glides by silently.[21]

24:21 The people challenge Joshua's unwelcome words. The object-first grammar captures the stress of this declaration: "Absolutely not! *As for Yahweh*, we will serve him." They choose the expected option that has unexpectedly been declared a mission impossible. The tension built as a result of this dialogue can no longer be held in check. It pulls even the most passive reader in multiple directions, forcing a choice in the end. One direction is the trajectory toward obedience, security, and unification. These values hinge on the words of the people — "we will serve the LORD" — and desperately requires them to be genuine. A second direction is the trajectory toward apostasy, insecurity, and fragmentation. Joshua's words in this speech and in the previous (in collusion with the narrator) project this end. For his vision to come to pass, the words of the people, either in this generation or some future one, must be regarded as disingenuous — viz., "we will not serve the LORD" —

---

[21]Modern scholarship regards parts of the text of Joshua (like this) as a late addition. As such, it points to the Babylonian captivity and, in part, is written to justify Yahweh's righteous choice to expel Israel from the land. Note how the calamity is described in passages like 2 Kgs 17:7-20.

I would agree with this goal for the text, although I would disagree with the conclusion that it must be an after-the-fact composition. See the discussion in the introduction concerning the "Deuteronomistic History."

bringing down a certain punishment. Again, the open-endedness of
the entire enterprise is sensed.

24:22-24 In a move that defuses the immediate conflict, Joshua
stands down and calls for two witnesses. The first is the witness of
communal memory. **You are witnesses against yourselves.** While on
the face of it, this statement is neutral enough, biblically, to "witness
against" a thing indicates wrongdoing.[22] In this case, the people know
what they have claimed; their own memory will become their harsh-
est critic. Following this, Joshua again appeals to Jacob's Shechem
experience: **throw away the foreign gods . . . and yield your hearts
to the LORD, the God of Israel.** For a second time now the call for
a "burial" is issued, and, for a second time, it passes ambiguously
without action. To cinch the parallel with Genesis 35, reference to
"the God of *Israel*" or "the God of *Jacob*" appears. Israel, the man,
responded to the exclusive demand involved in Yahweh-choosing;
can the same be said of Israel the people?

24:25-28 This tense dialogue fades with a return to narrative.
Beyond communal memory, a stone is called upon to serve as the
second witness. The passage begins with a now-familiar phrase, **on
that day**, this time connecting the moment with Joshua's charge to
"choose . . . this day" (v. 15). The site of Shechem is repeated again
(in deference to previous texts), as Joshua formalizes a covenant.
While the idea of "covenant" flavors the text of the entire book, the
word itself (בְּרִית, *bᵉrîth*) has limited use. Setting aside passages
where it appears in a descriptive formula attached to the Ark-box of
God ("the ark of the *covenant* of Yahweh"), the only other places
where the word for "covenant" (*bᵉrîth*) appears is the violation of
Achan (7:15), in the hasty agreement between the leaders of the people and the people of Gibeon (9:6,7,11,15,16), and in the warning
speech of Joshua (23:16). It is not until the textual moment of 24:25,
eight verses from the end of the book, that the people are called
upon to enter explicitly into a "covenant" relationship. Perhaps even
more surprising, the "text" of the covenant itself appears only indirectly. It is simply drawn up **for the people**[23] as unspecified **decrees**

---

[22]Cf. Num 5:13; Deut 19:16; 1 Sam 12:5; Prov 24:28; Micah 1:2. See also
BDB, s.v. עוּד.

[23]The phrase reads "to" or "for the people" (לְעָם, *lā'ām*), using a lamed of
interest or *benefactive dative*." See Waltke and O'Connor, *Biblical Hebrew
Syntax*, sec. 11.2.10d.

and laws and recorded **in the Book of the Law of God**. While the nature of these decrees and the document on which they are written is not known (is it possible that Joshua adds to *torah* at this point in time?), it likely concerns Israel's choice to be exclusively loyal to Yahweh. It may be that the precedent of scratching *torah* upon rock or plaster is followed, as inferred from 8:32.[24]

Finally, after all these things, the great stone is set up **under the oak**.[25] The final piece of direct linkage between the experience of Jacob and Joshua at Shechem comes by way of wood, earth, and stone. Markers of memory have been erected on many other occasions within the text of Joshua. This last one stands as a silent witness to promises made. It is placed, at least in a literary fashion, over the same earth — possibly commemorated by **the holy place of the LORD** — where the Israel of another generation buried the trappings of unfaithfulness in his household. With witnesses in place, the people are sent away to their uncertain future, **each to his own inheritance**.

3. Three Grave Signals at the End (24:29-33)

[29]**After these things, Joshua son of Nun, the servant of the LORD, died at the age of a hundred and ten.** [30]**And they buried him in the land of his inheritance, at Timnath Serah[a] in the hill country of Ephraim, north of Mount Gaash.**

[31]**Israel served the LORD throughout the lifetime of Joshua and of the elders who outlived him and who had experienced everything the LORD had done for Israel.**

[32]**And Joseph's bones, which the Israelites had brought up from Egypt, were buried at Shechem in the tract of land that Jacob bought for a hundred pieces of silver[b] from the sons of Hamor, the father of Shechem. This became the inheritance of Joseph's descendants.**

---

[24]The term translated "book" (סֵפֶר, *sēpher*) may simply refer to a tally or inscription.

[25]The Hebrew term אַלָּה (*'allāh*) is often translated into English as "oak," but is probably not to be understood as the local species known as the Tabor Oak (*Quercus ithaburensis*). Instead it is probably to be understood as the Atlantic terebinth (*Pistacia atlantica*). Like oaks, these trees grow to a great size and age, but have pinnate leaves and are a different species altogether. See Hepper, *Bible Plants*, pp. 32-33.

[33]And Eleazar son of Aaron died and was buried at Gibeah, which had been allotted to his son Phinehas in the hill country of Ephraim.

[a]30 Also known as *Timnath Heres* (see Judges 2:9)   [b]32 Hebrew *hundred kesitahs*; a kesitah was a unit of money of unknown weight and value.

To conclude, while the gods are not expressly buried, people are. Three burials are reported in succession; each independently told, yet masterfully linked together in a way that signals not just the end of a book, but the end of an era.

24:29-31 The first character to be buried is Joshua. This event comes on the heels of **these things** (or "words"), and notice is made of Joshua's long life of **a hundred and ten** years.[26] Interestingly, only in death does the narrator alter his title from the "aide to Moses" (1:1) to **the servant of the LORD**. This latter phrase has been used repeatedly and exclusively of Moses up to this point in the text. That Joshua receives an "upgrade" to this title can hardly be overlooked; it conveys the conclusion that, in the end, the man who was ordained as Moses' successor, who functioned as the legitimate interpreter of *torah*, and who became an agent of the Divine in this time of "a great commission," has become one with his mentor in the service of Yahweh.[27]

In contrasting the death of Joshua with the death of Moses, two issues may be noted. First, while the leadership transition from Moses to Joshua is clear, developing in snippets of texts from Exodus to Deuteronomy, no such mentoring role is described in the case of Joshua. No successor is named at the time of his death. This vacuum gives cause for alarm; who will follow Joshua? Who will pick up where he left off? A second contrast notes how the place of Moses' burial is shrouded in mystery while the place where Joshua's body is buried is known and is described as נַחֲלָתוֹ (*naḥălāthô*), "his inheritance." Buried in distant Nebo, Moses can only peer at the thought from afar. Clearly, the landless have landed; outsiders have become insiders. In the case of Joshua, his place in the earth corresponds with a requested allotment detailed in 19:49-50.

---

[26]Joseph also lived one hundred and ten years (Gen 50:26). Moses lived to be one hundred and twenty (Deut 34:7).

[27]This is Kissling's point in developing Joshua as a "reliable character." See the introduction to his chapter on Joshua, "The Reliability of Joshua," in *Reliable Characters*, pp. 69-70.

To Joshua's credit, those who experienced his leadership and that of the elders who outlived him are dubbed faithful: they **served the LORD** and **experienced everything the LORD had done**. This conclusion jolts the reader who has already seen the boomerang come round: Jericho's spies, Achan's thievery, the Gibeonite deception, God's repeated attempts to jump-start the settlement process. No one is fooled. Has the narrator resorted to painting with a larger brush? Is this passage to be read as obituary-style hyperbole for Joshua, speaking more of the leader than the led? Could the conclusion simply be carving a high-water mark on the post? This latter possibility is attractive, given the sentiment voiced above about how these people are unable "to serve the LORD" (24:19).[28] All who know the texts understand that pockets of unremoved locals dot the countryside, obnoxious gods-in-hand so to speak, ready to prey upon Israel's instincts to fracture and assimilate. A deflating spiral will be played out in the generation that follows as demonstrated by the overlap of Joshua 24:31 with Judges 2:6-15. Maybe it is in this sense — comparing this generation with those to come — that Joshua's congregation is given such accolades.

24:32 The second character to be buried is Joseph, son of Jacob. Many centuries previously, this patriarch extracted an oath that his body would not be covered in Egyptian sand (Gen 50:22-26). Carried into the wilderness at the time of the exodus (Exod 13:19), his sarcophagus was a regular feature of the wandering column. Now, at last, Joseph's remains are put to rest at Shechem, not just the place of covenant renewal as previously described, but perhaps even more provokingly, the plot of earth purchased by his father upon his return from abroad (cf. Gen 28:15,20; 33:18-20).[29] Like his father —

---

[28]The tension that this chapter presents with respect to Joshua's generation and "serving the LORD" has been variously interpreted by students of the text. L. Daniel Hawk offers an example of a deconstructionist reading and suggests that the text is "untidy" and "mirrors the difficulty of applying dogma to the experience of life" (*Every Promise Fulfilled: Contesting Plots in Joshua* [Louisville, KY: Westminster John Knox, 1991], p. 145). In an interesting play he contrasts the desire of Israel (security and life), with the desire of Yahweh (covenantal relationship), with the desire of the narrator (an ordered story, a happy ending?), and the desire of the reader. For him, in the end, the tension is maintained.

[29]A site found in modern Nablus is one of two in the *Heartland* honored as the tomb of Joseph. This place, known in Hebrew as *Kever Yosef*, has been

otherwise known as *Israel* — Joseph at last finds his way home. Explicitly, the report raises again the subject of tribal inheritance (נַחֲלָה, *naḥălāh*) and a demonstration of how promises ought to be kept. Implicitly, the report establishes Joshua's story as *Israel's* story.

24:33 The third character to be buried is Eleazar. Just as Aaron served as High Priest in the days of Moses, Eleazar's tenure as High Priest is intimately connected to the days of Joshua (14:1; 17:4; 19:51; 21:1) but not beyond. Mention is made of land assignments and the hill country of Ephraim. Finally, Phinehas, a personality already associated with bloody conflict, is brought to the fore.[30] That he would succeed his father in the role of High Priest and serve in the dark period of the judges must be discovered elsewhere (Judg 20:28). For the moment, it is enough to note that Eleazar's death, like the death of Joshua, marks the end of an era.[31] It is an appropriate, although ominous, conclusion indeed.

CONCLUDING STUDY

REREADING JOSHUA

The foundation story of the gospel message centers upon the mission of Jesus Christ. From this perspective, there is no doubt. He is *the* long-awaited *Messiah*, the God-answer for the problem of sin and brokenness. He comes to confront tyranny at its root, to cast a new vision for a purified land and people, and, by means of a sacrificial death and miraculous resurrection, to make this vision of restoration accessible to the whole of humanity. As viewed by the writers of the New Testament — and certainly by Jesus himself — it is a story without peer, but not without roots. Moved by the Spirit

---

a focus of recent dispute in the Israeli-Palestinian conflict. For a taste of the tradition, see G.R.H. Wright, "Joseph's Grave under the Tree by the Omphalos at Shechem," *VT* 22 (Oct 1972): 476-486.

[30]See notes at 22:13.

[31]Some LXX traditions add additional information to the end of the book with respect to the movements of the Ark-box of the covenant, Eleazar's succession, and Israel's apostasy. These additions more formally link the text of Joshua to the text of Judges. As such, they are regarded as late by most scholars. See, for example, the translation and comments by Nelson (*Joshua*, pp. 280-283).

of God, the first generation of Christ-followers quickly recognized
that they were the recipients of something more than an oral testimony. They discovered a deep literary heritage (Matt 5:17; Luke
24:27,44-45). This heritage was composed of many panels carefully
stitched together over the course of centuries: prose to poetry, *torah*
to prophecy, crisis to promise. What the Hebrew Bible offered was
indeed rich. What it lacked was a suitable conclusion.[32]

At once, they set about the task of completing that foundation
story, in part, by rereading old texts in new ways. As revealed, this
exercise required spiritual insight, a crisp memory, and creative
interpretation (not necessarily in that order!). Its result, to use a
familiar metaphor, was to put new wine in old wineskins: remarkably, their effort did more than fill the text to capacity, it burst the
skins! Old ideas were recentered, enriched, expanded, or, in some
cases, cast aside as obsolete.[33] The Kingdom of Israel grew into the
Kingdom of God. The mantle of Elijah drifted down and settled
upon the shoulders of John the Baptist. *Messiah* himself taught with
words that communicated both disorientation and reorientation:

---

[32]The Old Testament is a story in search of an ending. As others have
observed, it is a salvation account that oddly lacks salvation! Alternatives to
fill this void (apart from Christianity) were offered in the opening centuries
of the modern era. These include the apocalyptic dreams crafted by the
authors of the Dead Sea Scrolls, the more down-to-earth political hopes of
the Zealot movement, and a host of contemplations offered by Rabbinic
Judaism. All three of these options selectively and creatively reread Old
Testament texts in the effort to craft a fitting conclusion to the story.
Interestingly, while these examples look to the future for completion, Christianity alone looks back to the past. Suffice it to say, all of these trajectories
are possible due to the incomplete nature of the Old Testament.

[33]The practice of "deconstruction" as a reading strategy is well known in
the literature of biblical interpretation. While much of what happens as a
part of this strategy is viewed as dangerous (for good reason!), it is worth
noting that what one interpreter may consider to be "decentering" might be
considered "recentering" in the mind of another. To illustrate this point,
consider how the message of the gospel in the mouth of the Apostle Paul
might have sounded in a first-century synagogue somewhere in Asia Minor.
For the strict traditionalist, Paul's rereading of the Old Testament was a sub-
versive "deconstruction" to be rejected. For others, Paul's "connecting of
the dots" made sense and could be embraced. Needless to say, strategies of
"rereading" and "deconstruction" have been around for a long time, albeit
known under different labels.

"You heard it was said . . . but I say to you . . ."[34] The practice of temple sacrifice was written off as unnecessary ritual due to the once-and-for-all atoning work of the cross. How many more examples of such rereading can be found?

Two may help conclude the present work. They concern a rereading of God's *land* and a rereading of God's *people*. These are selected for no less than four reasons. First and most basically, they suggest the ongoing challenge of handling texts. Along the way, the nature of texts is sensed.[35] Second, study of God's *land* and God's *people* identifies the movement and distance between past and present appropriations. These concepts are far from static; God may be the same "yesterday, today, and forever," but this is hardly true with everything else. Third, these examples illustrate how a rereading of the book of Joshua recenters, enriches, and expands the message of the Old Testament. One cannot help but sense the tautness of the wineskins; old definitions are inadequate containers for a bold new message. Fourth and finally, thinking through a rereading of God's *land* and God's *people* scrapes at ideas embedded in segments of the evangelical church today. Such scraping, as argued here, is long overdue.

To begin, the larger contours of the Old Testament story of land and people must be recalled. Joshua readers are well aware of the promises offered to Abraham. Elements of it are narrowly focused on the *Heartland*: "To your descendants I give this land [הָאָרֶץ הַזֹּאת, *hā'āreṣ hazzō'th*], from the river of Egypt to the great river, the Euphrates" (Gen 15:18). Other elements, often overlooked, are much more expansive. Abraham is promised blessing for the sake of a larger pool: so that "every clan" or "all peoples" (כֹּל מִשְׁפְּחֹת, *kōl mišpǝḥôth*) "on earth will be blessed through you" (Gen 12:3).

---

[34]The text known as the "Sermon on the Mount" (Matthew 5–7) eloquently gives voice to Jesus' vision for the Kingdom of God. It is not a freshly invented thing, but as these phrases suggest, a rereading of ideas communicated long ago.

[35]Much ink has been spilled over the nature of biblical texts. Do they have just one meaning only (univalence) or many meanings (polyvalence)? Creative attempts have been made to satisfy both camps ("the text has one meaning with many applications"), but these seem to be little more than wordplay. Clearly, to even suggest that the text has one meaning for an Old Testament audience as well as an expanded meaning for a New Testament audience argues for the multivalent nature of these texts.

Throughout *torah* and on into Joshua the promise of land is repeatedly cast in theological terms, it is a "blessing," a "gift," or an "inheritance" offered to the people of God. If it is described as "holy" in any way, it is not because of some innate properties found in its soil, water, or rock, but because the land is God's and he is holy.[36] Like all that is good, holiness is derivative; it flows from the presence of Yahweh. Israel may temporarily possess land parcels, but only as aliens (גֵּרִים, *gērîm*) and tenants (תּוֹשָׁבִים, *tôšābîm*) who camp lightly upon its surface and operate at his bidding.[37] For this reason *torah* stipulates that this land can never be held absolutely, much less bought or sold permanently.[38] As for Joshua's story, the success of the "pedestrian expedition" is far from guaranteed. In fact, the *only* thing that is certain in the text (beyond the leadership of Yahweh) is the open-endedness of the entire enterprise. To put it differently, what is absolutely certain is the variable of human choice! How else can one explain the fiasco at The *'Ay*, the compromise made at Gibeon, the failure to fully occupy assigned tribal allotments, and the sound, running through it all, of Joshua's repeated urges that the people "*choose* carefully"?

If the successful occupation of Canaan is a question from the start of the book, its failure is a forgone conclusion by the end. Here, the speeches of the "departing patriarch" must be remembered. As leader, Joshua recognizes what Moses predicted (Deuteronomy 28): that the people would *not* choose Yahweh over the long run, nor would Yahweh sustain them in the *Heartland* indefinitely (Josh 24:19-20). Israel's staying power is like that of the Canaanites before them, and, not by accident, their loss is voiced in exactly the same terms (Josh 23:14-16; see also Lev 18:25-28; 20:22). With this, the Deuteronomic trajectory of "land acquired," "land held," and "land lost" arcs silently overhead again.

---

[36]Despite the fact that the phrase "holy land" is frequently used today, it appears only once (Zech 2:12) in the whole of the Hebrew Bible! The NIV brings forth "holy land" again in Ps 78:54 only after the editors supply an inferred "land." Needless to say, it is hardly a biblical term.

[37]Lev 25:23; cf. the parable of the Wicked Tenants in Matt 21:33-46.

[38]Consider the discussion of land tenure in the context of the Sabbath and Jubilee teachings of Leviticus 25. For more, consult C.J.H. Wright, *God's People in God's Land: Family, Land, and Property in the Old Testament* (Grand Rapids: Eerdmans, 1990).

The remainder of the Old Testament story bears this out. Because of persistent unfaithfulness, the gift of land is withdrawn and Israel is flung out to the nations (Jer 17:1-4; 15:1-14). Churning in the wake of this judgment are scraps of prophetic promise connected to "the last days" (הַיָּמִים אַחֲרִית, 'aḥărîth hayyāmîm), the Age to Come, or the end of exile. Might there be hope after all? Will forgiveness be found? Can Israel be restored? Perhaps. But one thing is clear from an Old Testament perspective: should this happen, the charter of a restored Israel will not be like that of the old. A new covenant is in order. This one will be marked by an obedience as deep as the human heart and a knowledge of God as near as personal experience (e.g., Jer 31:31-34; Ezek 11:17-20). Moreover, *Messianic* hopes must be realized.[39] Texts here are scattered and enigmatic, but hint that a David-like figure will liberate the people of God, rule from Zion (a codeword for Jerusalem), and establish Zion as both the source-point of salvation (Joel 2:32 [H 3:5]) and a magnet for all the peoples on earth (Isa 2:1-4; Micah 4:1-4). If such a Zion, such a *Messiah*, such a covenant, and such a "people of God" could ever be found, it would represent a radical — indeed, an *eschatological* — new turn. While it runs ahead of the present discussion, it is difficult to resist the observation that nowhere in Scripture is a secular and political "state of Israel" ever envisioned; the very idea is a contradiction of thought.

With Israel disintegrating, the Old Testament narrative drifts to the side of the road. A brief resurgence is felt when a few brave souls take up the challenge of returning from Mesopotamia to rebuild Jerusalem. Prophetic encouragement eventually stimulates the construction of a new, but lesser, temple. The reality on the ground prompts tears of joy and sorrow (Ezra 3:13). This is for good reason. Unlike the First Temple, no indwelling presence will ever be biblically noted; for all we know, the Holy of Holies of the Second Temple

---

[39]Academics struggle to identify the nature of Messianic expectation by the end of the Old Testament period. Identifying the character, mission, nature, installment(s), and even number of messiah(s) was obviously of great interest to Christians and Jews alike. Critical texts include 2 Samuel 7; Dan 7:13-14, Amos 9:11; and a host of passages in Isaiah (including Isa 53:2-12). For more on Messianic hopes, see N.T. Wright, *The New Testament and the People of God* (Minneapolis: Fortress, 1992), pp. 307-320.

was a dark and empty room, bereft of furniture, and, significantly, symbolic of a deeper hollowness. The Ark-box and its associated glory are long gone.[40] Likewise, when the hopes pinned to the person of Zerubbabel fail to materialize, it becomes clear that this is a temporary exercise at best, an anticlimactic spasm that fails on every score to measure up to "end of exile" expectations. Swathed in the acrid smoke of compromise and corruption, Israel takes its place in line beside other victims in the maw of Persian Imperialism. In the end, the anticipated restoration proves to be a no-show.[41] God's *land* is carved like a carcass and is incorporated into a less-than-holy Persian Empire. God's *people* either lose their identity altogether or are counted as just one more ethnic group contributing to the golden coffers of Persepolis. Hence, the Deuteronomic prediction and the historical reality finally meet; the Old Testament story exhausts itself on the side of the road.[42] It is tragedy at its best — or worst — and, is clearly a story in need of an ending.

Christian interpreters, prolific writers from the start, wasted no time in scripting this needed ending. In so doing, they reread many texts and demonstrated how the lines of Israel's story could be redrawn with Jesus of Nazareth in the center. By this strategy, they not only appropriated the whole of the Old Testament in a single sweeping move (no doubt to the chagrin of some), but demonstrat-

---

[40]Strikingly, Ezekiel describes the departure of the divine presence from the Jerusalem temple before it is destroyed by the Babylonians (Ezek 10; 11:16,22-25). Nowhere in the biblical text does it return again. Why? Because it is unnecessary (cf. Luke 23:45 and parallels). As Robertson writes, "Once this stage of consummate fulfillment has been reached, never again will the revelation from God suggest that his people should aspire to the old, typological ways of the old covenant. Progress toward consummation in the new covenant cannot allow for a retrogression to the older, shadowy forms." See Robertson, *The Israel of God*, p. 17.

[41]This is, of course, one way of looking at the so-called "postexilic" period. It follows the vigorous presentation of N.T. Wright, *New Testament and the People of God*. For critiques and adjustments, see John Nugent, "Biblical Warfare Revisited," or Brant Pitre, *Jesus, the Tribulation, and the End of Exile: Restoration Eschatology and the Origin of the Atonement* (Grand Rapids: Baker, 2005).

[42]Consider this text from the very end of the OT period: "See, we are slaves today, slaves in the land you gave our forefathers so they could eat its fruit and the other good things it produces. Because of our sins, its abundant harvest goes to the kings you have placed over us. They rule over our bodies and our cattle as they please. We are in great distress" (Neh 9:36-37).

ed why *their* ending fit better than others. It explained the obvious and not-so-obvious turns of the past: why Israel gained and lost the *Heartland*. It connected intellectually and emotionally with the present situation: the end of exile may be understood in the victory of Jesus and the arrival of the New Covenant. And, it anticipated events of the future: the inclusion of the Gentiles, the judgment of the wicked, and the renewal of all creation, etc. Study along each of these lines continues to be profitably conducted, but in light of the current work, a ready-made focus is available through the presentation known as Luke–Acts, here emphasizing the latter.[43] In the book of Acts, the Gospel writer (who, incidentally, is also a very careful storyteller) unobtrusively demonstrates how the mandate to Joshua may be understood in the ministry of the early church.[44] Or, to view it from the other end, Luke offers his account of Jesus and the Church in such a way so as to prompt a rereading of the text of Joshua.[45] Two overlapping elements of this proposal may be briefly considered: first, attention is given to the subject of God's *land*; and second, attention is given to the subject of God's *people*. In the case of both, expectations are exceeded as definitions are expanded.

It is difficult to overstate the importance of *land* for the text of Joshua. As already noted, territorial concerns drive the outline of the book and constitute a major theme within it. With respect to land as a theme, much has already been contemplated. The acquisition of land is simply one more step in the ongoing plan of God. As far as Israel is concerned, theirs is a grand "stamping expedition" where Yahweh executes judgment on the land's current residents. Israel's responsibility is to follow Yahweh's lead through the person of Joshua and to exhibit characteristics of strength, courage, care, and thoughtfulness with respect to *torah*.

Moving from theme to outline, three stages are suggested in the first major section (chs. 1–12): a central, southern, and northern

---

[43]David W. Pao works this same perspective, albeit toward a different end, in his careful study of *Acts and the Isaianic New Exodus* (Grand Rapids: Baker, 2000).

[44]I was first made aware of these connections through the work of Timothy G. Crawford, "Taking the Promised Land, Leaving the Promised Land."

[45]Mention has already been made of Luke 24:25-26,44. These examples, of course, are bigger than Joshua, but specifically demonstrate the dynamic of Christian rereading.

campaign. This progression is logical from a geographical perspective to be sure, but from the perspective of the narrative, is a point lightly passed. More textual energy is given to the demonstration of how the opposition, and hence, the external challenge, is "ratcheted up" in intensity with each stage. This drama is missed in the second major section of the book where land allotment rather than land conquest carries the story. Here, the presentation of land moves roughly from south to north, although one suspects other concerns are at work here as well. The fact that Judah is the first allotment described and is, in some ways, the most successful, while Dan is the last allotment described and is, without a doubt, the least successful, is hard to overlook. Hence, *land* is important in Joshua for the sake of theme and outline.

It is not possible to argue that the book of Acts mimics the geographical patterning of Joshua in any way. Still, it is clear that Luke uses *land* to orient the movement of the gospel in the book of Acts. Students have long recognized Acts 1:8 as thematic: "But you will receive power when the Holy Spirit comes on you: and you will be my witnesses in Jerusalem, and in all Judea and Samaria, and to the ends of the earth." The path of this new "campaign" is carefully noted. It begins in Jerusalem (1:1–2:41) with the transfer of leadership from one who is departing (Jesus of Nazareth) to one who is arriving (Holy Spirit). It proceeds from Jerusalem to Judea (3:1–8:3) and Samaria (Acts 8:4-25), before finally extending to the edges of the known world (ἐσχάτου τῆς γῆς, *eschatou tēs gēs*), e.g., Ethiopia and Rome (Acts 8:26–28:31). This series of concentric circles are laid down in order, both on the ground and in the text.

To be sure, there is a sense in which this spiraling movement resembles Old Testament expectations for a "Zion"-centered "last days" scenario. However, if approached in geographical terms alone, it suggests a careful reversal and a rereading of the theme of land. Instead of the edges flowing to the center, the center flows to the edges! Perhaps even more significantly, the "Zion" that is envisioned in Acts is also a part of the grander appropriation: rather than being a codeword for a literal or physical Jerusalem, the limits of "Zion" are now expanded to suggest the "place," "throne," or even "Kingdom of God." As the prophets anticipate it: "The *torah* will go out from Zion, the word of Yahweh from Jerusalem" (Isa 2:3; Micah

4:2). Similarly, the goal of "land" that is envisioned in Joshua, esca-
lates into the whole "earth" in the book of Acts. To minimize this
move as some kind of "spiritualization of Israel's territorial promise"
minimizes the power of the gospel! Moreover, this geographic liter-
alism misses an important wordplay tucked snugly into the Old
Testament text. The Hebrew 'ereṣ is flexible enough to suggest not
just the ground immediately beneath one's feet, but the whole of the
terrestrial creation. Yahweh encouraged Abraham to lift his eyes
from the *Heartland* to the "north and south, east and west" in order
to contemplate the larger picture (Gen 13:14). New wine bursts the
old wineskins every time!

What the book of Acts presents, therefore, is the initiation of a
"pedestrian conquest" that now has the whole earth in view. The
priming for this plot comes by way of *The* Great Commission where
divine directives are issued, distributed among the people of God,
and used to induce courage, comfort, and, above all else, obedience.
If there is any *Heartland* focus at all in the book of Acts (or indeed,
within the whole of the New Testament), it is short-term at best. The
Heartland appears neither as holy nor crucial to future moves in the
plan of God.[46] It is simply ground-zero for the much larger work of
blessing, redeeming, and renewing all creation. This "conquest"
begins in Acts and continues to the present.[47] Who can describe its
successful future completion in terms more glorious than those
selected by the prophet Isaiah?

---

[46]It is difficult to understand how/why some theologians wish to resurrect
a pre-Christian and pre-Pentecost view of God's "earth" by limiting it to an
Old Testament definition. Such is the case with interpretations that seize
upon (and celebrate) the creation of the modern state of Israel in 1948.
Even more repulsive are notions that understand the displacement of non-
Jewish—and at times, even Christian—inhabitants of the *Heartland* as a legitimate modern application of Joshua's conquest. This is no miracle of God;
it is the flash of teeth and muscle that accompanies the politics of power.
More to the point here, such interpretations seek to apply select portions of
old covenant theology in a new covenant situation. Robertson puts it in
these terms: such views prefer "type" over "reality" and "shadow" over "substance." See Robertson, *The Israel of God*, pp. 30-31.

[47]In his Pentecost speech, Peter rereads the text of Joel to suggest that this
first-century moment, the birth of the Church, corresponds with the beginning of "the last days." See Acts 2:17-21.

"Holy, holy, holy is the LORD Almighty; the whole earth [*ha'areṣ*] is full of his glory" (Isa 6:3).

The wolf will live with the lamb, the leopard will lie down with the goat, the calf and the lion and the yearling together; and a little child will lead them. The cow will feed with the bear, the young will lie down together, and the lion will eat straw like the ox. The infant will play near the hole of the cobra, and the young child put his hand into the viper's nest. They will neither harm nor destroy on all my holy mountain, for the earth [*hā'āreṣ*] will be full of the knowledge of the LORD as the waters cover the sea (Isa 11:6-9).

How wonderful is this future vision of a renewed earth! Everything else pales by comparison.

In shifting the discussion from the subject of God's *land* to the subject of God's *people*, much thought here, too, has already been invested. It is suggested that the identity of the people of God in the book of Joshua is a major theme, as assumptions are brought forward and carefully kneaded. Case studies, by way of Rahab, Achan, the Gibeonites, Caleb, the Cisjordan tribes, and the Transjordan tribes, are presented for contemplation. In what is no surprise by now, outsiders turn into insiders and insiders turn into outsiders. This flexing builds a case that those who *become* Israel are those who are chosen and rescued by Yahweh. Those who *remain* Israel are those who choose and serve Yahweh. The importance of *torah* loyalty, personal responsibility, and personal choice is thus played out. By the end, the conclusion that Israel is an ethnically defined people group becomes so unstable that it is difficult to maintain. If this were the end of the foundation story, it would be, without doubt, both confusing and disappointing.

However, in rereading Joshua from a New Testament perspective, Christian interpreters recognized this instability and provided an answer to resolve it. Here, as in the case of land, they scripted an ending by exceeding expectations and by expanding definitions. Clearly the book of Acts contains a "pedestrian expedition" of its own. Conversion accounts spiral outwardly from Jerusalem, not just in a series of geographical reaches across land and sea, but in a sequence of concentric circles that are ethnically or socially defined. Boundaries are penetrated. Walls are brought down. A New Covenant based upon the proposition of faith is outlined and enacted. Specifically, the gospel message glides from an exclusively Jewish (Jerusalem and Judea) context, to a "half Jewish" (Samaritan, Ethiopian) context, to an exclusively Gentile context (Caesarea, Greece, Rome). As in the book of Joshua, the people of God are encouraged to gear up, cross over, and faithfully follow the leading of God (via his Spirit).

In Acts, as in Joshua, case studies play a critical role by inviting comparisons and contrasts. Two apostles, Judas and Matthias are placed side by side, as are two groups: the Sanhedrin and the Pentecost crowd. Ananias and Sapphira contrast with Barnabas, while the Ethiopian eunuch and Cornelius function in similar roles. The same may be said of Stephen and Philip. Of course, the Saul/ Paul contrast is powerful enough to drive the book to another kind of open-ended conclusion. It may be remembered that the text of Joshua fades while sending "grave" signals of an ominous nature; the *Heartland* campaign has run its course. On the other hand, the text of Acts concludes while sending signals that the best is yet to come. Paul has overcome numerous obstacles and has finally arrived in Rome. There, the Kingdom of God is preached "boldly and with out hindrance" (Acts 28:31). Ethnicity and geography cannot contain it. While no dynamic similar to the *ḥāram*-warfare of Joshua is explicitly mentioned, it is clear that whenever the message of Jesus is presented, it has a powerful polarizing effect. It drives outsiders to become insiders and insiders to become outsiders. As such, it is a kind of self-administered blade yielding either personal salvation or personal destruction.

As one might expect, *torah* concerns with purity issues are raised repeatedly in Acts, specifically in dietary applications. This, however, is not done with the goal of expanding food rules, but for the purpose of setting up a metaphor of a different order. The injunction of the Jerusalem conference is hardly a checklist for salvation (Acts 15:20,29; 21:25). It is a concession for the sake of Jewish-Gentile fellowship. Similarly, the sheetful of animals in Acts 10:9-22 turns out to be less about food and more about people: "Do not call anything impure that God has made clean" (Acts 10:15). This admonition releases Peter from the conscience of his own upbringing; he is able to step over the short geographical distance between Joppa and Caesarea and, in so doing, cross the yawning cultural divide between the Jewish world and the Gentile one. In this, the ambiguity concerning God's people left dangling in the book of Joshua finds resolution: all who respond to the message of Jesus Christ are counted as members of the covenant community. As in the case of land, the definition of "Israel" is expanded in many new directions.[48] That which is chewed in Joshua is swallowed in Acts. Gentiles fill those seats abandoned at Abraham's eschatological table; the end of exile is celebrated and the ingathering begins. The *Messiah* has come; this changes everything! By this rereading of God's *land* and God's *people*, the Old Testament story, including the book of Joshua, is recentered, enriched, and expanded.

---

[48]Consider O. Palmer Robertson's chapter on "The Israel of God: Its People" in *The Israel of God*, pp. 33-51. More to the point of Luke's program within the book of Acts, see David W. Pao's work on "Who Is the 'True Israel'?" in *Acts and the Isaianic New Exodus*, pp. 59-68.